WOODWORKER'S HANDBOOK

Roger W. Cliffe

 Sterling Publishing Co., Inc.   New York

Library of Congress Cataloging-in-Publication Data

Cliffe, Roger W.
    Woodworker's handbook / Roger W. Cliffe.
        p.   cm.
    Rev. ed. of: Woodworking, principles and practices. c1981.
    ISBN 0-8069-7238-6
    1. Woodwork (Manual training)   I. Cliffe, Roger W.   Woodworking,
principles and practices.   II. Title.
TT180.C56   1990
684'.08—dc20   89-22019
                                                                    CIP

Copyright © 1990 by Roger W. Cliffe
Published by Sterling Publishing Co., Inc.
387 Park Avenue South, New York, N.Y. 10016
First edition published in hardcover under the title,
"Woodworking Principles and Practices," copyright
© 1981 by American Technical Publishers, Inc.
Distributed in Canada by Sterling Publishing
℅ Canadian Manda Group, P.O. Box 920, Station U
Toronto, Ontario, Canada M8Z 5P9
Distributed in Great Britain and Europe by Cassell PLC
Artillery House, Artillery Row, London SW1P 1RT, England
Distributed in Australia by Capricorn Ltd.
P.O. Box 665, Lane Cove, NSW 2066
Manufactured in the United States of America
All rights reserved
Sterling ISBN 0-8069-7238-6

Contents

WOODWORKER'S HANDBOOK

List of Projects

Acknowledgments

Adjustable Clamp Co.
American Forest Institute
American Forest Products Industries, Inc.
American Plywood Association
Andersen Corporation, Bayport, MN 55003
Bassett Furniture
Binks Manufacturing Co.
Black & Decker Manufacturing Co.
Boice Crane
Borden Chemical Division of Borden Inc.
Bostitch Division of Textron Inc.
California Redwood Association
The Cincinnati Tool Co.
Dexter Lock Division of Kysor Industrial Corp.
DeWALT Division of Black and Decker (U.S.) Inc.
Duo-Fast Corporation
Fanspray Danvern Valve (Sprayon Products Inc.)
Forest Products Laboratory (USDA Forest Service)
Georgia Pacific
Greenlee Tools
Henry L. Hanson, Inc.
Identical Construction Co.
Irwin Auger Bit Co.
Justrite Manufacturing Co.
Leichtung, Inc.

National Institute for Occupational Safety and Health (NIOSH)
National Kitchen Cabinet Association
National Particleboard Association
National Safety Council
Parker Manufacturing Co., Trojan Tools
Frank Paxton Lumber Company
Paxton-Patterson
P.X. Industries, Inc.
Red Cedar Shingle and Handsplit Shake Bureau
Reliance Universal Incorporated
Rockwell International, Power Tool Division
Sears, Roebuck and Co.
Spotnails, Inc.
Stanley Power Tools Division of The Stanley Works
St. Regis Paper Company
Toolmark Co.
TRW United-Carr Supply Division
Uni-Cut
United States Gypsum Co.
U.S. Forest Service, Southern Forest Experiment Station
Weyerhaeuser Company
Woodcraft Supply Corp.
The Woodworkers Store
Workrite Products Co.
X-ACTO®
Yorkite (NUF Company)

The author wishes to thank Dr. John R. Beck for his advice and critique of the manuscript, Mr. William Halfpenny for his assistance on the photographs, Ms. Loveda Paulus for typing the manuscript, and Mr. Don Simon, Mr. Ed Zydek, Mr. Constantine L. Wagner III, Mr. James Woodward, and Mr. John Stern for developing the project drawings.

Encouragement from my wife, Cathy, and my parents is also acknowledged.

The following photos are courtesy of Delta International Machinery Corporation: Figures 34-1, 34-14, 35-1, 36-1, 36-4, 38-1, 38-2, 38-6, 38-16, 39-1, 39-4, 40-1, 40-21, 40-25, 42-11, 42-14, 43-1.
Porter-Cable Corporation has provided the following photos: Figures 38-17, 44-1, 44-21, 46-2, 46-7, 46-14.

Production Credits

Production Coordinated by *Patricia L. Reband*
Designed by *Wm. T. Jaycox Associates*
Art Coordinator: *Carl Hudson, Jr.*

Composition furnished by *Black Dot Typesetting Co., Inc.*
using Computerized Typesetting. Text is set 10/12 Univers 55;
captions are 9 pt. Univers 56.

Introduction

Woodworker's Handbook is an introductory approach to woodworking. It covers the basic skills, principles and practices related to key woodworking topics.

The heavily illustrated text is organized in the same way you might build a project: planning, using hand tools, joining, using power tools, finishing and specialized topics. Key woodworking operations and jobs are illustrated. Each chapter builds on previous chapters, but each chapter stands alone. You can read only those chapters related to the project you are building, or you can read the book from beginning to end.

All chapters have *key terms, suggested activities* and *questions for review.* The key terms alert you to new words. These words are used in the chapter and may be found in the glossary. Questions for review help you check your learning, and the suggested activities provide some learning activities related to the chapter.

Woodworker's Handbook emphasizes safety. Illustrations show the safe or approved methods of working. The text provides safety rules for most machines and safe practices for use around woodworking tools and materials. These rules and practices will help you work safely in the wood shop.

Twenty-five woodworking projects are presented. These will help you apply your woodworking knowledge. There are drawings for each project. There are also photos of the project during construction or after completion. The drawing-photo combination helps you build the project with a minimum of error. The projects vary in difficulty, but they all offer opportunities for developing your woodworking skills.

SECTION 1

Planning Your Project

CHAPTER 1

Planning a Project

All woodworking projects require planning. A well-planned project is easy to build. A poorly planned project is difficult to build. Poor planning can cause errors. Errors in design or measurement can be wasteful and expensive. Every extra minute spent planning a project could reduce construction time by about four minutes. It will also reduce the chance of error. A well-planned project will give you a finished piece of which you can be proud (Figure 1-1).

Figure 1-1. *These well-constructed pencil boxes could not have been built without good planning.*

A woodworking project needs a "plan." A plan outlines the steps and details of construction. It may include a design sketch, drawings, and the types of wood, joints, finish and hardware. Figure 1-2 shows a typical project plan.

The plan may also outline construction steps. This is called the *plan of procedure.* The plan of procedure lists in sequence the steps in building a project. This saves time and makes the job easier.

KEY TERMS

project	creativity
plan	jigs
plan of procedure	fixtures
bill of materials	

BEGINNING TO PLAN

Designing the project is the first step in developing a plan. A good plan requires a good design. A good design follows standard design principles and styles. The organized method for designing a project is discussed in Chapter 2.

After a design is developed, the sketches are converted to drawings. The drawings include all construction details. The construction details give dimensions and help determine the order in which pieces should be built. The list of dimensions and materials is called the *bill of materials.* As you read further, you will learn how to design, sketch and lay out a project. This knowledge will help you develop a complete plan for projects you wish to build.

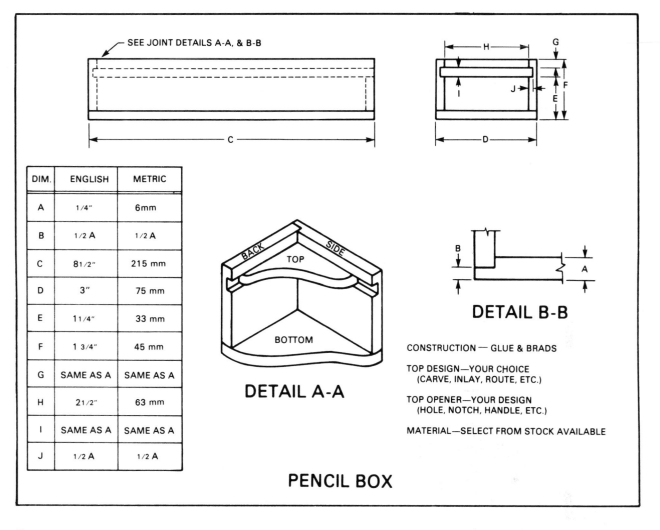

Figure 1-2. *Project plan for a pencil box. A woodworking plan contains the details needed for building the project.*

PLANNING A PROJECT

When you look at project designs or drawings, some parts may seem difficult to build. Wood allows great freedom of design because it can be bent, cut, shaped and glued easily. As you become an experienced woodworker, you will find that almost any shape or design can be made from wood.

Some woodworkers limit their design or plan to the operations and procedures with which they are familiar. Other woodworkers limit their design or plan to the woodworking machines available. Limiting your design or plan may restrict creativity. Creativity can be the most rewarding part of any work. Creating a project

with an original design can give you a feeling of pride and satisfaction.

A good way to learn and develop skills is to first copy the designs of others or use plans that have been proven. These projects, if well constructed, can provide a feeling of accomplishment and satisfaction. As you gain experience, creativity can increase with every project you plan.

You may want to design a project *without* any limitations. Experiment to find out if the project can be built. When you experiment in the shop, you *must* observe all safety precautions or rules. The safe procedures for most woodworking tools and machines are found in later chapters.

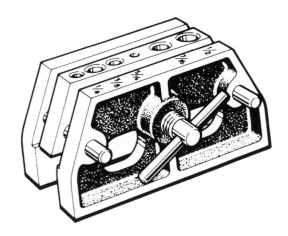

Figure 1-3. *This jig guides the drill into the work.*

Figure 1-4. *This fixture holds and guides the work over the blade.*

Knowing these procedures will help you plan your work for safety and will also save time.

Remember that the project can be built with either power tools or hand tools. You can also design holders that will guide the tools or the stock during machining. These holders are known as "jigs" or "fixtures". Jigs guide the tool (Figure 1-3), and fixtures hold or guide the work (Figure 1-4). Jigs and fixtures can improve accuracy and make the job safer.

If you are building jigs or fixtures, you should use a strong, hard wood, such as maple. Hard-

wood resists wear and retains its shape to maintain accuracy under hard use. Build jigs and fixtures carefully. It is important that a jig or fixture be accurate because errors in the jig or fixture will cause errors in the work.

As your woodworking skills increase, your projects can become more challenging and may require more experimentation. Try to learn something new with each project. Building a simple project again will do little to increase your woodworking skills or knowledge. Try to vary your woodworking experiences to increase your ability to plan and build more challenging projects.

QUESTIONS FOR REVIEW

1. Why is planning so important in woodworking?
2. What might be included in a woodworking plan?
3. What is the building sequence in a woodworking plan called?
4. What is the list of dimensions and materials in a woodworking plan called?
5. Why is creativity important in woodworking?
6. What is a jig?
7. What is a fixture?
8. Why must jigs and fixtures be accurate? How does a hard wood increase their accuracy?

SUGGESTED ACTIVITIES

1. Look at the projects and drawings in Chapter 54. See if you can identify any jigs or fixtures.

2. Look at the pencil boxes in Chapter 54. Can you suggest any other lid designs? Try to sketch your ideas.

3. Measure an unsharpened pencil. Will it fit into the pencil box in Figure 1-2? Is the pencil box well-planned?

A well-designed project has a pleasing appearance and serves its intended purpose. When a project does not function well or has an awkward appearance, it has been poorly designed. Therefore, design must consider both appearance and function.

As you read this chapter, you will learn what makes a good design. You will also learn design procedures. This knowledge will help you build a well-designed project.

KEY TERMS

line	balance
plane	proportion
form	function
surface finish	problem statement
texture	sketches
color	materials
variety	hardware
unity	finish samples
rhythm	project design

PRINCIPLES OF DESIGN

The principles of design become a part of the overall project design. The principles include line, plane, form, texture, and color.

Line is very important to design. A series of lines defines a *plane,* and a series of planes gives the design a *form* (Figure 2-1). Lines may be straight or curved. A designer may use lines to make an object appear larger or smaller (Figure 2-2). Line also adds interest to the design. An irregular or curved line can bring parts of the design together and improve overall appearance.

Form results from joining or intersecting lines and planes (Figure 2-1). Form is the shape of the

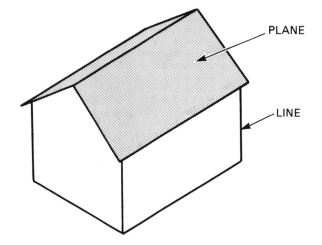

Figure 2-1. *Lines make planes, and planes give an object form.*

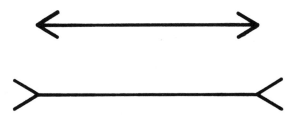

Figure 2-2. *One line looks longer than the other. Measure the lines. You will see that they are the same length. Lines can make your project look larger or smaller than it really is.*

design. Forms may be curved, round, cubic, pyramidal or any combination of these. Many architectural designs combine forms to develop an original shape.

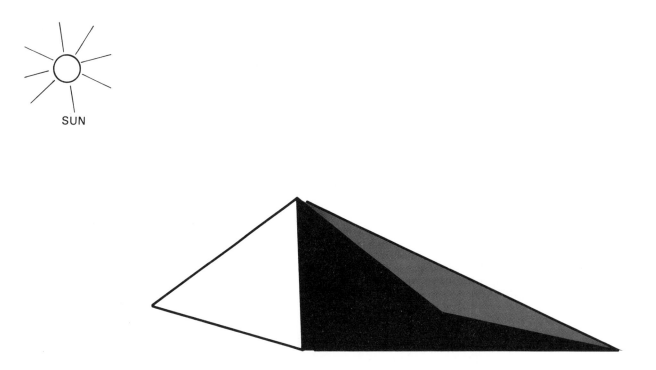

SUN

Figure 2-3. *Light affects form. The form may look different than it really is.*

The way in which light strikes will influence how a form appears. Some portions will be lit up, while other portions will be in shadows as shown in Figure 2-3.

Surface finish has texture and color. Both must be considered as part of the design.

Texture is any contrast in the appearance of a surface. Wood has natural texture due to its grain pattern. Some surfaces have a texture caused by the way the material is installed, for example, shingles and siding on a house.

Texture can add interest to a design. Some furniture uses the texture of wood grain to design a shape. A diamond shape can be made from four triangles of veneer by matching their grain patterns. This use of texture is found on doors and table tops (Figure 2-4).

Color affects overall appearance of a design. Many pieces of furniture are designed in earth tone colors such as brown or reddish-brown.

Colors for interior decoration are selected according to the purpose of each room. A dark

Figure 2-4. *Can you see how this diamond shape could add texture to your design?*

hallway may be painted a light color to brighten it. A bedroom may be painted blue. This is because blue is a cool, relaxing color. Color influences the appearance of the design.

ELEMENTS OF DESIGN

When you look at a finished piece you can see how the principles of design work together. Line, plane, form and surface finish provide the overall design of a piece. The overall design is then evaluated against the elements of design and other considerations. The elements of design include *variety, unity, rhythm* and *balance.*

Variety describes the use of different planes, lines, forms and surface finishes in the design. Variety makes a design interesting. A variety of shapes and texture is common in woodworking designs because of the natural wood grain and the ease in carving and shaping wood.

Unity describes how the lines, forms, planes, and surface finish blend together (Figure 2-5). All the design principles must work together to give the design a unified appearance or theme. Without unity, the design appears awkward.

Rhythm describes constancy in the design. It refers to identical, similar or agreeable parts of the design. For example, it may be the recurrence of a pattern, color, line, texture or form within the design. A flight of stairs containing steps of equal dimensions has rhythm. When the same form is used in various parts of a design, rhythm is added to the product.

Balance describes how planes, lines, forms or texture offset each other. Shapes, colors and textures should promote equality in the design. When the balance point seems to be in the center of the product, it is known as *symmetry* or *formal balance* (Figure 2-6). If the product is not

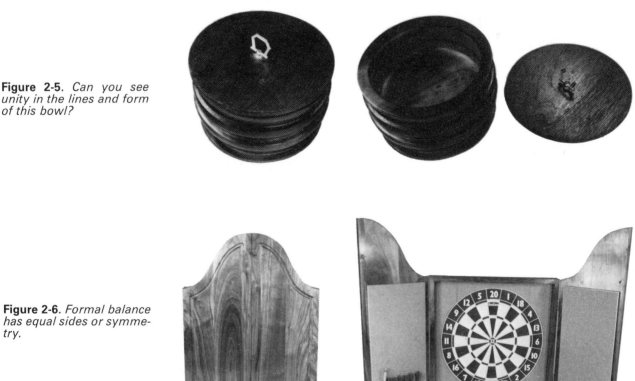

Figure 2-5. *Can you see unity in the lines and form of this bowl?*

Figure 2-6. *Formal balance has equal sides or symmetry.*

Figure 2-7. *Informal balance is not symmetrical but seems to be at rest.*

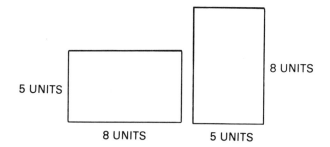

Figure 2-8. *The relationship between height and width is called "proportion." Proportions of 5 to 8, or 8 to 5, are considered good proportions.*

symmetrical but seems to be at rest then the design has informal balance (Figure 2-7).

Balance is a part of *proportion.* Proportion is the ratio of height to width. It may also be the relationship of height, width, and depth. If a product is not wide enough for its height, it is out of proportion.

Designers have found that the eye prefers a ratio of approximately 5 to 8 (Figure 2-8). This means if a product is 8 units tall, it should be 5 units wide. Products 5 units tall and 8 units wide also have correct proportion. Some products that do not have a proportion ratio of 5 to 8, however, may still appear in correct proportion. With

experience you will gain a feel for balance and proportion. The final test is overall appearance.

FURNITURE STYLES AND DESIGN

Many styles of furniture have been developed through the centuries. Furniture styles have developed from experimentation with the elements of design.

Some designers have copied parts of earlier designs and improved them by adding different lines, shapes, or textures. Each new design is then given a name representing the furniture design or style.

Furniture styles can be divided into the following groups: *traditional, provincial,* and *modern.* Each group has its own qualities. Figure 2-9 shows an overview of the major styles.

DESIGN CONSIDERATIONS

When you evaluate a product, consider the principles and the elements of design. If the product has a pleasing appearance, it will also have some of the elements and principles of good design. This is *harmony.* The product with harmony does not appear awkward, off-balance, or out of proportion.

Function is also an important design consideration. Function is how well the product does its job. If the product is well-designed, it will serve its purpose and be easy to use. If the function of a chair were evaluated, the height and comfort of the seat would be important in the evaluation. Function is always measured against intended use of the product.

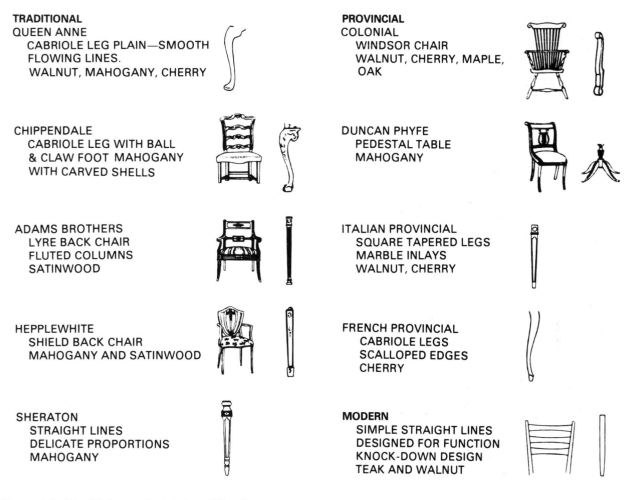

TRADITIONAL
QUEEN ANNE
    CABRIOLE LEG PLAIN—SMOOTH
    FLOWING LINES.
    WALNUT, MAHOGANY, CHERRY

CHIPPENDALE
    CABRIOLE LEG WITH BALL
    & CLAW FOOT MAHOGANY
    WITH CARVED SHELLS

ADAMS BROTHERS
    LYRE BACK CHAIR
    FLUTED COLUMNS
    SATINWOOD

HEPPLEWHITE
    SHIELD BACK CHAIR
    MAHOGANY AND SATINWOOD

SHERATON
    STRAIGHT LINES
    DELICATE PROPORTIONS
    MAHOGANY

PROVINCIAL
COLONIAL
    WINDSOR CHAIR
    WALNUT, CHERRY, MAPLE,
    OAK

DUNCAN PHYFE
    PEDESTAL TABLE
    MAHOGANY

ITALIAN PROVINCIAL
    SQUARE TAPERED LEGS
    MARBLE INLAYS
    WALNUT, CHERRY

FRENCH PROVINCIAL
    CABRIOLE LEGS
    SCALLOPED EDGES
    CHERRY

MODERN
    SIMPLE STRAIGHT LINES
    DESIGNED FOR FUNCTION
    KNOCK-DOWN DESIGN
    TEAK AND WALNUT

Figure 2-9. *Identifying period styles of furniture.*

Wood properties can also affect function. A hammer handle made of wood with low shock resistance will break during use. A handle made from wood with low shock resistance would be a design error of function.

DESIGNING A PROJECT

A project is built to satisfy some need. It should be designed specifically to meet that need. The process of designing a project follows a series of steps. These steps include: a need or problem statement; sketches of solutions to the problem statement; design or sketch evaluation; materials and cost consideration. Each of these steps helps you develop the best possible design for your project.

Problem Statement

You may have a general idea of the type of project you plan to build. For example, you may need a place to hang your coat or you may want a desk organizer to store pens, pencils, and other supplies. By writing a *problem statement,* you can focus on your specific need. This will help you develop a suitable design. The problem statement describes your needs and any limitations that might be related to those needs.

A problem statement for a coat rack could be written like this. *A unit for holding coats is needed near the door. It should hold at least 3 heavy coats and be mounted on the wall. The unit should not extend more than 8 inches from the wall.*

This problem statement guides the design procedure. By reading the problem statement, you know that the rack must hang from the wall and not extend more than 8 inches. Because the rack must hold three heavy coats, you will have to determine their maximum weight and how much space should be allowed for each coat. These size considerations help you design a coat rack that will serve its purpose.

Sketches

After writing the problem statement, make some sketches of possible solutions. These sketches help you design a project that serves its purpose and has a pleasing appearance. Some designers recommend that as many as 50 sketches be drawn for each problem statement. Figure 2-10 shows several designs for a coat rack.

The sketches are then evaluated against human factors and design considerations. This will eliminate some sketches. Other sketches will be combined to improve the design. Fellow students or your teacher may recommend improvements in the design or provide sketches. You

	HEIGHT	DEPTH	WIDTH
CHAIRS			
DESK	16 1/2	15-18	15-18
DINING	16-18	15-18	15-18
TABLES			
COFFEE	12-18	18-24	36-60
CARD	29	30	30
GAME	30	24	30
WRITING	30	24	36-40
KITCHEN	29-30	30	42
END	30	15	24
DINING	30	42	60
CABINETS			
SECTIONAL	30	12-14	ANY
CHINA STORAGE	54-60	20-22	ANY
KITCHEN	32-36	12-24	ANY
DRESSER	32-54	24	ANY
STUDY DESKS	30	24-30	40-60

Figure 2-11. *Common furniture dimensions that consider human factors.*

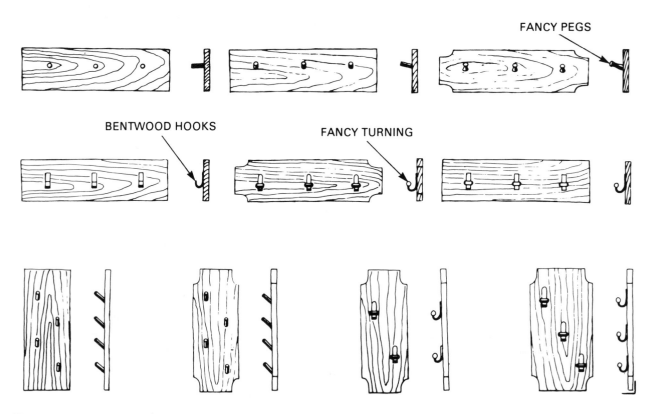

Figure 2-10. *These sketches answer the problem statement for the coat rack. Can you develop ten more?*

should evaluate sketches carefully before deciding upon a design.

Design or Sketch Evaluation

Evaluate sketches according to the principles and elements of design. You should consider design function first. Will the project do its intended job well? Do the dimensions consider the people using the product? For example, can the coat rack be reached easily by all family members? If you design a table, is the height comfortable? These are human considerations. Figure 2-11 gives common dimensions that take into account those who will use the product. You will also want to consider line, shape, texture, harmony, and balance in your design. By changing your sketch, you may improve these design elements.

Materials and Cost Consideration

After you have decided upon a sketch, determine what materials are suitable to your design.

WOOD SELECTION CHART

SPECIES	Comparative Weights[1]	Color[2]	Hand Tool Working	Nail Ability[3]	Relative Density	General Strength[4]	Resistance to Decay[5]	Wood Finishing[6]
HARDWOODS[7]								
ASH, tough white	Heavy	Off-White	Hard	Poor	Hard	Good	Low	Medium
ASH, soft white	Medium	Off-White	Medium	Medium	Medium	Low	Low	Medium
BALSAWOOD	Light	Cream White	Easy	Good	Soft	Low	Low	Poor
BASSWOOD	Light	Cream White	Easy	Good	Soft	Low	Low	Medium
BEECH	Heavy	Light Brown	Hard	Poor	Hard	Good	Low	Easy
BIRCH	Heavy	Light Brown	Hard	Poor	Hard	Good	Low	Easy
BUTTERNUT	Light	Light Brown	Easy	Good	Soft	Low	Medium	Medium
CHERRY, black	Medium	Med. Red-Brown	Hard	Poor	Hard	Good	Medium	Easy
CHESTNUT	Light	Light Brown	Medium	Medium	Medium	Medium	High	Poor
COTTONWOOD	Light	Grayish White	Medium	Good	Soft	Low	Low	Poor
EBONY	Heavy	Black	Hard	Poor	Hard	Good	Medium	Medium
ELM, soft, Northern	Medium	Cream Tan	Hard	Good	Medium	Medium	Medium	Medium
GUM, sap	Medium	Tannish White	Medium	Medium	Medium	Medium	Medium	Medium
HICKORY, true	Heavy	Reddish Tan	Hard	Poor	Hard	Good	Low	Medium
MAHOGANY, Genuine	Medium	Golden Brown	Easy	Good	Medium	Medium	High	Medium
MAHOGANY, Philippine	Medium	Medium Red	Easy	Good	Medium	Medium	High	Medium
MAPLE, hard	Heavy	Reddish Cream	Hard	Poor	Hard	Good	Low	Easy
MAPLE, soft	Medium	Reddish Brown	Hard	Poor	Hard	Good	Low	Easy
OAK, red *(average)*	Heavy	Flesh Brown	Hard	Medium	Hard	Good	Low	Medium
OAK, white *(average)*	Heavy	Grayish Brown	Hard	Medium	Hard	Good	High	Medium
PADAUK, African	Heavy	Orangish Red	Hard	Poor	Hard	Good	Medium	Medium
POPLAR, yellow	Medium	Lt. to Dk. Yellow	Easy	Good	Soft	Low	Low	Easy
ROSEWOOD, Indian	Heavy	Dark Purple	Hard	Poor	Hard	Good	Medium	Medium
TEAK	Heavy	Yellowish Brown	Hard	Poor	Hard	Good	High	Poor
WALNUT, black	Heavy	Dark Brown	Medium	Medium	Hard	Good	High	Medium
WILLOW, black	Light	Medium Brown	Easy	Good	Soft	Low	Low	Medium
SOFTWOODS[8]								
CEDAR, aromatic red	Medium	Red	Medium	Poor	Medium	Medium	High	Easy
CYPRESS	Medium	Yellow to Reddish Brown	Medium	Good	Soft	Medium	High	Poor
PINE, ponderosa	Light	Orange to Reddish Brown	Easy	Good	Soft	Low	Low	Medium
PINE, northern	Light	Creamy Brown	Easy	Good	Soft	Low	Low	Medium
PINE, sugar	Light	Creamy Brown	Easy	Good	Soft	Low	Medium	Poor
REDWOOD	Light	Deep Red-Brown	Easy	Good	Soft	Medium	High	Poor

[1] Kiln dried weight.

[2] Heartwood. Sap is whitish.

[3] Comparative splitting tendencies.

[4] Combined bending and compressive strength.

[5] No wood will decay unless exposed to moisture. Resistance to decay estimate refers to heartwood only.

[6] Ease of finishing with clear or "natural" finishes.

[7] Leaf bearing tree.

[8] Cone and needle bearing trees.

Figure 2-12. *A list of wood properties like this one can be found in most lumber catalogs. It will help you select the right wood for the job.*

Products designed for interior use will require different materials and finishes than those designed for exterior use. If you are building the project with hand tools, select a wood that works well with hand tools. Lumber catalogs will help you select the correct wood for the job.

You must consider the function of your project. A cutting board, for example, often gets wet. Figure 2-12 shows common wood characteristics. If you make a cutting board, there will be two material considerations: first, the wood strips should be able to stand up to water or moisture; second, the strips should be glued together with water-resistant or waterproof glue. If the wrong wood or glue is used, the cutting board will not function well. Besides the properties of the materials selected, you should also consider their cost. Certain materials may be too expensive for your project. Know the cost of the project before you begin to build it.

Hardware is also an important part of material selection. Hardware should complement or accent the design. Specialty hardware is sold by many large companies. By looking through their catalogs, you should be able to select appropriate hardware.

Figure 2-13. *These finish samples will help you select the right stain and finish for your project or design.*

Finish Samples

Finish samples (Figure 2-13) help you select an appropriate stain or finish for your design. By trying out stains and finishes, you can select a color that complements the design or gives it harmony in its surroundings.

QUESTIONS FOR REVIEW

1. What do the principles of design include? Discuss their effect on project design.
2. What are the elements of design?
3. How is proportion related to project design? How do you judge proportion?
4. Why is function important to project design?
5. Describe formal balance and informal balance.
6. How does a problem statement help you design a project?
7. Why are sketches so important to project design? How should sketches be evaluated?
8. How do available materials affect your design? How do you determine what materials are best suited to your design?
9. Why are finish samples important in project design?

SUGGESTED ACTIVITIES

1. Write a problem statement for a project you would like to build.

2. Try to sketch the project you outlined in your problem statement.

3. Turn to Chapter 54 and study Figures 54-80 to 54-83. Note how the numbers change the appearance of the clock. Suggest another way of showing the clock numbers.

Sketching and drawing are very important in woodworking. Sketching helps in designing a functional product and in planning all the construction details.

Sketching is less formal than drawing. No special drawing tools are used—only pencil and paper. Figure 3-1 shows a simple sketch of a pencil box. Drawings are made with instruments and are more exact. Figure 3-2 shows three views of the pencil box: front, top, and right. This instrument drawing helps you see all the details.

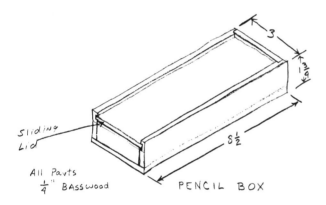

Figure 3-1. *A sketch is drawn without instruments. Lined paper can help you draw straight lines.*

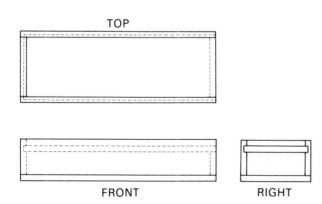

Figure 3-2. *Mechanical drawings are made with instruments. This drawing shows the front, top, and right-hand view. It is called an orthographic drawing.*

KEY TERMS

sketching	triangle
drawing	T square
mechanical drawing	French curve
orthographic drawing	architect's scale
isometric drawing	compass
oblique drawing	scale drawing

SKETCHING

Sketches help you choose the best design for a project. They also help you develop other elements of a plan such as the detail drawings, bill of materials, and plan of procedure.

Sketching is a form of communication which helps you display ideas in picture form. As others look at your sketches, they may suggest design improvements or different ideas. Sketches may be rough at first, but with practice they will become quite accurate. When you begin sketching, use lined paper to help you sketch straight lines and lay out your project easily.

All sketches should show the object as the eye sees it. Because it is not possible to show all planes of an object in a sketch, you should choose the surfaces that best describe the object. For example, a dresser front would have more detail than the back. Therefore, it would be better to show the dresser front in your sketch.

How To Sketch

Begin your sketch by lightly drawing an outline of the object. Make your lines light because you may want to erase them. Light lines are easy to make if you grip your pencil lightly 2 to 3 inches (50 to 75 mm) behind the point (Figure 3-3). To make a straight line keep your eye fixed on the point where you want the line to end. As you move your pencil toward the point, it will follow a straight line (Figure 3-3).

After the object is outlined, begin sketching in details. If circles or curved lines are required, lightly draw the center line of the circle or arc and mark the radius (Figure 3-4). This will keep the curve or circle uniform. Remember to keep lines very light until you have the object

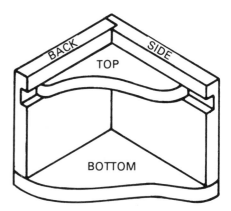

Figure 3-5. *Detail sketches or drawings make assembly of your project easier.*

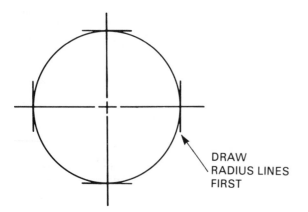

Figure 3-3. *Light lines can be drawn by gripping the pencil two to three inches (50-75 mm) behind the point. Straight lines can be drawn by looking at the point where the line ends.*

DRAW
RADIUS LINES
FIRST

Figure 3-4. *Circles are sketched after the center lines and radius have been marked.*

sketched correctly. All important lines can then be darkened and other lines can be removed. Darken lines by holding the pencil as if you were writing.

After you have selected a design, you may wish to sketch some details of construction such as the types of joints. These sketches will help plan the construction of your project (Figure 3-5).

DRAWINGS

Drawings are sometimes called mechanical drawings or detail drawings (Figure 3-2). The term *mechanical drawing* is used because the drawings are made with drawing tools. The term *detail drawing* is used because the drawings include all details required to build the object.

A drawing with three separate views is called an *orthographic drawing* (Figure 3-2). The three basic views in an orthographic drawing are the front, top, and right side. Each view is drawn as it appears in front of the eye. Orthographic drawings provide all dimensions and locate all holes, curves, or openings.

Lines in an orthographic drawing vary in thickness. Some lines are solid and others are broken. These lines all have a meaning in the drawing. As you become familiar with orthographic drawings, these lines will be easy to understand.

Some drawings have an isometric or oblique drawing in addition to an orthographic drawing. *Isometric* and *oblique* drawings look like sketch-

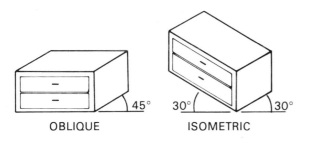

OBLIQUE   ISOMETRIC

Figure 3-6. *Isometric and oblique drawings look like a picture. They usually show three views of the object.*

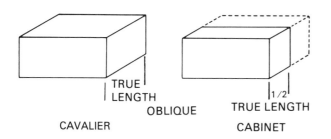

CAVALIER   CABINET

Figure 3-7. *A cabinet drawing is a form of oblique drawing. The depth is one-half actual size. It looks more like the eye would see it.*

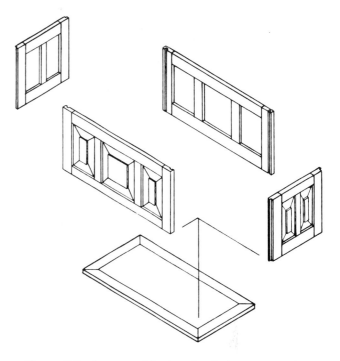

Figure 3-8. *An assembly drawing helps you see how parts fit together.*

es (Figure 3-6). For some projects an isometric or oblique drawing is all that is needed.

Oblique drawings show the front view full size or true to a scale. The right side and top view are shown by extending lines off the front view at a 45° angle.

Oblique (or cavalier) drawings often look out of proportion. The right side appears too wide when drawn to scale. To correct for this, some oblique drawings show the right side at one half of its depth or scale. Then the drawings are called *cabinet oblique drawings* (Figure 3-7).

Isometric drawings have both the front and right hand views turned 30° from the horizontal axis (Figure 3-6). All lines are true length in an isometric drawing. Isometric drawings appear to be in better proportion than oblique drawings.

Isometric drawings are often used to show how parts are assembled. These drawings are sometimes called assembly drawings (Figure 3-8). An assembly drawing helps visualize how a series of parts is joined together.

Drawing Tools

The most common tools used to make a drawing are 30°-60° and 45° *triangles* (Figure 3-9). These triangles are held against a *T square* (Figure 3-9) or a *drafting machine* (Figure 3-10). The T square or drafting machine helps you make horizontal and vertical lines. The triangles help you make vertical or inclined lines.

Figure 3-9. *Triangles are used to make vertical and angular lines. The T square is used for horizontal lines.*

15

Figure 3-10. *The drafting machine will make horizontal, vertical and angular lines.*

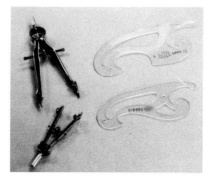

Figure 3-11. *The compass is used to make circles and curves. An irregular or French curve is used to make irregular lines.*

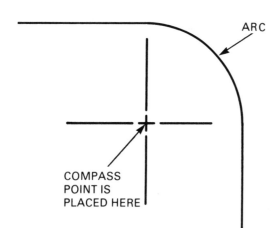

ARC

COMPASS POINT IS PLACED HERE

Figure 3-12. *An arc is a curved line.*

For circles and curved lines, a *compass* or *French curve* is necessary (Figure 3-11). Irregular curves are drawn with a French curve. The French curve is aligned with segments of the

irregular curve. A curve is then drawn lightly with a pencil. After the complete curve is drawn, the line is darkened.

Circles are drawn with a compass. The center of the circle is located and the compass is adjusted to the correct radius. The compass point is placed at the center of the circle and the lead or pencil draws the circle as the compass is swung around. An arc is drawn in the same way, as shown in Figure 3-12.

A ruler or architect's scale is used to measure lines. Inches or millimeters are used. The lines can be measured directly or may be marked off with a compass.

Scale Drawings

A scale drawing is a sketch or drawing that is larger or smaller than the actual project. For example, a cabinet that is 36″ high and 24″ wide, might be drawn 9″ by 6″. (A scale of 3″ = 1′ - 0″). That is, each 3″ on the sketch or drawing represents one foot on the actual cabinet.

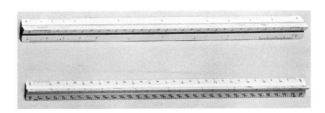

Figure 3-13. *An architect's scale is used to measure lines. It can measure actual object size when the drawing is not actual size.*

An *architect's scale* helps you measure lines at the correct scale. Figure 3-13 shows an architect's scale which includes several different scales.

LAYING OUT A DRAWING

A drawing should have a border around the edge of the paper, and all views should be spaced equally on the paper. Usually, a border of ¼ to ½ inch (6 mm to 12 mm) is used on an 8 ½″ × 11″ sheet of paper (Figure 3-14). When an orthographic drawing is made, the top view should be directly above the front view and the right side view should be located directly to the right of the front view (Figure 3-2).

Choose a scale for your drawing that fits your paper. It should be large enough so that all details are easy to understand. Isometric and oblique drawings should be centered on the paper. Space should be allowed for notes and dimensions around the drawing.

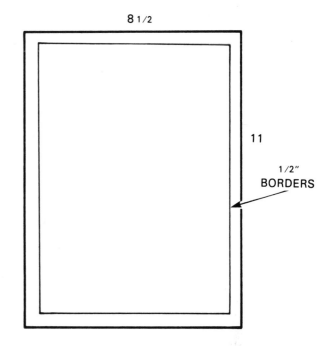

8 1/2

11

1/2″ BORDERS

Figure 3-14. *Borders measuring ¼″ to ½″ (6 mm to 12 mm) are used on most drawings.*

QUESTIONS FOR REVIEW

1. What is the difference between a sketch and a drawing?
2. Why is sketching so important in woodworking?
3. What are some general guidelines for sketching a project?
4. Why are drawings sometimes called mechanical drawings?
5. What is an orthographic drawing?
6. Describe an oblique drawing or sketch.
7. Describe an isometric drawing.
8. What are some common tools you would use to make a drawing?
9. How does an architect's scale help you make a drawing?
10. How is a drawing laid out on a sheet of paper?

SUGGESTED ACTIVITIES

1. Make a front view sketch of one of the projects in Chapter 54.

2. Sketch the isometric drawing shown in Figure 3-1 at twice the size of the sketch shown in this book.

Elements of a Plan

A complete woodworking plan contains many elements. Each element guides the builder through project construction. Plans for smaller projects usually do not contain every element of a plan. This is because the project is not complex. On the other hand, a large project would be difficult without all the elements of a plan. It would be like assembling a puzzle that had some pieces missing. Complex projects require all the elements of a plan.

As you read this chapter, you will see how the elements of a plan help the builder construct a project. You will also understand why each element of a plan is important to successful project completion.

KEY TERMS

presentation drawings   stock cutting sheet
detail drawings   template
section drawings   finishing schedule
bill of materials   finishing sample
plan of procedure   material order sheet

DRAWINGS

Drawings are the most important elements of a plan. They help you visualize how a project is to be built. Drawings include your presentation drawing and detail drawing.

Presentation Drawings. A *presentation drawing* is usually an oblique or isometric drawing. It provides an overall picture of how the assembled project will look (Figure 4-1). A presentation drawing helps the builder understand the detail drawings. Sometimes a photograph of the finished project is used instead of a presentation drawing.

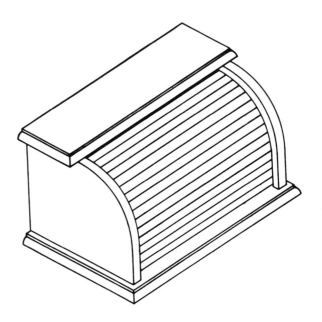

Figure 4-1. *The presentation drawing gives an overall picture of how the product will look.*

Detail Drawings. *Detail drawings* are usually orthographic drawings. They show all the details of construction in one or more views (Figure 4-2). These views may include the front, top, and right side. For some assemblies, a large scale detail drawing is included to show how pieces are joined or assembled (Figure 4-3).

Section Drawings. Sometimes you need to see inside the project. A cutaway or *section drawing* shows the inside. A section view is made as if the project were cut apart. This enables you to look into the project and see how the parts fit together. Figure 4-2, Section A-A, shows the

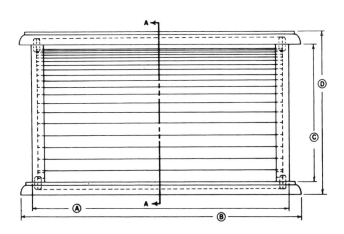

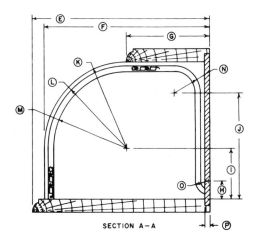

SECTION A-A

Figure 4-2. *Section A-A shows the inside of the bread box. The cutting line was line A-A front view. Large scale detail drawings show how pieces are joined or assembled.*

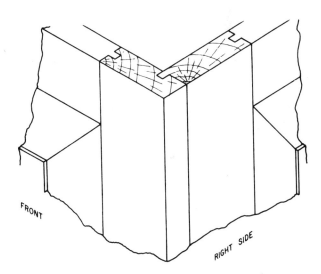

FRONT

RIGHT SIDE

Figure 4-3. *Detail drawings show all construction details in one or more views. Some details are also shown in an isometric drawing.*

inside of the bread box. The view is made as if the box were sawn on line A-A (front view).

There may be additional drawings for projects with many irregularly shaped pieces. Most projects, however, will require only a presentation and a detail drawing.

BILL OF MATERIALS

A *bill of materials* (Figure 4-4) is also an important element of a plan. The bill of materials lists all the parts included in the project. It tells you the name of the part, the size of the part and the number of parts required. The bill of materials

may also include items like dowels, glue, and hardware such as screws and hinges.

A bill of materials sometimes lists a rough and a finish dimension for each piece. The rough dimension is provided as a guide. It helps you select stock from short pieces that must be squared. It can also provide you with a cut out size for selecting parts from rough stock of varying sizes.

The bill of materials always lists the dimensions of a piece of stock in this order: thickness, width, and length. The grain of the wood always runs along the length of the piece.

19

BILL OF MATERIALS

PART NAME	SUB-ASSEMBLY	SPECIES	NUMBER NEEDED	FINISHED SIZE			DETAILS OR REMARKS
				T	W	L	

OTHER MATERIALS — DOWELS, NAILS, SCREWS, GLUE, HARDWARE

Figure 4-4. *A Bill of Materials form is used to list all the parts in a project. It also lists their sizes and species. This helps you select stock easily.*

PLAN OF PROCEDURE

PART OR PARTS	OPERATION	TOOLS AND MACHINES NEEDED	ALTERNATE PLAN	COMPLETE

Figure 4-5. *The Plan of Procedure lists all steps for building a project. It helps save time and reduce errors.*

PLAN OF PROCEDURE

A *plan of procedure* (Figure 4-5) provides a sequence of steps or events that guides the building process. The plan of procedure helps identify each step when you build a project. A plan of procedure may list all steps for building an entire project or for each assembly unit. Large projects can be divided into assembly units.

A plan of procedure may be difficult to develop at first. But, as you become an experienced woodworker, the plan of procedure will become easier. The first step in a plan of procedure is gluing up stock and machining the stock to size. The size is specified in the bill of materials.

Large panels may be glued while you are machining other pieces. This allows work to proceed while the glue cures. After all stock is machined to size; additional cuts are made. The sequence for these cuts will vary according to the final shape of the stock. If a machine is set up for a specific cut, all pieces should be machined at that time. This will reduce set-up time and ensure that all pieces have been machined to the same dimensions.

The plan of procedure will vary after stock has been machined. Some procedures will require sanding and others will require assembly of parts or possibly finishing. If internal parts will be difficult to finish, they may be sanded and finished before assembly.

Parts that must fit together accurately will affect the plan of procedure. An opening for a drawer should be built before the drawer. If the drawer is built first, it may be too big or too small for the opening.

STOCK CUTTING SHEET

A *stock cutting sheet* (Figure 4-6) is a plan for cutting sheet stock. A sheet of graph paper is used to develop a stock cutting sheet. Outline an area four inches by eight inches on the graph paper. This is a scale model of a 4' × 8' piece of sheet stock. If the sheet stock being cut has a grain pattern, draw the direction of the grain pattern on the paper. This will ensure the correct grain direction on pieces that you cut.

Be sure to make an allowance between pieces for the saw kerf (saw cut). You can lose from ¹⁄₁₆″

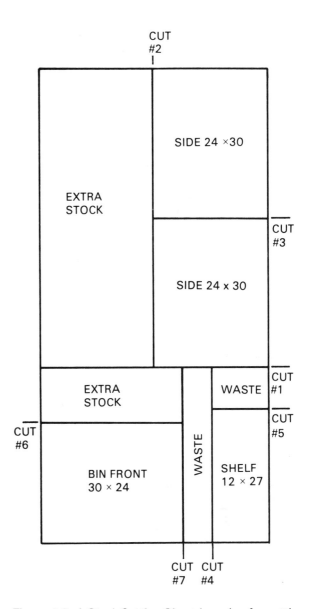

Figure 4-6. *A Stock Cutting Sheet is a plan for cutting sheet stock. Always allow for the saw cut when making a stock cutting sheet.*

to ⅛″ (2 to 4 mm) for each saw cut. After all pieces have been marked on the stock cutting sheet, number the cutting sequence. This will simplify stock handling and saw setup. The stock cutting sheet will save time and improve accuracy. It will also reduce waste and yield larger pieces of leftover sheet stock. These pieces can be used on other projects.

TEMPLATES

A *template* (Figure 4-7) is a pattern used to draw a curved line or a design onto your work. Templates can be made from heavy cardboard, plywood, or hardboard. By making a template before building your project, you can save time in the shop.

A template makes it easy to lay out stock and increases accuracy. Avoid using project drawings for layout. Using drawings to lay out curves will destroy the drawings.

Templates can be made for a complete design or for half of the design. If the design has left and right sides, a half template is made (Figure 4-8). The half template is used for both sides of the design. Line up the half template along the center of the workpiece. Then flip the template over for the other design.

FINISHING SCHEDULE AND SAMPLE

A *finishing schedule* (Figure 4-9) is a plan of procedure for finishing the surface of your project. It contains all finishing steps from final sanding through waxing or polishing. A finishing schedule can be developed by a manufacturer of finishing materials or by the builder. Figure 4-9 shows an actual finishing schedule for a project.

Finishing schedules are best developed after experimenting with various finishing materials on scrap stock. The scraps can then be used as samples. Be sure to label the samples.

Finish samples can be compared to other furniture, paint, or carpet to achieve color harmony. The samples also help the finisher discover any problems before actually finishing the project.

The finishing schedule becomes an important element of your plan. Any additional pieces will have a matching finish if you follow the finishing schedule. The finishing schedule also becomes a record that can be used for repairing the finish.

Figure 4-7. *A template makes layout easier. It saves time and improves accuracy.*

Figure 4-8. *This half template is used to lay out both sides of this end for a tool box.*

FINISHING SCHEDULE

POWER SAND WITH 80 GRIT GARNET.
POWER SAND WITH 100 GRIT GARNET.
BLOCK SAND WITH 100 GRIT GARNET.
HAND SAND WITH 120 GRIT GARNET.
STAIN WITH NUMBER 950 SALEM MAPLE PIGMENT
   WIPING STAIN IN THIS ORDER:
      LEGS
      BOTTOM FRAME
      TOP
      BOX (APPLY STAIN WITH BRUSH)
ASSEMBLE LEGS, BOTTOM, BOX AND TOP.
LAST INSPECTION BEFORE THE OIL FINISH.
RUB ON DANISH OIL FINISH. LET SOAK AND DRY
   OVERNIGHT.
RUB ON SECOND COAT OF OIL FINISH AND REMOVE
   EXCESS.
LET DANISH OIL DRY FOR AT LEAST 48 HOURS.
RUB OUT THE FINISH WITH WOOL WAX AND STEEL
   WOOL.
POLISH WITH PASTE WAX.

Figure 4-9. *A Finishing Schedule is a plan of procedure for the finish. It is also a written record. It is helpful if the finish must be repaired.*

MATERIAL ORDER SHEET

A *material order sheet* (Figure 4-10) is a shopping list for your project. The material order sheet lists all the materials required to build your project. It includes wood, hardware, glue, plastic laminate, paint or any other necessary material.

MATERIAL ORDER SHEET

SURFACED LUMBER

SPECIES	T	W	L	GRADE	QUANTITY	COST	TOTAL COST

TOTAL _____

ROUGH LUMBER

SPECIES	THICKNESS	GRADE	BOARD FEET	COST	TOTAL COST

TOTAL _____

PLYWOOD

SPECIES	GRADE	THICKNESS	QUANTITY	COST	TOTAL

TOTAL _____

OTHER MATERIALS
DOWELS, SCREWS, NAILS, GLUE, HARDWARE, FINISHING MATERIALS.

Figure 4-10. *The Material Order Sheet is a shopping list for your project. It will help you compare prices among dealers.*

TOTAL COST _____

The material order sheet enables you to have all materials available when construction begins. It also enables you to compare prices among lumber and hardware dealers. Comparison shopping may reduce material cost.

The material order sheet is adapted from the bill of materials. Material order sheets using hardwood may list the number of board feet required to build the project. If the project is made of softwood, it may list the number of lineal feet of a standard board size such as 1" × 4". Always allow 10 to 20 percent additional stock on your order. This will allow for machining and waste.

QUESTIONS FOR REVIEW

1. How does a plan help the builder complete a project?
2. What is the difference between a presentation drawing and a detail drawing?
3. What is a section drawing? When is it used?
4. Why is the bill of materials an important element of a woodworking plan?
5. What is contained in a bill of materials?
6. How does a plan of procedure help you complete your project?
7. What is a plan of procedure? What are the first considerations in a plan of procedure?
8. How does a stock cutting sheet save time and reduce waste?
9. How would you define a template? For what is a template used?
10. How is a half template used?
11. How do finish samples help you select the correct finish for a project?
12. How does a finishing schedule help in planning a finish?
13. What is a material order sheet? Why is it an important element of the plan?
14. What is used to develop a material order sheet?

SUGGESTED ACTIVITIES

1. Study the plan of procedure for the pencil box in Chapter 54. Write this up in your own words. Refer to Figure 4-5 for the proper form to use.

2. Study the bill of materials for the pencil box (Chapter 54). In your own words, write up the bill of materials. Refer to Figure 4-4 for the proper form to use.

Selecting materials for your project is an important part of planning and building. You must know how to select the correct material for the job. The function of the project determines the materials you will need.

If several materials gave the qualities required for your project, you should then consider cost. Less expensive materials will reduce the overall cost of your project.

This chapter covers most of the materials used in woodworking projects.

KEY TERMS

veneer	grain structure
plastic laminate	grain pattern
sheet stock	medullary rays
plywood	dimensional stability
particle board	quarter sawn
hardboard	flat sawn
paneling	tangential shrinkage
solid stock	radial shrinkage
hardwood	longitudinal shrinkage
softwood	board foot
dimension stock	lineal foot
board stock	square foot

PLASTIC LAMINATES AND VENEERS

Plastic laminates and veneers are thin materials which are glued to backing sheets for support. They have a decorative color or pattern. *Plastic laminates* are used for furniture, kitchen counters and table tops. They are easy to clean and resist stains or burns. Some plastic laminates have a wood grain pattern. They are used on furniture pieces such as dressers and chests.

Plastic laminates are usually ¹⁄₁₆″ (2 mm) thick. They are brittle and will break easily. All plastic

laminates are glued to sheet stock. This provides strength for the plastic laminate.

Plastic laminates are usually sold in sheets 4′ wide (1.2 m) and 8 to 12′ (2.4 to 3.6 m) long. They can be cut with most woodworking tools, but it is best to use tools with carbide cutters. This is because the plastic laminates are very hard and will dull tools quickly.

Veneers are pieces of wood less than ⅛″ thick. They also can be glued to inexpensive backing sheets (sheet stock) such as plywood or particleboard. The application of hardwood veneers makes the sheet stock look like an expensive piece of hardwood.

SHEET STOCK

Sheet stock includes all wood materials sold in sheets 4′ wide and 8′ to 12′ long. Common types of sheet stock include plywood, particleboard, hardboard and paneling.

Plywood

Plywood is made up of several layers of veneer glued together (Figure 5-1). Plywood sheets are commonly sold in thicknesses of ¼, ⅜, ½ and ¾

Figure 5-1. *Plywood is made of several layers of veneer glued together as a sheet.*

inch (about 6, 10, 13, and 20 mm). The center ply in a sheet is called the core (Figure 5-2).

Some plywood has a veneer core which is slightly thicker than the other plies. This is known as *veneer core* plywood. In some sheets, the core is made up of solid stock. This is known as *lumber core* plywood. Other types of plywood use a *particleboard* core and are called *particleboard core* plywood. See Figure 5-2.

THIS OPENED VIEW OF A PLYWOOD PANEL SHOWS HOW THE WOOD GRAIN OF THE PLIES RUNS IN OPPOSING DIRECTIONS TO EACH OTHER TO COUNTERACT WEAKNESS WITH THE GRAIN.

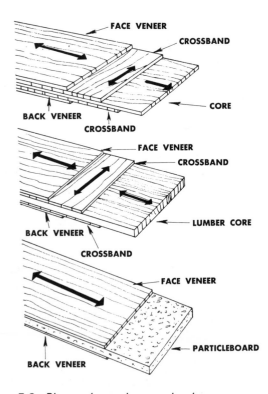

VENEER CORE: THE MOST COMMON PLYWOOD USES AN ALL VENEER CORE. THE NUMBER OF PLIES DEPENDS ON THE USE. THE MORE PLIES THE GREATER THE STRENGTH.

LUMBER CORE: THE CORE CONSISTS OF LUMBER STRIPS, ONE TO FOUR INCHES WIDE, EDGE GLUED TOGETHER. LUMBER CORES WITH FACE WOOD ON ALL FOUR EDGES MAY BE ORDERED.

PARTICLEBOARD CORE: THE CORE IS MADE OF WOOD FLAKES AND CHIPS BONDED TOGETHER WITH RESIN TO FORM A MAT. THREE TO FIVE PLY PANELS, ONE-FOURTH INCH OR MORE IN THICKNESS, ARE COMMON.

Figure 5-2. *Plywood can have a lumber core or a veneer core. The veneers laid perpendicular to the core are called the crossbands. The best exposed surface is called the* face. *The worst surface is called the* back.

The other internal veneers are called the "crossbands". The outer veneers are called the *face* and the *back.* The highest quality outer veneer is always the face. Figure 5-2 illustrates crossbands, face and back veneers.

There is always an odd number of layers in a plywood sheet. Alternating the grain of each layer increases the dimensional stability of the plywood.

PLYWOOD HAS MANY ADVANTAGES:
1. Less shrinkage and swelling than solid stock.
2. Uniform strength with and across the grain.
3. Large pieces available.
4. Better use of our wood supply.
5. Ease of machining with the same tools as solid stock. Plywood can be machined with most woodworking tools. Carbide cutters work best.

Hardwood Plywood. Hardwood plywood has face and back veneers of expensive hardwood. The face veneers are usually matched for grain and color. Figure 5-3 shows common grain matches. Hardwood plywood can have a lumber, veneer or particle core. It is not necessary that the core stock be hardwood. It may be made of softwood.

Hardwood plywood is graded according to the quality of face veneers used (Figure 5-4). Face veneers can be divided into five different grades. The two most commonly used are *premium* or *custom,* and *good. Sound, utility* and *backing* grades are not used for furniture.

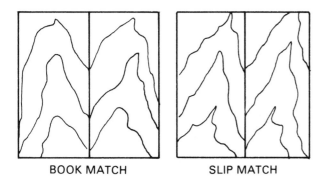

BOOK MATCH   SLIP MATCH

Figure 5-3. *Plywood veneers are usually matched for color and grain pattern. Book matches and slip matches are two common grain matches.*

HARDWOOD PLYWOOD GRADES

PREMIUM	SPECIAL GRAIN AND COLOR MATCH	VERY EXPENSIVE
GOOD	GRAIN AND COLOR MATCH	FOR FURNITURE
SOUND	POOR GRAIN AND COLOR MATCH	PAINTABLE
UTILITY	NOT DESIRABLE FOR WOODWORKING	FOR CRATES AND PACKING
BACKING	NOT DESIRABLE FOR WOODWORKING	FOR CRATES AND PACKING

Figure 5-4. *The first three grades of hardwood plywood are used for woodworking.*

Softwood Plywood. Softwood plywood is used for general construction and furniture. It usually has a veneer core, but may have a lumber or particleboard core. Softwood plywood is graded according to use. Appearance grades are used when the plywood surface will be seen. When the plywood surface is not visible, construction grades are used.

Appearance grades are sanded. The face and back veneer are graded according to the number of visible defects they contain. Each grade has a letter designation. A sheet of plywood will be graded with two letters such as A-C. The A represents the face veneer grade and the C represents the back veneer grade.

The highest quality appearance grade is N. This is not commonly found at lumber yards. The second highest quality grade is A. It has no visible defects. Other grades include B, C and D. The exact requirements of each grade are listed in Figure 5-5.

Appearance grades are designated as *interior* or *exterior* plywood. Exterior plywood is made with waterproof glue. Interior plywood is made with water-resistant glue. Construction grades of plywood are unsanded and are graded for strength only. They are made with waterproof glue.

PLYWOOD VENEER GRADES

Grade	Description
N	Special order "natural finish" veneer. Select all heartwood or all sapwood. Free of open defects. Allows some repairs.
A	Smooth and paintable. Neatly made repairs permissible. Also used for natural finish in less demanding applications.
B	Solid surface veneer. Circular repair plugs and tight knots permitted.
C	Knotholes to 1". Occasional knotholes $\frac{1}{2}$" larger permitted providing total width of all knots and knotholes within a specified section does not exceed certain limits. Limited splits permitted. Minimum veneer permitted in Exterior type plywood.
C Plugged	Improved C veneer with splits limited to $\frac{1}{8}$" in width and knotholes and borer holes limited to $\frac{1}{4}$" by $\frac{1}{2}$".
D	Permits knots and knotholes to 2-$\frac{1}{2}$" in width, and $\frac{1}{2}$" larger under certain specified limits. Limited splits permitted.

Figure 5-5. *A and B grades of softwood plywood are used for woodworking. C and D grades are used for carpentry.*

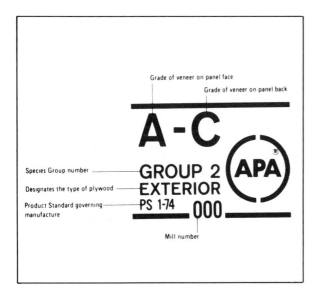

Figure 5-6. *A common plywood stamp.*

All plywood is stamped with the grade and type. Figure 5-6 shows a common plywood stamp. Various species of veneers are used in structural plywood. Each of these species is given a numerical grade according to strength and stiffness. Group 1 woods are the strongest and group 5 woods are the weakest.

Fastening Plywood. Plywood has good gluing characteristics. Any woodworking glue can be used on plywood. The nail- and screw-holding power of plywood varies. Veneer core and particleboard core plywoods hold nails and screws well in the face grain, but poorly in the edge grain. Lumber core plywood holds screws and nails well in both edge grain and face grain.

The best screws to use in plywood are sheet metal screws. They have threads that anchor well in plywood. Box nails and finishing nails hold well in plywood.

Particleboard

Particleboard (Figure 5-7) is a sheet material made from wood chips or wood particles. The particles are mixed with glue and pressed into sheets. Particleboard is very stable. It shrinks and swells very little. Usually the chips in the inside layer of the board are larger than the chips used on the face and back. The large chips in the center increase screw-holding power and the finer chips on the face and back make the sheet smoother.

Particleboard is used as a backing material for veneer and plastic laminates. Common thicknesses for particleboard are ½, ⅝ and ¾ inch

Figure 5-7. *Particleboard is a sheet material. It is made from wood chips and glue.*

(about 13, 16, 20 mm) thick. Particleboard can be machined or cut with most woodworking machines or tools, but for best results carbide-tipped tools and cutters should be used. Particleboard dulls steel cutters and tools quickly.

Fastening Particleboard. Particleboard does not glue as well as plywood, but it can be fastened with any woodworking glue. Often the particleboard sheets become glazed during manufacture. This glaze resists adhesion. Belt sanding the particleboard face can improve glue-holding characteristics.

Nails can be driven into particleboard, but they do not hold well. Screw-holding power of particleboard is better than nail holding power. Sheet-metal screws have better holding power than wood screws because of their finer threads.

Hardboard

Hardboard is remanufactured wood. Wood chips are reduced to wood fibers and *lignin* by a boiling process. The fibers and lignin are then pressed into sheets. Lignin is the natural glue in wood. It holds the wood fibers in the hardboard together.

Common hardboard sheet sizes run from ⅛″ to 1″ or more (about 3 mm to 25 mm). Hardboard is used for drawer bottoms, panel backing, siding and cabinet parts. Hardboard is high in dimensional stability and wear resistance. It bends easily and does not splinter when sawed.

Hardboard can be machined or cut with any woodworking tools, but carbide cutters work best. Hardboard is very hard and will dull steel cutters quickly.

Hardboard is sold with one side smooth or two sides smooth. If only one surface of the hardboard sheet will be seen, it is more economical to use hardboard that has only one smooth surface.

Some hardboard is sold with special surface treatments. For example, hardboard can be treated to make it suitable for wood siding or chalkboards.

Hardboard is sold in two common grades: *standard* and *tempered*. Tempered hardboard has increased surface hardness and moisture resistance. It has been treated with a drying agent and special additives.

Fastening Hardboard. Hardboard can be glued with most woodworking glues. The two most common glues used with hardboard are *panel adhesive* and *contact cement*. Panel adhesive is used to glue hardboard to walls or studs. Contact cement is used to secure plastic laminates or veneers to hardboard.

Other woodworking glues will yield poor to average results when used with hardboard.

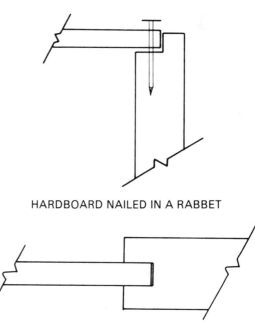

HARDBOARD NAILED IN A RABBET

HARDBOARD HELD IN A GROOVE OR DADO

Figure 5-8. *Hardboard is often nailed in a rabbet. It may also be held in a groove or dado joint. No glue is needed for these joints.*

Often hardboard is held in a grooved joint or nailed in a rabbet (Figure 5-8). This eliminates the need for glue.

Hardboard may be nailed to other wood materials easily. It is best to drive nails straight through the hardboard. Nailing at an angle will tear or break the hardboard. Keep nails at least ⅜″ from the edge of the panel.

The actual nail-holding strength of hardboard is quite low. Most hardboard used in woodworking is ¼″ thick or less. These sheets are not thick enough to hold nails well. If something must be fastened to hardboard, it is best to use staples.

Paneling

Paneling (Figure 5-9) is a name given to any sheet stock used to decorate walls of a home. Paneling may be designed for interior or exterior use. The panels are manufactured in many ways. Most panel stock is made of plywood, particleboard or hardboard. It is usually ³⁄₁₆″ to ¼″ (about 4 to 6 mm) thick. The exposed surface of the panel stock is covered with wood veneer or vinyl. The vinyl has a grain pattern printed on it.

Paneling is usually glued and nailed to walls or studs. Panel adhesive is used to glue the paneling in place. Special colored nails are used to hold the panels in place while the glue cures.

SOLID STOCK

Solid stock is the name for all lumber that has been cut into boards. Solid stock is sold according to species and grade. The species is the type of tree from which the lumber was cut. The grade indicates the quality of the wood. Hardwood and softwood have different grading procedures.

The classification hardwood or softwood is not a description of wood hardness. Hardwood and softwood trees are classified according to their leaf. Trees with needle-like leaves are classified as softwoods or coniferous trees. Trees with wide leaves that drop off during the fall are classified as hardwoods or deciduous trees. Some hardwoods such as balsa and basswood are actually softer than softwoods such as Douglas fir. Figure 5-10 shows leaves for common hardwoods and softwoods.

Figure 5-9. *Paneling is made of plywood, particle board or hardboard. The exposed surface is covered with wood veneer or vinyl. Small, colored nails are used to hold the panels in place while the glue dries.*

HARDWOODS
(BROAD LEAF)

Black walnut

Black cherry

Butternut

White oak

Sugar maple

American basswood

SOFT WOODS
(NEEDLE LEAF)

Eastern white pine

Douglas fir

Figure 5-10. *Hardwoods have broad leaves. Softwoods have needle-like leaves.*

HARDWOODS

There are many hardwoods used in woodworking. Those grown in the United States are called domestic hardwoods. Those grown in other countries are called imported hardwoods.

Hardwoods are further classified as open grain and closed grain. Open grain hardwoods have a porous grain (Figure 5-11). Closed grain hardwoods have a dense smooth surface after being planed. Closed grain woods are easier to finish, but do not always have as much grain figure as open grain hardwoods (Figure 5-12).

Hardwood Grading. Hardwood grades consider length, width and the amount of usable stock in the piece. The best hardwoods are classified as *first* and *seconds.* Firsts and seconds must be at least 8 feet long and 6 inches wide. Stock graded as firsts and seconds must yield at least 83⅓ percent clear usable stock.

Figure 5-11. *Open grain hardwoods have a porous grain. This piece of oak is an open grain wood.*

Figure 5-12. *Closed grain hardwoods such as basswood,* left, *do not have the grain figure of open grain woods like oak,* right.

HARDWOOD GRADES			
	PER CENT USABLE STOCK	MINIMUM SIZE	COMMENTS
FIRST & SECONDS	83⅓%	6″ W x 8′ L 150 mm x 2300 mm	VERY EXPENSIVE GRADE
SELECTS	83⅓% ON BEST FACE	4″ W x 6′ L 100 mm x 1830 mm	BACK SIDE MUST BE MINIMUM OF #1 COMMON
NO. 1 COMMON	66⅔%	3″ W x 4′ L 78 mm x 1220 mm	USED IN MOST SCHOOL SHOPS
NO. 2 COMMON	50%	3″ W x 4′ L 78 mm x 1220 mm	NOT USU-ALLY SOLD BY LUMBER DEALERS
NO. 3 COMMON	33⅓%		NOT USU-ALLY SOLD BY LUMBER DEALERS

Figure 5-13. *This chart describes common hardwood grades.*

The next grade is *selects.* Selects can be smaller, 6 feet long and 4 inches wide. The face must have 83 ⅓ percent clear stock, but the back may have more defects.

Lower grades include Number 1, Number 2, and Number 3 common. Number 1 common has stock 66⅔ percent clear. It is the grade often used in school shops. Figure 5-13 describes the characteristics of each hardwood grade.

Joining Hardwoods. Hardwoods can be glued with all woodworking glues. They are more difficult to glue than softwoods, but good glue joints are easy to obtain. Glue joints in hardwoods are often reinforced with wood screws. Wood screws or sheet-metal screws hold well in hardwood.

Nails are not commonly used in hardwood, but may be driven in softer hardwoods such as basswood. If hardwood must be nailed, it should be predrilled to avoid splitting. The hole must be slightly smaller than the nail diameter.

Softwoods

Almost all softwoods used in the United States are domestic, but some are imported from Canada. There are no open grained softwoods. All softwoods are close grained. The grain figure in softwoods varies considerably among species. Softwood is used principally for house construction, but also to make furniture.

Softwood Grading. Softwoods are divided into two groups, *select* and *common*. Select lumber is used for exposed work and common lumber is used for house framing. Select softwoods are divided into four groups (Figure 5-14). These groups are represented by the letters A to D with A being the highest select grade. In practice, A and B grades are combined and sold as B and

SOFTWOOD GRADES	
SELECT GRADES	
A SELECT	NO VISIBLE DEFECTS
B SELECT	SOME DEFECTS BUT ALMOST PERFECT
C SELECT	ALMOST PERFECT ON ONE FACE
D SELECT	SOME DEFECTS SUCH AS PIN KNOTS
COMMON GRADES	
NUMBER 1 COMMON	CONSTRUCTION GRADE
NUMBER 2 COMMON	STANDARD GRADE
NUMBER 3 COMMON	UTILITY GRADE
NUMBER 4 COMMON	ECONOMY ⎰ DIFFICULT
NUMBER 5 COMMON	ECONOMY ⎱ TO WORK WITH

Figure 5-14. *This chart describes common softwood grades.*

DIMENSION AND BOARD STOCK				
	Nominal Size		Actual Size	
Type	Thickness	Width	Thickness	Width
Dimension	2″	2″ 4″ 6″ 8″ 10″ 12″	$1\frac{1}{2}$″	$1\frac{1}{2}$″ $3\frac{1}{2}$″ $5\frac{1}{2}$″ $7\frac{1}{4}$″ $9\frac{1}{4}$″ $11\frac{1}{4}$″
Common Boards	1″	2″ 4″ 6″ 8″ 10″ 12″	$\frac{3}{4}$″ or $\frac{25}{32}$″	$1\frac{1}{2}$″ $3\frac{1}{2}$″ $5\frac{1}{2}$″ $7\frac{1}{4}$″ $9\frac{1}{4}$″ $11\frac{1}{4}$″
Shiplap Boards	1″	4″ 6″ 8″ 10″ 12″	$\frac{3}{4}$″ or $\frac{25}{32}$″	$3\frac{1}{8}$″ Face $5\frac{1}{8}$″ Width $7\frac{1}{8}$″ ″ $9\frac{1}{8}$″ ″ $11\frac{1}{8}$″ ″
T & G Boards	1″	4″ 6″ 8″ 10″ 12″	$\frac{3}{4}$″ or $\frac{25}{32}$″	$3\frac{1}{4}$″ Face $5\frac{1}{4}$″ Width $7\frac{1}{4}$″ ″ $9\frac{1}{4}$″ ″ $11\frac{1}{4}$″ ″

Figure 5-15. *Dimension and board stock are actually smaller than their nominal size.*

better. A grade lumber has almost no defects. B grade lumber has no major defects and C grade lumber has no major defects on one side. D grade lumber has more defects than C grade, but still has a sound surface. D grade defects are usually small knots.

Common grade softwoods have many defects, but are well suited to construction framing. Common grade softwoods are divided into 5 groups (Figure 5-14). These groups are numbered 1 through 5 with 1 being the highest common grade. Common lumber graded 1 through 3 is usually stocked at lumber yards. Common grades 4 and 5 are difficult to work with and are not in demand.

Dimension Stock. Many softwoods are sold as *dimension stock.* That means that the stock has been machined to a thickness of 2″ and width of 2″ or more. The stock is referred to by *nominal size* such as 2″ × 4″ (50 mm × 100 mm). The actual size of a 2″ × 4″ is 1 ½″ × 3 ½″ (38 × 90 mm). The difference between the nominal size and actual size is the *machining allowance.* This allowance is the stock removed during machining. Figure 5-15 lists common sizes of dimension stock. *Board stock* is also machined, but it has a thickness of 1″ and width of 2″ or more.

Joining Softwoods. Softwoods are very easy to glue with common woodworking glues. They are also easy to nail. For most house construction, softwoods are joined by nailing. Pre-drilling is not required to nail softwoods successfully.

Softwoods have good screw holding ability. All screws hold quite well in softwood. It is best to pre-drill softwoods when installing screws.

WOOD INDENTIFICATION

When you begin working with wood, it will be difficult to tell one wood from another. But as you gain experience, differences between species will become noticeable. Some noticeable differences include odor, weight, color, grain structure and grain pattern. Wood odor may be pronounced in some species such as aromatic red cedar. Other woods have an odor only when they are freshly sawn.

Some woods such as balsa and basswood are very light, and other woods, such as oak and

cherry, are quite heavy. A wood's weight is an indication of its hardness. A heavy piece of wood will have a hard surface.

Wood color helps you identify it. Some species are brown while others appear white or yellow. The older the tree, the more heartwood it will have. Figure 5-16 shows the location of the sapwood and heartwood. Heartwood is always in the center of the tree. Color in one species can vary between the heartwood and the sapwood. This is because the heartwood has certain deposits that make it darker.

Grain structure may help in wood identification. Certain hardwoods are open grained. Their porous surface and end grain can distinguish them from other hardwoods and softwoods.

Grain pattern is also an important aid to wood identification. The amount of *figure* in the grain can provide a clue to its species. Grain figure is caused by growth patterns of the tree. These growth patterns are regulated by tree diseases and the growing environment.

The grain figure will also vary according to how the wood is cut. *Flat sawn* lumber is cut so that

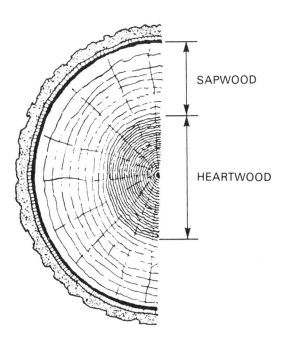

Figure 5-16. *Heartwood forms as a tree ages. The older the tree, the more heartwood it will have.*

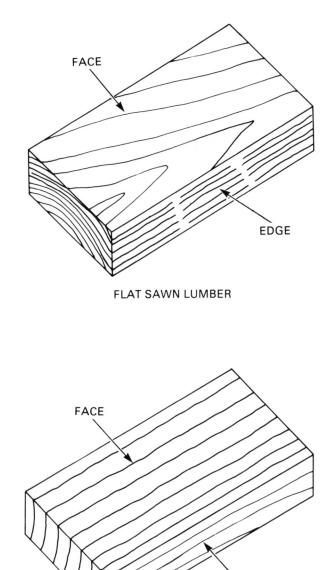

Figure 5-17. *Flat sawn lumber has annular rings that run from edge to edge. The faces have more figure than the edges.*

FLAT SAWN LUMBER

Figure 5-18. *Quarter sawn lumber has annular rings that run from face to face. The faces have less figure than the edges.*

QUARTER SAWN LUMBER

the annular rings run from edge to edge (Figure 5-17). The grain pattern has more figure than quarter sawn lumber. *Quarter sawn* lumber has the annular rings running from face to face (Figure 5-18). The grain pattern on quarter sawn lumber has little figure. It appears to be a series of straight lines.

Oak has an interesting grain figure when quarter sawn because of its *medullary rays.* Medullary rays appear as flakes on the face of the quarter sawn stock (Figure 5-19). Medullary rays are present in all woods, but are not always visible.

DIMENSIONAL STABILITY
Shrinkage and swelling in wood are caused by moisture. As wood takes on moisture, it swells. You may have noticed that a door or window sticks on a humid day. This is because the wood has absorbed some moisture.

Solid stock shrinks and swells. This is because of the wood cell arrangement in solid stock. The cell arrangement in a log causes three different types of shrinkage. Figure 5-20 shows the three types of shrinkage: *longitudinal*, *radial*, and *tangential*.

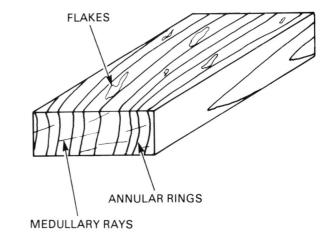

Figure 5-19. *Medullary rays appear as flakes in the faces of quarter sawn oak.*

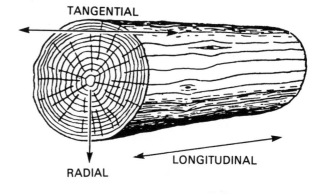

Figure 5-20. *There are three types of shrinkage in wood. Longitudinal shrinkage is very low. Tangential shrinkage is about twice radial shrinkage.*

Longitudinal shrinkage or swelling in wood is quite small. It is usually not a problem. Radial shrinkage or swelling, however, is somewhat larger and can cause dimensional changes in wood.

Tangential shrinkage and swelling can change stock dimensions significantly. Tangential shrinkage and swelling is about twice that of radial shrinkage.

Many wood floors are made from quarter sawn lumber to cope with tangential shrinkage. Shrinkage and swelling in quarter sawn lumber is greatest through its thickness. This means that quarter sawn flooring will change more in thickness than in width. The change in thickness will not damage the floor. If flat sawn stock was used, the stock would change more in width than in thickness. Figure 5-21 shows shrinkage and swelling in flat and quarter sawn flooring.

SOLID STOCK
Solid stock is sold either by the *board foot* or *lineal foot*. A lineal foot is a piece one foot long. Molding is commonly sold by lineal foot. A lineal foot is sometimes called a "running foot."

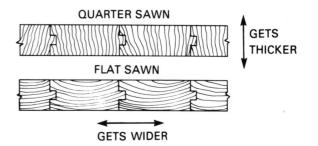

Figure 5-21. *Quarter sawn flooring gets thicker when it absorbs moisture. This does not affect the floor. Flat sawn flooring will get wider. This can cause the floor to "hump".*

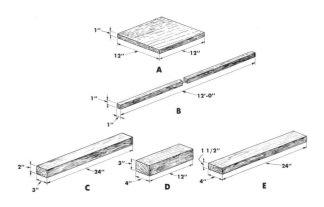

Figure 5-22. *The unit of measure for lumber is the board foot. Each of the above pieces is one board foot.*

A board foot measures volume. It considers stock thickness, width, and length. A board foot is the amount of wood in a piece of stock 1″ thick, 12″ wide, and 12″ long. Figure 5-22 illustrates board measure.

The formula for computing board footage is:
$$BF = \frac{T \times W \times L}{144}$$

where:

BF = board footage
T = thickness in inches
W = width in inches
L = length in inches

Suppose you have 2 pieces of stock 2″ thick, 6″ wide and 36″ long.

$$BF = 2 \text{ pieces} \times \frac{2'' \times 6'' \times 36''}{144}$$

$$BF = 2 \text{ pieces} \times \frac{2'' \times 6'' \times \overset{1}{\cancel{36''}}}{\underset{4}{\cancel{144}}} \qquad \text{Cancel by 36}$$

$$BF = 2 \text{ pieces} \times \frac{2'' \times \overset{3}{\cancel{6''}} \times 1''}{\underset{2}{\cancel{4}}} \qquad \text{Cancel by 2}$$

$$BF = 2 \text{ pieces} \times \frac{\overset{1}{\cancel{2''}} \times 3'' \times 1''}{\underset{1}{\cancel{2}}} \qquad \text{Cancel by 2}$$

$$BF = 2 \text{ pieces} \times \frac{1'' \times 3'' \times 1''}{1}$$

$$BF = 6$$

After you determine board footage, multiply it by the cost per board foot to determine cost.

Stock less than 1″ thick is always computed as 1″ thick. Stock over 1″ thick should be rounded to the nearest half inch. Stock 1¾″ thick would be rounded to 2″. Stock width should be rounded to the nearest inch.

If you are using the metric system, use the following formula to determine board meter measure (Bmm):

$$Bmm = \frac{T(mm) \times W(mm) \times L(m)}{1000}$$

where:
Bmm = board meter measure
T = thickness in millimeters
W = width in millimeters
L = length in meters (1,000 mm = 1 meter)

Suppose you have 2 pieces of stock 50 mm thick, 100 mm wide and 3 m long.

$$Bmm = \frac{2 \text{ pieces} \times 50mm \times \cancel{100}mm \times 3}{\underset{10}{\cancel{1000}}} \qquad \text{Cancel by 100}$$

$$= \frac{2 \text{ pieces} \times \overset{5}{\cancel{50}} \times 1 \times 3}{\cancel{10}} \qquad \text{Cancel by 10}$$

$$= \frac{2 \times 5 \times 1 \times 3}{1}$$

$$Bmm = 30$$

Surfaced Stock. Solid stock can be sold rough or surfaced. Rough stock has a rough surface from the saw. Surfaced stock has been planed smooth. Some stock has both faces planed and is called S2S (surfaced two sides) stock. Some stock is surfaced on all sides. This stock is called surfaced four sides or S4S stock. Figure 5-23 illustrates rough, S2S and S4S stock.

Hardwood is usually surfaced two sides (S2S) and sold in random widths and lengths. Most softwoods are surfaced four sides and sold in measured lengths of 2 feet multiples such as 6′, 8′ or 10′.

It may be difficult to purchase a piece of stock that is the exact size you need. Plan your work and your purchase so that you do not waste stock.

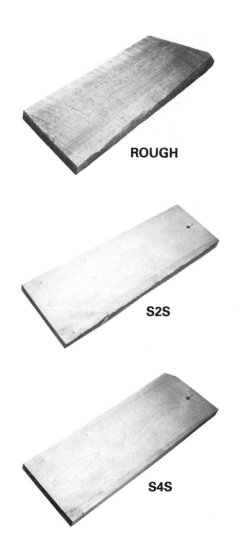

ROUGH

S2S

S4S

Figure 5-23. *Stock may be purchased rough, surfaced two sides (S2S) or surfaced four sides (S4S).*

Sheet Stock

Sheet stock is usually sold by the sheet. When you are working in the school shop, your instructor may have sheet stock by the *square foot* or the *square meter*. Square measure may also be used for veneer or plastic laminates.

To determine square footage, use the following formula:

$$SF = \frac{W \times L}{144}$$

where:

SF = square footage
W = width in inches
L = length in inches

Suppose you have two ¼″ pieces of plywood 18″ wide by 36″ long.

$$SF = 2 \text{ pieces} \times \frac{18'' \times 36''}{144''}$$

$$SF = 2 \text{ pieces} \times \frac{18'' \times \cancel{36}''}{\cancel{144}} \quad \text{Cancel by 36}$$

$$SF = 2 \text{ pieces} \times \frac{\overset{9}{\cancel{18}}'' \times 1''}{\underset{2}{\cancel{4}}} \quad \text{Cancel by 2}$$

$$SF = \cancel{2} \text{ pieces} \times \frac{9 \times 1}{2}$$

$$SF = \cancel{2} \text{ pieces} \times \frac{9}{\cancel{2}} \quad \text{Cancel by 2}$$

$$SF = 9$$

If you are using the metric system, use the following formula to determine square meter measure.

$$SMM = W \times L$$

where:
SMM = Square meter measure
W = width in meters (1,000 mm = 1 meter)
L = length in meters (1,000 mm = 1 meter)

Suppose you have 2 pieces of plywood each 1 meter wide and 3 meters long.
SMM = 2 × 1 × 3
SMM = 6 or 6 square meters

QUESTIONS FOR REVIEW

1. Why is material selection important to woodworking?
2. Of what importance is cost to material selection?
3. How would you define sheet stock? What woodworking materials could be defined as sheet stock?
4. What is the difference between lumber core and veneer core plywood?

5. How do the alternating layers of veneer affect plywood strength and stability?
6. How do hardwood plywoods differ from softwood plywoods? Which is most commonly used to build furniture?
7. How are plywoods graded? Can you name three systems for grading plywood?
8. How would you describe the fastening characteristics of plywood?
9. What is particleboard, and how is it manufactured?
10. What are some common uses for particleboard?
11. How is particleboard cut? What tools work best for machining particleboard?
12. How would you describe the fastening characteristics of particleboard?
13. What is hardboard? How does it differ from particleboard?
14. What are the common grades of hardboard and how do they differ?
15. How would you describe the fastening characteristics of hardboard? Does hardboard hold nails well?
16. What is solid stock? How is it sold?
17. What is the difference between hardwood and softwood? Are hardwoods actually harder than softwoods?
18. What considerations are made when grading hardwoods? Can you name the common hardwood grades?
19. Are hardwoods easy to fasten? Do nails work well in hardwoods?
20. Some softwoods are open grained. True or false?
21. What grade of softwood would you use for exposed work? What grade would you use for construction?
22. What is meant by the terms *dimension stock* and *board stock?*
23. What is the best fastener for softwoods?
24. What are some things that help you identify different wood species?
25. How would you describe flat sawn stock? How does it differ from quarter sawn stock?
26. How does the method of sawing lumber affect dimensional stability?
27. How is board footage computed? How many board feet are there in 2 pieces of stock 1" thick, 6" wide and 60" long?
28. Why are hardwoods sold in random widths and lengths? Are softwoods also sold in random widths and lengths?
29. How do you determine square measure? How does it differ from board measure?

SUGGESTED ACTIVITIES

1. Study the wood samples shown in the color chart. Can you find any of these woods in your shop?

2. Select three different samples of wood. Can you identify differences in weight, color, grain or odor?

Woods/Project Illustrations

WOOD SAMPLES

Every species (type) of wood has its own color. It also has its own grain pattern. Woods like walnut and willow look similar, but walnut is usually darker and heavier. Some woods such as basswood are almost white with very little grain pattern. As you work with wood, you will begin to identify wood by its color or grain pattern.

There are also some color differences within any species. All of the boards cut from a tree will not be the same color. The sapwood may be lighter than the heartwood. Other changes in color will also appear.

This section will show you some of the color differences in wood.* Notice that each kind of wood has its own color. Compare that color to some of the finished projects. You will see how stain and a finish change the wood's color.

The finished color of your project may not be the same as the wood you are using. You may have to darken the wood with stain. Before you stain your project, test some stains on a scrap piece. The test scrap should be the same kind of wood you used to build your project. This will help you select the best color.

Wood Samples: Frank Paxton Lumber Co.

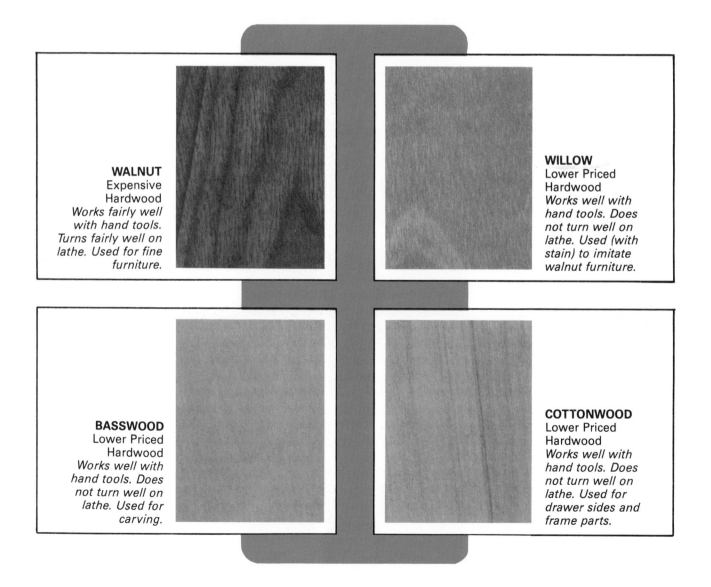

WALNUT
Expensive Hardwood
Works fairly well with hand tools. Turns fairly well on lathe. Used for fine furniture.

WILLOW
Lower Priced Hardwood
Works well with hand tools. Does not turn well on lathe. Used (with stain) to imitate walnut furniture.

BASSWOOD
Lower Priced Hardwood
Works well with hand tools. Does not turn well on lathe. Used for carving.

COTTONWOOD
Lower Priced Hardwood
Works well with hand tools. Does not turn well on lathe. Used for drawer sides and frame parts.

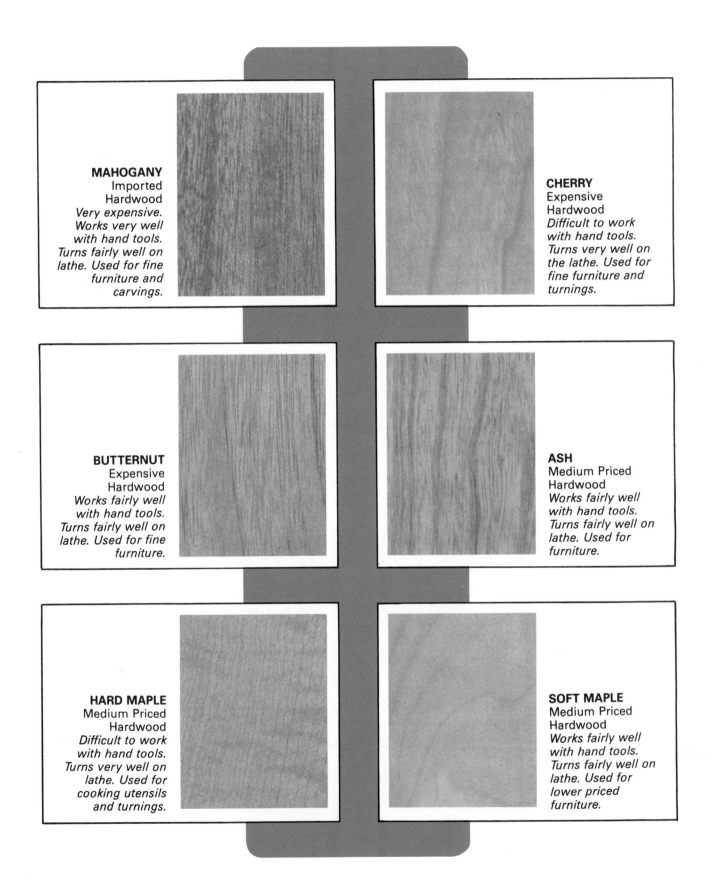

MAHOGANY
Imported
Hardwood
*Very expensive.
Works very well
with hand tools.
Turns fairly well on
lathe. Used for fine
furniture and
carvings.*

CHERRY
Expensive
Hardwood
*Difficult to work
with hand tools.
Turns very well on
the lathe. Used for
fine furniture and
turnings.*

BUTTERNUT
Expensive
Hardwood
*Works fairly well
with hand tools.
Turns fairly well on
lathe. Used for fine
furniture.*

ASH
Medium Priced
Hardwood
*Works fairly well
with hand tools.
Turns fairly well on
lathe. Used for
furniture.*

HARD MAPLE
Medium Priced
Hardwood
*Difficult to work
with hand tools.
Turns very well on
lathe. Used for
cooking utensils
and turnings.*

SOFT MAPLE
Medium Priced
Hardwood
*Works fairly well
with hand tools.
Turns fairly well on
lathe. Used for
lower priced
furniture.*

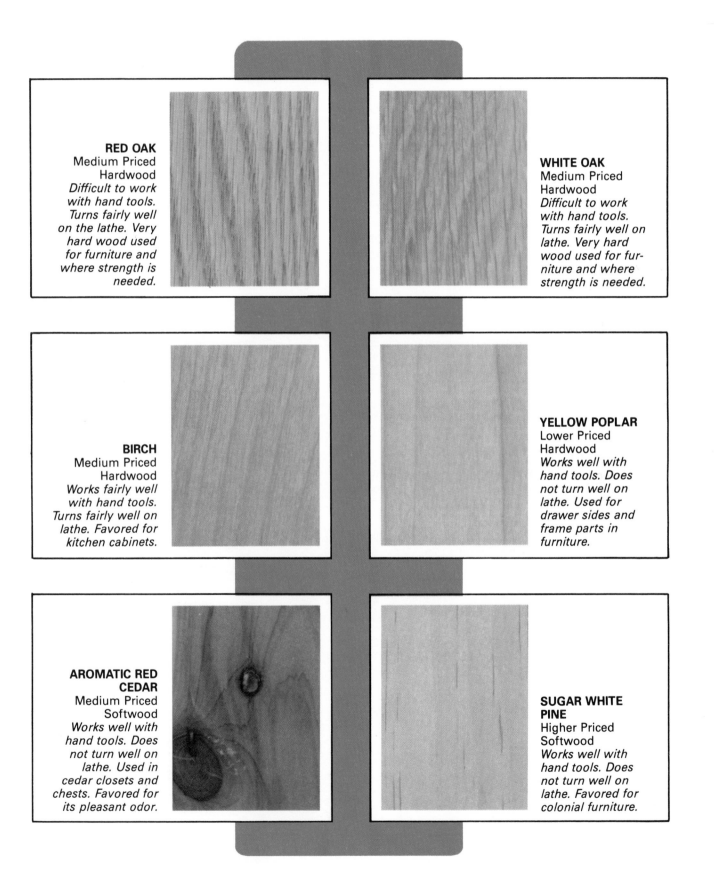

RED OAK
Medium Priced
Hardwood
Difficult to work with hand tools. Turns fairly well on the lathe. Very hard wood used for furniture and where strength is needed.

WHITE OAK
Medium Priced
Hardwood
Difficult to work with hand tools. Turns fairly well on lathe. Very hard wood used for furniture and where strength is needed.

BIRCH
Medium Priced
Hardwood
Works fairly well with hand tools. Turns fairly well on lathe. Favored for kitchen cabinets.

YELLOW POPLAR
Lower Priced
Hardwood
Works well with hand tools. Does not turn well on lathe. Used for drawer sides and frame parts in furniture.

AROMATIC RED CEDAR
Medium Priced
Softwood
Works well with hand tools. Does not turn well on lathe. Used in cedar closets and chests. Favored for its pleasant odor.

SUGAR WHITE PINE
Higher Priced
Softwood
Works well with hand tools. Does not turn well on lathe. Favored for colonial furniture.

PROJECTS

The projects pictured on these pages are built from the plans in Chapter 54. These projects can be built by you or they can be manufactured by your class.

Notice how the wood's color can change the look of a project. You can change the look of your project with stains or inlays. Carving and routing will also change the look of your project.

If you decide to build one of these projects, be sure to study the plans before you begin. You will also need to make a bill of materials, plan of procedure, and a finishing schedule. These are made before you begin working. They make the project easier to build. Section 1 tells you how to make a bill of materials, plan of procedure and finishing schedule.

Sanding Block
This sanding block can be used to finish other projects you build. Your class might want to manufacture them. This one is made of mahogany.

Coat Rack with Hooks
This is an oak coat rack with stain applied. The eagle is made of plastic. It has also been stained. The hooks are made by gluing five pieces of veneer into a hook shape.

Key Rack
These key racks are made from white pine. They have been stained with walnut stain. This project can be made easily with hand or power tools.

Oak Clock with Domino Numbers
The dominos show off well against the oak face. This would make a nice game room clock.

Maple Spoon
This spoon was carved from hard maple using hand tools. To carve maple tools must be sharp. An oil finish suitable for use with food was applied.

Bread Box
Mahogany or other fine wood may be used. This box has a hand-rubbed tung oil finish. The plastic tambours slide up and down.

SANDING BLOCK

COAT RACK

KEY RACK

OAK CLOCK

MAPLE SPOON

BREAD BOX

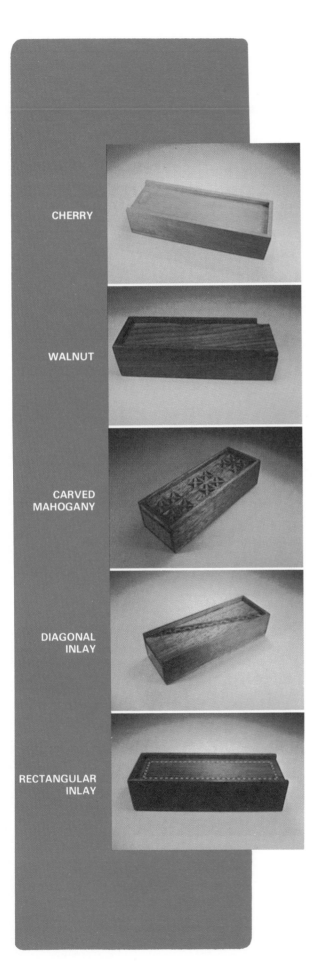

CHERRY

WALNUT

CARVED MAHOGANY

DIAGONAL INLAY

RECTANGULAR INLAY

PENCIL BOX PROJECT

These pencil boxes are easy to build. They can be made out of many kinds of wood. Woods like cherry and walnut are very hard. They should be worked with power tools.

Woods like mahogany and basswood are soft. They can be worked with power tools or hand tools. Softer woods work best for an inlay or chip carving.

Cherry Pencil Box
This pencil box has an oil finish. The box is made of cherry. Cherry is difficult to work with hand tools.

Walnut Pencil Box
This pencil box is made of walnut. The oil finish brings out the natural beauty of the wood.

Carved Mahogany Box
This pencil box is made of mahogany. It is soft and easy to carve. Chapter 11 tells you how to do chip carving. A shellac finish was used on this pencil box.

Mahogany Box with Inlay (Diagonal)
A colored inlay was glued into the lid of this pencil box. This pencil box is made of mahogany. It has a linseed oil finish.

Mahogany Box with Inlay (Rectangular)
This pencil box is made of mahogany. It has a tung oil finish. How would you cut the groove for the inlay?

PENCIL BOX CONSTRUCTION

These two pages show the key construction steps for a pencil box from layout through finishing. Follow the numbered sequence in building your project.

Hand tools have been used for all steps, but power tools may be used. Be sure to study the plans in Chapter 54 before you build this project.

Step 1. Lay out your stock with chalk first.

Step 2. Do your final layout in pencil.

Step 3. Crosscut the side to length.

Step 4. Plane side to exact width.

Step 5. Use a jig to hold the side. Two kerfs are made. The stock between them will be removed later.

Step 6. Make the shoulder cut for the end rabbet.

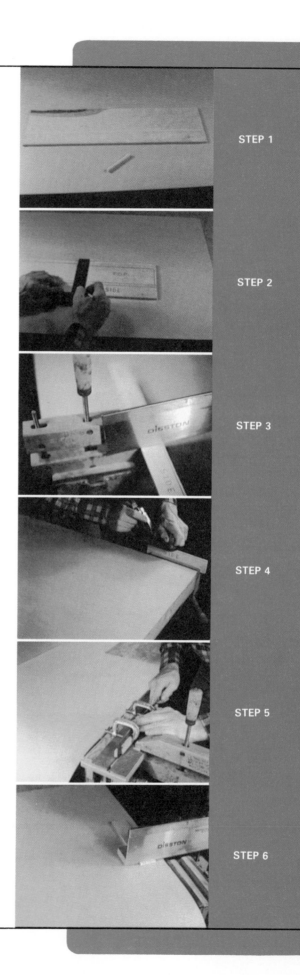

STEP 1

STEP 2

STEP 3

STEP 4

STEP 5

STEP 6

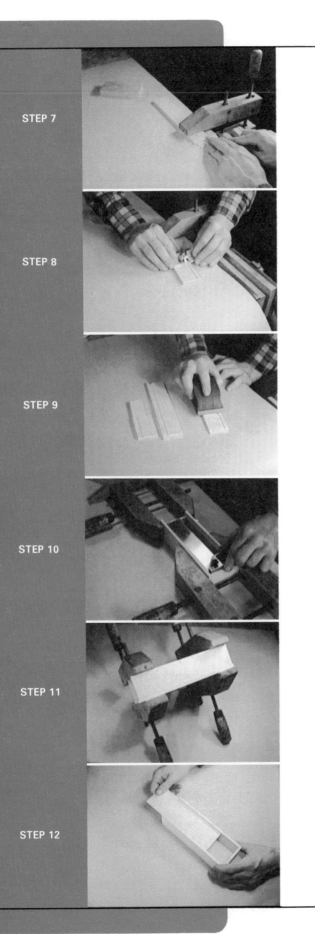

STEP 7

STEP 8

STEP 9

STEP 10

STEP 11

STEP 12

Step 7. Chisel out rabbet. Chisel stock to the shoulder cut; then use a palm router plane to clean up the rabbet.

Step 8. Use the palm router to clean out the groove. The two kerfs were cut in Step 5.

Step 9. After the sides and ends have been dry fitted, sand the inside of these parts. Also sand the inside of the bottom.

Step 10. Glue and clamp the sides and ends together. Use a try square to square the parts.

Step 11. After the glue dries on sides and ends, glue and clamp the bottom in place. Note that the bottom is slightly oversize. It can be sanded to exact size after the glue dries.

Step 12. Fit the lid to the assembled box. It should slide freely. If you have a tight fit, sand or plane the edges of the lid. Be careful not to remove too much stock.

Dart Board Case (Doors Open)
The dart board case was made from yellow poplar. A walnut stain and lacquer finish were applied. Would a light finish look as good next to the colors of the dart board?

Cherry Bowl
Three pieces of cherry were glued together to make this bowl. It was then turned on the lathe. An oil finish suitable for use with food was applied.

Ducks in a Pond
This project requires machine woodworking, carving and woodburning. A clock could be mounted in the center of the moon if desired. The ducks are carved from basswood. Use birch or maple for the other parts. An oil finish was used.

Step Stool
This step stool was made of yellow poplar. A walnut stain and lacquer finish were applied. How would you cut the curves on the sides of the step stool?

Dolphin
This dolphin was carved from basswood. It was cut to rough shape on the band saw. A nigrosine (black) stain was used for color. Three coats of lacquer from an aerosol can were applied after the stain dried. The base is also basswood. It has a walnut stain and oil finish.

Oak Tool Box
Oak was used to make this tool box. Oak is a strong wood. It will hold up well on the job. An oil finish was used on the tool box.

DART BOARD

CHERRY BOWL

WOOD DUCKS

STEP STOOL

DOLPHIN

OAK TOOL BOX

CHAPTER 6

After materials have been selected, they must be laid out and cut into usable sizes. To lay out stock requires you to know about lumber defects and layout tools. This chapter will provide that knowledge and help you learn to lay out stock with little or no waste.

KEY TERMS

stock layout	bench rule
try square	inches
try and miter square	millimeters
combination square	utility knife
framing square	scratch awl
compass	knot
divider	warp
trammel points	check
sliding T bevel	slake
marking gage	honeycomb
tape rule	pitch pocket

LAYOUT TOOLS

Woodworking layout tools are used to mark stock accurately. Each layout tool has a specific purpose. Knowing the purpose of each tool will help you to use it correctly.

Try Square

A *try square* (Figure 6-1) is used to mark right angles on stock. It may also be used to check a corner to see if it has been cut squarely (Figure 6-2). The try square is an important layout tool. Most work done in wood requires 90° corners. A try square ensures that all corners have a 90° angle.

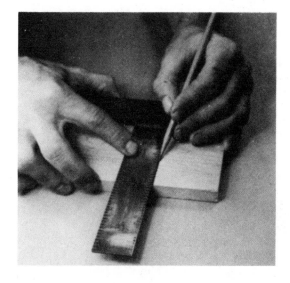

Figure 6-1. *A try square is used to mark right angles on stock.*

Figure 6-2. *A try square can check your work. Corners should be a right angle.*

Try and Miter Square

A *try and miter square* (Figure 6-3) looks like a try square, but may also be used to lay out 45° angles. The top of the handle on the miter gage is used to mark 45° angles. A 45° angle is one-half of a 90° angle and is commonly used in woodworking for miter joints (Figure 6-4).

Figure 6-3. *A try and miter square can be used to lay out angles of 90° and 45°. Notice the 45° angle on the head or handle.*

Figure 6-4. *The miter joint is a common woodworking joint. A try and miter square or combination square can be used to lay it out.*

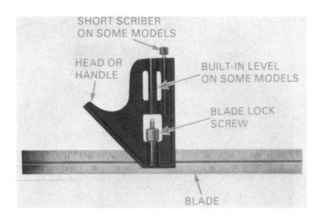

Figure 6-5. *The combination square has a steel blade that slides in the head. The blade is locked in place by tightening the blade lock screw.*

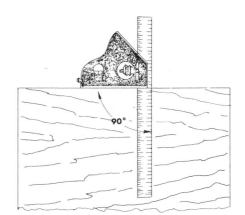

SQUARE A LINE ON STOCK

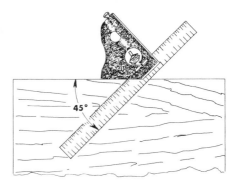

LAYING OUT A 45° ANGLE

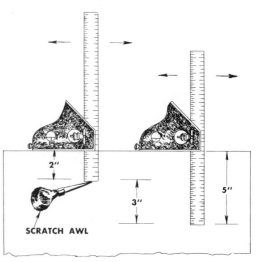

DRAWING PARALLEL LINES

Figure 6-6. *The combination square can be used for many layout jobs.*

Combination Square

A *combination square* has a blade that slides in the head of the square (Figure 6-5). The handle on the combination square can be locked to the blade by tightening the blade lock screw.

The combination square can measure the depth of a hole. It will also mark a line parallel to the edge of your work (Figure 6-6).

One face of the handle can be used to mark 90° angles and the other face can be used to mark 45° angles.

Framing Square

A *framing square* (Figure 6-7) is larger than a try square. This makes layout with a framing square very accurate for large pieces.

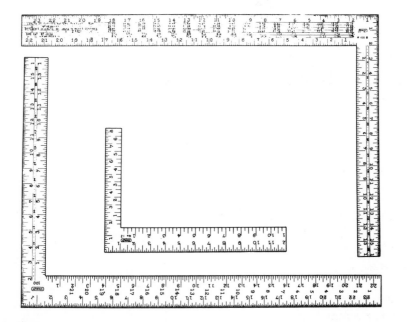

RAFTER OR FRAMING TABLE
THIS TABLE APPEARS ON THE BODY OF THE SQUARE.
IT IS USED TO DETERMINE THE LENGTH OF THE COM-
MON, VALLEY, HIP AND JACK RAFTERS AND THE
ANGLES AT WHICH THEY MUST BE CUT TO FIT AT
THE RIDGE AND PLATE.

OCTAGON SCALE
THIS SCALE IS ON THE TONGUE OF THE SQUARE. IT IS
USED TO LAY OUT A FIGURE WITH EIGHT EQUAL SIDES
ON A SQUARE PIECE OF TIMBER.

ESSEX TABLE
THIS TABLE APPEARS ON THE BODY OF THE SQUARE.
IT SHOWS THE BOARD MEASURE IN FEET AND TWELFTHS
OF FEET, OF BOARDS 1 INCH THICK OF USUAL LENGTHS
AND WIDTHS.

BRACE TABLE
THIS TABLE APPEARS ON THE TONGUE OF THE SQUARE.
IT SHOWS THE LENGTH OF THE COMMON BRACES.

Figure 6-7. *The framing square is larger than a try square. It is used by carpenters to lay out braces and rafters. The tables stamped on the square provide layout information.*

Figure 6-8. *Hold the square firmly. Make sure the head is against the machined edge of your stock. Use a sharp pencil or utility knife to make your line.*

Using a Square. All squares must be held firmly to obtain accurate layout lines. Make sure that the handle is held securely against the machined edge of your stock (Figure 6-8).

Mark the stock by pulling a sharp pencil or *utility knife* along the blade of the square (Figure 6-8). Do not make your layout line too wide. Narrow lines are more accurate.

Compass and Dividers
Both a *compass* and *dividers* have adjustable legs and are used to mark off distances (Figure 6-9). A compass has one leg that holds a pencil or lead.

It does not scratch the wood, but marks it with the pencil. The legs on dividers have sharpened steel points. They mark the wood by scratching it or piercing it.

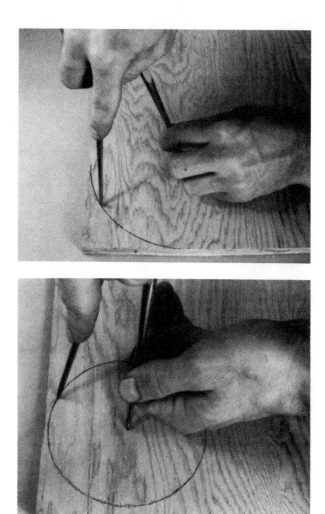

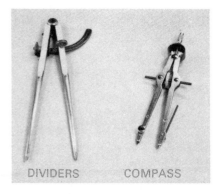

DIVIDERS   COMPASS

Figure 6-9. *A compass or dividers can be used to mark distances. The compass has a pencil or lead in one leg. The dividers have two pointed steel legs. The dividers mark the wood by scratching or making an indentation.*

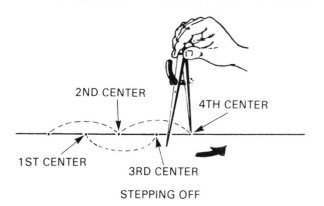

2ND CENTER

4TH CENTER

1ST CENTER

3RD CENTER

STEPPING OFF

Figure 6-10. *The compass and dividers can be used to lay out circles and arcs. They may also be used to step off equal distances.*

Figure 6-11. *Use a ruler to adjust a compass or dividers.*

Both the compass and dividers can mark circles or arcs (Figure 6-10). They may also be used to "step off" equal distances. Use a ruler to adjust the compass or dividers (Figure 6-11).

Trammel Points

Trammel points (Figure 6-12) are used to mark large arcs and circles. Trammel points are clamped to a wooden beam. One point remains stationary at the center of the arc or circle, while the other marks the stock. For pencil layout, one

of the trammel points holds a pencil in its clamping fixture. Figure 6-13 shows trammel points being used to lay out a circle.

Sliding T Bevel

The *sliding T bevel* (Figure 6-14) has a movable blade that can be clamped at any angle or

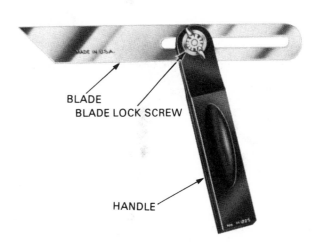

BLADE
BLADE LOCK SCREW

HANDLE

Figure 6-14. *The sliding T bevel has a movable blade that can be clamped at any angle.*

Figure 6-12. *Trammel points are used to mark large areas and circles. They are clamped to a beam.*

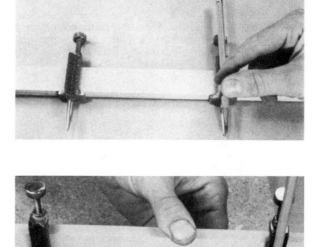

BEAM

Figure 6-13. *Laying out a circle with trammel points.*

length. It is used to lay out angles on stock (Figure 6-15) or adjust tools (Figure 6-16) to the correct work angle.

A *protractor* may be used to adjust the sliding T bevel to any desired angle (Figure 6-17).

Figure 6-15. *The sliding T bevel can be used to lay out angular cuts on wood.*

Figure 6-16. *The sliding T bevel can be used to adjust tools to the correct work angle. The miter gage angle is being adjusted with the sliding T bevel.*

Figure 6-17. *The sliding T bevel can be adjusted using a protractor.*

Marking Gage

A *marking gage* (Figure 6-18) is used to lay out lines parallel to the edge of a piece of stock. The beam slides in the head and may be adjusted to the desired measurement. Marking is done by the pin which protrudes through the beam. Keep the pin sharp by filing it. Figure 6-19 shows the correct use of a marking gage.

Rulers

Rulers are very important layout tools. Without rulers, accurate measurement would be difficult. The two most common rulers used in woodworking are the *bench rule* and the *tape rule* (Figure 6-20).

Bench Rule. The bench rule is made of wood. It is usually two feet (about 610 mm) long. The ends are capped in brass to protect them from wear and damage. A bench rule is divided into either one-eighth or one-sixteenth inch units. Metric bench rules are divided into one-millimeter units. The bench rule is used for layout at a workbench but is not commonly used elsewhere. This is because its length makes it difficult to carry.

MITER GAGE

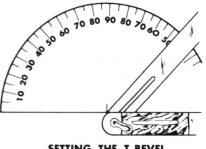

SETTING THE T BEVEL

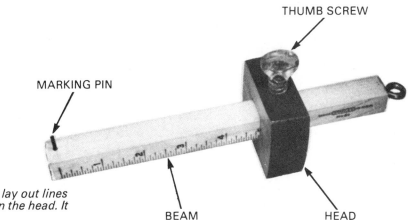

THUMB SCREW

MARKING PIN

BEAM

HEAD

Figure 6-18. *The marking gage is used to lay out lines parallel to stock edges. The beam slides in the head. It is locked in place with the thumb screw.*

Figure 6-19. *Tilt the marking gage slightly and pull it toward you. The pin will mark your stock.*

Tape Rule. A tape rule blade is made of metal. The blade winds into the protective case when not in use. The tape rule is easy to use and carry. Some tape rules have a clip attached to the case for carrying the tape rule on your belt (Figure 6-21). Locking tape rules allow the blade to be locked at any position. This can be useful for layout work. The tape rule is also divided into either one-sixteenth inch or one millimeter units.

When using the tape rule, be careful with the blade. Avoid sharp bends in the blade. Protect the end of the blade from breakage by feeding it slowly into the case.

Figure 6-20. *Rulers are important layout tools. They ensure accurate measurement. Pictured here are a bench rule and two tape rules.*

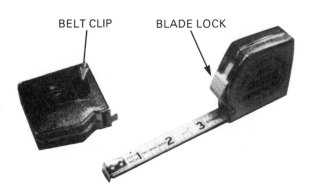

BELT CLIP   BLADE LOCK

Figure 6-21. *Some tape rules have a clip so they may be attached to a belt. A tape may also have a blade lock. This allows the blade to be locked in any position.*

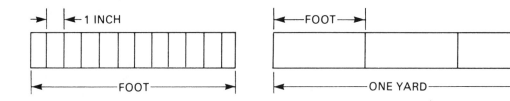

Figure 6-22. *The principle units in the customary system are the inch, foot and yard.*

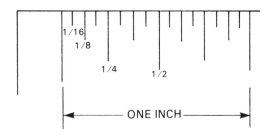

Reading a Ruler

Woodworkers traditionally used the customary inch system of measurement. You may encounter some metric measurement. If you know both systems of measurement, working from any plan will be easy.

Customary System. Principal length units in the customary system of measurement are the inch, foot, and yard (Figure 6-22). There are twelve inches in a foot and 3 feet in a yard. For dimensions smaller than one inch, the inch is divided into smaller parts. Figure 6-23 shows the relationship between the parts of an inch. The inch is commonly divided into two, four, eight or sixteen parts.

Count the spaces on the enlarged inch in Figure 6-23. There are sixteen equal units. Each unit is one sixteenth (¹⁄₁₆) of an inch. Four-sixteenths (⁴⁄₁₆) of an inch is equal to one-fourth (¼) of an inch and two-sixteenths of an inch is equal to one-eighth (⅛) of an inch.

Whenever there is an even number of parts to an inch such as ⁶⁄₁₆, ⁶⁄₈ or ²⁄₄, that number can be reduced to lower terms such as ⅜, ¾ or ½. Fractions in lowest terms are easier to lay out and are less confusing.

Metric System. Metric measure is based on the meter, which is slightly longer than a yard (39.97 inches). In a meter there are 100 centimeters or

FRACTION CONVERSIONS	
INCH FRACTIONS	LOWEST TERM
1/16	1/16
2/16	1/8
3/16	3/16
4/16	1/4
5/16	5/16
6/16	3/8
7/16	7/16
8/16	1/2
9/16	9/16
10/16	5/8
11/16	11/16
12/16	3/4
13/16	13/16
14/16	7/8
15/16	15/16
16/16	1

Figure 6-23. *The inch can be divided into two, four, eight, or sixteen parts. The inch is enlarged for illustrative purposes.*

MILLIMETERS

METRIC

0   10   20   30   40   50   60   70   80   90   **100**   110   120   130   140   150

1,000 MILLIMETERS = 100 CENTIMETERS = 1 METER

Figure 6-24. *All metric measurement is in units of ten. Millimeter is the accepted unit in woodworking.*

1,000 millimeters (Figure 6-24). All metric measurement is in units of 10. Metric woodworking plans use millimeters as the accepted unit. If you wish to convert them to meters divide by 1000.

Measurement problems are presented in Figure 6-25. Measure the lines in both inches and millimeters. Record your answers on a separate sheet of paper. The correct answers are printed upside down at the bottom of Figure 6-25.

Marking Stock

Stock can be marked during layout with several different tools. For a rough layout, white chalk works best. It is easy to see and can be rubbed off easily if the layout is changed (Figure 6-26).

A pencil can also be used for marking your layout. Keep pencils sharp so that they make a thin line. Thin lines are more accurate. When moving a pencil along the edge of a square, keep your eye on the pencil. Do not let it move away from the edge of the square. Keep all pencil lines light. If they cut into the wood it will be difficult to remove them.

A utility knife (Figure 6-27) can also be used for laying out stock. The blade cuts a very thin

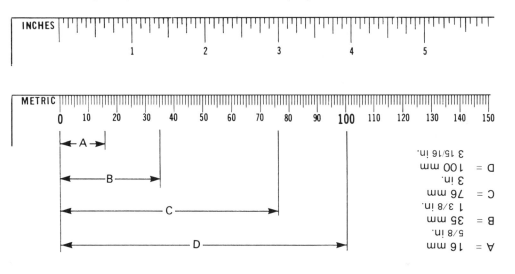

Answers:
A = 16 mm
5/8 in.
B = 35 mm
1 3/8 in.
C = 76 mm
3 in.
D = 100 mm
3 15/16 in.

Figure 6-25. *Measure these lines using both the metric and the customary systems. Record your answers on a separate sheet of paper. The correct answers are printed at the bottom.*

Figure 6-26. *White chalk works best for rough layout. It can be rubbed off if the layout is changed.*

Figure 6-27. *Marking stock with a utility knife leaves a fine line. Store the utility knife in a safe place when not in use.*

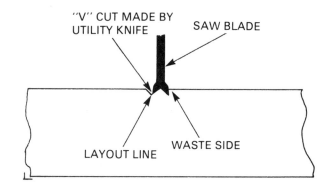

Figure 6-28. *The cut made by the utility knife reduces grain tear-out.*

layout line. The cut in the wood causes fibers to break at the line during sawing or chiseling. This reduces the possibility of grain tear-out. Figure 6-28 shows how the cut reduces grain tear-out.

Work carefully with the utility knife. It has a very sharp blade. Cut to your side away from your body. When the utility knife is not in use, store it in a safe place with the blade covered.

A *scratch awl* may also be used to mark stock (Figure 6-29). The scratch awl has a very sharp point that will scratch or indent the wood. It is commonly used to mark the center of a hole. The indentation made by the awl forms a starting point for a drill bit or wood screw. The scratch awl may also be used to scribe a straight line.

LUMBER DEFECTS

It is necessary to work around stock defects during layout. Stock defects make machining and finishing difficult. Although some stock defects give your work natural beauty, others can detract from its overall appearance. As you become an experienced woodworker, laying out defective stock will become easy. Higher grades of lumber will have less defects. But higher grades cost more.

Knots

Knots are caused by branches that have grown from the tree trunk (Figure 6-30). Some knots are loose while others are tight. If a branch dies before the tree is cut, the knot will be loose.

Figure 6-29. *The scratch awl can be used to mark stock. It is most often used to mark the center of the hole.*

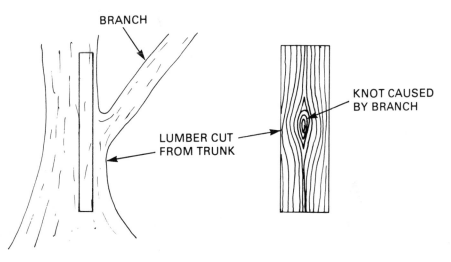

Figure 6-30. *Knots are caused by branches that have grown from the trunk.*

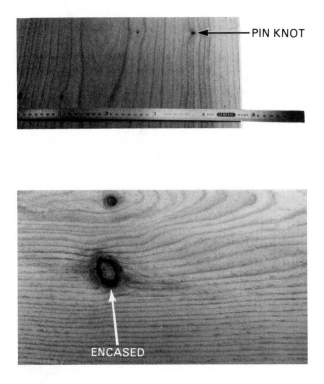

Figure 6-31. *Small knots are made by small branches. They are called "pin knots".*

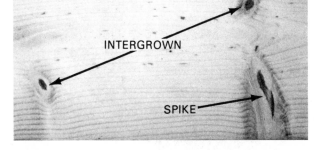

Figure 6-32. *Common types of knots are shown here.*

The grain around a knot runs at an angle to the grain of the stock. This causes the grain around the knot to tear or lift when the lumber is machined. Small knots (Figure 6-31) are called pin knots. They do not interfere with machining as much as larger knots do. Figure 6-32 pictures common types of knots.

Warp

Warp is any deviation from a true plane. There are four common types of warp: *cup, crook, bow,* and *twist* or *wind* (Figure 6-33). By cutting warped stock into smaller pieces there will be less waste. Figure 6-34 shows some methods of working with warped stock.

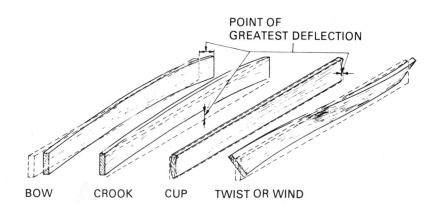

POINT OF
GREATEST DEFLECTION

BOW   CROOK   CUP   TWIST OR WIND

Figure 6-33. *Warp is any deviation from a true plane. Pictured are four common types of warp.*

Figure 6-34. *Cutting warped stock into smaller pieces increases usable stock.*

BOW

CROOK

CUT INTO NARROWER PIECES
AND GLUE UP A PANEL

CUT INTO SHORTER
PIECES

Figure 6-35. *Wane is bark on the edge of a piece of stock.*

WANE

Causes of warp. Warp may be caused by knots or uneven drying. Angular grain around a knot can cause stock to warp. Lumber should be stacked evenly with spacers between layers. This allows air to circulate keeping the wood dry and preventing warp.

Wane

Bark on the edge of stock is known as *wane*. Wane also describes the angular edge from which the bark has been removed (Figure 6-35). The angular edge is wasted stock since most products require a straight edge. It is good practice to cut wane away from the stock before it is laid out.

Checks

Checks are cracks that run perpendicular to the annular rings (Figure 6-36). Checks are usually found on the ends of solid stock. They are caused by the drying process. End grain dries quicker than face and edge grain. The quicker drying causes stresses and shrinkage which results in checks. Checks are cut off before laying out stock.

Shakes

Shakes are a separation between the annular rings (Figure 6-37). They are caused by a shock to a tree such as extreme wind or impact. Shakes can sometimes be removed by resawing. Stock with shakes is not suited to most woodworking projects, but may be used for practice or experimenting.

Honeycomb

Honeycomb is separation perpendicular to the annular rings (Figure 6-38). Honeycomb usually

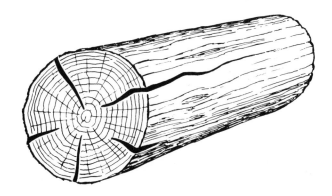

Figure 6-36. *Checks are cracks in the wood. They are perpendicular to the annular rings.*

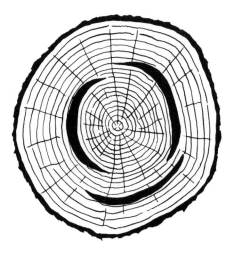

Figure 6-37. *Shakes are a separation between the annular rings. Wood with shakes is not suitable for most woodworking projects.*

Figure 6-38. *Honeycomb is a separation perpendicular to the annular rings. It usually follows the medullary rays.*

Figure 6-39. *Pitch pockets are cavities in the wood. They contain pitch, a sticky resin.*

Figure 6-40. *Stock with pitch pockets can be used if the pitch pockets are not visible.*

PITCH POCKET
ON BACK

occurs in the wood rays. They tend to separate. Honeycomb is not always visible from the wood's surface. Honeycombed stock is not suitable for most woodworking projects. Use it for practice or experimenting.

Pitch Pockets

Pitch pockets (Figure 6-39) are cavities in wood. They contain *pitch* which is a sticky resin common in softwoods. Lay out your pieces around pitch pockets. If the back side of a piece will not be visible, the pitch pocket can be laid out on that piece (Figure 6-40). Make sure the pitch pocket is located on the back side.

WORKING WITH LUMBER DEFECTS

When you lay out stock, study the wood carefully. Check both sides of the stock for defects. Plan your layout to avoid defects. Lay out your pieces with chalk. This allows you to change the layout as often as needed. Avoid waste whenever possible. But make sure you have allowed enough extra stock to square your piece.

Figure 6-41. *Glue narrow pieces together to obtain wide panels. This reduces waste.*

If you need wide panels, consider gluing several narrow pieces edge to edge (Figure 6-41). The narrow pieces will be less likely to warp and waste will be reduced.

Think before you cut. A careful layout saves time, energy, and money. Save your best stock for the most important parts of your project (Figure 6-42). Doors, drawers and tops should be made from pieces with the most figure (grain pattern) and best color. Do not waste beautiful wood on drawer sides or cabinet backs.

Figure 6-42. *Save your best stock for the visible parts of the project. The best stock was used for the panels.*

LAYING OUT SHEET STOCK

All sheet stock should be laid out according to the stock cutting sheet.

The edges and ends of sheet stock are precision cut so that the sheet is a perfect rectangle. These edges are called the *factory edges.* Use the factory edges for layout work. They will yield the most accurate layout.

Always make an allowance for the saw cut or kerf when you lay out sheet stock. Usually a quarter of an inch (6 mm) is enough.

QUESTIONS FOR REVIEW

1. Can you name some of the common layout tools used in woodworking and describe their use?
2. Why is a framing square more accurate than a try square for layout work?
3. What is the difference between a divider and a compass? For what are they used?
4. How are trammel points used? Can a pencil be used with trammel points?
5. For what type of layout work is a sliding T-bevel used?
6. What types of layout tools could be used to make a line parallel to the edge of a piece of stock?
7. Why is chalk used for rough layout work?
8. Why should layout lines in pencil be light and thin?
9. What precautions should be taken when using a utility knife for stock layout?
10. What causes knots in solid stock? Why does the grain around a knot tear or lift when planed?
11. How would you define warp? Can you name and describe four common types of warp?
12. What causes stock to warp?
13. What is wane? How is this defect removed?
14. What is a check? How does this defect differ from shake?
15. What is honeycomb? Is honeycombed stock suitable to woodworking projects?
16. Can you suggest any practices that should be observed when laying out defective stock? How do these practices save time and reduce waste?
17. How would you lay out sheet stock? Why is a stock cutting sheet used as a cutting plan?
18. What is a factory edge? How does a factory edge help you lay out stock?
19. Why is an allowance for the saw cut, or kerf important when laying out sheet stock or solid stock?

SUGGESTED ACTIVITIES

1. Using a straight edge, draw a line about six inches long. Use a ruler and mark off the following dimensions, reading from left to right: ½″, 1 ½″, 2 ⅝″, 3 ¼″, 3 ¹¹/₁₆″.

2. Select wood samples that show the following defects: knot, wane, warp.

3. Identify 3 layout tools in your shop. Describe how they are used.

4. Use a try square to check the end of a board for squareness.

CHAPTER 7

General Shop Safety

Before you enter the school shop, you should be aware of general safety precautions. These precautions will help you do a safer and better job.

Your instructor will provide you with safety rules for the shop. These may include rules for hand and power tools. There are also safety rules in this book for every hand and power tool. Be sure to follow these rules. If you do not understand them, ask your instructor.

KEY TERMS

safety rules   unsafe condition
housekeeping   unsafe act
personal protection   guards
shop courtesy

GENERAL SHOP SAFETY

1. Know where *safety rules* are posted in your shop. Study those rules before going to work.
2. Know where tools and materials are stored in your shop. Always return tools and materials to their proper storage space.
3. Work safely. Study the safety rules in this text before you go to work. If you do not know the safe way of using a machine or tool, ask your instructor.
4. Practice good *housekeeping* (Figure 7-1). Keep floors and machines clear of scrap and sawdust. Clean up any scrap or liquids on the floor before someone falls or trips (Figure 7-2).
5. Always wear *personal* protection. Eye protection must be worn in the shop at all times (Figure 7-3). You may also need a face shield, rubber gloves or hearing protection for certain jobs in the shop (Figure 7-4). Never perform a job without the proper protection.

Figure 7-1. *Practice good housekeeping.*

Figure 7-2. *Keep floors clean.*

Figure 7-3. *Always wear eye protection*

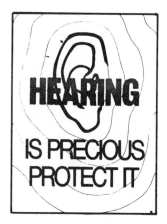

Figure 7-4. *Wear ear protection when necessary.*

6. Never work around machines when you are tired or when you are taking medication. It is too easy to make a mistake. Machine woodworking should be done only when you feel well and rested.

7. Lift objects carefully (Figure 7-5). Use your legs for lifting. Keep your back straight. Squat to grasp the object, then straighten your legs to lift it. If the object is too heavy for you, get help.

8. When handling or storing lumber, work carefully. Make sure everyone is clear of lumber before you begin moving it (Figure 7-6). Stack lumber carefully. It should be stacked in straight, even piles. Shorter pieces should be stacked on top of the pile. Remove or bend down nails that may be sticking out of the lumber (Figure 7-7).

9. Avoid horseplay in the woodworking shop. Never wrestle, abuse tools, or throw objects. Practice *shop courtesy* at all times. Help your classmates when necessary, but do not distract them.

10. Think safety. If you see an *unsafe condition* or an *unsafe act*, tell your instructor or supervisor.

11. Dress for safety. Remove neckties or scarves. Tie your hair back or wear a cap. Roll sleeves up above the elbow. Take off rings, watches and other jewelry. Avoid wearing sandals or other open shoes in the shop.

12. Know fire safety (Figure 7-8). Know where fire exits and fire extinguishers are located. Know how to report a fire and what to do if a fire alarm is sounded. Be able to identify all classes of fire.

13. Use all safety fixtures, devices, and *guards* when working (Figure 7-9). Never remove a guard without asking your instructor for permission.

Figure 7-5. *Lift objects in the proper way.*

SAFETY CHECK

Before you begin working in the shop, ask yourself these questions:

Do I know shop safety rules and what they mean?

Do I know the safety rules for tools and machines? Do I know what they mean?

Am I prepared with protective equipment such as: protective glasses, rubber gloves, faceshield, and hearing protection?

Do I have the correct mental attitude? Am I well rested and not taking medication?

Am I prepared to concentrate on my work observing all safety rules?

Am I dressed correctly? Sleeves rolled up, jewelry removed, hair tied back, neckties or scarves removed?

Have I studied my project or assigned work so I know what to do when I go to work?

Figure 7-6. *Watch for others when moving large materials.*

Figure 7-8. *Know what to do in case of fire.*

Figure 7-7. *Bend down nail points or remove nails in loose lumber.*

Figure 7-9. *Never remove guards or safety fixtures.*

QUESTIONS FOR REVIEW

1. Why is it important to know general safety precautions?
2. Where can you learn the safety for your shop?
3. If you do not understand the safety rules for a tool or machine, what should you do?
4. Why must floors be kept clear of scrap?
5. Why should machine woodworking be done only when you feel well and rested?
6. How should objects be lifted in the shop?
7. How should lumber be moved and stacked in the shop?
8. What should you do if you see an unsafe act or condition?
9. How do you dress for safety in the woodshop?
10. What must you know about fire safety in the woodshop?
11. What should you do before you remove a guard from a machine?

SUGGESTED ACTIVITIES

1. Identify the location of the fire extinguisher in your shop.

2. How do you report a fire? What is the phone number you call?

3. Identify guards on power equipment in your shop.

4. Demonstrate the correct way of lifting.

5. What personal protection do you use in your shop?

MY PLEDGE

Am I Ready to Work in the Woodshop?

Check If Ready

_____ I know shop, machine and tool safety rules.

_____ The phone number for reporting a fire is _____.

_____ I have the correct personal protection:
safety glasses
rubber gloves
faceshield
hearing protection

_____ I have the correct mental attitude:
well-rested
not taking medication

_____ I am prepared to concentrate on my work observing all safety rules.

_____ I am dressed correctly:
sleeves rolled up
hair tied back
jewelry removed
ties/scarves removed.

_____ I know what to do:
I have studied my assignment or project.
I have planned my work.
I know the safe way to do the job.

SECTION 2

Hand Tool Woodworking

CHAPTER 8

Hand Tool Safety

Safe use of hand tools requires that you plan your work carefully, use tools correctly and practice good working habits. As you read this chapter, you will become familiar with work safety. If you observe the procedures and practices listed in this chapter, you should know how to use hand tools safely and produce better work.

KEY TERMS

tang	secure footing
handle	cutting edge
mushroomed	dulling
brittle tools	personal protection

PLANNING YOUR WORK

A safe worker always plans a working sequence before beginning. There are many steps to planning the entire job. The stock must first be laid out accurately, and then the cutting, planing, boring, or shaping operations must be planned. First gather tools for the work and then inspect them (Figure 8-1). If tools are dull or in poor repair, sharpen or repair them before beginning the work.

It is also important to plan the best way of working the stock. When planing or carving, it is best to work with the grain. This helps you determine the best way of clamping your stock for easiest cutting. Clamp stock securely before you begin. If the work is complicated, the clamping sequence may require a plan.

USING TOOLS CORRECTLY

Using a tool correctly includes keeping it well maintained and using it for its intended purpose (Figure 8-2). Poorly maintained tools increase operator fatigue, decrease accuracy and cause accidents.

Figure 8-1. *Tools should be sharp and in good repair. Never use dull or damaged tools.*

Figure 8-2. *Follow these rules for safe tools operation.*

Hammering tools must have a well-fitted handle without defects. The head should not be chipped, cracked, or mushroomed (flattened outward).

The tip of a screwdriver should be undamaged. Use a screwdriver that fits the screw. Never hold the work while driving a screw. Do not use a screwdriver as a prybar or knife.

Chisels and other cutting tools must have a handle in good repair and a sharp cutting edge blade. Always use a handle over the sharp edge (tang) of a rasp or a file (Figure 8-3). A rasp or file without a handle may cause blisters or pierce your hand.

It is also important that a tool be used only for its intended purpose. Using the tool for any other purpose could damage the tool or cause injury. Brittle tools such as files may snap if they are used as prying tools.

Forcing a tool can also cause problems. You could slip while driving the tool, or the tool could break. Keep a secure footing and guide your tool into the work. Avoid forcing the tool.

When working with a hand tool, it is important that you guide the tool away from your body. Most hand tools have sharp cutting edges. If they are pulled toward your body, you could be cut. If the tool is designed to be pulled toward you, avoid forcing the tool. Keep your balance and pull the tool with moderate force. Tools are safest when guided away from your body.

When you work with chisels and carving tools, keep your hands behind the tool's cutting edge (Figure 8-4). This will protect you from injury if the wood splits or the tool slips.

Storing tools properly is important. When you are finished using a tool, put it away (Figure 8-5). Cover cutting edges when not in use (Figure

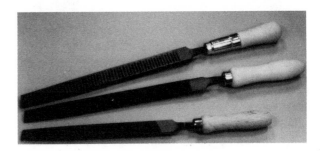

Figure 8-3. *A tool must have a well-fitted handle to be used safely.*

Figure 8-4. *When working with a sharp tool, keep your hands behind the cutting edge.*

Figure 8-5. *When you are finished using a tool, put it away.*

8-6). The cover protects the cutting edge from dulling, and protects you from being cut. A piece of wood, leather or cardboard can be used to cover the tool. Never put sharp tools into your pocket (Figure 8-7); a serious injury could result.

PRACTICING GOOD WORKING HABITS

Good working habits help you work safely. The first habit you should practice is *personal protection.* Always wear eye protection while working with wood and tools. Just a piece of sawdust in your eye can cause discomfort. It is important to protect your eyes at all times (Figure 8-8).

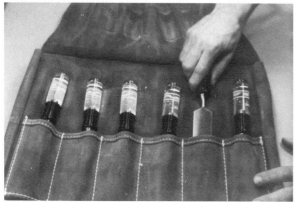

Figure 8-6. *Always cover cutting edges of tools when not in use.*

Figure 8-8. *Always wear eye protection.*

Figure 8-7. *Avoid carrying tools in your pocket. A serious injury could result.*

Figure 8-9. *Be sure you have adequate clearance and check that no one is in the way before you move long pieces of stock.*

Another important working habit is to keep the shop neat and clear of scrap. This helps guard against injuries caused by slipping or falling. When moving large pieces of stock always check the area before you swing or turn the stock (Figure 8-9). The stock could strike someone and cause serious injury.

Avoid distracting other workers. You could cause them to make a mistake or have an accident. Develop the habit of assisting other students when needed. Work cooperatively and the job can be done safely.

You should walk in the shop. Never run! Running does not save time. It may cause an injury (Figure 8-10). Work slowly and carefully. You will become faster with practice but not by rushing.

When working at a bench, keep your footing. Make sure that you are not off balance. If the tool slips, you could lose your balance and fall. A

Figure 8-10. *Running does not save time. It could cause injury.*

secure, balanced footing will eliminate the problem. Always clamp your material. This frees both hands for work.

QUESTIONS FOR REVIEW

1. Why should you plan your work?
2. How would you describe a well maintained tool?
3. Why must a tool have a handle to be used safely?
4. What can happen if you force a tool or use it for an unintended purpose?
5. What is the best direction for guiding hand tools?
6. Why is it important to store tools properly when they are not in use?
7. What are some of the working habits you should develop in the wood shop?

SUGGESTED ACTIVITIES

1. Check the tools in your home to see if they are in safe condition. Make a list of unsafe tools and note how they could be made safe.

2. Make a protective cover for any cutting tools you have. A simple protective cover can be made from cardboard and tape. Wrap the cardboard over the edge and tape the ends together.

CHAPTER 9

Hand Sawing Stock

Sawing stock is an important woodworking operation. A hand saw (Figure 9-1) is used to cut stock into manageable or usable pieces. Stock is usually cut to width or length but may also be cut to thickness.

KEY TERMS

rip sawing (ripping)	dovetail saw
crosscutting	miter box
teeth per inch	compass saw
saw set	keynote saw
kerf	coping saw
back saw	fret saw

The direction of the wood fibers in a piece of wood determines the grain of the piece. When stock is cut to width, it is sawn along the direction of the grain. This is called *rip sawing* or *ripping* (Figure 9-2). When stock cut to length it is cut across the grain. This is called *crosscutting* (Figure 9-3). There are special saws for ripping and crosscutting. A rip saw will not crosscut well, and a crosscut saw is not designed to rip.

The teeth on a rip saw and a crosscut saw are designed differently. This is because cutting across the grain or wood fibers is different than

cutting along the grain. Rip teeth cut like a chisel. They are filed to an edge instead of a point (Figure 9-2). The front of the tooth has a flat edge. It does not come to a point because the rip saw cuts with the wood fibers. Crosscut teeth are sharpened to a point. The sharp points cut the wood fibers easily (Figure 9-3).

ACTUAL CUT (RIPSAWING)

Figure 9-2. *Cutting with the grain is called* ripping. *Rip teeth are filed to an edge.*

ACTUAL CUT (CROSSCUTTING)

Figure 9-3. *Cutting across the grain is called* crosscutting. *Crosscut teeth are sharpened to a point.*

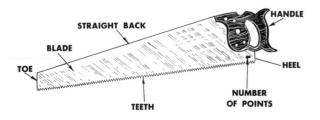

Figure 9-1. *The parts of a hand saw are shown.*

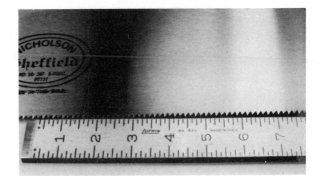

Figure 9-4. *There is always one more point than teeth per inch. This saw has eight points or seven teeth per inch.*

SAW TERMINOLOGY

Saw Size

There are two dimensions to saw size. They are blade length and teeth per inch. Blade length is measured along the cutting edge (Figure 9-4). A common length is 26 inches (660 mm).

The number of *teeth per inch* determines the smoothness of the cut. The more teeth, the smoother the cut. Some saws are sold by the number of points per inch. The number of points per inch is usually stamped on the blade near the handle. There is always one more point per inch than there are teeth per inch. A crosscut saw has 6 to 8 teeth per inch. A rip saw has 5 to 6 teeth per inch.

Saw Set and Kerf

Saw teeth are bent or offset to provide clearance (Figure 9-5). This is called the *set*. If the teeth were not offset, the blade would bind in the cut. Teeth are bent alternately away from the blade. This set makes the cut wider than the blade so the saw will not bind.

The cut made by the blade is called a *kerf*. The size of the kerf or cut is regulated by the saw set. The more set the teeth have, the wider the kerf will be. When sawing stock, make sure the cut is on the waste side of your layout line (Figure 9-6).

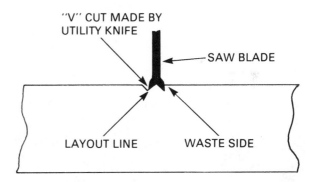

Figure 9-6. *Make sure the cut is on the waste side of your layout line.*

RIPPING STOCK TO WIDTH

Before ripping, lay out your stock and clamp it securely to a bench or sawhorse. You may hold stock on a sawhorse with your knee if the height is comfortable. Grasp the saw with a handshake grip. Begin your cut with short strokes at a low angle. You may want to start the kerf with a few back strokes. Pull the blade toward you until the kerf is started. Make sure the blade is on the waste side of your layout line.

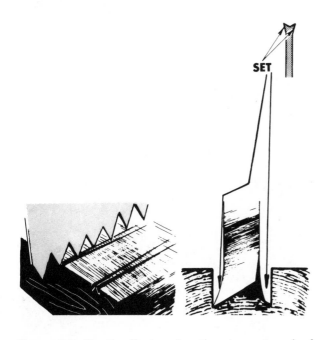

Figure 9-5. *Tooth offset makes the saw cut or kerf wider than blade thickness. Crosscut teeth are pictured.*

Figure 9-7. *Ripping is done at a 60° angle to the stock. Cut on the push stroke.*

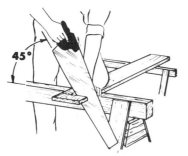

Figure 9-8. *Crosscutting is done at a 45° angle to the stock.*

Figure 9-9. *A saw blade may be twisted slightly to straighten the cut.*

As the kerf is made, raise the blade up so it is at a 60° angle to the stock and take longer strokes (Figure 9-7). Cutting is done on the push stroke. Make sure the blade is square with the edge you are cutting. If you travel off your layout line, you can twist the blade slightly. This will bring the saw back to the layout line. Let the teeth do the cutting. If you force the saw or take rapid strokes, you may become tired and less accurate.

CROSSCUTTING STOCK TO LENGTH

Before crosscutting stock, lay out your cuts and secure the piece to a bench or sawhorse. Grip the saw in the same way you would for ripping. Begin your cut at a low angle on the waste side of the line. Take short strokes until the kerf is out to a ¼" depth at the corner. Back strokes work well for making the kerf. Raise the blade to a 45° angle with the stock (Figure 9-8) and take longer strokes. Make sure the blade is square with the end you are cutting. You can correct for error by twisting the blade slightly as you are sawing (Figure 9-9). This will bring the blade back to the layout line.

SAWING PLYWOOD

Plywood is different from solid stock. Because of the different layers in plywood, the grain runs in two directions. The best saw to use when cutting plywood is the crosscut saw. Select a saw with 7 to 10 teeth per inch to reduce splintering.

Lay out the plywood with the good or exposed side up (Figure 9-10). Because the saw stroke is downward, any grain tearout will be on the under or unexposed side. To prevent tearout or the under side of the plywood, you can apply masking tape on the bottom side over the

Figure 9-10. *Use a crosscut saw to cut plywood. Make sure the good side is up before cutting.*

cutting line. The tape will hold the veneers in place as you saw through the tape. Scoring the underside of the stock along the cutting line with a utility knife will also reduce tearout.

SAWS AND ACCESSORIES

The Back Saw and Dovetail Saw
The back saw and the dovetail saw have crosscut teeth and are used chiefly for precision cuts and joinery work. Back saws and dovetail saws are rectangular and have a piece of steel fastened to the back or edge opposite the teeth (Figure 9-11). This piece of metal makes the saw rigid and increases sawing accuracy. It acts as a backbone.

Figure 9-12. *Dovetail saws and back saws are commonly used in a jig.*

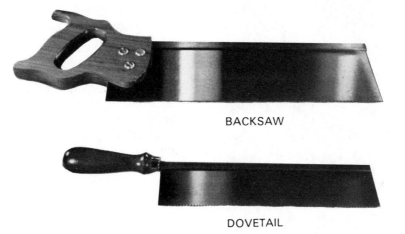

BACKSAW

DOVETAIL

Figure 9-11. *Back saws and dovetail saws have steel backs. This makes the saw blade rigid. Straight cuts are easier with a back saw or dovetail saw.*

The back saw and dovetail saw usually have more than 12 teeth per inch. The teeth are small and yield a very smooth cut. Both saws are frequently used with a fixture (Figure 9-12) or miter box. These devices help control the angle and depth of cut.

The back saw has a handle like most other crosscut and rip saws. The dovetail saw has a turned or dowel-shaped handle. This makes it easy to use in corners or tight spots. Both saws are started like a crosscut saw. Strokes are taken slowly. If you wish to control depth of cut, clamp a piece of stock to the blade (Figure 9-13). This will limit the cutting depth.

Figure 9-13. *A wood strip clamped to the blade limits the depth of cut.*

The Miter Box

The *miter box* is a fixture used with the back saw. It can be made from metal or wood. Wood miter boxes (Figure 9-14) are made from hardwood such as maple. They cut at 45° and 90° fixed angles. The metal miter box (Figure 9-15) can be adjusted to many angles and is more versatile. A longer back saw is used in a metal miter box. These back saws are usually over 16″ (406mm) long.

The miter box allows you to clamp your work and control the path of the saw. This improves accuracy. When you use a miter box, make sure that all adjustments are made before you begin.

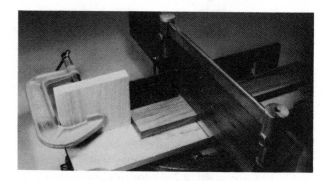

Figure 9-16. *Use a stop block or stop rod to locate your piece. You can also clamp stock to the miter box.*

Clamp your stock or use the stop rods attached to the miter box (Figure 9-16). Begin the cut as you would any other cross cut.

Metal miter boxes vary in operation and adjustment. Read the owner's manual or obtain proper instruction before using a metal miter box.

The Compass Saw

A compass saw (Figure 9-17) is a light-duty saw used for cutting curved, circular or irregular openings. Compass saws are 12 to 16″ (305 to 406 mm) long. A tapered blade can begin a cut in a small hole. The tapered blade also makes it easy to cut a sharp turn.

A compass saw blade has 7 or 8 teeth per inch. It is usually fastened in the handle with a wing nut. This is so it may be reversed in the handle for cutting in tight spaces.

Figure 9-14. *Wooden miter boxes are made from maple or other hard wood. A miter box is an easy project to build.*

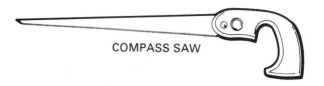

COMPASS SAW

Figure 9-17. *A compass saw is used to cut curved or irregular holes.*

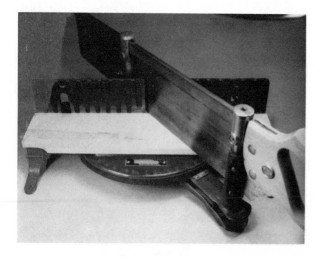

Figure 9-15. *A metal miter box can be adjusted to many angles.*

The Keyhole Saw

A keyhole saw (Figure 9-18) is like a compass saw, except that it has a shorter tapered blade with more teeth per inch. Some keyhole saws are sold with two blades, one for cutting metal and one for cutting wood. The blade in the

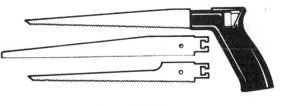

KEYHOLE SAW

Figure 9-18. *A keyhole saw is like a compass saw. The keyhole saw has a shorter blade with finer teeth.*

keyhole saw may be turned in its handle for use in tight spaces. Use a compass or keyhole saw in the same way as a rip or crosscut saw. The teeth are designed for cutting either with or against the grain.

The Coping Saw

The coping saw (Figure 9-19) is used for cutting fine curves. The blade is secured in a frame which makes it rigid. The blade can be rotated 360 degrees in the frame. This keeps the frame clear of the work. The frame height is usually 6 ½" (165 mm) and the depth of the frame is 4 ½ to 6 ½ inches (115 to 165 mm). A coping saw blade has a pin at each end to hold it in the frame. The frame handle is turned clockwise to tighten the blade. The teeth may point toward or away from the handle depending on the job. If the coping saw is used with an auxiliary table (Figure 9-20), the teeth point toward the handle. Coping saw blades are about 6 ½" (165 mm) long. A common blade has 15 teeth per inch.

The work is placed on the table and the saw cuts on the down stroke. When an internal cut is made, a hole larger than the blade pin is drilled in the waste stock (Figure 9-21). The blade is threaded through the hole and mounted in the frame. After the cut is complete, the blade is removed from the frame and pulled from the work.

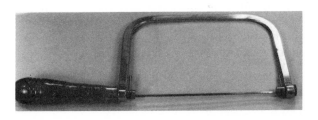

Figure 9-19. *The coping saw is used to cut fine curves.*

Take long strokes when using the coping saw, but do not force the blade into the stock. Let each tooth cut without becoming stuck in the work. Slow strokes will improve accuracy.

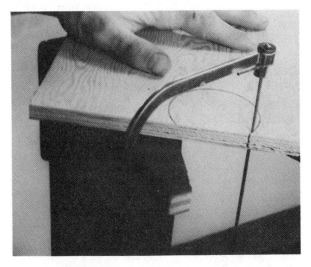

Figure 9-20. *If you use the auxiliary table, the saw teeth should point down.*

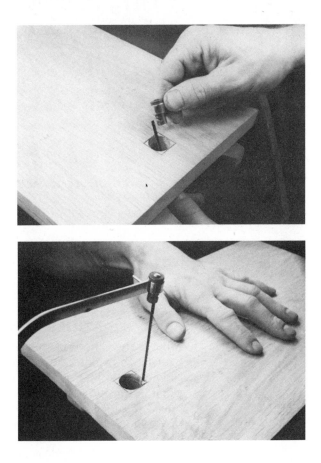

Figure 9-21. *Coping saw blades can be threaded through stock for internal cuts.*

The Fret Saw

The fret saw or jewelers saw (Figure 9-22) is like a coping saw except that it is used for finer, intricate work such as instrument making, jewelry and marquetry. Marquetry is the art of using

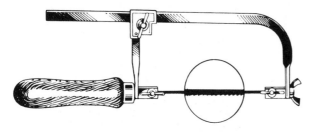

Figure 9-22. *A fret saw is like a coping saw. It is used for very fine work.*

Figure 9-23. *Marquetry is the art of using wood veneers to make a design or picture.*

wood veneers to make an illustration or design (Figure 9-23). Veneers in marquetry must fit together tightly. A fret saw makes a very fine kerf which allows tight fitting of veneers.

The fret saw has a chuck at each end of the frame that clamps the blade. The frame adjusts to blades 1" to 5" (25 to 125 mm) long. After the blade is clamped in both chucks, the frame clamping mechanism applies tension to the blade.

Blades used in the fret saw are up to 5" long and are finer than coping saw blades. They usually have 20 to 30 teeth per inch. Because the blades are so fine, they break easily. Use the fret like a coping saw, but be careful not to force the blade.

MAINTAINING YOUR SAW

Be sure to keep your saw well maintained. Keep the teeth protected so they will stay sharp. Wipe the saw blade with a light coat of oil. This will protect the blade from rust and make sawing easier. Avoid bending the blade or cutting painted stock. Paint will dull the blade and nails may be hidden under the paint. Always check stock for nails.

SAW SAFETY

Saw teeth are very sharp. When you use a saw, keep your hands clear of the teeth and avoid handling the saw by the teeth. When you prepare to saw stock, make sure it is clamped securely. Adjust your work so that you are comfortable and have good balance. This reduces fatigue and prevents slipping or falling.

QUESTIONS FOR REVIEW

1. What is the difference between rip sawing and crosscut sawing?
2. Sketch the profile of a rip tooth and a crosscut tooth.
3. How do you determine the size of a handsaw?
4. What is the difference between the number of teeth per inch and points per inch measured on a handsaw?
5. How would you describe saw set? What is the purpose of the saw set?
6. What is a saw kerf? How is it related to saw set?
7. Describe the procedures you would follow for crosscutting or ripping stock.

8. For what purposes are backsaws and dovetail saws used?
9. What is a miter box? For what purpose is it used?
10. When would you use a compass or keyhole saw? Are they designed for crosscutting or ripping?
11. How does the coping saw differ from the compass and keyhole saw?
12. What are some general practices you should follow to maintain your saw?
13. List some procedures that will help you saw stock safely.

SUGGESTED ACTIVITIES

1. Use a rip saw to rip a scrap of wood. Practice cutting a straight line. Keep the kerf on the waste side of the line. Also try crosscutting with a crosscut saw. Notice the difference between ripping and crosscutting.

2. Count the number of teeth per inch on a rip saw, crosscut saw and back saw in your shop. Which blade has the most teeth per inch?

3. Install a blade in a coping saw.

CHAPTER 10

Hand Planing and Smoothing Stock

It is difficult to work with rough, uneven lumber. For this reason, stock is smoothed or planed to uniform thickness. Smooth stock is easier to finish and requires less finishing materials. Rough stock is usually smoothed with a plane or scraper. There are many planes and scrapers on the market. In this chapter you will learn their names and how to use them.

KEY TERMS

block plane	mill marks
smooth plane	taper
jack plane	bevel
fore plane	chamfer
double plane iron	grinding
lever cap	honing
frog	scraping
rabbet plane	hand scrapers
router plane	cabinet scrapers
shooting board	burnisher
auxiliary fence	

COMMON PLANES: BLOCK, SMOOTH, JACK AND FORE PLANES

The four most common planes used in woodworking are the *block, smooth, jack* and *fore planes*. A block plane (Figure 10-1) is the smallest of the four. It is used for jobs where little planing is required. Carpenters and cabinetmakers often use block planes to trim pieces that do not fit. Block planes have a low blade angle. This enables them to work well on plywood and end grain (Figure 10-2). The blade in a block plane

Figure 10-2. *Block planes work well on end grain and plywood. This is because of their low blade angle. The blade has its bevel or cutting edge turned upward.*

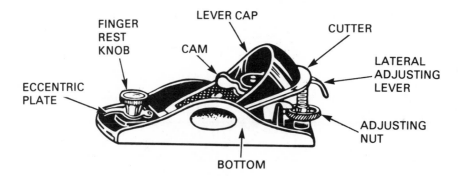

Figure 10-1. *The block plane is used to trim pieces to size. It has a low blade angle.*

Figure 10-3. *Smooth planes are used to take fine cuts. They smooth mill marks and saw cuts well.*

Figure 10-4. *The jack plane works well for smoothing rough stock.*

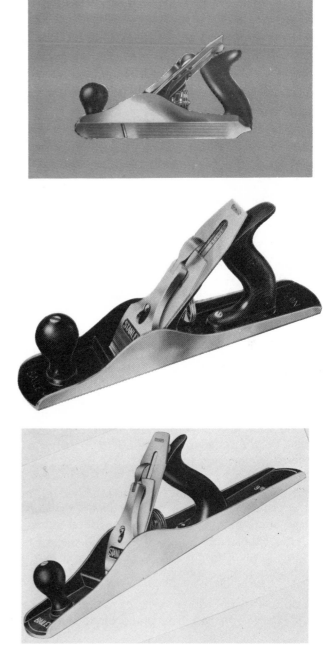

has the bevel turned upward. This allows close planing and planing of end grain. The blade bevel in jack, smooth and fore planes is turned downward. The adjusting nut or wheel behind the blade controls blade height on all planes.

The smooth, jack and fore planes have similar blade control mechanisms. The chief difference between these planes is their size. The smooth plane (Figure 10-3) is usually 6″ to 10″ (150 to 250 mm) long and 1 ½″ to 2″ (38 to 50 mm) wide. Jack planes (Figure 10-4) are 14″ to 17″ (350 to 430 mm) long and 2″ (50 mm) wide. The fore plane (Figure 10-5) is even larger; 2″ to 2 ⅜″ (50 to 60 mm) wide and 18″ (about 450 mm) long. A longer plane will produce a uniform, flat surface (Figure 10-6).

The smooth plane is used to remove *mill marks* (machine marks, waves) and to plane short stock. The jack plane works well for general smoothing of rough stock. It is also used to plane stock edges for edge gluing larger panels. The fore plane is often used on door and window edges. It can be used to smooth long boards and may be used in place of a power jointer or planer.

Figure 10-5. *A fore plane is larger than a smooth plane or a jack plane.*

Figure 10-6. *Longer planes produce a truer (uniform and flat) surface. A short plane follows any grooves in the wood.*

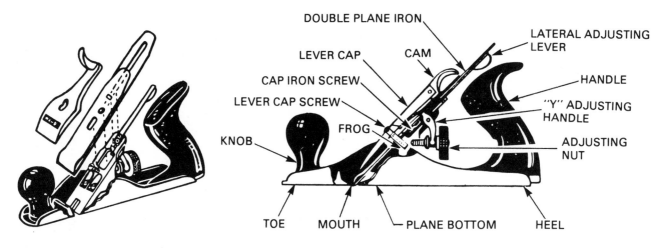

Figure 10-7. *The blade control system includes the frog, adjusting nut and lateral adjusting lever. The double plane iron is held in place by the lever cap.*

Blade Control

The blade control system for the smooth, jack and fore planes includes a frog, an adjusting nut and a lateral adjusting lever (Figure 10-7). The frog supports the double plane iron and lever cap. The lever cap holds the double plane iron on the frog. It has a lever that clamps the double plane iron into position. The lever cap screw may be tightened or loosened to increase or decrease clamping pressure.

The lateral adjusting lever is also attached to the frog which houses the adjusting nut that controls blade height. It controls horizontal adjustment of the blade (Figure 10-8). This keeps the blade parallel to the plane bottom and eliminates gouging of the work.

A double plane iron consists of the *plane blade* and *plane iron* cap. The plane blade does the

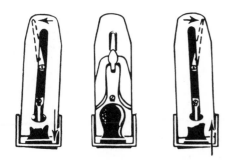

Figure 10-8. *The lateral adjustment lever controls horizontal adjustment of the blade. Adjust it so the blade is parallel with sole of the plane.*

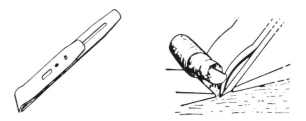

Figure 10-9. *The plane iron cap deflects the chip upward. This keeps the wood from splitting.*

cutting. The plane iron cap deflects the chips upward (Figure 10-9). This keeps the wood from splitting during planing. The plane iron cap is screwed to the plane blade with its edge $1/16''$ to $1/32''$ behind the cutting edge.

SPECIALTY PLANES

There are many specialty planes designed for specific planing operations. The most common of these include the rabbet plane, the side rabbet plane and the router plane.

Rabbet Plane

The rabbet plane cuts rabbets on stock edges (Figure 10-10). Rabbet size is controlled by the fence and depth stop. There are two blade positions on the rabbet plane. The front position is used for stop rabbets. All other cutting is done with the blade in the rear position.

The spur (Figure 10-11) on the rabbet plane is lowered when cutting rabbets across the grain. The spur cuts the wood fibers and eliminates tear-out. The spur must be kept sharp.

Cutting rabbets requires careful adjustment of the plane. Check your plane on scrap stock before planing your work. Take light cuts when using the rabbet plane.

Side Rabbet Plane

Side rabbet planes (Figure 10-12) are used for enlarging a rabbet or dado by trimming the sides. Side rabbet planes are not designed to cut a rabbet, but they work well for trimming them.

Figure 10-10. *The rabbet plane is used to cut rabbets.*

Figure 10-11. *The spur cuts the wood fibers. This eliminates tear-out on cross-grain cuts. Keep the spur sharp.*

Figure 10-12. *A side rabbet plane planes the sides of a rabbet. It can also plane the shoulders of a dado.*

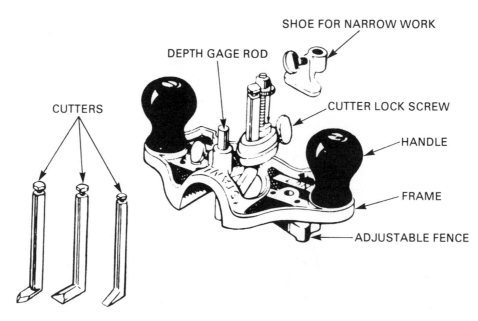

CUTTERS

SHOE FOR NARROW WORK

DEPTH GAGE ROD

CUTTER LOCK SCREW

HANDLE

FRAME

ADJUSTABLE FENCE

Figure 10-13. *The router plane can be used to deepen a dado or groove.*

Side rabbet planes have two blades. A side rabbet plane with two blades always cuts toward the center of the work. This eliminates grain tear-out or splintering. Side rabbet planes must be very sharp to trim end grain.

Router Plane

The router plane (Figure 10-13) can be used to deepen a "dado" or groove. It may also be used to cut a dado or groove after the shoulder cuts have been made with a back saw (Figure 10-14). The router plane has a ¼" and a ½" router blade and a ½" V-shaped smoothing blade.

Smaller router planes are also called "palm routers" (Figure 10-15). They work well on smaller pieces. Palm routers are often used for inlay work.

Figure 10-14. *The router plane can be used to cut a dado.*

Figure 10-15. *This small router plane is called a "palm router". It is used for inlay work.*

CONTROLLING THE PLANE

As you begin working with planes, it may seem difficult to control them. Let your fingers drop below the front of the plane, so you can feel the angle between the work and the plane (Figure 10-16). This will help you control the angle of cut.

Figure 10-16. *Your fingers can control the angle between the work and the plane.*

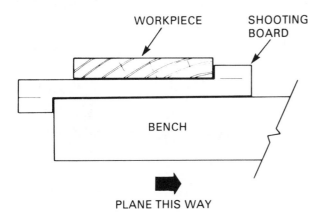

Figure 10-17. *A shooting board controls the angle at which the plane cuts the work.*

Shooting Board

A shooting board (Figure 10-17) may help to plane end grain perpendicular to the edge of the work. The shooting board is easy to build and controls the work quite well. Some shooting boards are built for planing miters to a 45° angle.

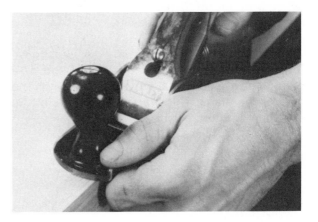

Auxiliary Fence

An auxiliary fence is designed to control the plane's cutting angle. The fence may be perpendicular to the bottom of the plane or it may be set at an angle (Figure 10-18). These shop-built devices are clamped to the plane with small C clamps. The plane is used in the normal fashion with the fence contacting the work.

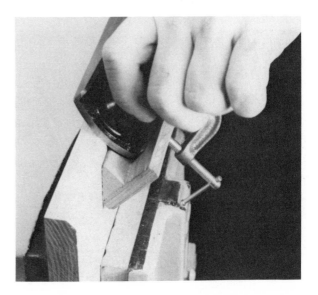

Figure 10-18. *The auxiliary fence controls the plane's cutting angle.*

PLANING TECHNIQUES

Clamp your stock securely at a comfortable height before planing. Make sure that you will be planing with the grain (Figure 10-19). Your feet should be parallel to your stock and point in the direction you intend to plane. Your plane should be turned slightly so that the blade is cutting at an angle (Figure 10-20). This will reduce grain lifting and make planing easier.

When you begin a planing stroke, exert more force on the toe of the plane. At the end of a planing stroke you must exert more force on the heel of the plane. This practice will plane a true surface with no taper or arc.

PLANE THIS WAY

ROUGH STOCK PLANING

First plane both faces of rough stock. Then plane one edge and cut the stock to size. Additional planing may be required after sawing. The rough edge left by a saw is removed by planing. Check your rough stock with a straight edge to find the truest face. This is where planing should begin. Clamp your stock securely and adjust a smooth or jack plane so that the blade extends 1/64" below the bottom. Begin planing with your plane turned at a slight angle (Figure 10-21).

Shavings should be light and feather-like. Heavy shavings tend to tear the grain. If the grain is tearing, reverse planing direction. You may be planing against the grain. Check the surface with a square or straight edge to find high and low spots. Continue working until the surface is true.

Figure 10-21. *Take a light cut on rough stock. Turn the plane at a slight angle.*

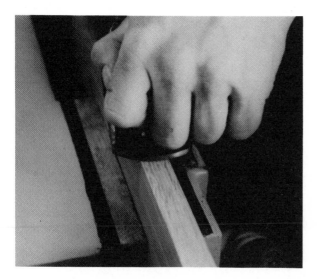

Figure 10-19. *Stock should be clamped for planing. Be sure to plane with the grain.*

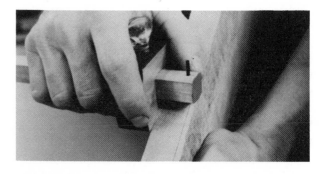

Figure 10-22. *The marking gage will scribe a line on the edge. This helps you plane the rough face parallel to the smooth face.*

Figure 10-20. *Turn the plane slightly when planing. This will make planing easier.*

You may then mark the edge opposite the trued surface with a marking gage (Figure 10-22). This mark tells you how much to remove from the opposite face. Clamp the piece and plane the other face to your mark. When both faces are parallel, plane one edge perpendicular to them. Then saw the piece to desired size.

REMOVING MILL MARKS

Mill marks are waves found on stock that has been planed by machine. If they are not removed, they will make the surface appear rough when it is stained and finished (Figure 10-23). It is not advisable to sand mill marks because they are deep. They may not be completely removed by sanding.

A smooth plane is used for removing mill marks. Set the plane iron cap 1/32" from the edge of the blade for best results. Make sure the blade is sharp. The blade should extend through the bottom of the plane about 1/64".

Plane with the grain until all mill marks are removed. Scraping may follow the planing operation if necessary. (Scraping is described later in this chapter.)

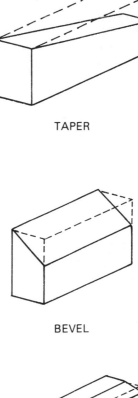

TAPER

BEVEL

CHAMFER

Figure 10-24. *Tapers, chamfers and bevels are all inclined surfaces.*

Figure 10-23. *Mill marks are waves on the wood's surface. They are caused by planing machines. Use a smoother plane to remove mill marks.*

CUTTING TAPERS, CHAMFERS AND BEVELS

Tapers, chamfers, and bevels are inclined surfaces (Figure 10-24). The relationship of the inclined surface to the stock differs. A taper is an inclined surface between the ends of the stock. A chamfer is an inclined surface that touches two perpendicular surfaces. A bevel is an inclined surface between two faces or edges. Smooth planes work best for cutting tapers, chamfers and bevels.

Planing a Taper

Lay out the taper on your stock. You should plane toward the end where the most stock is removed. Make sure that the grain is going in the proper direction.

Clamp the stock in a vise with the layout line parallel to the top of the vise. Take light cuts and pay attention to your layout lines. Check the surface frequently for flatness with the blade of a square.

Planing a Bevel

Lay out the bevel on your stock and secure it in a parallel clamp (Figure 10-25). Tighten the clamp in a vise so that your bevel is parallel to the floor. Begin planing; take light cuts and watch your layout line. A sliding T bevel may be used to check your work.

Planing a Chamfer

Chamfers are planed in the same way as bevels. Lay out the chamfer and follow the procedure for planing a bevel.

PLANING SHORT STOCK

Short stock is difficult to clamp. When you plane short stock, it is best to clamp the plane upside down and move the work across the sole of the plane (Figure 10-26). A smooth or jointer plane set for a light cut works best. You may use an auxiliary fence to help control the work. Be careful when you clamp the plane. You may crack the plane if you tighten the vise too much.

PLANING THIN STOCK

Thin stock bends easily and is difficult to clamp or plane. Some pieces may be clamped with a parallel clamp and secured to the top of the bench for planing. Other pieces will require the use of an auxiliary board. The sharp points on the auxiliary board hold the stock in position while planing (Figure 10-27). Plane the best side last. The rough side will have pin pricks left from the points on the auxiliary board. These can be removed by sanding or closed by applying water.

Figure 10-25. *The bevel or chamfer should be parallel to the floor for planing.*

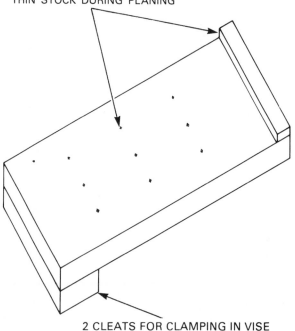

SHARP POINTS AND CLEAT HOLD
THIN STOCK DURING PLANING

2 CLEATS FOR CLAMPING IN VISE

Figure 10-27. *Thin stock can be planed with the auxiliary board. The sharp points hold the stock and keep it rigid.*

Figure 10-26. *Small stock can be moved across the sole of a stationary plane. Do not over-tighten the vise. This could crack the plane.*

PLANING END GRAIN AND PLYWOOD

End grain and plywood have a tendency to split at the ends during planing. Planing toward the center of the work (Figure 10-28) or clamping scrap stock to the end (Figure 10-29) will eliminate splitting. Block planes work best for end grain because of the low cutting angle. Take light cuts and frequently check your work with a square.

Figure 10-28. *Planing toward the center of your work will eliminate splitting.*

Figure 10-29. *Scrap stock will protect end grain from splitting.*

Figure 10-30. *Lay the plane on its side when not in use. This will keep the blade from becoming dull.*

CARE OF THE PLANE

A plane will last many generations if cared for properly. The blade should be kept sharp at all times. Lay the plane on its side when not in use (Figure 10-30). This will keep the blade from dulling due to contact with the bench. Be careful not to drop your plane. It is made from cast iron which is brittle. The plane should be kept clean. Apply a light coat of oil or paste wax to prevent rust.

Sharpening Plane Blades

Two operations are required to sharpen a plane blade. They are *grinding* (Figure 10-31) and

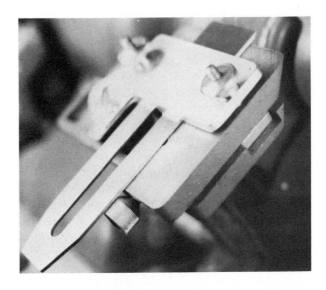

Figure 10-31. *Plane blades require grinding when they become nicked. Remove the plane iron cap before grinding the blade.*

Figure 10-32. *Honing sharpens the edge of the plane blade. Only the cutting edge should touch the stone. The rest of the bevel should be slightly above the stone.*

Figure 10-34. *Lay the blade flat on the stone. Honing in this position will remove the wire edge.*

honing (Figure 10-32). Blades are ground only when they become nicked. They are ground to a 25° to 30° angle on a grinder. You probably will not have to grind your plane blade. If you do, ask your instructor for help.

Honing is done frequently to bring the cutting edge to a 45° angle. Honing is done on a honing or sharpening stone (Figure 10-32). Begin with a coarse stone. Apply some oil to it. This will keep the metal chips from clogging the stone. Set the blade bevel down on the stone. Tilt the blade forward slightly. The cutting edge is now at the correct honing angle. Move the blade back and forth across the length of the stone until the entire cutting edge has been honed. A metal burr or wire edge will appear behind the cutting edge after honing (Figure 10-33). The wire edge must be removed to complete the honing operation. Lay the blade flat on the stone with the bevel up. Move the blade back and forth across the length of the stone until the wire edge is

removed (Figure 10-34). Repeat the honing operation on a finer stone to obtain a sharper edge. Wipe the oil from the stones and put them away.

SCRAPERS

Scrapers are used to remove a small amount of stock. They usually have a hooked edge that cuts with a scraping action. Scrapers will not lift the

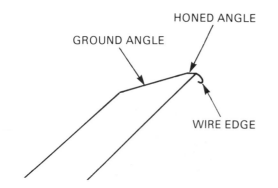

Figure 10-33. *Honing the cutting edge leaves a wire edge on the back of the blade.*

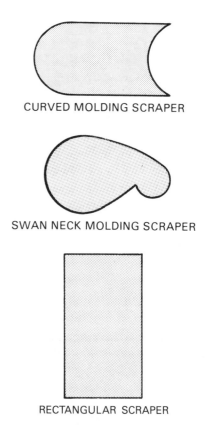

CURVED MOLDING SCRAPER

SWAN NECK MOLDING SCRAPER

RECTANGULAR SCRAPER

Figure 10-35. *Hand scrapers.*

grain. They are often used instead of abrasives to prepare a surface for finishing. The two principal types of scraping tools are hand (Figure 10-35) and cabinet scrapers (Figure 10-36).

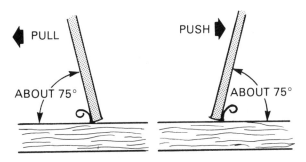

Figure 10-37. *The hand scraper can be pushed or pulled. Hold it at a 75° angle. Sharp scrapers lift a shaving.*

Figure 10-36. *Cabinet scraper.*

Hand Scrapers

Hand-held scrapers or *hand scrapers* are rectangular or irregularly curved (Figure 10-35). They are used to smooth small areas. Hand scrapers are pulled or pushed across the work at a 75° angle (Figure 10-37). A hand scraper should remove a shaving. If it removes sawdust, it is dull. Hand scrapers are usually sold in a set. The set includes a curved scraper, a swan neck scraper, and a rectangular scraper.

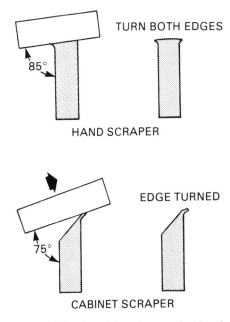

Figure 10-38. *The adjusting screw causes the blade to bend slightly. This bend improves the scraping action.*

Cabinet Scrapers

Cabinet scrapers (Figure 10-36) use a blade similar to a hand scraper. The blade is housed in a two-handled frame. The frame allows more working pressure and greater control. The blade is clamped into the frame with the cutting edge even with the bottom of the cabinet scraper. The adjusting screw is tightened slightly to arc the blade (Figure 10-38). The cabinet scraper is normally pushed across the work.

Sharpening Scrapers

The scraper's hooked edge does the cutting. The edge is sharpened or renewed by burnishing. A *burnisher* is a hardened steel tool that forms the hook on a scraper. It is pushed across the edge (Figure 10-39). The burnisher is held at an 85° angle. It slides along the scraper edge to form the hook.

The cabinet scraper has a 45° angle on the cutting edge and is burnished away from the bevel. A hand scraper has a flat cutting edge and may be burnished in either direction.

Figure 10-39. *The burnisher forms the hook on the scraper.*

QUESTIONS FOR REVIEW

1. Why is planing an important operation to learn?
2. Name and describe the four most common planes used for woodworking.
3. Discuss blade control in the smooth, jack and fore plane. List the functions of the frog, the adjusting nut and the lateral adjusting lever.
4. How are the plane iron cap and plane blade assembled? How are they installed in a plane?
5. How is the lever cap adjusted if it is too loose or too tight?
6. What is the difference between a rabbet plane and a side rabbet plane?
7. What is the function of a router plane?
8. Name and describe two shop-built devices that will help you control the plane.
9. What are some planing techniques that will help you plane your work correctly?
10. How is rough stock planed? What is the correct sequence for planing the surfaces?
11. If the grain is tearing as you plane, what must you do to correct this problem?
12. What are mill marks? How do you remove them?
13. How do chamfers, bevels, and tapers differ? How are they planed?
14. Why are plywood and end grain difficult to plane? How should they be planed?
15. Discuss care of your plane. How do you hone the blade?
16. What are scrapers and how are they used? How do they remove stock?
17. Discuss the procedure for sharpening a cabinet scraper or hand scraper.

SUGGESTED ACTIVITIES

1. Demonstrate the correct way of adjusting a hand plane in your shop.

2. Demonstrate the correct way of honing a hand plane blade. (Have your teacher check your technique.)

3. Lay out a taper, bevel or chamfer on a piece of scrap. Use the correct plane to shape the scrap to the layout line.

Shaping and Carving Stock

Woodworking projects often require a carved design or an irregular shape. Craft activities such as whittling require the use of many shaping and carving tools. When joints must be trimmed, a chisel is used to cut away a small amount of stock. There are many uses for shaping and carving tools in woodworking. It is important that you learn their names, how to use them and how to sharpen them.

Before shaping or carving stock, be sure that you have selected the correct tool and that it is sharp. Lay out your work accurately and clamp it securely. Work slowly and carefully. Make sure the sharp edge of the tool points away from you. Always keep your hands behind the cutting edge!

KEY TERMS

shaping	spokeshave
carving	file
chisel	rasp
tang	carving tools
gouge	chip carving
honing	whittling
drawknife	
multi-blade forming tool	

CHISELS

Chisels are edge-cutting tools used for *shaping* and *carving* stock. They are often used for removing stock in joint construction. A chisel has a forged steel blade. The steel is hardened to hold a sharp cutting edge. There are many types of chisel blades and chisel handles to perform various jobs. Figure 11-1 shows the most common chisel types: bench or paring chisel, butt chisel, firmer chisel and mortising chisel.

BENCH OR PARING CHISEL

BUTT CHISEL

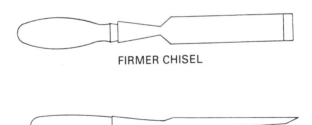
FIRMER CHISEL

MORTISING CHISEL

Figure 11-1. *Common chisel blades: bench or paring chisel, butt chisel, firmer chisel, and mortising chisel.*

Blade Types

There are many types of chisel blades. Each type of blade is designed to do a specific job. Chisel blades are sized by the width of the blade. Chisel blades range from ¼" to 2" (6 to 50 mm) in width.

Bench or paring chisels (Figure 11-1) have blades that are thin and have beveled sides. They are driven by hand and are used for making light cuts.

Butt chisels (Figure 11-1) have a slightly thicker and shorter blade than bench chisels. They also have beveled sides. A butt chisel may be driven with a mallet or by hand. The short blade permits use in tight spaces. Butt chisels are very popular among carpenters and cabinetmakers.

Firmer chisels (Figure 11-1) are designed for heavy cuts. The blade has a thick rectangular shape designed to take heavy blows. There are no bevels on the sides of the blade. These chisels are popular for rough work such as house framing.

The *mortising chisel* (Figure 11-1) is long and has a thick blade. The mortising chisel is designed to cut mortises, which are deep, square holes often used to make joints. The sides of the mortise chisel are square. Most mortising chisels are of a nominal width such as ⅜″, ½″, or ¾″.

Handle Types

Handles found on chisels can be classified as *socket, tang, or heavy* duty. A socket handle (Figure 11-2, *top*) fits into a tapered opening formed in the end of the chisel blade. The handle

may be wood or plastic. It it tapered for a tight fit in the blade. Socket handles are designed to take heavy blows from a mallet.

When a tang handle (Figure 11-2, *center*) is used on a chisel, part of the blade, called a *tang*, is inserted into the handle. Tang handles may be wood or plastic. Wooden tang handles are not designed for use with a mallet. Plastic handles with a metal striking face can be used with a mallet.

Heavy duty handles (Figure 11-2, *bottom*) are designed for the hardest use. The blade tang extends through the handle and forms a striking face on top. Because the tang goes through the handle, the full impact of the mallet is transmitted to the blade.

Cutting with a Chisel

Always clamp stock before you begin to chisel. Try to chisel with the grain. If this is not possible, take light cuts and work slowly.

A concave cut can be made by placing the bevel against the stock (Figure 11-3, *left*). A convex cut

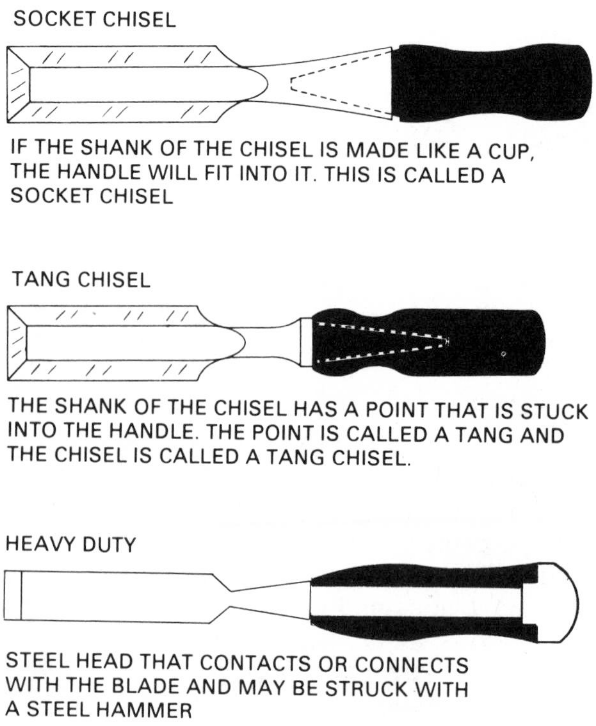

Figure 11-2. *Common chisel handles: socket, tang and heavy duty.*

SOCKET CHISEL

IF THE SHANK OF THE CHISEL IS MADE LIKE A CUP, THE HANDLE WILL FIT INTO IT. THIS IS CALLED A SOCKET CHISEL

TANG CHISEL

THE SHANK OF THE CHISEL HAS A POINT THAT IS STUCK INTO THE HANDLE. THE POINT IS CALLED A TANG AND THE CHISEL IS CALLED A TANG CHISEL.

HEAVY DUTY

STEEL HEAD THAT CONTACTS OR CONNECTS WITH THE BLADE AND MAY BE STRUCK WITH A STEEL HAMMER

CONCAVE CUT

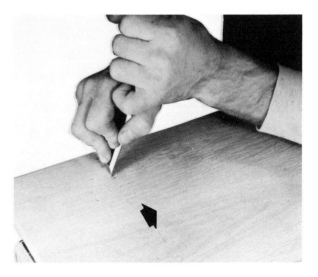

CONVEX CUT

Figure 11-3. *Concave cuts are made with the bevel against the work. Convex cuts are made with the bevel up.*

is made with the bevel up (Figure 11-3, *right*). You can drive the chisel with a mallet or with your hands. Remember to keep your hands behind the cutting edge.

Chisels can be used to remove stock left in the corner of a rabbet, lap, dado or mortise joint. This is done by tilting the chisel and pulling the

cutting edge through the corner of the joint (Figure 11-4). This cuts the wood fibers and makes it easy to pare them away.

In some cases, the chisel can be used as a scraper. When held upright and pulled toward you, the chisel will scrape a small area (Figure 11-5). The bevel must face away from you when scraping. Scraping with a chisel will level an irregular spot on your work. It will also remove glue spots on the wood.

Figure 11-4. *A chisel can be used to clean out a corner. Tilt the chisel and pull it through the cut. The chisel cuts like a knife.*

Figure 11-5. *A chisel can be used to scrape a small area*

GOUGES

Gouges are forged cutting tools. They look like chisels with curved blades (Figure 11-6). They have either socket or tang type handles.

The size of a gouge is measured across the blade. The curve in a gouge is called the *sweep.* Sweeps are numbered from 1 to 11. The higher the sweep number, the more curve the gouge has (Figure 11-7).

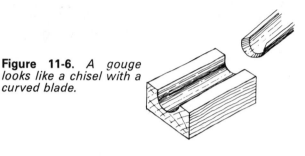

Figure 11-6. *A gouge looks like a chisel with a curved blade.*

A gouge may be beveled on the inside or outside. A gouge with an inside bevel (in cannel blade) makes concave cuts such as grooves and coves. A gouge with an outside bevel (out cannel blade) can be used for convex cuts such as reeding (Figure 11-8).

Cutting With a Gouge

A gouge can be driven with a mallet or by hand. Make sure that stock is clamped securely before you begin. A *concave cut* is started with a small gouge (Figure 11-9). Select a gouge with an inside bevel. The cut is enlarged using bigger gouges. Finish the cut with a gouge that is the same shape as the desired cut. Work with the grain whenever possible. Always drive gouges away from your body. Keep your hands behind the cutting edge.

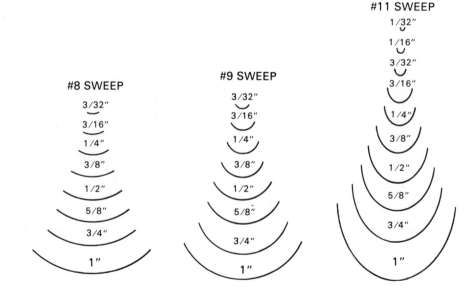

Figure 11-7. *The sweep of a gouge describes the curve in the blade.*

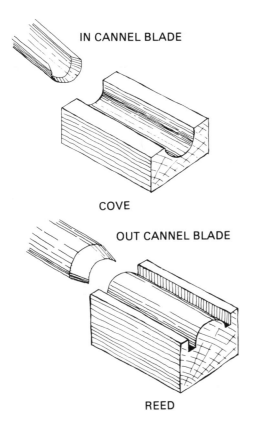

IN CANNEL BLADE

COVE

OUT CANNEL BLADE

REED

Figure 11-8. *Reeds and coves can be cut with gouges.*

Figure 11-9. *Begin a cove cut with a small gouge. Make sure the gouge has an inside bevel.*

When you make a convex cut, select a gouge that has an outside bevel. Work the gouge around the curve (Figure 11-10). Pare away stock until the desired shape is obtained. Check your work frequently to be sure the curve is in the correct shape.

Figure 11-10. *Making a convex cut with the gouge. Choose a gouge with a sweep slightly larger than the shape desired. Make sure the gouge has an outside bevel.*

SHARPENING CHISELS AND GOUGES

Chisels should be ground at an angle of 25° to 30°. Gouges should be ground at an angle of 30° to 35°. If used and cared for correctly, chisels and gouges seldom require grinding. They are usually sharpened by *honing* the cutting edge.

Honing a chisel or gouge is much like honing a plane iron. Begin with a coarse stone. Apply some oil to it. Set the blade bevel down on the stone and tilt the blade forward slightly (Figure 11-11). The cutting edge is now at the correct honing angle. Move the blade back and forth across the length of the stone until the entire edge has been honed.

Figure 11-11. *Gouges are honed like chisels. A rolling motion is needed to sharpen a gouge.*

When sharpening a gouge, you will have to roll it in order to hone the entire radius of the cutting edge. A gouge slip (Figure 11-12) may be used instead of a flat stone. You will not have to roll the gouge when you use a gouge slip. Gouges with an inside bevel can be honed with a slipstone (Figure 11-13). Tilt the slipstone so that it hones only the cutting edge. Apply some oil to the stone before you begin.

After honing the cutting edge, a wire edge will be raised on the opposite side. When the wire edge is on the outside of the gouge, remove it by laying the wire edge against the stone and moving the gouge back and forth. When the wire edge is inside a gouge, a slipstone can be used to remove the wire edge (Figure 11-14). Repeat the honing operation on a finer stone to obtain a sharper edge. Wipe the stones after honing and cover them to protect from dust and sawdust.

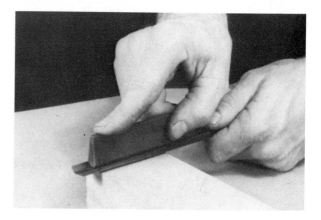

Figure 11-14. *The wire edge on an outside bevel gouge can be removed with a slipstone.*

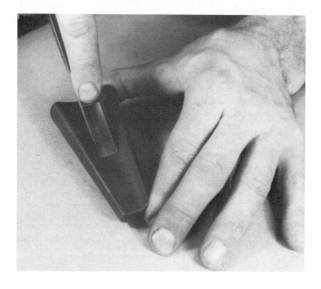

Figure 11-12. *A gouge slip sharpens gouges with an inside or outside bevel.*

Figure 11-13. *A slipstone may be used to hone gouges with an inside bevel.*

DRAWKNIFE AND SPOKESHAVE

The drawknife (Figure 11-15) and spokeshave (Figure 11-16) are shaping tools. The *drawknife* is used for rough shaping. Drawknives have various handle shapes and blades about 14" (350 mm) long. The cutting edge is shaped like that of a chisel. The blade is pulled toward you for

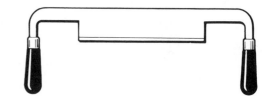

Figure 11-15. *A drawknife.*

Figure 11-16. *A spokeshave.*

shaping stock. The angle at which the blade enters the work controls the depth of cut. Take light cuts for best results.

When you use a drawknife, be sure your stock is clamped securely. Keep your balance and footing as you pull the drawknife toward you (Figure 11-17). The drawknife is honed with a hand stone. If there are nicks in the blade, they must be ground away.

Figure 11-17. *Pull the drawknife toward you. Keep your balance and footing when using a drawknife.*

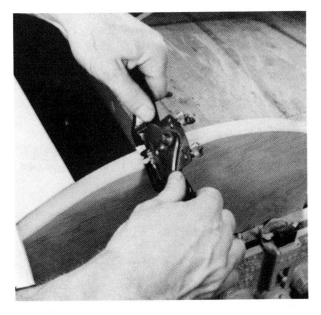

Figure 11-18. *A spokeshave may be pushed or pulled. Cutting with the grain gives best results.*

The *spokeshave* is used to shape stock. It was originally designed to shape spokes for wooden wagon wheels. A straight blade or a concave blade is used. A spokeshave is easier to control than a drawknife. It has a blade similar to a plane blade. Depth of cut is controlled by blade height.

The spokeshave may be pushed or pulled (Figure 11-18). Cut with the grain for best results. Set the blade for a light cut and begin shaping the stock. Be sure your footing is secure to keep your balance. Check your work frequently to obtain the desired shape.

FILES AND RASPS

Files and rasps are hardened pieces of steel with raised teeth. Files and rasps shape stock. Each tooth removes a small shaving. A file has rows of teeth. A rasp has larger individual teeth. Rasps are coarser than files and remove more stock.

Files and rasps have many shapes. The most common are flat, half round, and round (Figure 11-19). Those which have one flat side and one curved side are called "half round."

Figure 11-20 shows a file with the basic parts identified. A rasp uses the same terms to describe the parts. In use, a handle always goes on the tang.

Figure 11-19. *Flat, half round, and round cross-section shapes are used for files and rasps.*

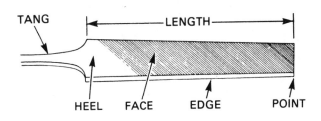

Figure 11-20. *Files are hardened pieces of steel with raised teeth set in rows.*

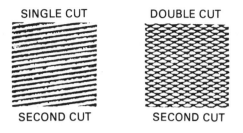

SINGLE CUT   DOUBLE CUT

SECOND CUT   SECOND CUT

Figure 11-21. *Common file cuts. For woodworking, coarse and bastard files work best.*

The angle between the rows of teeth and the edge of the file varies between 65° and 85°. When teeth cross a file in one direction it is called a "single cut" file. When the teeth cross in both directions it is called a "double cut file" (Figure 11-21).

Files commonly used in woodworking are classified as *coarse, bastard, second cut* and *smooth*. These classifications designate tooth size. Coarse and bastard files are most commonly used on wood. A 16″ bastard file has larger teeth than an 8″ bastard file.

Using a File or Rasp

Before you use a file or rasp, be sure a handle has been placed over the tang. This will protect your hands and make the tool easier to control. Clamp your stock securely at a comfortable height. Use the flat files and rasps for convex

Figure 11-22. *Tilt the file at a slight angle and push it away from your body.*

and flat cuts. Use round or curved files and rasps for concave cuts.

The file or rasp cuts on the forward stroke and should point away from your body. Turn the tool to a slight angle as you work (Figure 11-22). This will make the cut smoother. Do not force the tool or use it as a lever. Files and rasps are brittle. They will break easily. If the teeth clog, clean them with a file card (Figure 11-23).

Figure 11-23. *A file card is like a stiff wire brush. It is used to clean the teeth of a file.*

MULTI-BLADE FORMING TOOL

Multi-blade forming tools (Figure 11-24) cut like a file or rasp. Each tooth is like a plane blade. The teeth are stamped through the blade. This pre-

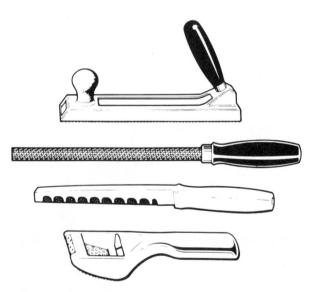

Figure 11-24. *Multi-blade forming tools have many small teeth. The teeth are stamped through the blade. This eliminates clogging.*

vents the teeth from clogging. Multi-blade forming tools come in many shapes.

The blade used in a multi-blade forming tool is made from hardened steel. It is brittle and will break easily if it is forced. Make sure the blade is installed securely to avoid vibration which could break the blade.

The multi-blade forming tool is used in the same way as a file or rasp. Observe the same cutting procedures.

CARVING TOOLS

Carving tools (Figure 11-25) are used to cut designs into wood. They look like small chisels and gouges although some have different shapes. Some carving tools have replaceable blades (Figure 11-26) which do not require sharpening. Other tools have blades that are

sharpened by grinding and honing. Use the same general procedures for sharpening carving tools as you use for chisels and gouges. Check the carving tool before you begin sharpening. Make sure you know the correct angles for grinding and honing.

CHIP CARVING AND WHITTLING

Chip carving is the process of making designs in wood. Usually three cuts are made for each section of the design (Figure 11-27). A triangular chip is removed at the intersection of the three

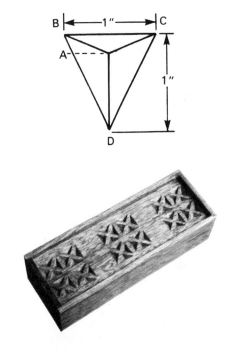

Figure 11-25. *Carving tools look like small chisels and gouges. They have shapes suited to carving wood.*

Figure 11-27. *Chip carving can create an interesting design. Three cuts are used to remove a triangular chip (top). Practice on scrap stock before you begin chip carving.*

Figure 11-26. *Some carving tools have replaceable blades. These blades do not require sharpening.*

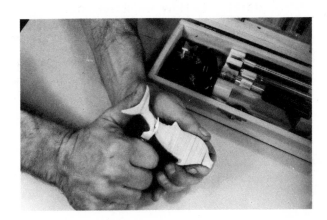

Figure 11-28. *Whittling is a form of carving done with knives. Most knives can be used for whittling.*

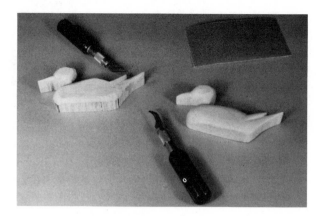

cuts. The recess cut into the wood adds interest to the design because each surface reflects light differently.

Whittling (Figure 11-28) is a form of carving done with knives instead of carving tools. There are many knives which are suitable for whittling. No special tools are needed.

Before you whittle or chip carve, practice on scrap. Select softer woods such as basswood, poplar or mahogany. Lay out your design carefully and clamp your stock securely. Keep your tools sharp. Always cut away from your body. Take light cuts for best results.

QUESTIONS FOR REVIEW

1. Can you name some woodworking projects that require a carved design or irregular shape.
2. What are some procedures that you should observe for safe shaping or carving of stock?
3. What types of blades and handles are used on chisels? How do they differ?
4. How does a gouge differ from a chisel? How do you determine the size of a gouge?
5. What type of gouge would you select for a concave cut? For a convex cut?
6. How are chisels and gouges sharpened? What stones are used to hone them?
7. For what purposes are a drawknife and a spokeshave used? How are they controlled?
8. How do a file and a rasp differ? How are they classified by size?
9. How does a multi-blade forming tool differ from a file or rasp?
10. What is the purpose of carving tools?
11. What is the difference between chip carving and whittling?

SUGGESTED ACTIVITIES

1. Identify the types of chisels you have in your shop.

2. Demonstrate the correct way of honing a chisel. Have your teacher check your technique.

Drilling and Boring Stock by Hand

Holes in wood are either *drilled* or *bored*. Holes under ¼" (about 6 mm) in diameter are usually drilled. Holes over ¼" (about 6 mm) in diameter are usually bored. Holes are drilled or bored in wood for many reasons, such as the installation of fasteners or hardware, to provide an access hole for a saw blade or to join two pieces of wood together.

Regardless of the purpose of the hole, it is important that it be laid out accurately. Locate the centers of all holes and mark them with an *awl* (Figure 12-1). The awl makes an impression or indentation in the stock. This helps start the bit at the proper center. Make sure that you select the correct bit for the job.

KEY TERMS

awl	brace
drilling	auger bits
boring	expansive bits
twist drills	lockset bits
hand drill	forstner bits
drill points	bit extensions
push drill	screwdriver bits
gimlet bits	

DRILLING

Holes are drilled in wood with the following types of bits: twist drills, drill points and gimlet bits.

Twist Drills

Twist drills (Figure 12-2) are steel bits with flutes that twist around the body. These flutes carry chips out of the hole. The point and the lips cut the stock and the flutes move the chips out of the hole.

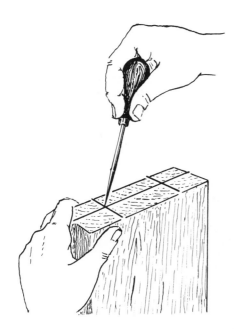

Figure 12-1. *Hole centers should be marked with an awl.*

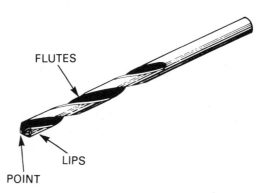

Figure 12-2. *A twist drill bit point centers the bit and the lips do the cutting. The flutes remove the chips.*

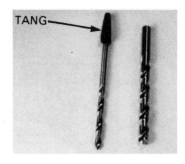

Figure 12-3. *Twist drill bits with a tang, left, are used in a brace. Those with a plain shank are used in hand drills or power drills.*

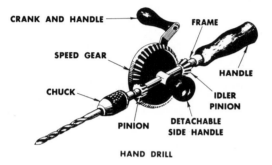

Figure 12-4. *The hand drill drives twist drill bits. Make sure the bit is centered before drilling.*

Twist drill bits are commonly sold in sizes from 1/64" to 1/2" (0.4 to 12 mm) in 1/64" graduations. The twist bit may have a tang for use in a brace or the shank may be round for use in a hand drill, portable drill, or drill press (Figure 12-3).

A hand drill (Figure 12-4) provides the motion for driving the twist drill bit. Hand drills are sized by the maximum chuck opening which is either 1/4" or 3/8" (about 6 mm or 9 mm). The chuck has self-centering jaws which grip the drill bit. Make sure the bit is centered in the jaws before tightening the chuck.

When using a hand drill with a twist bit, crank the handle and feed the bit into the work. Keep the hand drill perpendicular to the work for straight holes (Figure 12-5). Avoid forcing the bit. Excess force may bend or break the bit. Place a piece of scrap stock under the good stock to prevent the bit from tearing through the work when the bit comes out the opposite side.

Figure 12-5. *Crank the hand drill and push it into the work. Use a square to check your work.*

Drill Points

Drill points are pointed steel bits with straight flutes (Figure 12-6). The shank of a drill point is designed to be inserted into the chuck of a push drill (Figure 12-7). Drill points range in size from 1/16" to 11/64" diameter. They are often stored in the handle of a push drill when not in use.

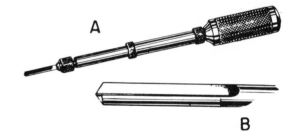

Figure 12-6. *Drill points are pointed steel bits with two flutes.*

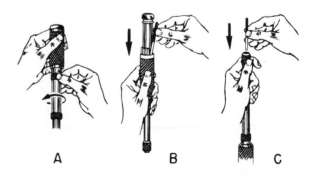

Figure 12-7. *The shank of the drill point is inserted in the chuck. Pull back on the chuck to insert or release bits.*

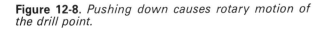

Figure 12-8. *Pushing down causes rotary motion of the drill point.*

A *push drill* provides rotary motion to drive the drill points (Figure 12-8). Pushing down on the handle causes rotary motion of the drill point. When drilling with a push drill, do not twist the drill point. Drill points are brittle and will break easily. Oil the shaft of your push drill occasionally to keep it operating freely.

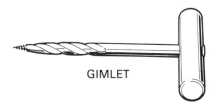

Figure 12-9. *Some gimlet bits have a T handle. Others have a square tang for use in a brace.*

Gimlet Bits

Gimlet bits are used to drill holes up to ¼″ (about 6 mm) in diameter. Gimlet bits may have a square tang for use in a brace or they may have a T handle (Figure 12-9). Gimlet bits have a tapered point similar to a wood screw (Figure 12-10). Gimlet bits range from ⅛″ to ¼″ (about 3 mm to 6 mm) diameter in 1/32″ graduations. Gimlet bits are numbered by 32nds. For example, a number 7 gimlet bit has a diameter of 7/32″.

BORING

Boring bits include auger bits, expansive bits, lockset bits, and forstner bits. All of these boring bits if they have a tang may be driven by a brace.

The Brace

A *brace* (Figure 12-11) provides rotary motion for any bit with a tang end. The square tang is inserted into the V-shaped notches in the *chuck*

Figure 12-10. *Gimlet bits have a tapered point like a wood screw. They work well for starting screws.*

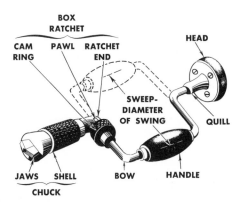

Figure 12-11. *The brace provides rotary motion for any bit with a tang end.*

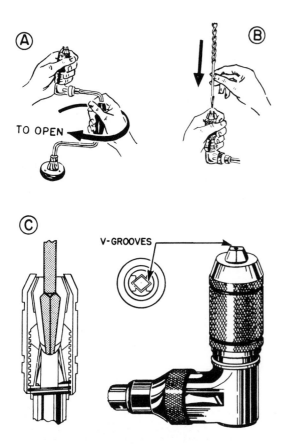

Figure 12-12. *The jaws of the chuck are tightened against the tang of the bit.*

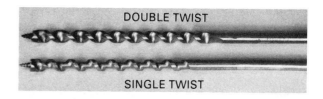

Figure 12-13. *An auger bit is the most common type of bit used in a brace.*

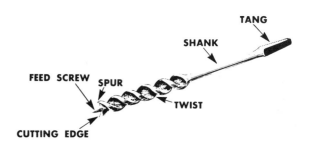

Figure 12-14. *The feed screw pulls the bit into the work. The spurs score the hole. The auger lifts chips from the hole.*

jaws. The chuck is tightened to pull the jaws securely against the *tang* (Figure 12-12).

The size of a brace is determined by its *sweep.* Sweep is the diameter of the circle made by a full revolution or swing of the brace handle (Figure 12-11). Braces vary in sweep from 8″ to 14″ (about 200 to 350 mm).

Some braces have a *ratchet mechanism* (Figure 12-11). This enables you to drive a bit when a full rotation of the brace is not possible. Ratchet mechanisms are convenient in tight spaces. A well-made brace will have bearings in the *head* and *handle*. The bearings reduce friction and make it easier to operate.

Auger Bits

Auger bits are the most common bits used in a brace. Auger bits may be single or double twist (Figure 12-13). Double twist bits are slower than single twist bits, but they are more accurate.

All auger bits have a threaded feed screw (Figure 12-14). After the feed screw pulls the auger bit into the work, the spurs score the hole. The lips then lift chips from the hole. These chips are carried up the auger away from the hole.

Auger bits are numbered. The number indicates bit size in sixteenths of an inch. For example, a number 9 bit would equal $\frac{9}{16}″$ diameter and a number 8 bit would equal $\frac{8}{16}″$ or $\frac{1}{2}$. The number is usually stamped on the tang. Auger bits range from $\frac{1}{4}″$ to 1 $\frac{1}{2}″$ diameter (about 6 to 38 mm).

Boring with Auger Bits. Mark all holes with an awl and secure the auger bit in the brace. Clamp your stock securely. You may want to back up your work with a piece of scrap (Figure 12-15).

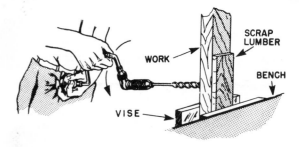

Figure 12-15. *Scrap stock will prevent tear-out.*

This will prevent the auger bit from tearing your stock as it cuts through.

If you are not boring all the way through your stock, you may attach a depth gage (Figure 12-16) to control the limit boring depth. The depth gage attaches to the auger bit. The depth of the cut is measured from the cutting edge on the auger bit to the bottom of the depth gage.

Insert the feed screw in the dimple made by the awl. Place some pressure on the head of the brace. Turn the handle in a clockwise direction. Keep the auger bit perpendicular to the work for straight holes. You can check the angle with a try square (Figure 12-17). After the auger bit is started, the feed screw will pull the bit into the work. It is not necessary to force the bit.

As soon as the feed screw comes through the stock, remove the auger bit by backing it out (Figure 12-18). Turn the brace counter clockwise to remove the bit. Then start the feed screw in

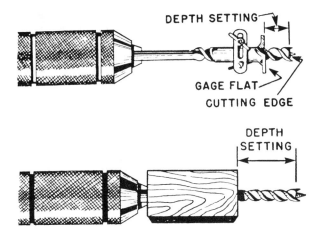

Figure 12-16. *Depth gages limit boring depth.*

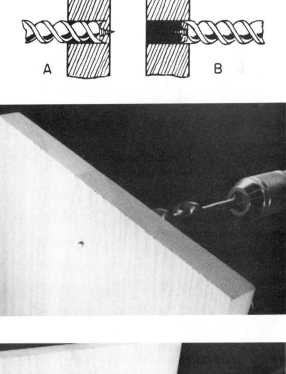

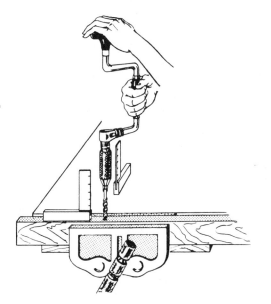

Figure 12-17. *A try square will help you bore a straight hole.*

Figure 12-18. *Boring from both directions will eliminate tear-out.*

the hole on the opposite side of the work. This technique eliminates splitting and tearing. When boring near the edge of the stock, place a clamp across the work to avoid splitting.

Holes can be bored at an angle when using auger bits. A sliding T bevel can be used to guide the boring. When several holes must be bored, you can make a boring jig (Figure 12-19).

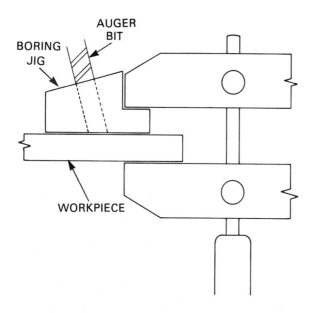

Figure 12-19. *A boring jig helps you bore holes at an angle.*

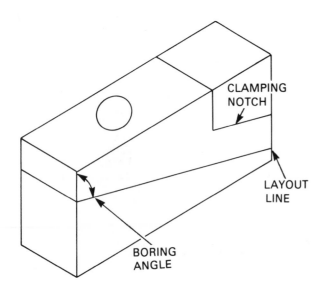

Figure 12-20. *Making a boring jig.*

To make a boring jig bore a hole through a piece of stock and lay out the boring angle on the bottom (Figure 12-20). Cut the piece off on the layout line with a back saw. Saw out a clamping notch. The jig may be clamped to the work to guide the bit.

Counterboring. Counterboring (Figure 12-21) is the process of boring 2 holes with different diameters and depths but with the same center line. Counterboring is done to bring bolts and nuts below the surface of the wood. The larger hole is always bored first. The feed screw of the larger hole locates the center of the smaller hole. If the smaller hole is bored first, the larger hole cannot be centered.

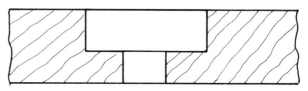

DRILL LARGER HOLE FIRST

Figure 12-21. *When counterboring, the larger hole is drilled first. Use a depth gage to limit hole depth.*

Countersinking. Countersinking is done to provide a seat for flathead wood screws (Figure 12-22). This seat makes the screw head rest even with the surface of the wood. Some countersinks are used in a brace. Others are used in a hand drill (Figure 12-23). After the hole is drilled, the seat for the screw head is made with the countersink. The countersink is placed in the hole and

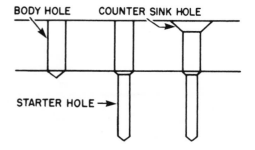

Figure 12-22. *Countersinking provides a seat for flat head screws.*

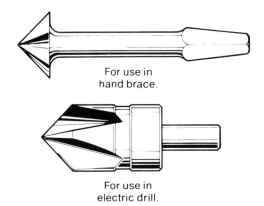

Figure 12-23. *Common types of countersinking bits.*

For use in
hand brace.

For use in
electric drill.

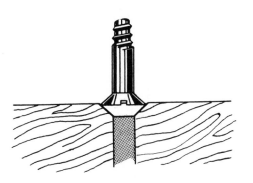

Figure 12-24. *The screw head should be the same diameter as the countersunk hole.*

turned. Compare the top of the countersunk hole in the screw head. Countersinking is complete when they are the same diameter (Figure 12-24).

Expansive Bits

Expansive bits (Figure 12-25) cut in the same way as auger bits. Expansive bits are adjustable. They will bore holes from ⅝" to 3" (about 12 to 77 mm) in diameter. An expansive bit will do the work of many auger bits. It may also be adjusted to diameters for which no auger bit is sold.

The cutter provided with the expansive bit is stamped like a ruler. When these lines are adjusted with the mark on the bit, the expansive bit will cut a hole of the indicated diameter (Figure 12-25). Bore a hole in scrap stock to be sure the expansive bit is adjusted correctly.

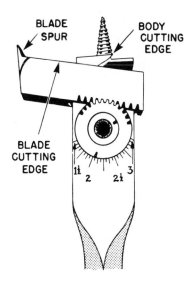

Figure 12-25. *Expansive bits are like auger bits but hole size is adjustable on an expansive bit.*

Expansive bits are used in the same way as auger bits. Let the feed screw guide the cutter into the stock. Do not force the bit.

Lockset Bits

Lockset bits (Figure 12-26) are similar to auger and expansive bits except they are shorter. Lockset bits are specifically designed for installing locks of a given size. Lockset bits are usually distributed by lock manufacturers. They are used in the same way as an auger bit.

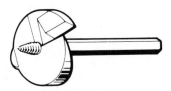

Figure 12-26. *Lockset bits are designed for installing locks of a given size.*

Forstner Bits

Forstner bits (Figure 12-27) are also boring tools. They have a square tang end for use in a brace. A forstner bit cuts a flat-bottomed hole because it

Figure 12-27. *Forstner bits cut flat bottomed holes. There is no feed screw on a forstner bit.*

has no feed screw. Flat-bottomed holes are often needed in counterboring operations. The edge or periphery of the bit scores the wood and the lips lift and remove the chips.

Forstner bits are numbered in the same way as auger bits. The number is stamped on the tang or shank. This number represents the diameter size in sixteenths of an inch. Forstner bits are available in sizes from ¼″ to 2″ in diameter.

Forstner bits work well in end grain because there is no feed screw. On an auger bit the feed screw could not pull the bit into the end grain. The feed screw would strip or pull out of the wood. Feed screws often strip in knots, but a forstner bit will cut through knots. A coarse feed screw will often split stock when a hole is bored near an edge. The forstner bit will cut these holes without splitting.

A forstner bit is difficult to start because it has no feed screw. You can draw a circle on your work that is the same size as the hole. This will help you line up the bit correctly. When you bore a hole at an angle, you may want to start the hole with an auger bit. Auger bits are easier to start and they will help you align the forstner bit correctly. The forstner bit may then be used to finish the hole (Figure 12-28).

Care of Boring Bits

All boring bits require similar care. Keep the bits clean and lightly oiled so they will not rust. Store bits separately in a protective case. If bits are dropped or hit each other, the cutting edges will become dull and may bend.

The lips of all boring bits are filed on the upper or tang side. File the lips until an edge is formed. Spurs are filed to a sharp edge on the inside only (Figure 12-29). Filing the outside of spurs will change the diameter of the bit. Sometimes a small stone is used to hone the cutting edges. This will improve the sharpness of a filed surface.

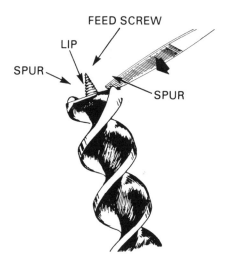

Figure 12-29. *Use this method to sharpen auger bits.*

Accessories for Boring

Bit extensions (Figure 12-30) are a popular boring accessory especially for drilling deep holes. Bit extensions are 12 to 18 inches (about 305 to 460 mm) long and may be used to extend the depth of holes 11/16″ in diameter or larger.

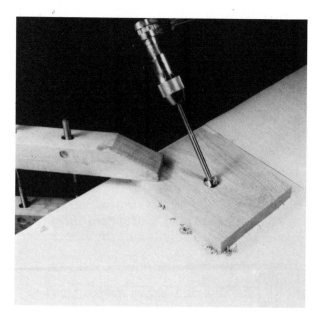

Figure 12-28. *Using a forstner bit for angular holes. Start the hole with an auger bit.*

Figure 12-30. *Bit extensions help you bore deep holes.*

Figure 12-31. *Screwdriver bits can be used in a brace. These bits are used to drive large screws.*

Screwdriver bits (Figure 12-31) with tang ends are available for braces. They are not boring accessories, but they may be used to drive screws into a hole you have bored. Screwdriver bits reduce fatigue when driving larger screws. They are available in various sizes for slotted and recessed head screws.

QUESTIONS FOR REVIEW

1. What is the difference between drilled holes and bored holes?
2. Why are hole centers marked with an awl?
3. Name and describe bits used for drilling holes. What types of tools are used to drive the bits?
4. What are grooves on a drill bit called?
5. Name the parts of a brace and describe its use.
6. How do you determine the size of an auger bit?
7. When you bore a hole with an auger bit, should you apply plenty of force with the brace? Why or why not?
8. Why is scrap stock used to back up a hole bored through your work?
9. Define counterboring and countersinking. What is the purpose of each?
10. What is the correct procedure for counterboring a hole?
11. What is an expansive bit? How is it adjusted and used?
12. Do expansive bits cut in the same way as auger bits?
13. For what purpose is a lockset bit used?
14. What are the advantages and disadvantages of using forstner bits?
15. Discuss some of the procedures you should follow to care for your boring bits correctly?
16. What is a bit extension and when is it used?

SUGGESTED ACTIVITIES

1. Install a twist drill bit in a hand drill and drill a hole in a piece of scrap.

2. Check the tang of an auger bit in your shop. See if you can find a number that indicates its size.

3. With a brace and auger bit, bore a hole in some scrap stock.

Cutting Joints with Hand Tools

Often joints are cut with power tools, but there also are reasons for cutting them with hand tools. If power or power tools are not available, hand tools will do the job. When pieces of stock are too large or too small to handle safely on a power tool, they may be clamped and cut safely with hand tools.

As you become experienced with hand tools, you may find that hand tools will do the job faster and more accurately than power tools.

KEY TERMS

butt joints	groove joints
dowel joints	dado joints
dowel centers	mortise and tenon
dowel jigs	joints
rabbet joints	dovetail joints
lap joints	miter joints

The accuracy of any joint made with hand tools depends upon how well it is laid out and cut. Use a sharp pencil or utility knife to mark layout lines. Be sure that stock is straight and square before you begin your layout. Layout tools should be held securely against stock while it is marked. If the layout line is incorrect, the joint will fit poorly. Measure and mark your stock carefully. Check your work as you progress. This will help you notice errors early.

BUTT JOINTS

Butt joints (Figure 13-1) require very little hand tool work. Two pieces of stock are butted together and held with glue or fasteners. Butt joints require that the faces or ends of the stock be planed or sawed to a flat surface. The surfaces

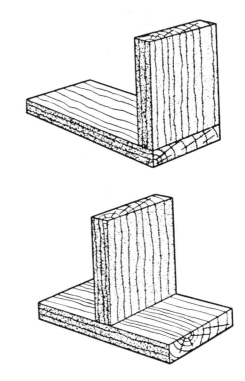

Figure 13-1. *Plain butt joints require little tool work.*

must fit together perfectly. Select a smoothing or jack plane for this task. Check the surfaces with the blade of a square or straightedge and check the fit of the two pieces. When they fit together without any gaps they are ready for fastening.

DOWEL JOINTS

Dowel joints are reinforced butt or miter joints. Dowels are placed into the parts of the joint for added strength (Figure 13-2). The diameter of the dowel you select should equal one-half the

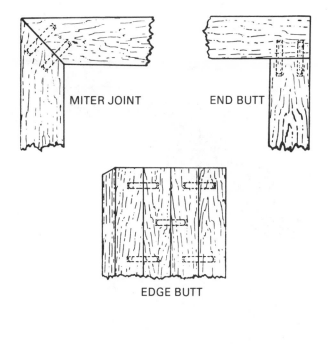

Figure 13-2. *Dowelled butt joints.*

MITER JOINT

END BUTT

EDGE BUTT

Figure 13-3. *Dowels should fit into the piece a distance 2½ to 3 times their diameter.*

HOLD DEPTH = 2 1/2 to 3 TIMES DIA OF DOWEL

thickness of the stock you plan to join. If the pieces you plan to join are of different thicknesses the dowel diameter should be one-half the thickness of the thinnest piece.

Wood dowels are usually made of birch. They are ¼", ⅜" or ½" in diameter and 1 ½" to 2" long, although longer dowel rods can be purchased. The length of the hole for the dowel should be 2 ½ to 3 times the diameter (Figure 13-3).

The dowels are usually grooved to allow for glue to flow (Figure 13-4). Often water-based glues will cause the dowel to swell.

Place dowels four to six inches apart on edge joints and at least one-half inch from the ends. When dowels are used in an end butt joint they may be spaced one inch apart.

Lay out dowel positions with a ruler, square, marking gage and awl. Bore the dowel holes with an auger bit or forstner bit. You can control

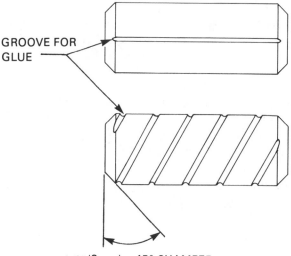

GROOVE FOR GLUE

1/8" (3mm) × 45° CHAMFER

Figure 13-4. *Some dowels are grooved to allow air and glue to flow out.*

hole depth by clamping a depth gage to your bit. The holes should be bored ¹⁄₁₆" deeper than the dowel length to allow for the glue.

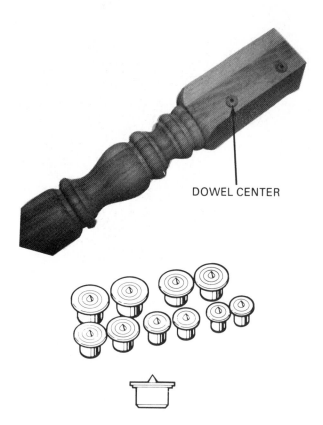

DOWEL CENTER

Figure 13-5. *Dowel centers transfer hole locations from one piece to another.*

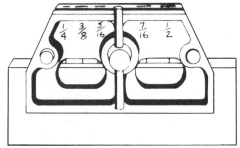

Figure 13-6. *The self-centering dowel jig.*

Dowel Centers

Dowel centers (Figure 13-5) are used to transfer hole locations from one piece of stock to another. Holes are bored in one of the pieces. The dowel centers are inserted into the holes and the piece is aligned with the opposite part of the joint. The pieces are pressed together. The points on the dowel centers mark the center of the holes on the opposite piece. These holes may now be bored accurately.

Dowel Jigs

A *dowel jig* is used to guide the drill bit into the work. It also locates holes in the center of the piece or at a uniform distance from the edge.

There are many types of dowel jigs, but the two most common are the self-centering jig (Figure 13-6) and the adjustable, single-hole jig (Figure 13-7). The self-centering jig centers on the work when you tighten the clamping screw. The mark stamped on the jig should line up with the layout line. The self-centering jig always adjusts for boring in the exact center of the work.

Figure 13-7. *The adjustable single hole dowel jig.*

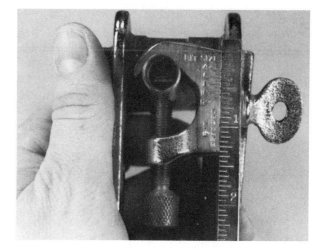

Figure 13-8. *The inside rail of the dowel jig must be adjusted before using.*

The adjustable, single-hole dowel jig has a series of drill guides of various diameters. First you install in the jig drill a guide of the same diameter as the dowel being used. The jig has two rails. The diameter of the dowel or bit size is stamped on the inside rail. Dimensions equal to one-half stock thickness are stamped on the outside rail (Figure 13-8). When you line up the two rails the jig is centered. Tighten the clamp. Figure 13-8 shows a ⅜" dowel set for the center of a ¾" piece of stock.

Mark the faces of the stock and be sure that the stationary jaw of the adjustable dowel jig is always located on the exposed side of your stock. This will eliminate any adjustment error.

Preparing Dowels For Use
Some dowels are sold cut to length and others are sold in 36" lengths. After you cut the dowel to length, the dowel ends must be chamfered. This makes the dowel easier to start and drive. The ends can be chamfered with a file. A ⅛" (3mm) x 45° chamfer is suitable (Figure 13-4).

RABBET JOINTS
Rabbet joints (Figure 13-9) are used to recess the back of a cabinet or to reduce exposed end grain at a corner. A rabbet joint also increases gluing surface, which increases the strength of the joint. Rabbet joints are cut to a maximum depth of one-half stock thickness.

Edge rabbets can be cut with a *rabbet plane*. Adjust the plane to cut along the layout lines (Figure 13-10). Begin planing with a light cut.

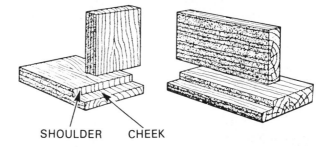

SHOULDER   CHEEK

Figure 13-9. *Rabbet joints reduce exposed end grain. Rabbet joints are often used on cabinet backs.*

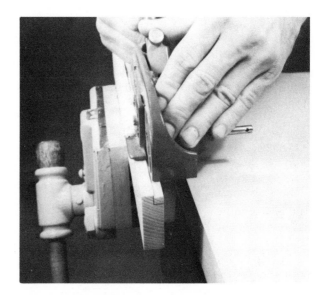

Figure 13-10. *Adjust the rabbet plane to cut along layout lines.*

Keep the plane in contact with the face and edge of the stock. This will ensure that the rabbet is square.

End rabbets may also be cut with a rabbet plane. In order to cut the wood fibers, the spur on the plane must be lowered before the rabbet is cut. End rabbets may also be cut with a back saw (Figure 13-11). Cut the shoulder first. Then cut the cheek. Remember to keep the back saw on the waste side of the line. The rabbet can be trimmed to exact size with a chisel or a side rabbet plane.

Figure 13-11. *A back saw can be used to cut rabbets. The shoulder is being cut first. Keep the blade on the waste side of the line.*

LAP JOINTS

Lap joints are used to make strong corners in furniture webs (Figure 13-12). The lap joint may also be used wherever two pieces of stock cross or lap over each other. Lap joints are cut like a rabbet joint except both pieces of the joint have stock removed.

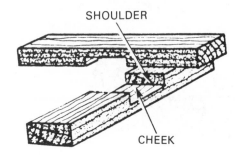

Figure 13-12. *Cross lap joints may be used anywhere two pieces of stock cross or lap over each other.*

Lay out stock with a marking gage. Do not remove more than one half of stock thickness from either piece. Lay out shoulder cuts and cheek cuts. Shoulder cuts can be laid out to the width of the stock (Figure 13-13). Cheek cuts can be laid out to one half of stock thickness or less. The shoulder cut is made first with a back saw. On a cross lap (Figure 13-12) make two shoulder cuts. Then make the cheek cut. The cheek cut cannot be cut with a back saw, so the stock is removed from a cross lap joint with a chisel (Figure 13-14) or a router plane.

Final fitting of the two pieces can be done with a chisel, file or side rabbet plane. Remember to make all saw cuts on the waste side of the line.

Figure 13-13. *The stock width can be used to lay out shoulder cuts.*

Figure 13-14. *A chisel is often used to complete a cross lap joint.*

GROOVE AND DADO JOINTS

Groove and dado joints (Figure 13-15) form a channel through the stock. When the joint is cut with the grain, it is called a *groove*. If the joint is cut across the grain, it is called a *dado*.

Groove and dado joints are cut to secure shelves and drawer bottoms. A dado or groove should not be deeper than one-half the stock thickness. In plywood the groove or dado should not cut the core or center ply (Figure 13-16).

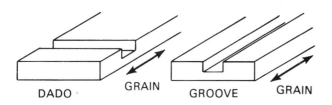

Figure 13-15. *Groove and dado joints form a channel through the stock. Groove joints are cut with the grain.*

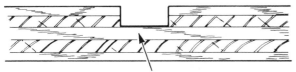

CENTER PLY OR CORE

Figure 13-16. *A dado joint in plywood does not cut the center core.*

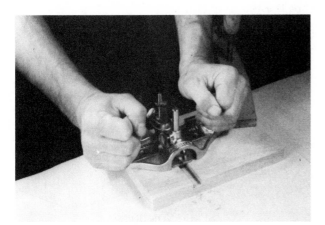

Figure 13-17. *A router plane is used to clean out a dado. Shoulder cuts must be made first.*

Shoulder cuts are made with a back saw. Cut on the waste side of the line so that the mating piece fits correctly. You can clamp a piece of stock to the back saw to control the depth of cut. A jig may also be built to control the saw.

After the shoulder cuts are made, the waste stock is removed with a chisel and a router plane (Figure 13-17). If the shoulders require trimming, use a side rabbet plane (Figure 13-18). When a blind dado or groove is made, the blind or closed end is squared with a chisel.

Figure 13-18. *The shoulders of a dado may be trimmed with a side rabbet plane.*

MORTISE AND TENON JOINTS

The *mortise and tenon joint* (Figure 13-19) is a two-part joint. One part, the tenon, is inserted into its mating part or mortise. Some mortise and tenon joints are round, while others are

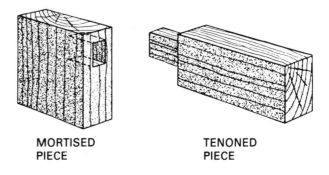

MORTISED
PIECE

TENONED
PIECE

Figure 13-19. *The mortise and tenon is a two-part joint.*

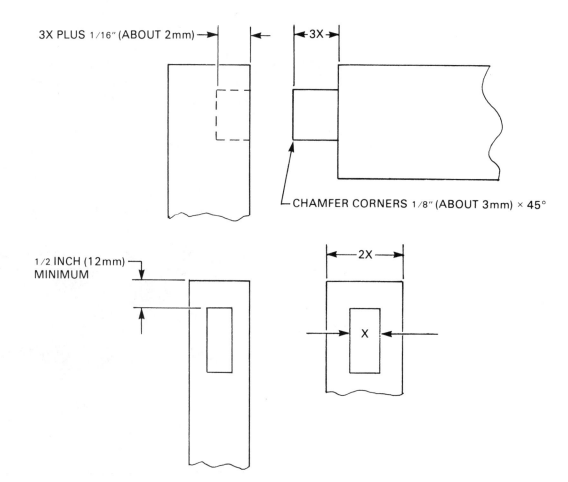

Figure 13-20. *Typical mortise and tenon layout.*

rectangular or square. Mortises are no wider than one-half stock thickness. Mortise depth is usually 3 times mortise thickness or greater (Figure 13-20). Mortises should always be ½" or more from the end of a piece of stock.

The mortise is cut first and should be started with a forstner bit or auger bit. A doweling jig can be used to guide the bit for greater accuracy. The ends of the mortise may be half round or square. After boring the mortise, the ends of the mortise may be squared with a chisel. The mortise must then be cleaned out and fitted to receive the tenon.

The tenon is cut to fit into the mortise. Use the same procedures for cutting a tenon as you used for cutting a rabbet joint or lap joint. Cut the shoulders first, then cut the cheeks. Fit the tenon to the mortise with a chisel or file. The shoulders

can be trimmed with a side rabbet plane. If you make an open mortise and tenon joint, (Figure 13-21), you can cut the mortise in the same way that the tenon is cut.

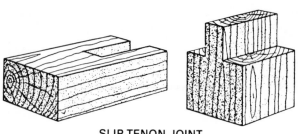

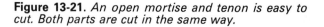
SLIP TENON JOINT

Figure 13-21. *An open mortise and tenon is easy to cut. Both parts are cut in the same way.*

DOVETAIL JOINTS

A *dovetail joint* (Figure 13-22) is a two-part joint. One part, the tail, is fitted to the mating part, the pin. Dovetail joints are often used for drawer corner joints. They are used on drawers because the joint is designed to resist pushing and pulling forces. The angle of the pins and tails is usually 10° to 25°, but this varies with the size of the dovetail.

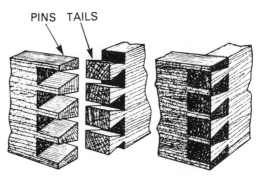

Figure 13-22. *The dovetail joint has two parts: the pin and the tail.*

Figure 13-23. *Tails are cut first when making a dovetail joint.*

Tails are cut first and used to lay out the pins. Lay out the tails with a sliding T-bevel or a template. The sockets or the stock between the tails is removed with a backsaw and a coping saw (Figure 13-23). The socket is then trimmed to the finished dimension with a file or chisel.

Cut the pin sides with a backsaw (Figure 13-24). Remove the waste stock with a coping saw and trim the pins to size with a chisel and file.

Dovetails require careful layout and fitting. Work slowly and carefully. Do not force the pieces together, or you may split the wood. Make a final fit before assembling. The pieces should not

Figure 13-24. *The sides of the pins are cut with a backsaw or dovetail saw. Keep the blade on the waste side of the line.*

Figure 13-25. *Make a trial fit. Trim the pins and tails for a perfect fit.*

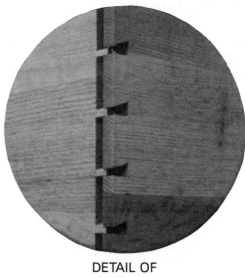

DETAIL OF
DOVETAIL
JOINT

have to be forced together. Use a chisel for final wood trimming. Figure 13-25 shows a well-fitted dovetail joint.

MITER JOINTS

A *miter joint* (Figure 13-26) is designed to hide end grain. The miter joint is used on picture frames. This is because all four corners have the end grain hidden. Miter joints do not have to form a 90° angle.

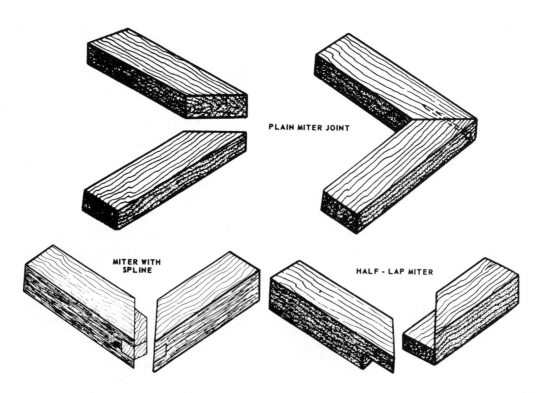

PLAIN MITER JOINT

MITER WITH
SPLINE

HALF - LAP MITER

Figure 13-26. *The miter joint is used to hide end grain. It is often used on picture frames.*

Figure 13-27. *A combination square can be used to lay out a miter joint.*

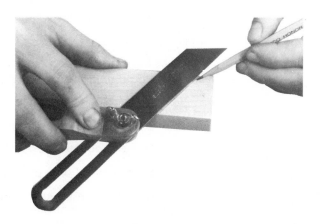

Figure 13-28. *A sliding T bevel may also be used to lay out a miter joint.*

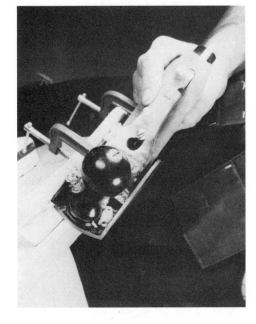

Figure 13-29. *A smoothing plane with an auxiliary fence can be used to cut an edge miter.*

Lay out the miter joint with a combination square (Figure 13-27) or sliding T bevel (Figure 13-28). End miters can be cut with a backsaw and trimmed with a block plane. A miter box may be used to control the cut for greater accuracy.

An edge miter can be cut with a smoothing plane (Figure 13-29). An auxiliary fence clamped to the plane will increase accuracy.

QUESTIONS FOR REVIEW

1. What determines the accuracy of any joint?
2. For adequate strength in a dowel joint, how long should a dowel be?
3. How do you determine the correct dowel diameter and dowel spacing?
4. How do dowel centers and doweling jigs increase accuracy in a dowel joint?
5. How are dowels prepared for use in a dowel joint?
6. What tools are required to cut an edge rabbet or an end rabbet?
7. How do lap joints differ from rabbet joints? Sketch and label a rabbet joint and a lap joint.
8. What is the difference between a dado and a groove? How are they cut?
9. How is a mortise and tenon joint made? Which piece is cut first?
10. What tools are required to make a mortise and tenon joint?
11. How are dovetails cut? How would you lay out the pins?
12. What tools are used to cut a dovetail joint?
13. How would you describe a miter joint?
14. How would you cut an end miter? How is an edge miter cut?

SUGGESTED ACTIVITIES

1. Describe the procedure for cutting a dado joint with handtools.

2. Lay out a dado joint on a piece of scrap. Cut the joint and test the fit.

3. Check the furniture in your home. Make a list of the joints used to construct four different pieces of furniture.

SECTION 3

Joining Stock

CHAPTER 14

Wood Joinery

In this chapter you will learn the importance of wood joinery and how to select the correct wood joint for the job.

Figure 14-1. *Dovetail joints can add strength.*

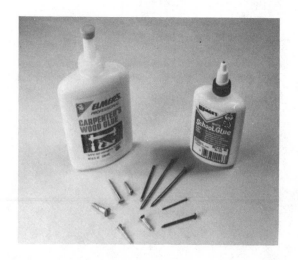

Figure 14-2. *Glue and metal fasteners can strengthen simple joints.*

Wood joints affect a product's appearance and strength. Certain joints add beauty to a wood product (Figure 14-1). Joints such as the mortise and tenon can be as strong as the wood itself.

Joints may be simple or complex. *Complex joints* are stronger but more difficult to construct. *Simple joints* can be strengthened by using metal fasteners and an adhesive (Figure 14-2). Simple joints with reinforcement are easy to construct and are strong enough for general use.

KEY TERMS

butt joints	dowels
dowelled butt joint	dado joint
mortise and tenon	groove joint
glue blocks	tongue and groove
gussets	joint
nails	rabbet joints
screws	lap joints
miter joints	dovetail joint

JOINERY CONSIDERATIONS

Wood joints join one piece of stock to another. The strength of the joint is determined by how well the pieces remain joined during use. There are several possible directions in which the members of a wood joint can move. Figure 14-3 shows the six major directions of movement. A strong joint can control movement in all six directions. Complex joints control more directions of movement. Greater control of movement means greater joint strength.

Making a *mortise and tenon joint* requires more stock than a *dowelled butt joint*. Both joints control the same amount of movement, but the mortise and tenon joint requires more stock. Shorter pieces of stock can be used for the dowelled butt joint. This is an important consideration when using lower grades of lumber.

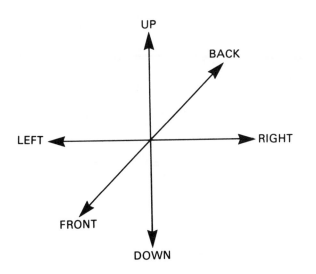

Figure 14-3. *Joints can move in six major directions.*

Another joinery consideration is the amount of glue surface between the joinery members. Large glue surfaces can increase joint strength. The strongest glue joint occurs when face grain is glued to face grain. Gluing end grain surfaces does very little to increase joint strength because end grain has poor gluing characteristics.

It may be difficult to decide which type of joint is best suited to your work. As a beginner, the best practice is to choose the simplest joint that will do the job.

CONTROLLING MOVEMENT IN JOINERY

Butt Joints

End *butt joints* control little movement (Figure 14-4). Increased control of movement can be obtained by installing *dowels* (Figure 14-5). In some butt joints a *glue block* (Figure 14-6) or a *gusset* (Figure 14-7) is used for reinforcement.

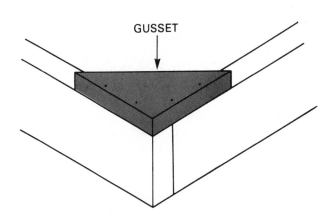

Figure 14-6. *A glue block can be used to strengthen a butt joint.*

Figure 14-4. *Butt joints control movement in one direction only.*

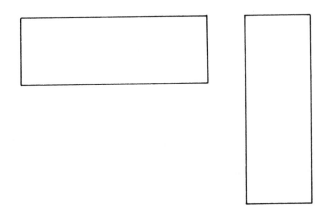

Figure 14-5. *By adding dowels, the butt joint controls more movement.*

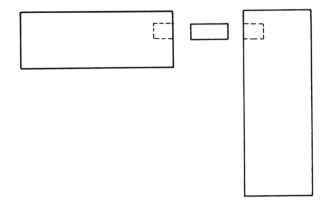

Figure 14-7. *A gusset can be glued and nailed to both members of a butt joint. The gusset makes the joint very strong.*

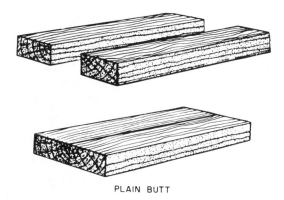

PLAIN BUTT

Figure 14-8. *Edge butt joints are very strong when only glue is used.*

Figure 14-9. *A miter joint controls little movement.*

Glue blocks are glued into the corner of the butt joint. Gussets can be glued and nailed to the joinery. Gussets are usually made of plywood.

Reinforcement with glue blocks or gussets helps control movement in butt joints. Nails may also be used to control movement in butt joints. Screws do not hold well in end grain and are seldom used to reinforce butt joints.

Edge butt joints (Figure 14-8) are very strong when glued. Edge grain gluing is very strong and controls movement effectively. If reinforcement is needed, dowels are commonly used. A tongue and groove joint may also be used in place of an edge butt joint.

Miter Joints

End *miter joints* (Figure 14-9) control little movement. Because end miter joints have end grain to end grain gluing, they should be reinforced with a nail or key. A key (Figure 14-10) may be glued between the two joinery members. The key controls movement and strengthens the joint. Keys are glued face grain to face grain. This is much stronger than end grain joinery.

A *spline* (Figure 14-11) may also be used to reinforce a miter joint. A spline should be as wide as the stock thickness. Half of the spline is glued into each joinery member.

End miter joints may also be strengthened with dowels or nails. Screws do not work well in end grain and should be avoided. Edge miter joints are quite strong when glued. If reinforcement is needed, dowels or splines are commonly used.

KEY

Figure 14-10. *A key strengthens the miter joint. Keys are glued face grain to face grain. This is the strongest type of gluing.*

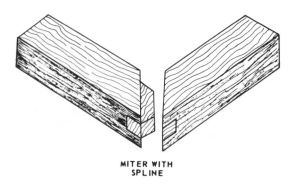

MITER WITH SPLINE

Figure 14-11. *A spline may be used to reinforce a miter joint.*

DADO   GROOVE

Figure 14-12. *Grooves are cut with the grain. Dadoes are cut across the grain.*

Dado and Groove Joints

Dado and *groove joints* (Figure 14-12) control more movement than butt joints. Dadoes go across the grain and grooves go with the grain. Glue, wood screws or nails can be used to control movement in other directions. Groove and dado joints are commonly used to secure a shelf in place. Glue holds these joints quite well.

Tongue and Groove Joints

Tongue and groove joints are often used to strengthen flooring (Figure 14-13). The pieces of flooring are nailed into place. The tongue and groove joint keeps the pieces of flooring from warping. In some edge grain gluing applications, such as chair seats, tongue and groove joints are used.

Tongue and groove joints control movement and hold pieces in place while the glue cures. It takes more stock to make a tongue and groove joint than an edge butt joint. Unless extra strength is needed, choose an edge butt joint because there is less waste.

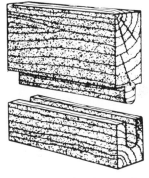

TONGUE AND GROOVE

Figure 14-13. *A tongue and groove edge joint is very strong. It requires more stock than an edge butt joint.*

Rabbet Joints

Rabbet joints (Figure 14-14) control little movement. Rabbet joints are commonly used for cabinet backs and drawer fronts. Rabbet joints are reinforced with glue, nails or dowels. The glue strength of an end rabbet joint is low. This is because of the large amount of end grain. Edge grain rabbet joints are much stronger.

Figure 14-14. *Rabbet joints control movement in two directions.*

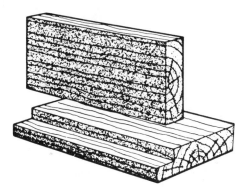

Lap Joints

An end *lap joint* (Figure 14-15) controls little movement. It can be glued, nailed or screwed together for increased control. End lap joints use more stock than end butt joints but have increased face grain glue surface. End lap joints are commonly used for furniture webs. A furniture web is a frame-like horizontal divider between drawers.

A cross lap joint (Figure 14-16) controls movement in four directions. It is used when two pieces must cross at an angle. The cross lap joint has a large face-to-face gluing surface and is very strong.

Dovetail Joints

Dovetail joints control movement in most direc-

tions. If the joint is pinned with a dowel (Figure 14-17), movement is controlled in all directions without glue.

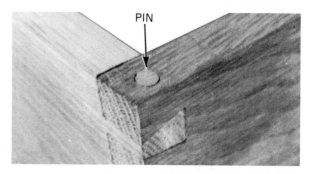

Figure 14-17. *When a dovetail joint is pinned, it controls movement in all directions without glue.*

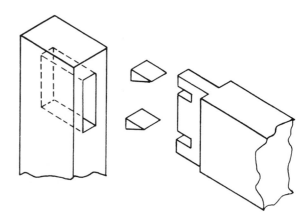

WEDGED MORTISE AND TENON

Figure 14-15. *An end lap joint controls little movement. Glue and nails can be used to strengthen this joint.*

PINNED MORTISE AND TENON

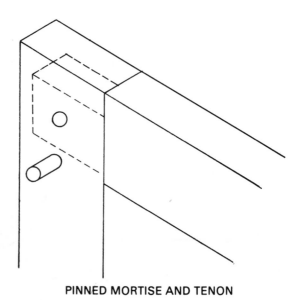

Figure 14-16. *Cross lap joints control movement in four directions.*

Figure 14-18. *A wedged or pinned mortise and tenon controls movement in all directions.*

Dovetail joints are complex. They require careful layout. A dovetail joint uses slightly more stock than a rabbet joint and is much stronger. The appearance of a dovetail joint is also pleasing.

Mortise and Tenon Joint

The *mortise and tenon joint* is a complex joint. It controls movement in most directions. If the joint is pinned or wedged (Figure 14-18), it will control movement in all directions without glue.

A mortise and tenon joint must be laid out carefully. The joint must be accurate to be strong. First layout the mortise and then cut the tenon to fit the mortise.

The mortise and tenon joint has a large surface area for face-to-face gluing. This also increases the strength of the mortise and tenon joint.

QUESTIONS FOR REVIEW

1. How does the selection of wood joinery affect your project?
2. How does a simple joint differ from a complex joint? How can a simple joint be reinforced?
3. How is the strength of a wood joint determined?
4. How do directions of movement affect joint strength?
5. How does gluing surface affect joint strength? Is end grain gluing stronger than face grain gluing?
6. What is the best practice for choosing the correct joints for your project?
7. How would you describe a key, spline, and gusset? How do they help reinforce simple joints?
8. Discuss how butt, dado, and dovetail joints control movement in wood.
9. Discuss how lap, rabbet, and mortise and tenon joints control movement in wood.
10. How can pinning a joint reduce the directions of movement in a joint?

SUGGESTED ACTIVITIES

1. Check the furniture in your home. See if you can find a gusset or glue block reinforcing a wood joint.

2. Look at a wooden picture frame to see if it has keys in the miter joints. If not, was anything else used to strengthen the miter joint?

CHAPTER 15

Adhesives

Adhesive is a general term. It refers to any material that joins two or more substances together. Many adhesives are known as glues or cements. Joining wood pieces together is called gluing. Adhesives may be solid, powdered or liquid. Figure 15-1 shows various types of adhesives used for woodworking.

Gluing is an important part of woodworking. A good glue joint strengthens the product; a poor gluing makes a poor bond. A sloppy glue joint suggests poor work. Using too much glue will cause drips and *glue blemishes* (Figure 15-2). A glue blemish does not take stain or finish. It will cause a light spot on your product.

Strength is very important if the piece will be machined or put under stress after gluing. Make sure that the glue joints are tight and strong because a weak joint will not hold up under stress. For safe machining, joints must be strong.

KEY TERMS

adhesive	hide glue
gluing	plastic resin glue
glue blemishes	urea resin glue
assembly time	resorcinol resin glue
clamping time	contact cement
pot life	epoxy
shelf life	hot melt glue
mastic adhesives	
white glue (polyvinyl resin)	
yellow glue (aliphatic resin)	

Figure 15-1. *The glues pictured here are common woodworking glues.*

Figure 15-2. *Glue will not take stain. A blemish will appear when stain is applied over glue.*

GLUING TERMINOLOGY

It is important to understand gluing terminology. This terminology is used by glue manufacturers to explain the use of their product. It is also used to describe glues discussed in this chapter.

Assembly Time

Assembly time is the amount of time you have to put stock into clamps after glue is spread. Stock should be clamped into the desired position before the assembly time has lapsed. After the assembly time has lapsed, the glue begins to harden or cure.

Some manufacturers divide assembly time into *open assembly time* and *closed assembly time.* Open assembly time is the amount of time allowed to spread the glue and put the pieces together. Closed assembly time is the amount of time allowed to shift the glued pieces into position for clamping.

Clamping Time

Clamping time is the amount of time the glued pieces must be held together under pressure. Clamping time is not required for some glues such as *contact cement* and *hot melt* glue. Other glues require 6 to 10 hours of clamping time.

Pot Life

Pot life is the length of time a glue can be used after mixing. Some glues such as plastic resin must be mixed before use. The pot life for most glues that require mixing is about 4 hours. Mix only as much glue as you can use in 4 hours.

Shelf Life

Shelf life is the length of time a glue may be stored before use. Some glues will lose their adhesive qualities if they are not used in a specified length of time. Most glues manufactured today have a long shelf life. Always use the oldest glue first to make sure that no old glue remains on the shelf.

COMMON WOODWORKING GLUES

There are many common woodworking glues (Figure 15-1). Each of these glues has been developed for use under different conditions. Knowing the qualities of each glue will help you use them correctly. Figure 15-3 lists the qualities of common woodworking glues. Before you use any glue, you should read the manufacturer's directions so that you use the product correctly and safely.

Some adhesives may irritate your skin. It is best to wear rubber gloves when you use them. Other adhesives are extremely flammable and should not be used near fire or flame. When using flammable adhesives, be sure to extinguish all pilot lights. Always wear safety glasses when using any adhesive.

GLUE TYPE	HOW SOLD	QUALITIES	PRECAUTIONS
VINYL RESIN (WHITE)	READY TO USE IN SQUEEZE CONTAINERS. ALSO SOLD IN BULK.	GENERAL-DUTY. WATER-SOLUBLE. SOFTENS WHEN HEATED. DRIES CLEAR. WILL REACT WITH METAL CLAMPS TO STAIN WOOD. ONE AND 1/2 HOUR CLAMPING TIME. SHORT ASSEMBLY TIME.	NOT FLAMMABLE. SAFE WHEN USED ACCORDING TO MANUFACTURER'S DIRECTIONS.
ALIPHATIC RESIN (YELLOW)	READY TO USE IN SQUEEZE CONTAINERS. ALSO SOLD IN BULK.	GENERAL-DUTY. WATER-SOLUBLE. LESS CREEP THAN WHITE GLUE. ONE-HOUR CLAMPING TIME. SAME GENERAL CHARACTERISTICS AS WHITE GLUE.	NOT FLAMMABLE. SAFE WHEN USED ACCORDING TO MANUFACTURER'S DIRECTIONS.
HIDE GLUE	SOLD IN FLAKES FOR MIXING ON THE JOB. ALSO SOLD IN READY-TO-USE SQUEEZE CONTAINERS.	WATER-SOLUBLE. LONG ASSEMBLY TIME. GOOD GAP FILLING QUALITIES. THREE-HOUR CLAMPING TIME. HAS AN AMBER COLOR WHEN DRY.	NOT FLAMMABLE. SAFE WHEN USED ACCORDING TO MANUFACTURER'S DIRECTIONS.
CONTACT CEMENT	READY TO USE. IN QUART CONTAINERS OR LARGER.	WATER-RESISTANT. STICKS TO ITSELF. ADHESION OCCURS WHEN TWO PIECES COME IN CONTACT. MOST OFTEN USED FOR GLUING LAMINATES AND VENEERS TO BACKING. MATERIAL. NOT AN ASSEMBLY GLUE.	POSSIBLE SKIN IRRITANT—WEAR RUBBER GLOVES. SOME CONTACT CEMENT IS FLAMMABLE. AVOID USE NEAR FIRE OR FLAME. FOLLOW MANUFACTURER'S DIRECTIONS. DOES NOT HAVE THE STRENGTH TO GLUE LARGE WOOD AS-SEMBLIES. FOR VENEERS AND LAMI-NATES ONLY.
HOT MELT GLUE	GLUE PELLETS THAT ARE INSERTED IN THE GLUE GUN.	WATERPROOF. SOFTENS WHEN HEATED. MAY BECOME BRITTLE IN FREEZING TEMPERATURES VERY SHORT ASSEMBLY TIME. CLAMPING NOT REQUIRED. FULL STRENGTH IN ONE MINUTE.	BURN HAZARD IF YOU CONTACT HEATED GLUE OR GUN. USE ACCORDING TO MANUFACTURER'S DIRECTIONS.
PLASTIC RESIN GLUE	SOLD BY THE POUND.	WATER-RESISTANT. LONG ASSEMBLY TIME. DOES NOT WORK WELL ON OILY WOODS. HARD BRITTLE GLUE LINE. DRIES A DARK BROWN COLOR. REQUIRES ONE TO TWO HOUR CLAMPING TIME. FOUR HOUR POT LIFE AFTER MIXING.	POSSIBLE SKIN IRRITANT. WEAR RUBBER GLOVES. USE ACCORDING TO MANUFACTURER'S DIRECTIONS.

Figure 15-3. *Woodworking glues.*

GLUE TYPE	HOW SOLD	QUALITIES	PRECAUTIONS
EPOXY	TWO-PART LIQUID. SOLD IN SMALL TUBES AND BULK.	WATERPROOF. SHORT ASSEMBLY AND CLAMPING TIME. SETS UP QUICKLY. DRIES CLEAR. OFTEN USED TO FASTEN WOOD TO OTHER MATERIALS.	POSSIBLE SKIN IRRITANT. USE ACCORDING TO MANUFACTURER'S DIRECTIONS. WEAR RUBBER GLOVES.
RESORCINOL	TWO CANS OF LIQUID, SOLD IN SMALL CANS AND BULK.	WATERPROOF. LONG ASSEMBLY TIME. SIX TO TEN HOURS CLAMPING. BROWN TO MAROON GLUE LINE. FOUR-HOUR POT LIFE AFTER MIXING. SIX HOUR CLAMPING TIME.	POSSIBLE SKIN IRRITANT. WEAR RUBBER GLOVES. USE ACCORDING TO MANUFACTURER'S DIRECTIONS.
UREA RESIN	SOLD BY THE POUND.	WATER-RESISTANT. LONG ASSEMBLY TIME. TAN TO BROWN GLUE LINE. CLAMP ONE TO THREE HOURS. FOUR HOUR POT LIFE AFTER MIXING.	POSSIBLE SKIN IRRITANT. WEAR RUBBER GLOVES. USE ACCORDING TO MANUFACTURER'S DIRECTIONS.
MASTIC OR PANEL ADHESIVE	SOLD IN TUBES.	WATER-RESISTANT/ WATERPROOF DEPENDING ON THE BRAND.	POSSIBLE SKIN IRRITANT. WEAR RUBBER GLOVES. SOME BRANDS ARE FLAMMABLE. AVOID USE NEAR FIRE OR FLAME. USE ACCORDING TO MANUFACTURER'S DIRECTIONS.

Figure 15-3. *Continued.*

Polyvinyl Resin Glue (white glue)

Polyvinyl resin glue (Figure 15-4) is white in color and is often called "white glue". This glue dries clear. It is a strong, general purpose glue. Polyvinyl resin glue does not require mixing. It has an assembly time of about six minutes and requires 1½ hours of clamping time.

Polyvinyl resin glue will react with iron in the presence of wood. This reaction will stain the wood black. When gluing lumber that has been planed to thickness, protect the wood with waxed paper to prevent the metal clamps from touching the wood.

Polyvinyl resin glue is water soluble and should not be used in damp or wet conditions. The glue will also soften when heated. This softening causes the glue to load abrasives ("gumup") during sanding operations.

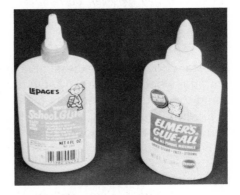

Figure 15-4. *Polyvinyl glue.*

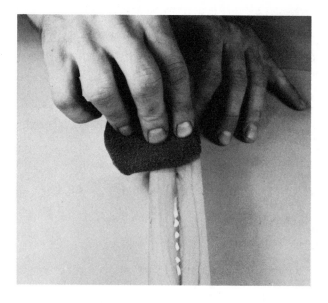

Figure 15-5. *Wet glue can be removed with a damp rag.*

Figure 15-7. *Aliphatic resin glue is like polyvinyl resin glue. Aliphatic resin glue has less tendency to "creep".*

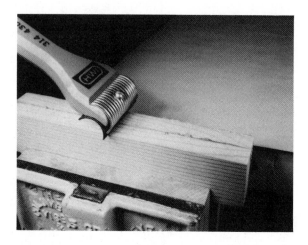

Figure 15-6. *Hardened glue can be removed with a paint scraper.*

It is important to remove excess glue before machining the wood because polyvinyl glue will dull cutting tools quickly. When the glue is wet, remove it with a damp rag (Figure 15-5). Glue that has cured can be removed with a paint scraper (Figure 15-6).

Aliphatic Resin Glue (yellow glue)

Aliphatic resin glue is light yellow in color (Figure 15-7). Aliphatic resin glue is much like polyvinyl resin glue except it is stronger and has less creep. Creep means the sliding that occurs between two pieces during clamping.

Aliphatic resin glue has an assembly time of about six minutes and requires 30 minutes to 1 hour of clamping time. Aliphatic resin glue should not be used in damp or wet conditions because it is water soluble.

Aliphatic resin glue will load abrasives and dull cutting tools. Remove excess glue with a damp rag when it is wet. After the glue has cured, remove it with a paint scraper.

Hide Glue

Hide Glue (Figure 15-8) is made from animal hides and bones. It is sold in both flake and ready-to-use form. The *ready-to-use* form is most popular. This is because mixing hide glue flakes is time-consuming and requires heat. After mixing, the hide glue has a pot life of only four hours. Ready-to-use hide glue has a much longer shelf life.

Hide glue leaves a light brown glue line. It is water soluble and should not be used in damp or wet conditions. The assembly time for hide glue is 10 to 15 minutes. This long assembly time

Figure 15-8. *Hide glue is made from animal hides and bones.*

Figure 15-9. *Plastic resin glue is sold in powder form. It is mixed with water.*

makes hide glue well suited to complicated glue jobs. Hide glue requires a clamping time of at least three hours. This is much longer than polyvinyl and aliphatic resin glue. Hide glue has good gap-filling properties. It is well suited to loose-fitting joints.

Ready-to-use hide glue may be somewhat lighter in color at the bottom of the container. This color difference will not affect the properties of the glue.

Plastic Resin Glue

Plastic resin glue (Figure 15-9) is sold in powder form and requires mixing. The pot life for plastic resin glue is about four hours. Plastic resin is a hard, brittle glue. Excess glue will dull cutting tools rapidly if it is not removed. Wet glue can be wiped with a damp rag. After the glue has dried remove it with a paint scraper.

Plastic resin glue is water-resistant and heat-resistant. It is well suited to wooden tableware such as cutting boards and salad bowls. Plastic resin glue has a 10 to 15 minute assembly time and requires 1 to 2 hours clamping time.

Plastic resin glue leaves a dark brown glue line. It works best on tight fitting joints. In industry, plastic resin glues are cured quickly in gluing machines (Figure 15-10). These machines reduce

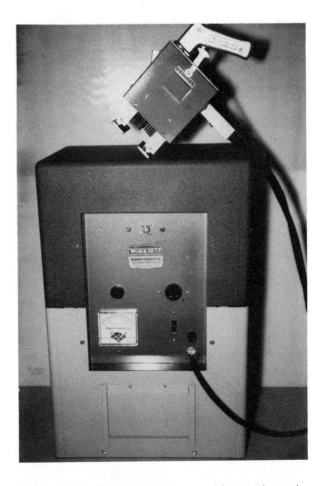

Figure 15-10. *Electronic gluing machines reduce gluing and clamping time to minutes.*

135

clamping time to minutes. Plastic resin glue may irritate your skin. Wear rubber gloves when you mix and apply plastic resin glue (Figure 15-11).

Figure 15-11. *Wear rubber gloves when mixing or using glues that may irritate your skin.*

Figure 15-12. *Resorcinol resin is a two-part glue. It is used for boat building because it is waterproof.*

Urea Resin Glue

Urea resin glue is much like plastic resin glue. It comes in a powder form and must be mixed. Urea resin has a four-hour pot life. It leaves a tan or brown glue line. Urea resin glue is heat- and moisture-resistant. It may be used for wooden tableware. Assembly time for urea resin glue is 10 to 15 minutes. Clamping time is 1 to 3 hours. Urea resin glue may be cured in high frequency electronic gluing machines.

Urea resin glue may irritate your skin. Wear gloves when you mix and apply urea resin glue.

Resorcinol Resin Glue

The outstanding quality of *resorcinol resin glue* (Figure 15-12) is that it is *completely waterproof.* Steam and heat will not affect its strength. Resorcinol resin glue is very popular for exterior and marine use. This glue is a two-part glue that has to be mixed. Mix only what you need. Resorcinol glues are not commonly used because they are expensive.

Resorcinol resin glues have a four-hour pot life and a 15-minute assembly time. The assembly must be clamped for six hours.

These glues are red in color. They leave a maroon or brown glue line. They are a potential skin irritant. Wear protective gloves when you mix and apply them.

Contact Cement

Contact cement (Figure 15-13) is used to apply plastic laminates and veneers to a backing of plywood or particleboard. The outstanding qual-

Figure 15-13. *Contact cement is used to apply plastic laminates and veneers.*

Figure 15-14. *Contact cement should be applied with a brush or roller.*

ity of contact cement is that it requires no clamping. Contact cement sticks to itself. Contact cement is applied to both pieces and allowed to dry. After drying, the coated pieces will adhere to each other upon contact. The bond is instant. The cemented pieces will not move without breaking.

Contact cements may be flammable or non-flammable. Flammable contact cements are solvent-based. They work well for both veneer and plastic laminates. Avoid fire and flame when using flammable contact cements. Non-flammable contact cements are water-based. They do not work well on veneers because the water causes the veneer to swell and curl. Non-flammable contact cements work well on plastic laminates.

All contact cements are sold ready-to-use. No mixing is required. Some contact cements may cause skin irritation. Wear rubber gloves when you use them. Read the manufacturer's directions to determine if the contact cement is a skin irritant.

Contact cement is applied to both surfaces and allowed to dry. Two coats may be necessary on

porous surfaces. Use a brush to apply the contact cement (Figure 15-14).

Epoxy
Epoxy (Figure 15-15) is a strong two-part liquid glue. It is mixed immediately before use. The pot life of epoxy varies but is seldom more than ten minutes. Assembly time is usually no more than 3 minutes. Clamping time is 30 minutes.

Epoxy dries with a clear line. It is waterproof and makes a very strong joint. Epoxy is most commonly used to join wood to metal, concrete or other material. It is not generally used for wood-to-wood joints because of its short assembly time and high cost.

Epoxies may cause skin irritation. Wear protective gloves and glasses when working with or mixing them.

Hot Melt Glues
Hot melt glues are applied hot. They cure by cooling. Hot melt adhesives have an assembly time of fifteen seconds. This short assembly time limits hot melt glues to small jobs.

Figure 15-15. *Epoxy is a two-part glue. It is used to glue wood to metal or other materials.*

Hot melt glue is applied to one surface and then the two surfaces are joined together (Figure 15-16). This must be done in fifteen seconds. After the surfaces are joined together, complete bonding occurs in sixty seconds.

Figure 15-16. *Hot melt glues are heated in the gun. They cure by cooling. They are applied to only one surface. The two pieces must be joined in 15 seconds. Be careful! The glue and the gun are very hot.*

Figure 15-17. *Hot melt glue can provide clamping action while stronger glues cure.*

Hot melt glue is waterproof, but will soften when it becomes hot. Some hot melt glues become extremely brittle when subjected to freezing temperatures.

The hot melt glue can be used with other glues. The surfaces are tacked together with hot melt glue while the other glue has time to cure (Figure 15-17).

The hot melt gun and glue get very hot during use. Avoid contact with the glue or gun nozzle because they can burn your skin. Unplug the electric glue gun when not using it.

Mastic Adhesives

Mastic adhesives (Figure 15-18) are sometimes called "panel adhesives." They are used chiefly for installing construction materials such as drywall, paneling and floor tile. Panel adhesives are ready to use. No mixing is required. They are usually sold in tubes for easy application. Most mastic adhesives are water-resistant or waterproof. They produce a thick, colored glue line. Mastic adhesives have an open assembly time of

CAULKING GUN

Figure 15-18. *Mastic adhesives may be used for assembling projects.*

15 minutes and a closed assembly time of 15 minutes. This long assembly time makes it popular for construction jobs.

If the two parts fit together well, clamping is not necessary. Nails hold the panels in place while the adhesive cures (Figure 15-19). Occasionally, panels are wedged into place with 2 × 4 braces. Mastic adhesives reach full strength in 48 hours.

Figure 15-19. *Nails will hold paneling in place while the panel adhesive cures.*

Panel adhesives will dissolve some building materials such as plastic foam insulation. Read the manufacturer's directions before using any mastic adhesive.

Some panel adhesives are flammable. They will burn. Before using flammable panel adhesives extinguish all pilot lights. Keep fire and flame away from the panel adhesive.

Panel adhesives may be skin irritants. Read and follow the manufacturer's directions. If skin irritation is possible, wear protective gloves.

PREPARING JOINERY FOR GLUING
In order for any glue to work well, the pieces must fit together well. Mating surfaces should have no gaps. All glue surfaces should be planed but not sanded. Sanding can seal the wood and make adhesion difficult.

When you glue a mortise and tenon or dowel joint together check the "dry fit" first. The pieces should be snug, but not too tight. If the dry fit is tight without glue, it may be impossible to assemble the pieces after gluing. This is because the water in the glue will cause the wood to swell.

Dowels may have grooves cut into them to allow glue and air to escape from the hole in which the dowel is inserted. Pre-chamfered and grooved dowels are available in many sizes.

When assembling several pieces, try to divide the job into several smaller units (Figure 15-20). Large assemblies are difficult with fast curing glues. If a large assembly must be glued in one operation, choose a glue with a long assembly time. This will make it easier to achieve good results.

Figure 15-20. *Glue a large assembly in small units or subassemblies.*

Always protect benches with paper when gluing. Never allow glue to drip on other objects. Always clean up your work area after gluing. Avoid using too much glue to prevent a difficult clean-up job. There is also a chance that glue spots will be left on the wood. These spots will make finishing difficult. They resist stain penetration and cause glue blemishes.

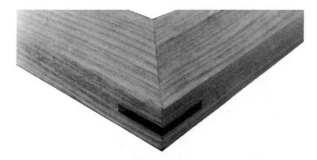

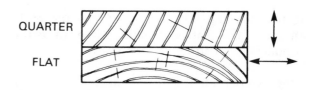

Figure 15-22. *Flat sawn and quarter sawn woods expand and contract in different directions. This can break a glue joint.*

Figure 15-21. *This end grain glue joint was strengthened with a key.*

End grain gluing often presents problems because end grain adhesion is low. It is best to double-coat both pieces before gluing. The double coating allows the glue to penetrate into the end grain. Reinforce end grain joinery whenever possible (Figure 15-21).

Temperature and moisture content of wood can also affect glue joint strength. Temperatures below 70°F (21.1°C) can affect glue joints ad-

versely. Low temperatures can cause glue to cure slowly or loose strength. Freezing temperatures can cause glues containing water to freeze. This destroys the adhesive properties of the glue. It is always best to glue stock at temperatures above 70° F (21.1° C).

High moisture content (above 10 percent) will cause the wood to shrink as it dries. This shrinkage will crack the joint. If you glue flat sawn stock to quarter sawn stock, joints may crack with changes in moisture (Figure 15-22).

QUESTIONS FOR REVIEW

1. Define the term adhesive.
2. How do assembly time, pot life and shelf life affect an adhesive?
3. Two common hazards of woodworking glue are skin irritation and flammability. What precautions should be taken when using glues with these hazards?
4. Why is it important to remove excess glue from stock before the stock is machined?
5. Which woodworking glues are water soluble? Can these glues be used in damp or moist conditions?
6. Which woodworking glue would be best for boat building and marine use?
7. What is the chief reason why resorcinol resin glue is not commonly used in woodworking?
8. Which woodworking glues tend to load abrasives during sanding?
9. What is the chief advantage of ready-to-use hide glue over hide glue flakes?
10. For what purpose is contact cement used?
11. Which type of contact cement works best with wood veneer?
12. Why is epoxy seldom used for wood-to-wood glue jobs?
13. What hazard is involved with the use of hot melt glues?
14. How long an assembly time is required for hot melt glues?
15. For what purposes are mastic adhesives commonly used?
16. What woodworking glues do not require clamping?

17. How tight should joinery parts fit before glue is applied?
18. Why are grooves cut into dowels before they are used in glue joints?
19. What type of glue would you select for gluing a large assembly together?
20. How do temperature and moisture content affect gluing and glue joints?

SUGGESTED ACTIVITIES

1. Read the manufacturer's instructions for at least three different types of wood glue. List the method of application for each type.

2. Cut a miter joint in scrap stock and glue the parts together. Break the joint after the glue dries. Compare its strength to that of a lap joint. Which is stronger?

3. Identify the types of glue used in your shop. Discuss any safety precautions that should be followed when using each type.

Clamping

Proper *clamping* is an important part of project assembly (Figure 16-1). Clamps hold stock in the correct position while glue cures or while nails and screws are driven.

If clamps are used incorrectly, they can damage your work. The clamps can mar your wood or cause incorrect alignment of parts. If the clamps are tightened too much, they will squeeze all of the glue from the joint causing a weak glue joint. These problems can be eliminated if you follow the correct clamping procedures.

This chapter will describe the correct procedures for clamping wood. Read the chapter carefully and study the illustrations. After mastering this material, you should know how to clamp almost any project correctly.

KEY TERMS

clamping
bar clamps
pipe clamps
clamp stands
parallel clamps
C clamps

spring clamps
adjustable frame
 clamps
web clamp
band clamp
edging clamp

GLUING AND CLAMPING PRECAUTIONS

Before beginning the gluing and clamping operation, take the following precautions:

1. Assemble the pieces without glue. Make sure all pieces fit correctly. Joints should be snug but not tight. Figure 16-2 illustrates this procedure.

Figure 16-1. *Clamps hold your work while glue cures or nails and screws are driven. It is important to use clamps correctly.*

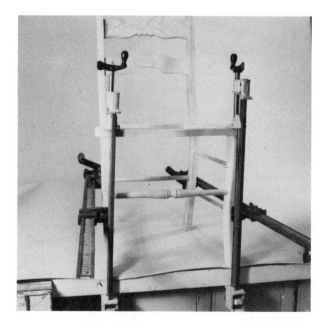

2. Inspect all surfaces that are to be glued. They should be dry and clean.
3. Mark all pieces to assure correct assembly. Chalk can be used to mark finished surfaces. Figure 16-3 shows the correct marking procedure.

Figure 16-2. *Parts should slide together easily. They should not need to be forced. Trim all tight-fitting joints.*

MASKING TAPE

Figure 16-3. *Use chalk to mark your parts. This helps you assemble the parts correctly. The masking tape helps eliminate glue blemishes on the wood.*

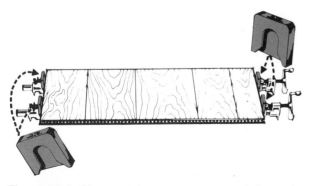

Figure 16-4. *Clamp pads protect your work from the hard clamp jaws. Thin scraps of plywood may also be used as clamp pads.*

4. Select an adhesive that is correct for the job. You may need a glue that is waterproof, or you may need a glue with a long assembly time. Make sure the adhesive is correct for the job.
5. Follow the manufacturer's instructions for mixing and applying the glue. Be sure to leave the pieces clamped for the recommended clamping time.
6. If you are assembling a project with a box shape, be sure that all internal surfaces have been sanded. You may want to stain internal surfaces or mask them (Figure 16-3) before assembly. This will eliminate glue blemishes on the inside of the cabinet. Do not stain rabbets and dadoes where glue holds the pieces together.
7. Gather all equipment before you begin gluing and clamping. Use the list below to determine whether you have the proper equipment:
   • Clamp pads to protect the work (Figure 16-4);

CLAMPSTAND

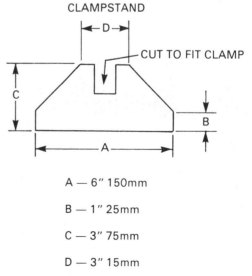

CUT TO FIT CLAMP

A — 6" 150mm

B — 1" 25mm

C — 3" 75mm

D — 3" 15mm

USE 2 PIECES OF SCRAP PLYWOOD OR PARTICLEBOARD 1/2" THICK OR GREATER

Figure 16-5. *Clamp stands make your work easier. The clamp will not tip over while you are working.*

- Clamp stands to make handling easier (Figure 16-5);
- Clamps of correct type and size, open to correct distance and ready to use (Figure 16-6);
- Rubber or wooden mallet (Figure 16-7) to drive pieces into position when necessary;

- Square (Figure 16-8) to check fit and align pieces;
- Glue and applicator (Figure 16-9);
- Damp towel or sponge to remove glue that squeezes out of the joints.

8. Have an assistant ready to help if the assembly is difficult.

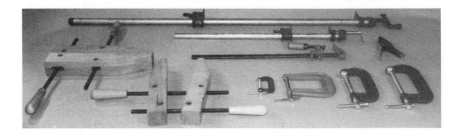

Figure 16-6. *Choose the correct size and type of clamp for the job. Be sure to open the clamp the correct distance before you begin.*

Figure 16-7. *A mallet can be used to drive pieces into position. Use a softwood block to protect your work if you use a wood mallet.*

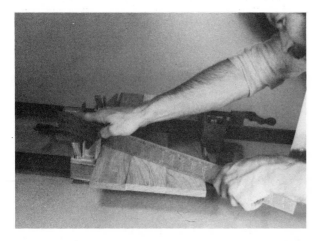

Figure 16-8. *A square may be used to check the fit or alignment of pieces.*

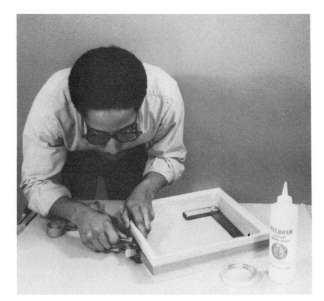

Figure 16-9. *Use the correct glue and applicator for the job.*

Figure 16-10. *Stock is glued edge to edge to make wide pieces.*

CLAMPING PROCEDURES

Each type of glue job requires different clamping procedures. There are many types of clamps and each can be used in several different ways. Clamping procedures can be divided according to the type of glue job performed. There are also some general clamping procedures that apply to all glue jobs.

General Procedures

Before applying clamps, make sure that glue has been applied to both surfaces. The glue should coat the surface, but should not drip from the surface. Use enough clamps to join the pieces. Clamps should be placed 4 to 12 inches (100 to 300 mm) apart. This distance depends on what type of glue job you are doing. Clamps should be on alternate sides of the assembly to provide uniform pressure and reduce warpage.

After the pieces are joined and clamped, remove excess glue from the work and the clamps with a damp rag. After the glue cures, any excess must be scraped with a paint scraper.

You should always leave the clamps on your work for the recommended clamping time. Removing the clamps too quickly may weaken the glue joint and cause it to fail during the machining process or after the project is finished.

Edge Gluing for Greater Width

To make wide pieces stock is glued edge-to-edge. These pieces may be used for chest and dresser lids, or table tops (Figure 16-10). Using a single piece of stock for a table top is not practical. A wide piece warps more than several pieces glued edge-to-edge.

Edge joints are usually clamped with either *bar clamps* or *pipe clamps*. Bar clamps (Figure 16-11) have two jaws—one of which moves on a

Figure 16-11. *Bar clamps have two jaws. One jaw moves on a wooden or metal bar.*

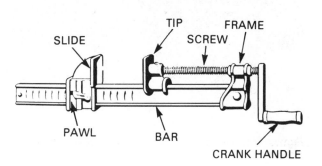

SLIDE   TIP   FRAME   SCREW

PAWL   BAR   CRANK HANDLE

Figure 16-12. *Pipe clamps use a metal pipe as a bar.*

wooden or metal bar. On pipe clamps (Figure 16-12), one jaw moves on a pipe. That jaw is adjustable to the size of the work. The other jaw provides clamping pressure. It is attached to a threaded rod. The jaw advances or retracts when the handle is turned.

Pipe and bar clamps come in sizes from 2' to 8' (600 mm to 2400 mm) long. Clamps over 4' (1200 mm) long tend to bow or bend under full pressure. Some clamps (Figure 16-13) have two bars or pipes to eliminate bowing or bending.

Begin edge gluing by placing the clamps into *clamp stands.* These stands hold the clamps upright when gluing. Set your stock in the

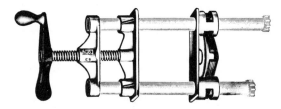

Figure 16-13. *Clamps with two bars or pipes will not bow or bend under pressure.*

Figure 16-14. *Alternate clamps for uniform clamping pressure.*

clamps and adjust the jaws. For finished work, make sure the edges of your work are protected with clamp pads.

Apply glue to the stock and set it in place. Tighten all clamps lightly. If the pieces tend to slip, drive them into place with a rubber mallet. Tighten the clamps securely and remove all glue that squeezes out of the joint. Clamps should be alternated along the assembly for uniform clamping pressure (Figure 16-14).

FACE GLUING FOR GREATER THICKNESS

Stock is face glued to make large squares for turnings such as table legs. It is best to glue up thin stock to make thick pieces. Using thick stock is not practical. Thick pieces do not dry uniformly and may check or twist. Face-glued stock is usually clamped with parallel clamps or C clamps (Figure 16-15).

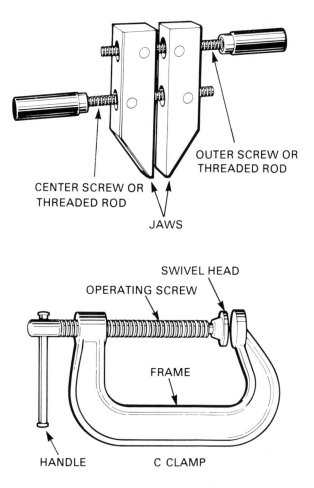

Figure 16-15. *C clamps and parallel clamps are commonly used for face gluing.*

Parallel clamps have broad wooden jaws. They help distribute the clamping pressure and do not mar the wood surface easily. Parallel clamps can be adjusted to clamp pieces that do not have parallel faces. The two threaded rods can be adjusted separately (Figure 16-16).

When clamping stock with parallel clamps, adjust the jaws so that they are in contact with the

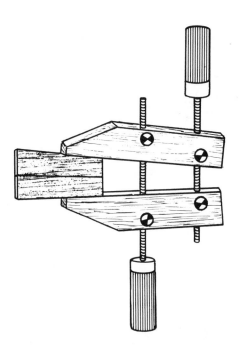

Figure 16-16. *Parallel clamps may be adjusted to clamp pieces that do not have parallel faces.*

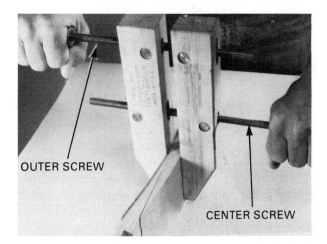

OUTER SCREW

CENTER SCREW

Figure 16-17. *Jaws should be adjusted parallel to the edges of your work. Tighten the center rod first. Then clamp the outer rod.*

work. Tighten the center screw first, then tighten the outer screw (Figure 16-17). After the clamp is tightened securely, the jaws should be parallel to the work surfaces.

Parallel clamps have jaws that range in length from 4" to 24" (100 mm to 600 mm). The most popular sizes are 4" to 12" (100 mm to 300 mm).

C clamps provide clamping pressure to a very small area (Figure 16-18). C clamps are easy to adjust and use in tight spots. They are commonly used for face gluing or for securing jigs, fixtures or fences to woodworking machines.

C clamps range from 1" to 12" (25 mm to 300 mm) between the jaws. One jaw is part of the C frame and remains stationary. The other jaw is attached to a threaded rod. It provides adjustment and clamping pressure. The throat depth varies among brands. Some clamps are sold with a deep throat feature. Deep throat clamps can be placed closer to the center of wide stock but are more likely to bend or bow under pressure.

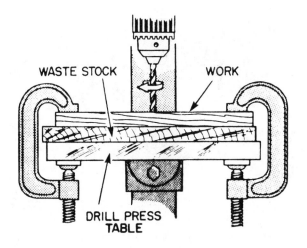

WASTE STOCK   WORK

DRILL PRESS TABLE

Figure 16-18. *C clamps are often used to secure fences or fixtures to a machine.*

Face Gluing Procedure. After you have selected pieces that are to be face glued, check the fit between pieces. There should be no gaps. The faces should fit together tightly. The pieces should be marked so they can be glued in the correct sequence.

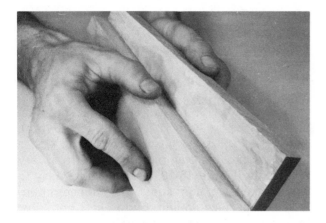

Figure 16-19. *Apply glue to both faces. Rub the pieces together to obtain even spreading.*

Open all clamps wide enough to accommodate the stock. Apply glue to both surfaces and rub them together to obtain an even spread (Figure 16-19). Apply the clamps and tighten them lightly. Drive pieces into place with a rubber mallet if necessary (Figure 16-20). Tighten all clamps securely. Work from the center outward. Be sure to wipe excess glue from the assembly after all the clamps have been applied.

Figure 16-20. *Use a rubber mallet to drive pieces into place.*

Clamping Corner Joints
Corner joints are found on many types of frames such as picture frames, furniture webs, and frame and panel furniture parts. The corner joints in these frames differ and determine the type of clamping method used. For dowel joints or mortise and tenon joints in the corners, bar or pipe clamps may be used (Figure 16-21). For end lap joints, parallel clamps (Figure 16-22) or C clamps can be used.

Figure 16-21. *Bar clamps are used on corners using dowel or mortise and tenon joints.*

Figure 16-22. *Lap joints may be clamped with a parallel clamp.*

Spring clamps (Figure 16-23) may also be used on end lap joints. Spring clamps work like a clothespin. They exert pressure between the jaws. Spring clamps are sometimes used to attach molding to larger pieces. Some spring clamps have barbed jaws. These barbs dig into the wood and pull the pieces together. Barbed spring clamps work well on miter joints.

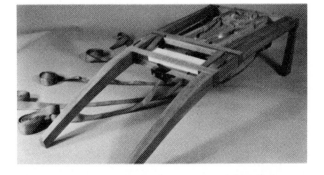

Figure 16-23. *Spring clamps work like a clothespin. They work well on lap joints.*

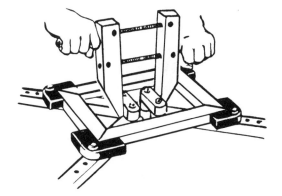

Figure 16-24. *An adjustable frame clamp can hold four miter joints. A single parallel clamp provides clamping pressure.*

Miter joints may also be clamped with an *adjustable frame clamp* (Figure 16-24) or a corner clamp (Figure 16-25). The clamp is adjusted to the frame size. It is held in position with a single parallel clamp.

Web clamps or *band clamps* (Figure 16-26) may also be used for frames and furniture. Pressure is exerted on the perimeter of the frame as the clamp is tightened. The band, usually made of nylon or canvas, is tightened with a ratchet mechanism or a threaded rod.

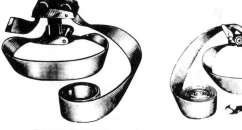

BAND CLAMP   WEB CLAMP

Figure 16-25. *Corner clamps are used on miter joints.*

Figure 16-26. *Band and web clamps may be used for frames. Band clamps are designed for heavy use.*

Figure 16-27. *The miter vise will clamp two pieces at a 90° angle.*

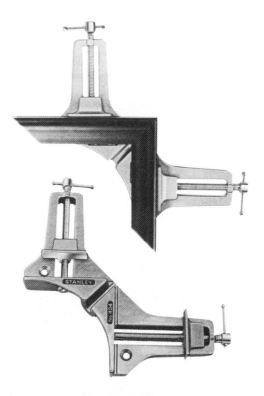

Figure 16-28. *Corner clamps work well on miter joints. Four clamps are needed for an entire frame.*

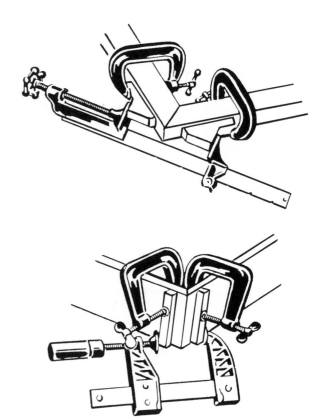

Figure 16-29. *Miters may be held with these clamping methods.*

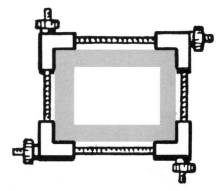

Figure 16-30. *Metal frame clamps also work well for gluing frames or rectangular objects.*

A *miter vise* (Figure 16-27) or *corner clamps* (Figure 16-28) may also be used for corner joints. They secure one corner at a time. For an entire frame, four vises or clamps must be used. Miter vises and corner clamps ensure that the two pieces are perpendicular when clamped. Other methods (Figure 16-29) may be used to clamp a miter joint.

Metal frame clamps are also available for gluing frames (Figure 16-30). They have threaded rods that provide clamping pressure. The rods have a nut on the end. The nut is tightened to clamp the frame. Metal frame clamps are designed for frames up to 9″ × 12″ (230 mm × 300 mm). They can be used for larger frames if longer threaded rods are used.

Clamping Miter Joints. Miter joints absorb glue rapidly. This is because of end grain gluing. End grain should be coated with glue before assem-

Figure 16-31. *A clamping corner holds the object square.*

Figure 16-32. *A web clamp is used with an adjustable frame and parallel clamp to hold this circular object.*

bly. After the clamps are adjusted, the end grain should be recoated. Then assemble and clamp the parts. Remove excess glue after the clamps are tightened.

Clamping Chests and Cabinets

Large assemblies, such as a chest or cabinet, have many parts. It is important that all parts be square and pre-sanded. Internal pieces may be stained and finished before assembly.

Whenever possible, the glue job should be divided into subassemblies. This will simplify gluing and clamping. Assemblies are usually held with pipe or bar clamps. Other clamps may also be used when required.

Web clamps are sometimes used to hold parts together. If web clamps are used, check the corners to be sure they are square. Clamping corners (Figure 16-31) are used with parallel clamps to hold corners square while the glue cures. On finished pieces, joints may be masked to protect surfaces from glue squeeze-out.

Clamping Irregular Surfaces and Edges and Veneers

Irregular surfaces and edges require that you use clamps and clamping accessories in many different ways. Irregular shapes may require more than one clamp (Figure 16-32). A *veneer press* (Figure 16-33) can be used for gluing veneers or other large flat surfaces.

Edging clamps (Figure 16-34) can be used to clamp veneer or molding to stock edges. The two opposing screws adjust the clamp to the

Figure 16-33. *The veneer press can be used for gluing veneers or other large flat surfaces.*

correct position. The right angle clamp can then be used to hold the molding or veneer in place. Be sure to use clamp pads to protect the wood surfaces from damage.

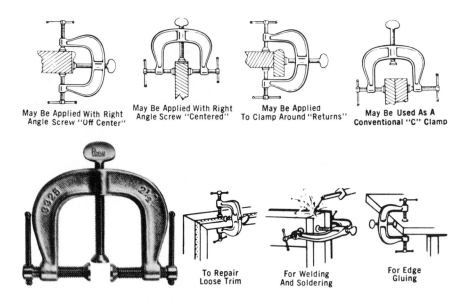

May Be Applied With Right Angle Screw "Off Center"

May Be Applied With Right Angle Screw "Centered"

May Be Applied To Clamp Around "Returns"

May Be Used As A Conventional "C" Clamp

To Repair Loose Trim

For Welding And Soldering

For Edge Gluing

Figure 16-34. *Edging clamps are used to clamp veneer or molding to stock edges. Use clamp pads to protect finished stock.*

QUESTIONS FOR REVIEW

1. How do clamps help you assemble projects?
2. What precautions should be taken prior to gluing and clamping stock?
3. What are some general gluing and clamping procedures that should be observed when joining stock?
4. What types of clamps are used to glue stock edge-to-edge?
5. What is the advantage of a double-bar or pipe clamp when compared to a single-bar or pipe clamp?
6. What should be done when pieces tend to slip or creep as the clamps are tightened?
7. Why is it impractical to use thick stock for turning?
8. What types of clamps are commonly used for face-gluing stock?
9. For what purpose are clamp pads used?
10. What type of clamps are used for dowelled corner joints?
11. On what type of corner joints are spring clamps used?
12. How does an adjustable frame clamp work?
13. What special treatment should be given to miter joints during gluing and clamping?
14. How are irregular edges and surfaces clamped into place? How are clamping accessories used on irregular surfaces?
15. How is molding attached to an edge?

SUGGESTED ACTIVITIES

1. Identify the clamps found in your shop. List at least one use for each clamp.

2. Ask your instructor if you may check the clamps in your shop. Make sure they are lubricated and free of rust and glue. Clean them if needed.

3. Is there a savings when you buy glue in larger containers? Compare prices in your local hardware store.

Metal fasteners are used to join wooden parts, reinforce joints or attach hardware. Metal fasteners may be installed manually or with power. The metal fasteners are designed for a specific job or purpose. It is important to know the purpose of the metal fasteners and how to use them.

KEY TERMS

nails	wood screw
aluminum nails	countersinking
galvanized nails	counterboring
hammer	screw starter
nailing patterns	screwdriver
toenailing	staples
clinching	repair plates
nail set	chevrons
ripping bar	corrugated fasteners
nail nippers	Teenut® fasteners
brads	jack nuts
escutcheon pins	

NAILS

There are many types of nails in use today. They vary in size, type of point, finish, type of head and metal used. Most nails are made from mild steel. *Galvanized nails* and *aluminum nails* will not rust. Aluminum nails are commonly used to install aluminum siding. Some nails are coated to increase holding power.

Nail Size

The most widely used types of nails include *common*, *box*, *casing* and *finishing* (Figure 17-1). All of these nails vary in head type and diameter. Length for these nails is designated by the *penny* (d). This is an old English system. Figure 17-2 shows the relationship between the penny, inch,

and millimeter. Most nails used in woodworking are 8d or shorter.

Types of Nails

Common Nails. Common nails (Figure 17-1) are general duty nails. They have the largest diameter for their length of all nails sold. Common nails tend to split thin stock. This is because their large diameter and sharp point act as a wedge. Common nails have great holding power also due to their large diameter. Common nails are most often used for general carpentry.

Box Nails. Box nails (Figure 17-1) have a smaller diameter than common nails of the same length. Box nails do not have as much holding power as common nails but are less likely to split the stock. This is because of their smaller diameter.

Casing Nails. Casing nails (Figure 17-1) have a smaller diameter than box nails. Casing nail

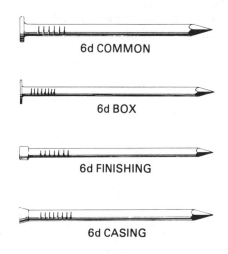

6d COMMON

6d BOX

6d FINISHING

6d CASING

Figure 17-1. *The nails pictured above are widely used in woodworking: common, box, casing and finishing.*

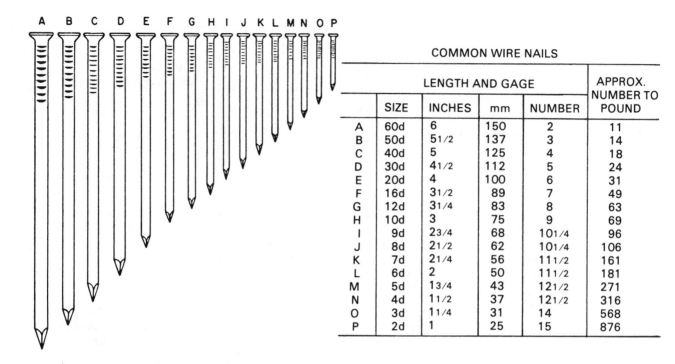

Figure 17-2. *Nail sizes are given by the "penny". Woodworkers use from 2d to 8d.*

		COMMON WIRE NAILS			
		LENGTH AND GAGE			APPROX. NUMBER TO POUND
	SIZE	INCHES	mm	NUMBER	
A	60d	6	150	2	11
B	50d	5 1/2	137	3	14
C	40d	5	125	4	18
D	30d	4 1/2	112	5	24
E	20d	4	100	6	31
F	16d	3 1/2	89	7	49
G	12d	3 1/4	83	8	63
H	10d	3	75	9	69
I	9d	2 3/4	68	10 1/4	96
J	8d	2 1/2	62	10 1/4	106
K	7d	2 1/4	56	11 1/2	161
L	6d	2	50	11 1/2	181
M	5d	1 3/4	43	12 1/2	271
N	4d	1 1/2	37	12 1/2	316
O	3d	1 1/4	31	14	568
P	2d	1	25	15	876

heads also differ from the heads on box and common nails. The head on a casing nail is designed to be driven slightly below the surface of the wood. The nail can be hidden with wood filler. Casing nails are used to install baseboard, door trim and other decorative molding.

Finishing Nails. Finishing nails (Figure 17-1) are similar to casing nails except they have smaller diameters and heads. Finishing nails are designed to be driven below the surface. The head of the nail may then be hidden with wood filler.

Finishing nails are used for light assembly work such as picture frames and other small products. Finishing nails are sometimes used to install molding.

Selecting Nails
Nails are selected according to the requirements of the job. If rusting will be a problem, aluminum or galvanized nails should be used. If splitting could be a problem, a nail with a small diameter will work best. Blunting the nail point (Figure 17-3) will also reduce splitting.

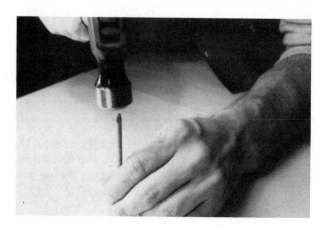

Figure 17-3. *Blunting a nail point will reduce splitting of the wood.*

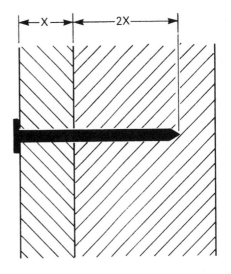

Figure 17-4. *The nail length should be 3 times the thickness of the piece being attached. Always nail the thinner piece to the thicker piece.*

For maximum holding power, choose a nail that is three times as long as the thickness of the piece being attached (Figure 17-4). It may not always be possible to do this, but shorter nails will not hold as well. The thinner piece of stock should always be nailed to the thicker piece.

Driving Nails

All nails should be driven with a *hammer* selected according to the job and the nail size.

For general nailing, a *curved claw* hammer (Figure 17-5) is used. The curved claw makes it easier to remove nails in case of error. Curved claw hammers have a *head* that weighs from 13 to 16 ounces (370 to 450 grams). The lighter head is best suited to general nailing.

Figure 17-5. *Curved claw hammers are used for general nailing. Hammer handles may be made of metal, fiberglass or wood.*

Hammers may have a wood, fiberglass or steel handle. Steel and fiberglass handles have rubber grips to help reduce shock to the hand. Select a handle that feels comfortable to you. Before using your hammer, make sure that the head is securely attached to the handle. A loose head could fly from the handle and cause serious injury.

Before you begin nailing, be sure to put on a pair of protective glasses. The hammer head is made of hardened steel and could chip. A flying chip could strike your eye. Nails can also strike your eye. When a nail is started improperly, it can fly from the wood when struck with a hammer.

Hold the nail and set it with light blows. The nail is *set* when the nail has been driven into the wood ⅜″ (9 mm). Begin swinging the hammer after the nail is set (Figure 17-6). Grip the

Figure 17-6. *Swing the hammer from your elbow. Be sure the nail is set before taking a full swing.*

155

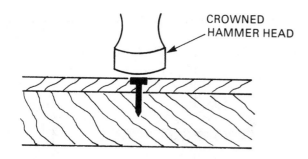

Figure 17-7. *The crowned head sinks the nail without denting the wood.*

hammer low on the handle and swing from the elbow. The hammer should do the work. Let the weight of the hammer drive the nail. Extreme force will bend the nail or cause the hammer to slip off the nail head.

When the head of the nail is about ¼" (6 mm) away from the wood surface, you should lighten the blows. The nail should be driven flush with the wood surface without denting the wood. The crowned head of the hammer makes this possible. (Figure 17-7). Denting the wood makes the job look poor. Before driving nails into your project, practice with scrap stock. Nail one piece of scrap to another.

Nailing Patterns. Driving nails in a straight line should be avoided. The nails can act as a wedge and cause the wood to split. It is better to stagger nails in an irregular *nailing* pattern (Figure 17-8). An irregular pattern will increase strength and reduce the chance of splitting.

STAGGERED NAILING PATTERN

Figure 17-8. *Nails should be staggered when joining pieces. Straight line nailing can cause the wood to split.*

Toenailing. Nail holding strength is increased when nails are driven at an angle (Figure 17-9). *Toenailing* (Figure 17-10) is a method of driving nails at an angle. Toenailing is used in rough carpentry. It usually leaves hammer marks because the nails are driven at an angle. Toenailing is not used for finish work where hammer marks might be visible.

Clinching Nails. Nails are sometimes *clinched* for added strength (Figure 17-11). Nails should be ½ to 1 inch (12 to 25 mm) longer than the thickness of the pieces being joined. The nails are driven through the wood and then bent. Bend the nails across the grain to avoid splitting. Clinched nails resist pulling and increase

Figure 17-9. *Nails driven at an angle make a stronger joint.*

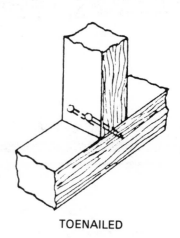

TOENAILED

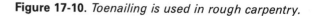

Figure 17-10. *Toenailing is used in rough carpentry.*

Figure 17-11. *Clinched nails resist pulling. Clinch nails across the grain to reduce the chance of splitting.*

strength. Wooden crates often have clinched nails.

Using a Nail Set. Finishing and casing nails are driven below the wood surface so they may be concealed with wood filler. A *nail set* (Figure 17-12) is used to drive nails below the surface.

A nail set is made from hardened steel. It has a point that is cupped. The cupped point grips the

nail as it is driven. Nail sets come in sizes from 1 to 5. The higher the number, the larger the diameter.

Wear eye protection when using a nail set. Place the point of the nail set against the nail head. *Hold the nail set firmly so that it does not slip off the nail head.* Drive the nail set with a hammer until the nail head is slightly below the wood surface.

Nail-Holding Strength

Nails driven at an angle have more holding power. This is because they resist withdrawal when a strain is placed on the joint. Certain coatings will also help nails resist withdrawal. Cement-coated nails have a rosin coating that increases nail-holding strength. Galvanized nails also have increased nail-holding strength because of their rough surface. Rough surfaces provide a better grip in wood.

Some nails are made with rough gripping surfaces. Ring shank nails (Figure 17-13) and spiral thread nails (Figure 17-14) have additional holding power. The threads and rings both grip the wood better than a smooth nail.

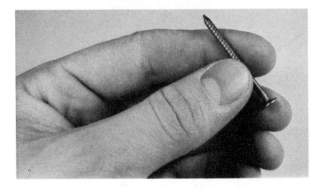

Figure 17-13. *Ring shank nails have more gripping surface than smooth nails.*

Figure 17-12. *A nail set is used to drive nails below the surface.*

SPIRAL

Figure 17-14. *Spiral nails turn as they are driven. They must also turn when removed. This requires extra force.*

If the wood splits when any type of nail is driven into it, strength is lost. Splitting can cause a strength loss of fifty percent or more. Splitting is most likely to occur near the edges of the stock. If splitting is likely, pre-drill the nail hole. Make the hole slightly smaller than the nail diameter. Pre-drilling is also advisable when nailing hardwood and edge-nailing plywood. The nail point may also be blunted to reduce splitting. Nail-holding strength is also much lower in end grain than it is in face or edge grain.

Removing Nails

If you bend a nail while driving it, it must be removed. A curved claw hammer may be used. You can place a block of wood under the head of the hammer for extra leverage (Figure 17-15). The block of wood will also protect finished surfaces from damage.

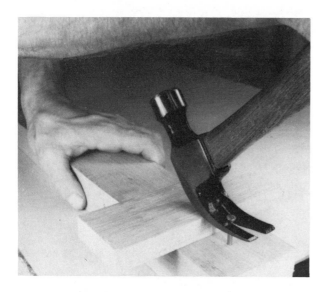

Figure 17-15. *A block of wood provides extra leverage. It also protects the wood surface.*

Figure 17-16. *When nail heads are buried, a hammer claw will not lift them. A ripping bar,* top, *or a nail claw,* bottom, *must be used.*

When the head of a nail has been buried below the surface a *ripping bar* or *nail claw* must be used to remove it (Figure 17-16).

If a piece of molding has been removed, casing and finishing nails are best taken out from the back side. There is less damage to the molding and nails are easier to remove. Use a pliers or *nail nippers* (Figure 17-17) to remove the nails. Be sure to pick up any nails you remove. They could injure someone.

Figure 17-17. *Finishing and casing nails should be pulled through the molding. This reduces splitting and damage. Nail nippers or pliers may be used for this job.*

BRAD

Figure 17-18. *Brads look like small finishing nails.*

Brads

Brads (Figure 17-18) look like small finishing nails. A brad has two measures of size: the length and the wire gage or diameter. Brads are usually less than 1¼" (30 mm) long. They are driven with a light claw hammer or a brad pusher (Figure 17-19). The brad pusher drives the brad without bending it.

Escutcheon Pins

Escutcheon pins (Figure 17-20) are small, round-head nails made of brass or coated with brass. They are used for decorative work such as metal

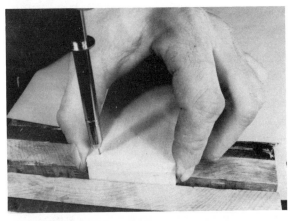

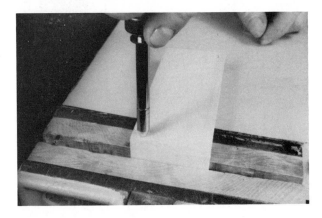

Figure 17-19. *The brad driver makes it easy to drive brads without bending. Top, loading the brad pusher; middle, starting the brad; bottom, driving the brad.*

molding and trophy plates. Escutcheon pins also have two measures of size: length and wire gage. Pre-drill holes before installing escutcheon pins. Use a brad pusher or light hammer to drive the escutcheon pins.

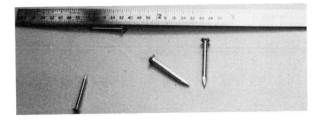

Figure 17-20. *Escutcheon pins are used in decorative work. They are usually brass-coated steel.*

WOOD SCREWS

Wood screws have different heads, driving slots, lengths, and diameters. Wood screws are commonly made from mild steel, but may also be made from brass and other metal alloys.

Wood Screw Size

Wood screws are available with *flat, round* and *oval* heads. Figure 17-21 illustrates the types of screw heads and how each is measured for

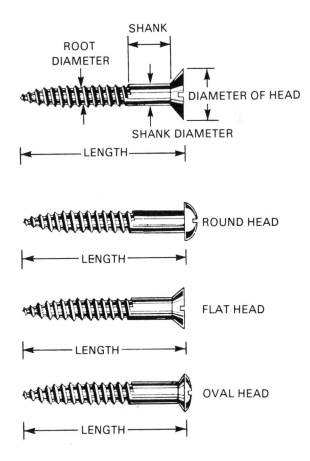

Figure 17-21. *Common wood screws.*

length. Screw heads are either *slotted* or *recessed* (Phillips). These heads require different screwdrivers. Slotted screws are driven with a regular screwdriver. Recessed screws are driven with a Phillips screwdriver. Figure 17-22 shows both types of screwdrivers.

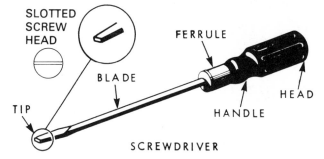

Figure 17-22. *Types of screwdrivers in common use.*

BIT SIZES FOR BORING PILOT HOLES AND SHANK CLEARANCE HOLES FOR WOOD SCREWS.

Number of Screw	For Shank Clearance Holes		For Pilot Holes — Hardwoods				For Pilot Holes — Softwoods				Number of Auger Bit (To counterbore for sinking head by 16ths) Slotted or Phillips
	Twist Bit (Nearest size in fractions of an inch) Slotted or Phillips	Drill Gauge No. or Letter (To be used for maximum holding power) Slotted or Phillips	Twist Bit (Nearest size in fractions of an inch) Slotted	Twist Bit Phillips	Drill Gauge No. (To be used for maximum holding power) Slotted	Drill Gauge No. Phillips	Twist Bit (Nearest size in fractions of an inch) Slotted	Twist Bit Phillips	Drill Gauge No. (To be used for maximum holding power) Slotted	Drill Gauge No. Phillips	
0	1/16	52	1/32	—	70	—	1/64	—	75	—	—
1	5/64	47	1/32	—	66	—	1/32	—	71	—	—
2	3/32	42	3/64	1/32	56	70	1/32	1/64	65	75	3
3	7/64	37	1/16	1/32	54	66	3/64	1/32	58	71	4
4	7/64	32	1/16	3/64	52	56	3/64	1/32	55	65	4
5	1/8	30	5/64	1/16	49	54	1/16	3/64	53	58	4
6	9/64	27	5/64	1/16	47	52	1/16	3/64	52	55	5
7	5/32	22	3/32	5/64	44	49	1/16	3/64	51	53	5
8	11/64	18	3/32	5/64	40	47	5/64	1/16	48	52	6
9	3/16	14	7/64	3/32	37	44	5/64	1/16	45	51	6
10	3/16	10	7/64	3/32	33	40	3/32	5/64	43	48	6
11	13/64	4	1/8	7/64	31	37	3/32	5/64	40	45	7
12	7/32	2	1/8	7/64	30	33	7/64	3/32	38	43	7
14	1/4	D	9/64	1/8	25	31	7/64	3/32	32	40	8
16	17/64	I	5/32	1/8	18	30	9/64	7/64	29	38	9
18	19/64	N	3/16	9/64	13	25	9/64	7/64	26	32	10
20	21/64	P	13/64	5/32	4	18	11/64	9/64	19	29	11
24	3/8	V	7/32	3/16	1	13	3/16	9/64	15	26	12

Figure 17-23. *Common screw sizes and bit sizes for pilot holes and shank clearance holes.*

Screws have two dimensions: length and wire gage or diameter. Common screw lengths range from ¼" to 6" (6 mm to 150 mm). Wire gage numbers range from 0 to 24. The larger the wire gage number is, the larger the screw diameter.

Selecting Wood Screws

Wood screws are selected according to the requirements of the job. Mild steel screws are selected for general use. When rusting is a problem, brass screws are usually selected. Chrome-plated or brass screws are often chosen for decorative work.

A screw should be at least three times as long as the thickness of the piece being attached. The screw gage varies with the screw length.

Installing Screws

Wood screws cannot normally be driven into wood without *pre-drilling*. Driving a screw without pre-drilling may either twist off the head of the screw or cause the wood to split. The shank on a wood screw has a larger diameter than the threaded portion (Figure 17-21). A pre-drilled screw hole must have two different diameters to accommodate the shank and threads.

The shank hole (the larger hole) is drilled first. It is the same diameter as the screw shank. It is drilled to a depth equal to the length of the shank. This hole is called the *clearance* or *shank hole.* The smaller hole is drilled. It is called the *pilot hole* and is drilled to the root diameter (Figure 17-21). Figure 17-23 will help you select the correct drills for shank or pilot holes.

When using brass screws or working seasoned hardwood, you may have to enlarge the root diameter. If possible, test the screws in scrap stock.

Countersinking and Counterboring. Flat head and oval head screws must be *countersunk* for correct installation. Countersinking makes a seat for the flat or oval head screw. Countersinking allows the flat head to remain flush with the surface (Figure 17-24, *left).*

When the screw is to be hidden below the wood surface, the screw hole must be *counterbored* (Figure 17-24, *right).* After the screw is installed, the hole can be filled with wood filler or a wooden plug. When counterboring, drill the

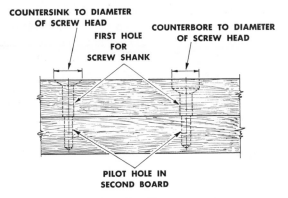

Figure 17-24. *Drilling details for wood screws.*

largest hole first. This will keep all the holes centered.

Special bits designed to drill all countersinking or counterboring diameters at one time are available. These bits make screw installation simpler. Use these bits carefully. They are more fragile than a twist drill bit.

Screw starters. In extremely soft woods such as pine, a shank or pilot hole is not necessary. Screws can be started in soft woods with a *screw starter* (Figure 17-25). The screw starter has a threaded point much like an auger bit. It is driven into the wood to form a starting hole for the wood screw. Avoid using the screw starter in hard woods. The screws are likely to break when driven into the wood.

Screwdrivers. *Screwdrivers* are used to drive screws. Some have tips for driving Phillips head

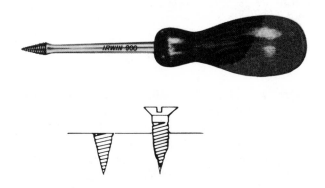

Figure 17-25. *Screw starter.*

screws and others have tips for driving slotted screws. Screwdrivers are sold by blade length and tip size. Blade length is measured from the ferrule to the tip. Figure 17-22 shows common screwdrivers and terms used.

Blade width on a regular screwdriver is the distance in inches across the tip. Phillips screwdrivers have sizes numbered from 0 to 4. Four is the largest, and 2 and 3 are the most common sizes.

Select a screwdriver that fits the screw slot. If the screwdriver is too small, it will damage the screw slot. If the screwdriver tip is too wide it will damage the wood. Do not use a screwdriver with a twisted or nicked blade. It can damage the screw slot.

Cabinet screwdrivers (Figure 17-26) are used for driving slotted screws. The tip of a cabinet screwdriver has parallel sides. It was designed for driving screws in countersunk holes without damage.

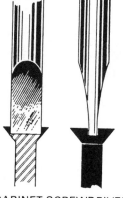

CABINET SCREWDRIVER

Figure 17-26. *The cabinet screwdriver blade has parallel sides.*

Using a screwdriver. When driving a screw, begin by holding the screw against the blade of the screwdriver with one hand (Figure 17-27), and turn the screwdriver with the other hand. This will start the screw. After the screw is started, move your fingers away from the tip of the screwdriver. They can now guide the blade from the shank of the screwdriver (Figure 17-28).

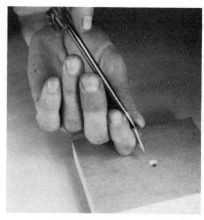

Figure 17-27. *Starting a screw.*

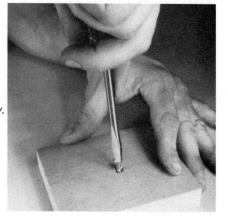

Figure 17-28. *Driving a screw.*

A little wax on the threads will make the screw easier to drive. This is very important when driving brass screws. They have a tendency to twist off if there is too much resistance. Sometimes the pilot hole has to be enlarged for brass screws.

SHEET METAL SCREWS

Sheet metal screws (Figure 17-29) are becoming popular as a woodworking fastener. The sheet metal screw has a uniform diameter. This reduces drilling operations. Only a pilot hole needs to be drilled.

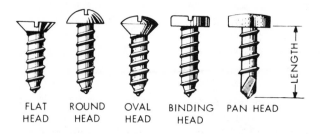

FLAT HEAD   ROUND HEAD   OVAL HEAD   BINDING HEAD   PAN HEAD

LENGTH

Figure 17-29. *Sheet metal screws are also used for joining wood.*

Sheet metal screws are harder than wood screws. They are less likely to snap or break. Sheet metal screws also have finer threads than wood screws. This increases their holding power in end grain and particleboard. Wood screws cause particleboard to crumble because of their coarse threads. Some sheet metal screws can tap or cut their own pilot hole. These screws will work well only in soft wood.

Sheet metal screws range from ⅛" to 2" (3 mm to 50 mm) in length and use the same wire gage diameters as wood screws. For sheet metal screws drill pilot holes about 60 percent of the screw diameter.

Sheet metal screws come with different heads such as *flat, round, oval,* and *pan* (Figure 17-29).

POWER DRIVER FASTENERS

Self-Threading Screws

There are many types of self-threading screws (Figure 17-30). These screws are made of hardened steel and are able to drill their own pilot hole as they are driven. Self-threading screws are driven with an electric or pneumatic driver. The driver is powerful enough to drive the screws into hardwood. Power screw drivers may also be used to drive wood and sheet metal screws, but generally only after a pilot hole has been drilled.

Self-threading screws are commonly used for installing drywall and assembling kitchen cabinets. They usually have a Phillips drive because it is less likely to slip under power.

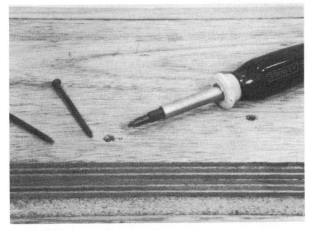

Figure 17-30. *Self-threading screws. Sharpened points act as drills.*

Power-Driven Nails and Staples

Power-driven nailers and staplers (Figure 17-31) are very popular woodworking tools. They can drive fasteners rapidly with little operator fatigue. Power-driven fasteners are less likely to bend than hand driven fasteners. Power is supplied by electricity or compressed air.

By changing the size of staple or nail, a variety of woodworking jobs can be done. *Staples* are commonly used for installing insulation and ceiling tile. They are also used for upholstery and cabinet work. There are many types of staples and staplers used today. Power-driven nails are commonly used for carpentry. Smaller T shaped nails (Figure 17-32) are used for cabinet work and finish carpentry.

Figure 17-31. *Power-driven stapler.*

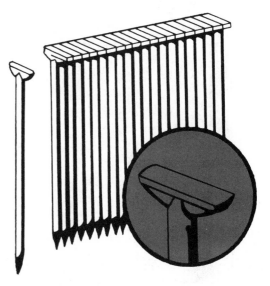

Figure 17-32. *T nails are used for cabinetwork and finish carpentry.*

Safety With Power-Driven Fasteners

The following precautions will help you operate power fastening tools correctly and safely.

1. Always wear safety glasses when operating power fastening tools.
2. Be sure to read the manufacturer's directions before using any power fastening tool. The directions will tell you about safe operation and which fasteners are correct for the job.
3. Make sure all safety features are operating correctly. Take a test firing in scrap stock.
4. Disconnect the electric or air power from the gun when loading the gun or when the gun is not in use.
5. Use the recommended amount of air pressure and no more.
6. Keep the nose of the gun firmly in contact with the work when firing. Do not point the gun at yourself or others for any reason. Keep your hands behind the gun during operation.
7. Make sure that the fasteners will be driven into a backing piece. Some fasteners can actually be driven through the piece. Always check the location of the backing pieces.

REPAIR PLATES

Repair plates (Figure 17-33) are fastening accessories commonly used with wood screws. They are metal plates used to reinforce wood joints. The plates are punched to accommodate flat head screws.

MITER JOINT FASTENERS

Chevrons (Figure 17-34) and *corrugated fasteners* (Figure 17-35), are commonly used to reinforce miter joints. These fasteners pull the pieces together as they are driven. A hammer is commonly used to drive both types. Some corrugated fasteners can be driven with a power nailer.

Figure 17-34. *Chevron fastener.*

Figure 17-35. *Corrugated fastener.*

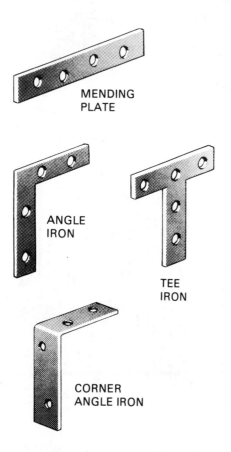

MENDING PLATE

ANGLE IRON

TEE IRON

CORNER ANGLE IRON

Figure 17-33. *Common repair plates.*

Figure 17-36. *Teenut® fasteners allow metal-to-metal fastening in wood.*

TEENUT® FASTENERS AND JACK NUTS

Teenut® fasteners (Figure 17-36) and *jack nuts* (Figure 17-37) allow metal to metal fastening in wood. These fasteners are common on articles that are frequently disassembled.

A Teenut® fastener is driven with a hammer. The hole into which it is driven must be slightly larger than the threaded screw used with it. The barbs on the Teenut® fasteners hold it in the wood.

A jack nut secures itself by bending as it is tightened. The threaded portion of the jack nut must face away from the mating surfaces to secure itself correctly.

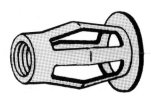

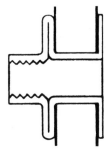

Figure 17-37. *Jack nuts allow metal-to-metal fastening in wood.*

QUESTIONS FOR REVIEW

1. What are some common types of nails? For what purpose is each of these nails used?
2. How is the size of a nail determined?
3. How would you decide what type of nail to use for a job? How long should the nail be?
4. How is a nail started? How is it driven?
5. How does a nailing pattern affect strength between the joined pieces?
6. How do toenailing and clinching of nails affect nail-holding strength?
7. For what purpose is a nail set used?
8. For what purposes are nails coated?
9. How do a ripping bar and nail claw help you remove nails? How should finishing and casing nails be removed?
10. For what purposes are brads and escutcheon pins used? How do you determine their size?
11. What types of heads are common on wood screws? How are these screws driven?
12. How should wood screws be selected for a job?
13. Why must screws be driven into pre-drilled holes? What will happen if screws are driven without pre-drilling?
14. How would you describe countersinking and counterboring? For what purposes are holes countersunk or counterbored?
15. How is a screw starter used? In what types of wood does a screw starter work best?
16. How do you determine the size of a screwdriver? How do you select a screwdriver for driving a wood screw?
17. What is a cabinet screwdriver? How does it differ from other screwdrivers?
18. How are wood screws driven? How does wax make driving screws easier?
19. What advantages do sheet metal screws have that wood screws do not? What are the common sizes of sheet metal screws?

20. What advantages do self-threading screws have that wood and sheet metal screws do not?
21. For what purposes are power-driven nails and staples used?
22. What are some precautions that should be observed to drive power-driven fasteners safely?
23. How are repair plates used to reinforce wood joints?
24. For what purpose are chevrons and corrugated fasteners used?
25. What are jack nuts and Teenut® fasteners? When are they used?

SUGGESTED ACTIVITIES

1. Identify the types of nails and screws found in your shop. Measure the nails to determine their penny size.

2. Drill a shank hole and pilot hole in a piece of scrap. Select the proper screwdriver and install a screw.

3. Visit your hardware store to determine how nails and screws are sold. Is it cheaper to buy nails and screws in large quantities?

SECTION 4

Preparing to Finish

CHAPTER 18

Coated Abrasives

Coated abrasives are used to smooth or prepare wood for finishing. Coated abrasives are sometimes called *sandpaper.* This term originated when only sand was used as an abrasive. The use of coated abrasives is called *sanding.* Sanding operations are classified as either *hand* (Figure 18-1) or *power* sanding (Figure 18-2).

It is important to know the types of abrasives used for sanding. The information in this chapter will help you select the correct abrasive for any job. Using the correct abrasive is essential for a beautiful finish.

KEY TERMS

coated abrasives	aught grit size
sanding	mesh system
flint	open coat abrasives
garnet	closed coat abrasives
aluminum oxide	stearated abrasives
silicon carbide	flexing
nominal grit size	

TYPES OF ABRASIVES

The four common woodworking abrasives include *flint, garnet, aluminum oxide* and *silicon carbide.* Flint and garnet are natural abrasives.

Aluminum oxide and silicon carbide are synthetic abrasives. They are both manufactured in electric furnaces. Aluminum oxide and silicon carbide are much harder than flint or garnet.

Flint

Flint is a form of quartz. It is white in color and the most inexpensive abrasive available today. Flint dulls rapidly during use and does not have a very long life. Flint is often used to remove paint and other finishes before refinishing.

Flint is rarely used for finishing fine woodwork because the grits are not uniform in size. This lack of uniformity causes scratching of the wood. It is difficult to obtain a surface smooth enough for stain or a clean finish when flint is used.

Figure 18-1. *Hand sanding.*

Figure 18-2. *Power sanding.*

Garnet

Garnet is a semi-precious stone with a reddish color. It is harder and remains sharper than quartz. Garnet grits tend to fracture when they become dull. When they fracture, new cutting edges are exposed. These new edges increase the life of the garnet abrasive. Garnet is an excellent choice for wood preparation. It cuts well and leaves the surface smooth and uniform.

Aluminum Oxide

Aluminum oxide has a reddish brown color. Because of its toughness, it is frequently used for machine sanding. Aluminum oxide grits do not fracture as they become dull. Their cutting surfaces become rounded. Machine sanding with rounded abrasives will *burnish* or glaze the wood's surface.

Burnishing or glazing of the wood surface is caused by excess heat. The heat brings lignin and resins in the wood to the surface. The lignin and resins seal or glaze the wood's surface. This makes it difficult to stain because the stain will leave light and dark blotches. Color will not be uniform when stain is applied to a burnished surface.

If the wood surface becomes burnished with aluminum oxide abrasives, hand sand the surface with a piece of garnet abrasive. This will cut through the glaze.

Silicon Carbide

Silicon carbide is the hardest woodworking abrasive in common use. It does not burnish wood like aluminum oxide does because the abrasive is brittle. Edges fracture exposing new cutting edges. The new cutting edges do not generate enough heat to cause burnishing. Silicon carbide abrasives are commonly used to rub out a finished surface.

ABRASIVE GRIT SIZE

There are three common methods of describing *grit size:* the *aught, mesh* and *nominal.* Figure 18-3 explains the size relationship between the three methods. The mesh system has recently become the most popular method of indicating grit size, but the other two methods are still used.

APPROXIMATE COMPARISON OF GRIT NUMBERS.

MESH	AUGHT	NOMINAL
400	—	
360	—	
320	7/0	
280	6/0	VERY FINE
240	5/0	
220	4/0	
	3/0	
180	—	
150	—	
	2/0	FINE
120	—	
	0	
100	—	
	1/2	
80	—	
	1	MEDIUM
60	—	
50	1 1/2	
	2	
40	—	
	2 1/2	COARSE
36	—	
30	3	
24	—	
20	—	VERY COARSE
16	—	
12	—	

Figure 18-3. *Abrasive grit size may be classified as mesh, aught or nominal.*

Nominal Grit Size

Nominal grit size is described with words such as *fine, medium* and *coarse.* The grits included in each nominal grade are not as uniform in size as grits rated by the mesh or aught method. The nominal grit method is commonly used for flint abrasives.

Aught Grit Size

The *aught* method uses 0 as a base for indicating grit size. Grit sizes range from 3 (coarse) to % (fine). Grit size decreases as the number of zeros increases. For example, % abrasive would be finer than a % abrasive. Coarse abrasives have no zeros in their grade. These grades include 1, 2 and 3. The aught system is used to grade all abrasives except flint.

Mesh System

Abrasive grits graded by the *mesh* system are sifted through a silk screen. The screen has the same number of openings per linear inch as indicated by the mesh number. For example, a screen with 80 openings per linear inch would yield abrasives classified as 80 grit or mesh.

ABRASIVES BACKINGS

Backings for abrasives are either *paper* or *cloth*. Paper backings are used for hand sanding and some portable power sanders. Cloth backings are used on power sanders such as the belt sander and other industrial machines.

Paper Backings

Paper backings come in a number of weights. These weights are classifed with a letter. The lightest paper is classified as *A* weight. Other weights include *C, D* and *E. E* weight is the heaviest paper backing in common use.

Paper of *E* weight is used on stationary sanding machines such as the disc sander. *C* and *D* weight papers are commonly used for portable power sanders and hand sanding. *A* weight paper is too light for power sanding. The movement of the power sander would rip the paper. *A* weight paper can be bent and folded easily. This makes it desirable for sanding moldings and carvings. Letter size is specified on the back of the abrasive paper (Figure 18-4).

Paper sheets measure 9″ x 11″ (230 mm x 280 mm) except for flint. Flint sheets measure 9″ x 10″ (230 mm x 255 mm). Portable finishing sanders are usually designed to use ¼, ⅓ or ½ sheet of coated abrasive. Lay out the paper carefully so that you get the most from each sheet of abrasive.

Cloth Backings

Cloth backings are tougher than paper backings. Cloth-backed abrasives are used on belt sanders where extra strength is needed. Many industrial machines also use cloth-backed abrasives.

There are two cloth backing weights: *jeans* and *drills* cloth. Jeans cloth is a lighter fabric. It is used on some belt sanders. On some belts, the letter *J* is used to indicate jeans cloth.

Drills cloth is identified with the letter *X.* It is heavier than jeans cloth and is used for belt sanders and industrial machines such as the abrasive planer.

ABRASIVE GLUES

Abrasives are glued to the cloth or paper backing by two coats of glue. The first coat is called the *bond* coat, and the second coat is called the *size* coat (Figure 18-5).

Hide glue and *synthetic resin glue* hold the grits to the backing. Hide glue is used for most common abrasive sheets. For wet or dry abrasives, a synthetic resin glue is used. The synthetic resin glue is waterproof. It will not break down during wet sanding.

Figure 18-4. *A-weight paper is flexible. It is used to sand irregular shapes. A-weight paper cannot be used for power sanding.*

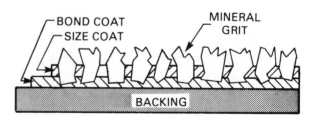

Figure 18-5. *Two coats of glue hold the abrasive grits in place.*

OPEN AND CLOSED COAT ABRASIVES

Open and *closed* coat abrasives differ in the amount of abrasive grits on the sheet. An open coat sheet of abrasive has about 70 percent as much abrasive as a closed coat sheet.

Open coat abrasives provide more space between abrasive grits for chip removal. Open coat abrasives are used for removing old finishes and for rough work.

Closed coat abrasives yield a smoother finish, but they tend to burnish the surface. Closed coat abrasives are used for most wood sanding jobs.

STEARATED ABRASIVES

Some abrasives are coated with a *stearate.* A stearate is a soap-like material derived from stearic acid. It keeps the abrasive from loading or clogging when sanding wood finishes. Stearated abrasives are commonly used to sand finishes between coats. This treatment increases abrasive life.

CUTTING AND FLEXING ABRASIVES

A 9″ x 11″ (230 mm x 280 mm) abrasive sheet must be cut into smaller pieces to be used efficiently. Often a fixture (Figure 18-6) is built for tearing abrasives to a desired size. Before the sheet is torn or cut, it is *flexed.*

Figure 18-7. *Flexing the abrasive sheet makes it easier to cut or fold.*

An abrasive sheet is flexed by pulling the paper side across the sharp corner of a bench or counter (Figure 18-7). The flexing action breaks the sizing coat of glue and makes the sheet more flexible. Flexing makes the sheet easier to cut or fold. It also increases the life of the abrasive sheet.

Abrasive sheets may be cut or torn. It is better to cut an abrasive sheet (Figure 18-8). When the sheet is cut, the edges remain smooth. When the sheet is torn, the edges may be ragged. Ragged edges will scratch the wood. You cannot do a

Figure 18-6. *This fixture makes tearing abrasive sheets easier and more accurate.*

Figure 18-8. *Cutting abrasive sheets leaves a smoother edge.*

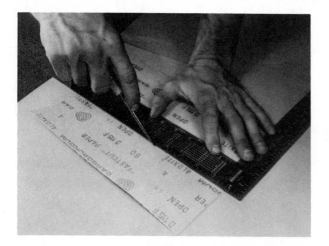

good sanding job using abrasives with a ragged edge. Before tearing an abrasive sheet, fold or score the back side along the line on which you plan to tear it (Figure 18-9). This will reduce the chance of a ragged edge.

STORING ABRASIVES

Abrasives will break down quickly if they are exposed to extreme heat or humidity. Store abrasives in a cool, dry place away from sunlight. Abrasives will last a long time when they are stored properly.

Figure 18-9. *Score the sheet before tearing. This produces a smoother edge.*

QUESTIONS FOR REVIEW

1. What are the four common woodworking abrasives? Which of these abrasives are natural? Which are synthetic?
2. For what purpose is flint commonly used?
3. What causes burnishing? How can it be eliminated?
4. For what purpose is silicon carbide used?
5. What are the three methods of describing abrasive grit size? Which is most commonly used?
6. What weights of paper are commonly used for coated abrasives? Which weight is best for sanding moldings and carvings?
7. For what purpose are cloth-backed abrasives used? Which weight would be used on industrial machines?
8. What types of glues are used to fasten abrasives to the paper or cloth backing?
9. What is the difference between an open coat and a closed coat abrasive sheet? For what purpose is each used?
10. For what purpose are stearated abrasives used?
11. Why are abrasive sheets flexed before use?
12. Why is it better to cut than to tear an abrasive sheet?
13. How should coated abrasives be stored?

SUGGESTED ACTIVITIES

1. See if you can identify the types of abrasives found in your shop.

2. Read the printed information on the back of an abrasive sheet. Discuss what this information means.

3. Demonstrate the correct way of flexing an abrasive sheet.

4. Look at the sanding block in Chapter 54. You may want to make one for use in the shop.

CHAPTER 19

Hand sanding is done before applying a finish. All hardware should be fitted and removed before hand sanding. Hand sanding removes the swirl marks left by machine sanders (Figure 19-1). Hand sanding breaks through a *burnished* surface so that stain can be applied uniformly. The sharp abrasive grits will cut through the glazed or burnished surface in a few strokes.

Hand sanding also removes "fuzz" and smooths raised grain. As wood absorbs moisture from the air, wood fibers on the surface swell and raise. This makes the wood feel rough to the touch. Grain is sometimes raised by dampening the wood with a sponge (See next chapter). After the surface dries, a final sanding removes the raised grain. Be sure to wear a dust mask (Figure 19-2) while sanding.

KEY TERMS

burnished surface   hand sanding
sanding blocks

ABRASIVE GRIT SEQUENCE

Hand sand after mill marks have been removed with a hand plane, scraper or power sander. Before you begin sanding, select the correct abrasive grit size. An abrasive that is too coarse will cause extra work. An abrasive that is too fine will not remove heavy surface flaws.

The species of wood should also affect the selection of abrasive. Begin sanding hardwoods with a 60 or 80 grit (or mesh) abrasive. Softwoods will require an 80 or 100 grit abrasive.

When the surface has been sanded uniformly, change to an abrasive about 20 grit (or mesh) finer. For example, if you began with 60 grit, change to 80 grit. If you began with 100 grit, change to 120 grit. Avoid over-sanding your wood. Softwood rarely needs sanding finer than 150 grit. Hardwood should be sanded to about 120 grit.

Figure 19-1. *Hand sanding will remove swirls left by power sanders.*

Figure 19-2. *A dust mask provides protection. You should wear it when sanding.*

SANDING BLOCKS

Use sanding blocks (Figure 19-3) whenever possible. A sanding block helps produce a smooth, flat surface because the flat block does not flex and follow the grain. Hand sanding with finger tip pressure allows the abrasive to flex and follow the grain of the wood. This can cause a wavy surface (Figure 19-4). Sanding blocks cut down the high spots and span the low spots (Figure 19-5). This produces a more uniform

Figure 19-3. *A sanding block helps produce a smooth surface.*

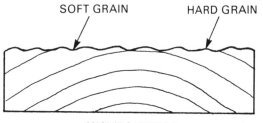

SOFT GRAIN   HARD GRAIN

WAVY SURFACE

Figure 19-4. *Without a sanding block, the abrasive sheet follows the grain causing the softer grain to wear quickly. This causes a wavy surface.*

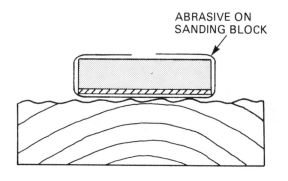

ABRASIVE ON
SANDING BLOCK

Figure 19-5. *A sanding block will span low spots and cut down high spots.*

surface. Sanding blocks can increase the life of the abrasive. The felt or rubber pad protects the paper backing from wear (Figure 19-3).

Sanding blocks come in many shapes and sizes (Figure 19-6). The shapes can be made to fit molding or other irregular pieces. Most sanding blocks use ¼ to ⅛ of an abrasive sheet.

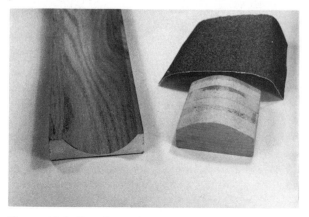

Figure 19-6. *Sanding blocks come in many shapes.*

SANDING SOLID STOCK

Always sand with the grain. Abrasives cut best with the grain. Cross-grain sanding leaves scratches which are difficult to remove. The scratches are visible when stain and finish are applied.

Take long strokes on the stock (Figure 19-7). Overlap your strokes slightly. Be careful when sanding an edge. Keep one half of the sanding block on the surface (Figure 19-8) to avoid rounding the edges. An edge should have a slight radius (Figure 19-9), but it should not be rounded.

When sanding edges and ends, you can clamp stock to the work. This will prevent rounding of the edges (Figure 19-10). It is best to sand end grain in one direction only. This lays the fibers down and yields a smoother surface.

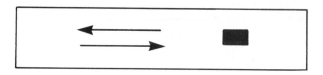

Figure 19-7. *Take long strokes. Overlap each stroke slightly.*

Figure 19-8. *Keep one half of the sanding block on the surface. This will keep the edges from rounding.*

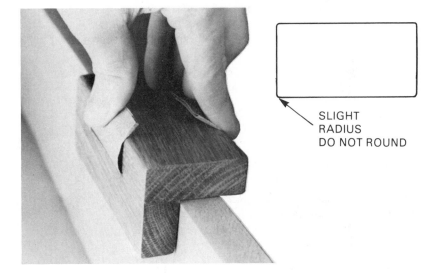

Figure 19-9. *Corners should have a slight radius. They should not be rounded.*

SLIGHT
RADIUS
DO NOT ROUND

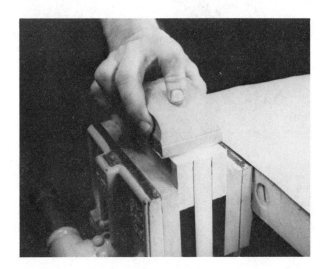

Figure 19-10. *Protect edges and ends from rounding with scrap stock.*

SANDING PLYWOOD

Plywood comes pre-sanded. If it is handled carefully, it should need very little additional sanding. All plywood sanding should be done with a sanding block. A wavy surface is produced if a sanding block is not used.

Over-sanding plywood may remove most of the face veneer. The glue behind the veneer then resists stain penetration. Thin veneers will then appear burnished when stain is applied.

SANDING IRREGULAR SHAPES

Irregular shapes are difficult to sand. Use *A* weight abrasive because they are flexible and follow irregular shapes best. Dowels and other wood shapes can be used as sanding blocks for some shapes (Figure 19-11). A deck of cards (Figure 19-12) can also be used as a block to sand shapes and moldings. Wrap a piece of abrasive around the deck of cards.

If a block cannot be used, fold two ¼ sheets of abrasive together (Figure 19-13). The thickness of the two sheets makes the abrasive stiffer. Alternate the folding pattern as the abrasive wears. Avoid over-sanding molding and irregular shapes. Over-sanding will cause the pieces to lose their sharp detail.

Figure 19-12. *A deck of cards will conform to an irregular edge. Wrap A weight abrasive around the deck of cards.*

Figure 19-13. *Fold two ¼ sheets of abrasive for hand sanding with finger pressure. The extra thickness helps spread the pressure.*

Figure 19-11. *Dowels can be used on a cove or curved edge. Use A weight abrasives over dowels.*

SANDING SMALL PARTS

Small parts may be clamped or placed in a fixture for sanding. It is also possible to move the part across a stationary piece of abrasive (Figure 19-14). Glue or nail the abrasive sheet to a flat surface. When you sand parts on a stationary abrasive sheet, check them often. If not, they may be sanded incorrectly. The edges may wear down too quickly or become rounded.

Figure 19-14. *Some small pieces can be sanded by moving them over a stationary abrasive.*

Figure 19-15. *Brushing dust from an abrasive sheet makes the abrasive sheet last longer.*

WASTING ABRASIVES

Use abrasives until they are completely worn. Brushing abrasive sheets to remove wood dust (Figure 19-15) will increase their life. Used abrasive sheets from power sanders work well for hand sanding. Use them until they no longer cut.

Abrasives are used mainly for smoothing wood. Do not use abrasives as a replacement for the plane and scraper. If wood has been scraped and planed, very little sanding will be needed. Do not waste time and abrasives removing heavy surface flaws such as mill marks.

QUESTIONS FOR REVIEW

1. When is hand sanding done?
2. Why must the raised grain be removed before finishing?
3. What causes wood grain to raise?
4. What abrasive grit should be used for initial sanding of hardwood?
5. How does a sanding block help produce a smooth surface? What can happen when a sanding block is not used?
6. How should solid stock be sanded? How are edges treated?
7. How much sanding does plywood require? What can happen if plywood is over sanded?
8. How are irregular shapes sanded? What special sanding blocks are used?
9. How are small pieces sanded? How might a fixture be used for sanding small pieces?
10. How can you increase the life of coated abrasives? Should coated abrasives be used to remove mill marks?

SUGGESTED ACTIVITIES

1. Hand sand one scrap of softwood plywood without a sanding block and one with a sanding block. Which method leaves the plywood smoothest?

2. Demonstrate the method of folding two sheets of abrasive for hand sanding.

3. Design and sketch a sanding block for sanding an irregular shape.

CHAPTER 20 — Preparing Surfaces for a Finish

Before you apply a finish, all surface imperfections must be repaired or removed. Dents must be raised, holes must be filled and glue must be removed from finish surfaces. These operations are very important. If done incorrectly, defects will appear in the finish.

KEY TERMS

plugs	wax sticks
plastic wood	raising the grain
wood putty	tack cloth
stick shellac	burn-in knife

RAISING DENTS

During the construction of your project dents may appear in the wood. Softer woods dent more easily than harder woods. Dents can be raised by swelling the wood cells with steam or water.

A small dent (Figure 20-1) can be raised with a few drops of water. The wood cells absorb the water and swell. This raises the dent. In a large dent use a small pin to make some holes (Figure 20-2). This will cause the wood to absorb water faster.

When water does not raise the dent, steam may be used. Steam may be generated with a damp towel and a soldering iron (Figure 20-3). Place the paper towel on the dent. Touch the

Figure 20-1. *A few drops of water will raise the dent.*

Figure 20-2. *Perforating a dent with a small pin will cause it to absorb water faster.*

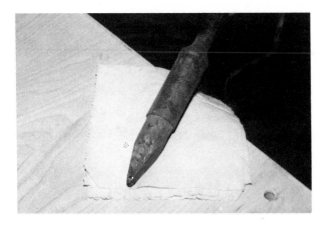

Figure 20-3. *Use a soldering iron and a damp towel to steam a dent.*

soldering iron to the towel, to force steam into the wood.

After the dent has been raised, let the wood dry overnight. When it is dry, sand the wood thoroughly. If the dented area is not sanded, it will absorb stain differently than the rest of the surface.

FILLING HOLES IN WOOD

Holes in wood may be filled in many different ways. Each method of filling holes has some advantages and disadvantages. Study Figure 20-4. This information will help you select the correct filler for each job you do.

TYPE OF FILLER	DESCRIPTION	ADVANTAGES	DISADVANTAGES
PLUGS	ACTUAL PIECE OF WOOD THAT IS DRIVEN INTO A HOLE.	HAS GRAIN AND TAKES STAIN LIKE THE REST OF THE SURFACE	MUST BE GLUED IN PLACE AND THEN FILED OFF. INSTALLATION IS TIME CONSUMING. COME ONLY IN SIZES SUCH AS 1/4", 3/8", 1/2"
PLASTIC WOOD (WOOD DOUGH)	COMBINATION OF WOOD POWDER AND PLASTIC HARDENER. COMES IN MANY COLORS. CAN BE COLORED WITH COLORS IN OIL.	QUICKLY APPLIED DRIES QUICKLY	DOES NOT TAKE STAIN SHRINKS ABOUT 10% NO GRAIN PATTERN
WOOD PUTTY	MIXTURE OF WOOD AND ADHESIVE IN A POWDER FORM. MIXED WITH WATER TO A DOUGH-LIKE CONSISTENCY.	EASY TO APPLY INEXPENSIVE MIX ONLY WHAT YOU NEED DRIES QUICKLY	DOES NOT TAKE STAIN CAN BE COLORED WITH WATER STAINS. MUST BE MIXED SHRINKS ABOUT 10% NO GRAIN PATTERN
STICK SHELLAC	COLORED SHELLAC APPLIED WITH A HEATED KNIFE. MUST MATCH FINISHED COLOR OF THE WOOD.	HARD, DURABLE FILLER. NO DRYING TIME	DOES NOT TAKE STAIN MUST BE APPLIED WITH A HEATED KNIFE. TIME CON-SUMING APPLICATION NO GRAIN PATTERN
WAX STICKS	COLORED WAX MUCH LIKE A CRAYON. FORCED INTO A HOLE AND WIPED WITH A SOFT CLOTH.	EASY TO APPLY NO DRYING TIME	DOES NOT TAKE STAIN MANY FINISHING SOLVENTS WILL DISSOLVE WAX STICKS. WAX STICKS NEVER HARDEN. NO GRAIN PATTERN MELT WHEN HEATED

Figure 20-4. *Wood fillers, their advantages and disadvantages.*

Plugs

Wooden *plugs* are cut from a piece of scrap stock (Figure 20-5). The scrap should be of the same species as the piece that must be filled. This will ensure that the plug matches the wood. For accent, you may want to cut the plugs from a different species. Installing plugs with the grain perpendicular to the surface grain (Figure 20-6) also provides accent.

Plugs are installed in hole diameters of ¼″, ⅜″, or ½″. The hole must be drilled to exact size to install a plug. The plug is driven into the wood with a mallet. Check the grain direction before

Figure 20-6. *Plugs of another species provide accent. So do plugs with the grain perpendicular to the surface grain.*

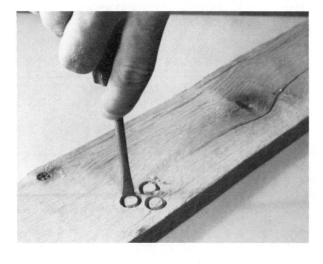

Figure 20-5. *Plugs cut from scrap stock are used to fill holes in wood.*

Figure 20-7. *Cut off the plug close to the surface.*

you install the plug. Use very little glue when installing plugs. Excess glue could spill out onto the wood. Cut the plug off with a coping, dovetail or backsaw (Figure 20-7). File the plug down even with the surface (Figure 20-8) and sand. Plugs are more pleasing to the eye than other types of fillers because they have a grain pattern and will take stain.

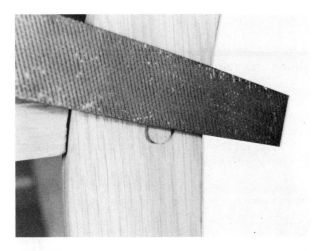

Figure 20-8. *File the plug even with the surface, then sand.*

Figure 20-9. *Plastic wood is used to fill holes in wood. It comes in several colors.*

Plastic Wood

Plastic wood or "wood dough" (Figure 20-9) is a combination of wood powder and plastic hardener. Plastic wood does not take stain. However, it may be colored with special colorants to match a stained surface (Figure 20-10). The two most common colorants are colors-in-oil or universal colorant. Make the plastic wood slightly darker than the wood color. It will lighten slightly when it dries. Plastic wood is also sold in various pre-mixed colors.

Plastic wood has no grain pattern, so large patches will not match the wood. Apply plastic wood with a putty knife (Figure 20-11) or your fingers. If you apply plastic wood with your fingers, moisten them first. This will keep the plastic wood from sticking to them.

Be sure to mound the plastic wood slightly when it is applied. It will shrink slightly. Allow the plastic wood to dry for 16 hours before sanding.

Wood Putty

Wood putty is a mixture of wood and an adhesive in powder form. It is mixed with water for use. Mix only what you need or what you can use in one hour. Wood putty can be colored by using powdered water stain. Wood putty has no grain pattern and will not take stain.

PLASTIC WOOD **COLORED PLASTIC WOOD**

Figure 20-10. *Plastic wood can be colored with colors-in-oil or universal colorant.*

PLASTIC WOOD

Figure 20-11. *Plastic wood can be applied with a putty knife. Be sure to mound the plastic wood to allow for shrinkage.*

Figure 20-12. *Mix water putty to the thickness of dough.*

Wood putty is commonly used to fill holes under painted surfaces. It also works well for filling the edges of plywood or particleboard. Mix the wood putty with water to a dough-like consistency (Figure 20-12).

Apply the wood putty with a putty knife or your fingers. Mound the wood putty slightly to allow for shrinkage. Drying time for wood putty varies, so be sure to follow the manufacturer's directions. After drying, sand the wood putty even with the surface.

Stick Shellac

Stick shellac (Figure 20-13) is a colored shellac in solid form. It is applied with a hot burn-in knife

(Figure 20-14). Stick shellac has no grain pattern and cannot be stained. It is available in over 50 colors. Two or more colors can be mixed to obtain any color that is not available.

To obtain the correct color, stain and seal a scrap of wood. Match the stick shellac to the color of the finished scrap (Figure 20-15). The stick shellac does not take stain so it must be the color of the finished wood.

Figure 20-14. *Stick shellac is applied with a hot burn-in knife.*

Figure 20-13. *Stick shellac can be clear or colored. It is used to fill holes in wood.*

Figure 20-15. *Match stick shellac to the finished color of the wood. Stick shellac will not take stain.*

Figure 20-16. *Smooth the stick shellac by scraping. Use a sharp chisel for this job.*

The stick shellac is melted and leveled with a burn-in knife. Be careful when using stick shellac. Both the stick shellac and the burn-in knife can burn your skin. *Do not* use a soldering iron to apply stick shellac. It is too hot. The heat burns or boils the stick shellac. This leaves black spots or pinholes in the repair.

If the stick shellac is not perfectly smooth after application, scrape it with a sharp chisel (Figure 20-16) and then sand it.

Wax Sticks

Wax sticks (Figure 20-17) are soft like a crayon. They are available in more than 15 different colors. Some wood finishing solvents dissolve wax sticks. Wax sticks do not take stain and have no grain pattern.

Wax sticks work well for filling nail holes in paneling and molding. They are pushed into the nail hole and then leveled with a soft cloth (Figure 20-18).

Figure 20-17. *Wax sticks are like crayons. The soft wax is forced into a nail hole.*

Figure 20-18. *Wax sticks are commonly used to fill nail holes on paneling. The wax is leveled with a soft cloth.*

RAISING THE GRAIN

After holes have been filled, dents raised and the rough sanding completed, start *raising the grain.* Dampen all wood surfaces with a sponge that has been wrung dry (Figure 20-19). This causes wood fibers on the surface to swell. Sanding off the swollen fibers will make the surface smoother.

Figure 20-19. *Raising the grain.*

Figure 20-20. *Glue blemishes can be removed with a cabinet scraper or a chisel.*

While dampening the wood, watch for glue blemishes. Many glue blemishes will turn white or yellow when they are wet. Circle any glue blemishes with chalk. Before sanding, remove the glue blemish with a cabinet scraper (Figure 20-20) or a sharp chisel. If not removed, glue blemishes cause uneven staining.

After the wood dries, hand sand all surfaces thoroughly with the grain. Check your work carefully. Make sure that the wood is smooth.

DUSTING YOUR PRODUCT

Before you begin finishing your product it should be dusted. Dust can mix with the stain or finish if it is not removed. This can mar the finish. Use a vacuum cleaner or a dust cloth to remove the dust. A commercial tack cloth may also be used to remove the dust. A *tack cloth* is a treated cloth. The treatment leaves it in a sticky condition. Dust is gathered and held on the tack cloth due to this stickiness. When all dust is removed, you are ready to stain or finish your project.

QUESTIONS FOR REVIEW

1. Describe the procedure for raising dents in wood.
2. How are plugs used to fill holes in wood? What advantages do plugs have over other fillers?
3. Can plastic wood be stained? How is plastic wood applied?
4. For what purposes is wood putty commonly used?
5. What is stick shellac? How is it applied?
6. Are wax sticks commonly used for wood patches? Why?
7. Why must the grain be raised before the final sanding? How is the grain raised?
8. How are glue blemishes removed? What will happen if they are not removed?
9. Why must wood surfaces be dusted prior to application of stain or finish?
10. What is a tack cloth? How is it used?

SUGGESTED ACTIVITIES

1. Demonstrate the procedure for raising dents in a scrap of wood.
2. Drill several holes in a scrap of wood and practice applying wood fillers.
3. Drill a hole in a piece of scrap and fill it with a plug.

SECTION 5

Wood Finishing

CHAPTER 21

Finishing Safety

Finishing materials can be hazardous. The chemicals in many finishing materials can burn or injure the skin. Others, if they are absorbed, breathed or swallowed, can cause damage to your internal organs. In addition, most finishing materials are flammable. This means that there is always a possibility of fire.

You should always be concerned with *personal protection* and *fire safety.* Bodily harm and fire are common hazards when working with finishing materials. Personal protection will guard you from bodily harm. This chapter will describe the correct personal protection and tell you when to use it. This chapter will also discuss fire prevention. It will help you identify and eliminate fire hazards before they cause a fire.

KEY TERMS

ventilation	oxygen
respirator	housekeeping
fuel	fire extinguisher
heat	

PERSONAL PROTECTION

The chemicals in many finishing materials can burn your eyes or skin. *Protective glasses* and *gloves* (Figure 21-1) must be worn when there is any danger of a burn. Always read the manufacturer's instructions to determine if there is a *burn hazard.* Even when there is no burn hazard, you should wear your protective glasses. They protect your eyes from hazardous finishing materials used by others in the shop.

If you are ever burned by a finishing material, immediately flush your skin with running water. Run water over it for at least fifteen minutes. Special eye wash stations (Figure 21-2) are set up in modern finishing shops. They are designed to rinse your eyes in the event of burn.

An *apron* also affords some protection from burns. It is a good idea to wear one. It will also protect your clothes from damage.

Breathing dust or vapors can be harmful to your lungs and other internal organs. Always wear a

Figure 21-1. *Protective glasses and gloves protect you from injury and burns. Always wear them.*

Keep eyelids open

Figure 21-2. *Eye wash stations enable you to flush your eyes of hazardous liquids.*

Figure 21-3. *The respirator protects your lungs from dust and vapors.*

respirator (Figure 21-3) when spraying a finish or sanding bleached surfaces. Spray vapors and dust from bleached wood can be harmful to your lungs.

Proper *ventilation* will also reduce the amount of vapor or dust you breathe. Make sure the spray booth is well ventilated and that the dust collection system is working. Good ventilation and dust collection reduce but do not eliminate the hazard. Always wear a respirator when spraying or sanding bleached surfaces.

Do not smoke while sanding or spraying. The dust or vapor will mix with the smoke. This could be very harmful to your lungs. There is also the possibility of fire. Be sure to wash well before

eating or smoking. Any finishing material on your hands or face could be inhaled or swallowed when you smoke or eat.

FIRE SAFETY

For a fire to start, there must be *fuel, heat,* and *oxygen.* This is known as the *fire triangle* (Figure 21-4). If fuel, heat or oxygen is not present, a fire cannot start. Good *housekeeping* practices can reduce the chance of fire.

Store finishing materials properly (Figure 21-5) and away from heat. Also, keep cabinet doors closed to reduce the amount of available oxygen. Store rags in a closed container to eliminate oxygen (Figure 21-6). By emptying the container every day, the amount of fuel is also reduced. As long as these housekeeping practices are observed, there is little chance of fire.

The finishing area should be a "no smoking" area. Spray vapors can cause an explosion if ignited. In addition, a careless smoker could provide the flame that starts a fire. Never smoke while working with finishing materials.

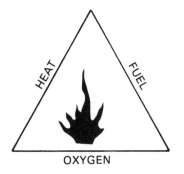

Figure 21-4. *This triangle represents the three elements of a fire. Remove any one of the three and there can be no fire.*

Figure 21-5. *Finishing materials should be stored in approved metal cabinets. Make sure you use approved containers.*

Figure 21-6. *Closed containers for rags prevent fires. Empty the container daily. Be sure it is an approved container.*

Fires can also be caused when *used solvents* are not disposed of correctly. Solvents should be collected in an approved container and discarded each night. Never pour solvents into sinks or drains connected to the sewer system. This will contaminate our water and could cause an explosion within the sewer. Make sure that all used solvents are disposed of correctly. Check local ordinances or consult with the fire department. They will tell you the correct way to dispose of solvents.

TYPES OF FIRE

Not all fires are the same. For this reason fires have been divided into classes (Figure 21-7). You can properly extinguish the fire if you know its class. Using the wrong type of *fire extinguisher*

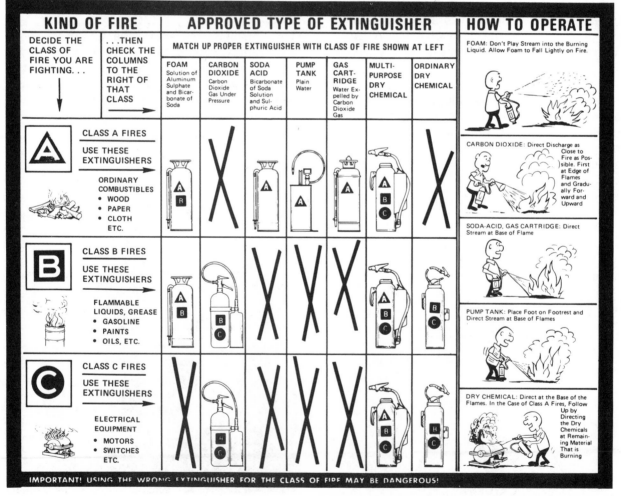

NATIONAL INSTITUTE FOR OCCUPATIONAL SAFETY AND HEALTH

Figure 21-7. *Using the wrong extinguisher for the class of fire may be dangerous!*

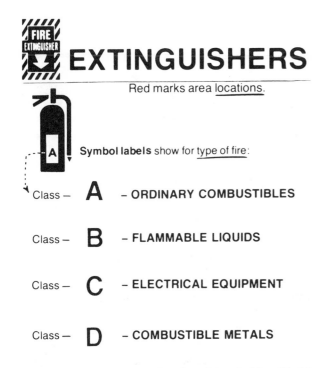

EXTINGUISHERS

Red marks area locations.

Symbol labels show for type of fire:

Class — **A** – ORDINARY COMBUSTIBLES

Class — **B** – FLAMMABLE LIQUIDS

Class — **C** – ELECTRICAL EQUIPMENT

Class — **D** – COMBUSTIBLE METALS

Figure 21-8. *The type of extinguisher is identified by letter, symbol and color.*

on a fire could spread the fire or cause injury. Study Figure 21-7 to find out what type of extinguisher to use on a fire.

After you learn what types of extinguishers to use on the various classes of fires you should learn where these extinguishers are located. Check through the shop and finishing area. Identify the type of extinguisher and what class of fire it will extinguish (Figure 21-8). Read the label on the extinguisher. It will tell you how the extinguisher is operated.

You should also know how to report a fire. Place the phone number for reporting a fire near the phone and be sure you know the address of the shop and finishing room. A fire should be reported before any attempt is made to extinguish it. This will assure fire department support if the fire is difficult to extinguish.

QUESTIONS FOR REVIEW

1. What are two common hazards associated with the use of finishing materials?
2. What types of personal protection should be worn when working with finishing materials?
3. What should you do if your skin or eyes became burned by a finishing material?
4. Why is proper ventilation important in the finishing area?
5. Why is it important to wash well after working in the finishing room? What could happen if you did not wash before eating or smoking?
6. Sketch the fire triangle. What happens if any part of this triangle is missing?
7. How can good housekeeping prevent fires?
8. How should used solvents be discarded?
9. How should rags be stored and discarded?
10. What are the three classes of fire? How would you describe each?
11. What type of extinguisher should be used on burning wood? On burning liquid?

SUGGESTED ACTIVITIES

1. Check your shop to see where the fire extinguishers are located. Which extinguishers are designed to fight a fire caused by finishing liquids?
2. Make sure you know how to report a fire. Post the phone number on the bulletin board and next to the phone.
3. Make a list of the types of protective equipment found in your finishing room. Discuss the purpose of each piece of equipment.

Bleaches and Stains

Clear finishes are best for some species of wood because of their dark natural color or grain. Among those species are cherry, walnut and mahogany. Other woods, such as pine, poplar and oak, lack color. These woods may be colored with wood stain to increase their appeal. Wood stain is also used to obtain a uniform color between two or more species of wood.

Figure 22-1. *Two-part wood bleach will lighten the wood's color.*

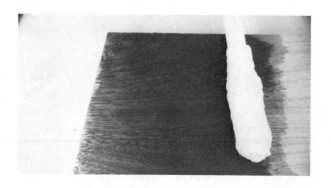

Figure 22-2. *Throw-away applicators are used to apply bleach. Wear protective glasses and gloves to apply bleach.*

Unlike stain, wood bleach is used to remove color from wood. Bleach reacts with wood chemically to remove color. Bleached wood appears white. Bleach may be used to remove color from an entire project, or it may be used to remove dark spots on a light-colored wood. Bleach is also sometimes used to reduce the color difference between sapwood and heartwood.

Furniture refinishing also uses bleach. It can usually remove stains from glassware, heat or cigarette burns. Before you use any bleach or stain, read the manufacturer's instructions. Wear protective glasses and rubber gloves when using stain or bleach.

KEY TERMS

bleach	solvent
wood stain	vehicle
pigmenting stain	pigments
penetrating stain	dyes

BLEACH

There are many types of wood *bleach* available today. Even commercial laundry bleach will work on wood. The most effective wood bleach is the two-solution bleach (Figure 22-1). Two-solution bleach requires a two-step application. The first solution conditions the wood and the second solution neutralizes the chemicals.

Throw-away applicators (Figure 22-2) work best for applying bleach. Use different applicators for each of the two solutions. If the same applicator is used for both solutions, the chemicals will react with each other and no bleaching will result. Do not use paint brushes to apply bleach.

The two solutions are swabbed onto the wood following the manufacturer's instructions. Use non-metallic containers for the bleach solutions. Bleaches will corrode metal containers. The corrosion will discolor the bleaching solutions and cause them to stain the wood.

Always wear protective glasses and gloves when applying any type of bleach. Bleach can irritate your eyes and hands if they are not protected.

After the second solution begins to dry, sponge the surface with water to remove chemical residue (Figure 22-3). If the surface is not light

Figure 22-3. *Sponge the wood with water when the second chemical begins to dry. This removes the chemical residue.*

enough, repeat the bleaching process. Allow the surface to dry completely before sanding the raised grain.

Figure 22-4 shows a piece of walnut. The right half of this piece has been bleached. Bleach does not have deep penetration. It is possible to sand through the bleached wood while sanding away the raised grain. Sand only enough to remove the raised grain. You can apply a thin coat of shellac to the surface before sanding. This will hold the raised grain upright during sanding. There is less chance of cutting through the bleached surface when a thin coat is applied.

Whenever you sand a bleached surface, be sure to wear a respirator. The respirator protects your lungs from the harmful bleach residue that remains in the sanding dust.

STAIN

There are many types of *stain* sold commercially today. Each type has a different *solvent* or *vehicle*. The solvent or vehicle is the liquid that allows the stain to flow onto the wood. The vehicle evaporates and causes the stain to dry.

The vehicle can be used as a solvent to reduce stain thickness or make a lighter stain. It will also clean brushes or spray equipment used to apply the stain.

NATURAL WALNUT BLEACHED WALNUT

Figure 22-4. *The right half of this piece of walnut has been bleached.*

STAIN TYPE	VEHICLE SOLVENT	STAINING ACTION	APPLICATION	QUALITIES
WATER	WATER	PENETRATING	SPRAY OR BRUSH	SLOW DRYING. DOES NOT FADE. TRANSPARENT: DOES NOT HIDE THE GRAIN. WATER IN THE STAIN RAISES THE GRAIN. SOLD IN POWDER FORM. MIX AND STORE IN NON-METALLIC CONTAINER. NON-FLAMMABLE USES NO HYDROCARBON SOLVENTS.
ALCOHOL	ALCOHOL	PENETRATING	SPRAY OR BRUSH. SPRAY WORKS BEST	DRIES QUICKLY. FADES EASILY. OFTEN USED FOR STAINING SAP-WOOD. SOLD IN POWDER FORM. MIX AND STORE IN NON-METALLIC CONTAINER. STAIN POWDER CAN BE MIXED WITH SHELLAC OR LACQUER TO MAKE A SHADING COAT. MAY RAISE GRAIN SLIGHTLY.
NON GRAIN RAISING	ALCOHOL GLYCOL	PENETRATING	SPRAY OR BRUSH. SPRAY WORKS BEST	DRIES QUICKLY. DOES NOT FADE. USUALLY SOLD IN THE LIQUID FORM. STORE IN NON-METALLIC CONTAINER. DOES NOT RAISE THE GRAIN.
OIL STAIN (PENE-TRATING)	MINERAL SPIRITS OR TURPENTINE	PENETRATING	SPRAY OR BRUSH	DRIES QUICKLY. FADES EASILY. DOES NOT RAISE THE GRAIN. TENDS TO MIX WITH THE FINISH (BLEED). SOLD IN LIQUID FORM.
OIL STAIN (PIG-MENTING)	MINERAL SPIRITS OR TURPENTINE	PIGMENTING	SPRAY OR BRUSH	SLOW DRYING. DOES NOT FADE. SOLD IN LIQUID FORM. MUST BE MIXED WELL BECAUSE THE PIGMENTS TEND TO SETTLE. LIES ON THE SURFACE AND TENDS TO HIDE THE GRAIN. COLORS WOOD UNIFORMLY.
LATEX STAIN	WATER	PIGMENTING	SPRAY OR BRUSH	SLOW DRYING. DOES NOT FADE. SOLD IN LIQUID FORM. MUST BE MIXED WELL BECAUSE THE PIGMENTS TEND TO SETTLE. LIES ON THE SURFACE AND TENDS TO HIDE THE GRAIN. COLORS WOOD UNIFORMLY. NON-FLAMMABLE USES NO HYDROCARBON SOLVENTS.
GELLED WOOD STAIN	MINERAL SPIRITS OR TURPENTINE	PIGMENTING	WIPE. THIN TO BRUSH OR SPRAY	SLOW DRYING. DOES NOT FADE. SOLD IN A GELLED FORM. REQUIRES NO MIXING BECAUSE THE PIGMENTS CANNOT SETTLE. COLOR REMAINS UNIFORM THROUGHOUT THE CAN. MUST BE THINNED FOR BRUSHING OR SPRAYING.

Figure 22-5. *Wood stains.*

Figure 22-5 lists the vehicle for most common stains. It also describes their qualities. Use this table to select the correct stain for the job you are doing. It will also show the correct solvent for cleaning brushes or spray equipment.

Stains may color wood with *pigments* or *dyes.* Dyes penetrate into the wood fibers. Stains made with dyes are called *penetrating stains.*

Stains made with pigments are called *pigmenting stains.* Pigmenting stains stay on the wood's surface. They do not penetrate into the wood. A pigmenting stain provides uniform color but tends to hide the grain. With penetrating stains, the wood color is less uniform, but the grain shows. Pigmenting stains must be stirred well before use. The pigments are heavier than the vehicle. They drop to the bottom of the can.

PRE-STAINING OPERATIONS

Sap staining is a staining operation performed only on the lighter colored sapwood (Figure 22-6). After the sapwood is stained a color similar to the heartwood, the entire project may be stained again for a darker overall color. Overall color will be quite uniform due to the sap staining.

Figure 22-6. *Sapwood is darkened by sap staining. Use an alcohol penetrating stain for this job.*

End grain usually becomes darker than face or edge grain when stained. It absorbs stain faster than edge or face grain. You can coat end grain to resist stain penetration. The coating you use

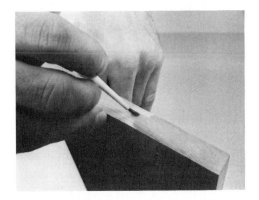

Figure 22-7. *Use a solvent on end grain before staining. This keeps the end grain from becoming too dark.*

should be the same as the stain's vehicle (Figure 22-7). Figure 22-5 will help you select the correct vehicle.

APPLYING STAIN

Stain is either brushed or sprayed onto the wood. Gelled wood stain may be wiped on with a rag. Because of its consistency, it will not drip. If other pigmenting or penetrating stains are applied with a rag, stain drips from the rag may cause dark spots in the wood. These spots are very difficult to remove. Brushing or spraying gives better stain control.

Make sure that the stain is mixed well (Figure 22-8) and that you wear protective glasses and gloves. Treat end grain and sapwood before you

Figure 22-8. *Make sure the stain is well-mixed before use. Wear protective gloves and glasses.*

Figure 22-9. *Brush the stain into the wood. Work slowly. Be sure all surfaces are coated.*

Figure 22-10. *When wiping the stain, use a soft cloth and wipe with the grain.*

begin. Work slowly to be sure all surfaces are coated (Figure 22-9). When the stain begins to dry, wipe the stain with a soft cloth (Figure 22-10). Work with the grain. Wipe the stain until the color is uniform.

If the wood is not dark enough, it can be stained again. If the wood is too dark, dampen a rag with the stain's solvent and wipe the wood. This will lighten the color if the stain is not dry. The color should be correct if you have experimented with the stain. Always test the stain on a scrap to be sure color is correct for the job. A finish schedule can help you apply the finish correctly. Always place used rags in a covered container to prevent fire.

Most stains should dry overnight before the surface is sealed. Alcohol and NGR (non grain raising) stains can be sealed in four hours. Use a commercial sealer or a shellac washcoat (thin coat of shellac) to seal the surface. The sealer prevents the stain from mixing with the top coat or paste wood filler. A paste wood filler or top coat may now be applied.

QUESTIONS FOR REVIEW

1. For what is stain used? What wood species are usually stained? What species are usually not stained?
2. What are some common uses of bleach? How is bleach used to remove color from the wood?
3. What type of bleach is most effective on wood? How is it applied?
4. What are some precautions that should be taken to apply bleach safely?
5. Why must bleached surfaces be sanded carefully? How does a thin coat of shellac help when sanding a bleached surface?
6. Why must a respirator be worn when sanding bleached surfaces?
7. How does a penetrating stain color wood? How does it differ from a pigmenting stain?
8. What is the function of the vehicle or solvent in a wood stain?
9. What advantages are there to stains using water as a vehicle and solvent?

10. What is sap staining? What type of stain is used for sap staining?
11. Why must pigmenting stains be mixed thoroughly? What pigmenting stain requires no mixing?
12. How is end grain treated before staining?
13. Why is it poor practice to apply stain with a rag?
14. Discuss the procedure for applying wood stain. What can be done if the stain is too dark or too light?
15. How long should wood stain dry before applying a sealer? Why is a sealer applied?

SUGGESTED ACTIVITIES

1. Make a finish schedule for use with finishing materials found in your shop.

2. Apply two or three types of stain to a wood scrap. Compare the differences.

CHAPTER 23
Paste Wood Filler

Open grain woods, such as oak, walnut and mahogany, have a porous surface. The application of a paste wood filler will fill the wood pores and make the surface smoother. A smooth surface requires less finishing material to obtain uniform coverage.

KEY TERMS

paste wood filler	mineral spirits
linseed oil	catalyst
silex	bleeding
drier	

Paste wood fillers are available in colors. Most colored paste wood fillers have a matching wood stain. The paste wood filler can be used to match the color of the wood or accent the grain (Figure 23-1). The natural color of paste wood filler is beige or tan. Colors-in-oil and universal colorants (Figure 23-2) can be used to color paste wood filler.

Paste wood fillers contain *linseed oil,* a solvent, *silex* and commercial *driers.* Boiled linseed oil is the vehicle. It is the liquid portion that makes paste wood filler easy to spread. As the linseed oil dries, it expands slightly. This expansion packs the paste wood filler into the wood pores.

The solvent in paste wood filler reduces the thickness of the linseed oil. It evaporates after the paste wood filler is applied. The solvent most commonly used is *mineral spirits,* but turpentine may also be used. If the paste wood filler is too thick, mineral spirits or turpentine may be added. These solvents can be used to clean your brush.

Figure 23-1. *Paste wood filler can be used to match the color of the wood or accent the grain.*

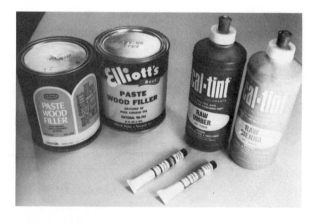

Figure 23-2. *Paste wood filler can be colored. Universal colorants and colors-in-oil may both be used.*

Figure 23-3. *Stir paste wood filler well before use.*

Silex is the solid portion of the paste wood filler. Silex is ground quartz. It is a fine powder that can easily be forced into the wood pores. Whenever paste wood filler is left unused, the silex will drop to the bottom of the container. For this reason, you must mix the paste wood filler well before use (Figure 23-3).

Commercial driers make up about ten percent of the paste wood filler. Driers act as a *catalyst*. They cause the linseed oil to mix with oxygen at a much faster rate. This speeds the drying of the linseed oil.

APPLICATION OF PASTE WOOD FILLER

Make sure that the paste wood filler has been mixed thoroughly and that all surfaces have been sealed before you begin. A commercial sealer or a shellac washcoat (thin coat of shellac) may be used to seal the surface.

It is important to seal the wood surfaces. If the wood is not sealed, the pigments in the paste wood filler will seep into the wood. This is called *bleeding*. When this happens, the wood becomes darker in color and the paste wood filler becomes lighter in color. This produces an uneven color contrast between the stain and paste wood filler.

Paste wood filler is applied with a paint brush (Figure 23-4). Use an inexpensive brush. Do not use your best brush for applying paste wood filler because some silex may remain in the bristles after the brush is cleaned. The silex could ruin the finish if that brush is used to apply the finishing material. Use the brush for paste wood filler only.

Brush the paste wood filler onto the surface with the grain (Figure 23-4). Apply the paste wood filler to a small area. If you cover a large area, the paste wood filler will dry and it will be difficult to wipe off.

Figure 23-4. *Brush paste wood filler onto the work. Cover a small area. After paste wood filler dries, it is difficult to remove.*

After brushing the paste wood filler with the grain, brush it across the grain (Figure 23-5). This will force it into the wood pores. When the paste wood filler loses its gloss or appears flat, it is dry enough to be removed.

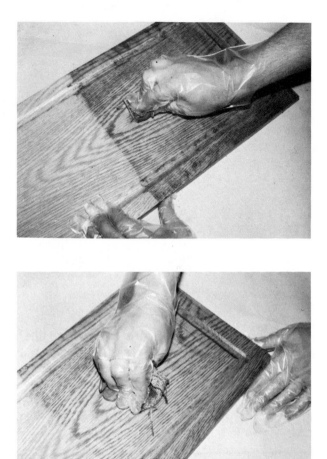

Figure 23-6. *Wipe paste wood filler across the grain first. Then wipe it with the grain.*

Figure 23-5. *Brush across the grain. This forces the filler into the wood pores.*

Wipe the paste wood filler across the grain with a coarse cloth or piece of burlap (Figure 23-6). Be sure to protect your hands with gloves. Wiping paste wood filler across the grain packs it into the wood pores. After wiping the surface across the grain, wipe it with the grain (Figure 23-6). This will remove the excess paste wood filler.

If paste wood filler becomes lodged in a corner or molding, remove it with a pointed dowel (Figure 23-7). Wrap a cloth around the point and pull it through the corner.

If paste wood filler hardens, it will be difficult to remove. You may soften it somewhat if you dampen it with mineral spirits. For best results cover small areas until you become experienced with paste wood filler.

Allow the paste wood filler to dry for 16 hours before sealing the surface. Sealing will prevent the paste wood filler from bleeding (seeping) into the top coat. Use a shellac wash coat or commercial sealer for this job. After sealing the surface, a top coat may be applied.

Figure 23-7. *A pointed dowel will remove paste wood filler from molded edges. Wrap the dowel with a rag before use.*

QUESTIONS FOR REVIEW

1. On what types of wood is paste wood filler used?
2. How are paste wood fillers colored?
3. What materials are contained in paste wood fillers? What is the purpose of each material?
4. Why is it important to seal the wood before applying paste wood filler?
5. Why is an inexpensive paint brush used to apply paste wood filler?
6. How is paste wood filler applied?
7. Why should paste wood filler be applied to a small area?
8. How is paste wood filler removed from corners or molding?
9. How long must paste wood filler be allowed to dry before sealing?
10. What solvent is used to clean a brush used to apply paste wood filler?

SUGGESTED ACTIVITIES

1. Make a list of the types of wood found in your shop that require paste wood filler.

2. Read the manufacturer's directions on a can of paste wood filler. Why is it important to stir paste wood filler?

3. Select a scrap of open grained wood and apply paste wood filler as a part of the finishing schedule.

Penetrating Oil Finishes

Penetrating oil finishes (Figure 24-1) are *wipe-on finishes.* Wipe-on finishes are easy to apply. They are rubbed into the wood with a soft cloth.

Penetrating oil finishes flow into the wood. They do not coat the wood's surface. Penetrating oil finishes dry rapidly and do not attract dust. No brushing or spraying defects can occur because they are wiped on. Most penetrating oil finishes have low flammability and are not a serious fire hazard.

Oil finishes may be applied to small pieces by dipping them. This makes finishing of small parts much easier. Penetrating oil finishes will not crack with age and are easy to repair. An application of the finish over a scratch will repair it. Oil finishes are water and alcohol-resistant, but they can be damaged by frequent exposure to alcohol or water.

Penetrating oil finishes are only as hard as the wood they protect. This is because the oil lies below the wood's surface. Coatings that lie on the wood's surface can be harder than the wood. Surface finishes will also provide greater depth and luster than penetrating oil finishes.

Some commercially prepared penetrating oil finishes have dyes mixed with them. Those finishes do the work of a stain and a finish.

KEY TERMS

penetrating oil finishes
wipe-on finish
boiled linseed oil
tung oil

mineral spirits
drier
catalyst
wax

PENETRATING OIL FINISHES

Penetrating oil finishes are a mixture of an oil and its solvent. Common penetrating oils are *boiled linseed oil* and *tung oil* (Figure 24-2). Both of these oils dry by *oxidation.* As oxygen in the air combines with the oil it hardens below the wood's surface.

Figure 24-1. *Penetrating oil finishes are rubbed into the wood with a soft cloth. They dry rapidly and do not attract dust.*

Figure 24-2. *Two common penetrating oils are boiled linseed oil and tung oil.*

Figure 24-3. *These commercial penetrating oil finishes dry faster and harder than tung oil.*

The solvent used with boiled linseed oil or tung oil is either *turpentine* or *mineral spirits.* The solvent thins the oil and makes it easy to spread. After the oil is spread, the solvent evaporates and the oil oxidizes.

A drier is sometimes added to the oil. The drier is a catalyst that accelerates oxidation (drying) of the oil. Oxidation causes the oil to harden.

Danish oil, Minwax, and Okene are commercial penetrating oils (Figure 24-3). They dry faster and harder than tung or linseed oil. This is because the oils have been modified to improve their characteristics.

Salad bowl finish (Figure 24-4) is a specialized penetrating finish. It has been approved by the United States Food and Drug Administration for use on wooden tableware such as spoons, bowls and cutting boards. After salad bowl finish dries, it becomes non-toxic. Salad bowl finish is expensive, but it is the safest finish for wooden tableware.

APPLYING PENETRATING OIL FINISHES

Stain the wood before applying the penetrating oil. Alcohol and water stains work best with penetrating oil finishes. This is because they will not bleed (seep) into the oil. Pigmenting stains do not work well with penetrating oil finishes. Some commercial penetrating oils have dyes in them to color the wood. A stain is not needed with these oils. They will do the work of both a stain and a finish.

Apply the penetrating oil with a soft cloth. Be sure to wear protective glasses and gloves during application. Coat the entire surface and allow the oil to soak into the wood (Figure 24-5).

Figure 24-4. *Salad bowl finish is a penetrating oil used for wooden tableware. It has been approved by the United States Food and Drug Administration.*

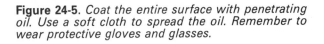

Figure 24-5. *Coat the entire surface with penetrating oil. Use a soft cloth to spread the oil. Remember to wear protective gloves and glasses.*

Leave the oil on the wood for about ten minutes and then wipe it off. For additional luster, the surface can be recoated after twelve hours. Sanding between coats with a 220 or 320 grit abrasive will improve the finish.

Figure 24-6. *Penetrating oil finishes should dry for 24 hours before waxing.*

After the finish has dried completely, it can be *waxed* (Figure 24-6). The wax will protect the finish and increase its beauty. Allow 24 hours for complete drying before applying the wax.

Be sure to place all rags in a covered container after use. Oily rags can be a fire hazard if they are not stored in a covered container.

Keep all penetrating oil finishes covered when they are not in use. The oil will mix with oxygen in the air and begin to dry. This will cause the oil to thicken and form a skin on the surface. The skin must be discarded because it will not dissolve.

Penetrating oil finishes cannot be applied to woods that have been sealed. If the wood is sealed, the oil cannot penetrate into the wood. Penetrating oil finishes should be applied to raw wood or applied over penetrating oil.

Before you apply any penetrating oil finish, read the manufacturer's instructions. This will ensure safe application and best results.

QUESTIONS FOR REVIEW

1. What are some advantages of a penetrating oil finish?
2. What oils and solvents are common in a penetrating oil finish? How do commercial penetrating oils differ?
3. What does a drier do to the oil in a penetrating oil finish?
4. What penetrating oil finish is considered safest for wooden tableware such as salad bowls? Why?
5. What stains work best with penetrating oil finishes? What stains should not be used with penetrating oil finishes?
6. How is a penetrating oil finish applied?
7. What safety precautions should be observed when applying penetrating oil finishes?
8. How long should a penetrating oil finish dry before it can be waxed?
9. Can penetrating oil finishes be applied to surfaces that have been sealed? Why?

SUGGESTED ACTIVITIES

1. Read the manufacturer's instructions on the penetrating oil found in your shop. Can you determine what oil and solvent were used to make it?

2. Compare prices of commercial penetrating oil finishes at your paint store. What finish is least expensive, most expensive?

Shellac finishes are surface coatings. They dry by *evaporation* of their solvent, denatured alcohol. The shellac resin is a product of the *lac bug,* an insect found in India and Siam. It secretes the lac resin onto twigs. This resin is then gathered and processed into shellac.

Shellac is usually bleached before being sold. This is done because shellac has an orange tint that is not desirable for many finishes. Various thicknesses or cuts of shellac are available. The most common cuts are 3- and 4-pound. A 3-pound cut has 3 pounds of shellac cut or mixed into a gallon of alcohol.

Shellac is a fast drying finish. It dries to the touch in 15 to 30 minutes. It dries hard in two hours. The shellac finish lies on the wood's surface and may be rubbed out to a deep luster.

Shellac is not resistant to moisture or alcohol. Water turns shellac white and alcohol will dissolve a shellac finish. Shellac has a *shelf life* of about six months. If shellac is kept too long, it will not dry. It will remain sticky.

KEY TERMS

shellac	runs
evaporation	washcoat
denatured alcohol	French polish
shelf life	

APPLYING A SHELLAC FINISH

A shellac finish may be brushed or sprayed. Two thin coats are better than one thick coat. Thick coats will cause runs, drips or thick spots in the finish. When brushing shellac, work quickly. Use long strokes. Avoid repeating brush strokes. The shellac dries so quickly that repeated strokes will leave brush marks. Sand the surface between coats with 220 to 320 grit silicon carbide abrasive. This will improve adhesion.

The second and third coats may be thicker than the first coat. But, remember that thinner coats provide better results. After the final coat, the finish may be rubbed out with pumice and rottenstone or steel wool. Clean your spray equipment or brush after use with denatured alcohol.

SHELLAC WASHCOAT

Shellac can be used as a sealer or *washcoat.* Sealers are used to stop bleeding between finishing materials. A shellac washcoat is a very thin solution. Washcoats are made by adding additional alcohol to 3- or 4-pound cut shellac. Four to six parts of denatured alcohol to one part shellac should be enough.

A washcoat may be used as a wood sealer. It may also be used as a sealer over stain or paste

Figure 25-1. *A shellac washcoat acts as a sealer. It keeps stain or paste wood filler from mixing with the finish.*

wood filler (Figure 25-1). Shellac washcoats are a popular sealer because they dry quickly. A washcoat will dry in 15 minutes. This enables the finishing process to progress rapidly.

Shellac washcoats may be sprayed or brushed. They are applied in the same way as a shellac finish. Clean your brush or spray equipment with denatured alcohol after use.

FRENCH POLISH

French polish is a mixture of shellac (thinned with alcohol) and boiled linseed oil. It is rubbed onto the wood with a pad (Figure 25-2). The pad is made from a soft cloth (coarse cotton) wrapped in a finely woven cloth (linen or tightly woven cotton).

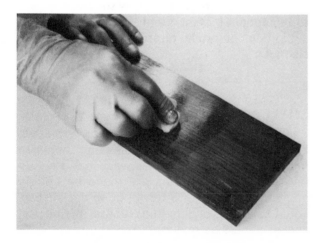

Figure 25-2. *French polish is a mixture of shellac, alcohol, and boiled linseed oil. It is rubbed onto the wood with a special pad.*

The linseed oil acts as a lubricant while the French polish is spread. The friction of the pad heats the surface and speeds the drying of the shellac. French polish is applied with a circular motion (Figure 25-3). Be sure to wear protective gloves and glasses when applying French polish.

As the polish builds on the surface, a gloss will appear. If the pad sticks, place a few drops of linseed oil on it. This will reduce friction as the surface is polished. Any swirls left by the pad may be rubbed out with a cloth dampened in denatured alcohol. When not in use, store your pad in a covered jar (Figure 25-4). This will eliminate the chance of fire.

Figure 25-3. *Use a circular motion when applying French polish.*

Figure 25-4. *Store your pad in a covered jar. This will keep it soft and eliminate a fire hazard.*

French polish is a mixture of two parts 3- or 4-pound cut shellac, two parts denatured alcohol and one part (or less) boiled linseed oil. This mixture may vary slightly according to individual preference and use. Best results on raw wood are obtained when a shellac washcoat is applied before the French polish.

French polish is used to repair damaged finishes. It is also used to finish projects that have been turned on a lathe. French polish works well as a finish on small projects such as jewelry boxes. It is rarely used on furniture-size projects.

COMMERCIAL FRENCH POLISHES

Commercial French polishes are sold under trade names such as Seal-A-Cell and Lac-French (Figure 25-5). These French polishes are made from modified or synthetic materials. Be sure to read the manufacturer's instructions before use. Wear protective glasses and gloves when applying a commercial French polish.

When using any French polish make sure you try the finish on a scrap before you begin to finish a project. Your experience finishing the scrap will help assure good results when you finish your project.

Figure 25-5. *These are commercial French polishes. They are sometimes used to repair scratches in a finish. Read the manufacturer's instructions before use.*

QUESTIONS FOR REVIEW

1. What is shellac? How is it obtained?
2. Why is shellac bleached before it is sold?
3. What are the most common shellac cuts?
4. Is shellac a penetrating finish or a surface finish?
5. What are some advantages of shellac? What are some disadvantages?
6. How is shellac applied? What safety precautions should be observed?
7. How is a shellac washcoat mixed? What is the purpose of a washcoat?
8. What are some common uses of French polish? How is French polish made?
9. How is French polish applied? How do you make an applicator for French polish?
10. How do you remove swirls from a surface that has been French polished?

SUGGESTED ACTIVITIES

1. Mix a shellac washcoat from 3- or 4-pound cut shellac. Use the formula found in this chapter.

2. Make a pad for applying French polish.

3. Use the pad to practice applying French polish to a scrap of wood.

4. Read the manufacturer's instructions on any commercial French polish. Describe how it differs from French polish mixed in the shop.

Varnish Finishes

Varnish finishes are tough surface finishes. They form a thick surface film when they dry. Varnish finishes are resistant to water and alcohol.

A varnish finish may be sprayed or, more commonly, brushed. The drying time for varnish finish varies, but it is usually longer than other clear finishes.

KEY TERMS

varnish	modified varnish
oil	polyurethane
short oil varnish	rosin
long oil varnish	turpentine
resin	mineral spirits
solvent	stain varnish

Figure 26-1. *Varnish is a clear, waterproof finish. It is favored for marine use. Varnish is made of resin, oil, solvent and a drier.*

Varnish (Figure 26-1) is a combination of *oil, resin, solvent,* and drier. It is a clear, waterproof finish.

Some varnishes are natural and others are modified. *Modified varnishes* are like natural varnishes except that the oils and resins have been altered.

Modified varnishes are altered to improve the natural qualities. Modified varnishes may have improved weather resistance or better drying properties. Two common modified varnishes are alkyd resin and oil modified urethane varnish (polyurethane).

The *oil* used in varnish is usually boiled linseed oil or tung oil. High quality varnish is made with tung oil. Varnishes with a large percentage of oil such as spar or marine varnish are tough and flexible. These varnishes are called *long oil varnishes.* They are used for exterior work and for boats.

Varnishes with a small percentage of oil such as cabinet or rubbing varnish are hard and brittle. These varnishes are called *short oil varnishes.* Short oil varnishes produce a high gloss. This is due to the high percentage of resin.

Resins may be fossil deposits of trees that died centuries ago or they may be the sap of living trees. Rosin is a resin produced from living trees. It is a by-product of the solvent *turpentine.* Turpentine is made by distilling the sap of the long-leaf pine tree. Turpentine makes an excellent solvent for natural varnish.

TYPE OF VARNISH	COMPOSITION	USE
LONG OIL MARINE OR SPAR VARNISH	40 TO 100 GALLONS (151 TO 378L) OF OIL PER 100 LBS. (45 Kg) OF RESIN.	WEATHERPROOFING BOATS AND OTHER MARINE EQUIPMENT. FORMS A DURABLE, FLEXIBLE COATING.
MEDIUM OIL FLOOR VARNISH	12 TO 40 (45 TO 151L) OF OIL PER 100 LBS. (45 Kg) OF RESIN.	FINISHING HARDWOOD FLOORS AND HAND RAILS. FORMS A HARD, DURABLE COATING.
SHORT OIL CABINET OR RUBBING VARNISH	5 TO 12 GALLONS (19 TO 45L) OF OIL PER 100 LBS. (45 Kg) OF RESIN.	FINISHING FURNITURE AND CABINETS. FORMS A VERY HARD, BRITTLE COATING. EASILY RUBBED AND WAXED TO A HIGH LUSTER.

Figure 26-2. *Varnishes.*

Some *modified varnishes* use turpentine for their solvent, but others use *mineral spirits.* Mineral spirits is a petroleum-based solvent with qualities like turpentine. The driers found in varnish cause the oil to oxidize (mix with oxygen in the air) and harden more quickly. Figure 26-2 lists the varnish types and their uses. Use this for planning your work.

STAIN VARNISH

Stain varnish (Figure 26-3) is a varnish product that does the job of both staining and varnishing. The varnish contains dyes or pigments. The dyes and pigments give the varnish color. When stain varnish is applied, the wood takes on the color of the stain varnish.

Stain varnish provides a uniform color even when two or more woods of similar color are used. The grain will be visible through the stain varnish coating. This is because the pigments or dyes are only a small percentage of the varnish. Stain varnish is thinned with mineral spirits.

Stain varnish is not considered to be a high quality finish. This is because any scratch in the finish will show the original color of the wood. Always mix stain varnish well or the dyes and pigments will not be distributed evenly in the finish. Stain varnish is applied in the same way as other varnishes.

APPLYING VARNISH FINISHES

Varnish finishes may be applied by brushing or spraying. Varnish must be thinned for spray application. Follow the manufacturer's instructions for thinning the varnish. When brushing varnish, the first coat should be thinner than the second coat.

Figure 26-3. *Stain varnish is colored with dyes or pigments. It produces a uniform color on wood.*

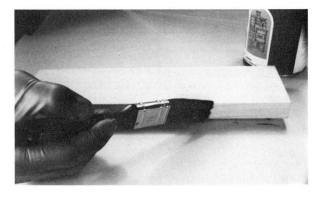

Figure 26-5. *Brush edges and ends first.*

Figure 26-4. *Stir varnish before use. Do not shake. Shaking puts bubbles in the varnish.*

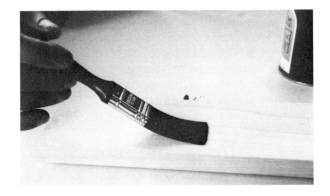

Figure 26-6. *Apply varnish along the grain. Light coats are easier to apply.*

Stir the varnish gently before using (Figure 26-4). Do not shake it. Shaking causes bubbles to form. These bubbles will damage a brushed finish because they burst after the varnish is applied. This produces a rough or pitted surface.

Select a high quality brush for applying varnish. Any loose bristles may come out in the varnish. If the bristles are blunt ended, the finish will be rough. Brush edges and ends before doing a surface (Figure 26-5). Apply the varnish with the grain (Figure 26-6). Brush strokes may then be blended by lightly brushing across the grain. Use the tip of the bristles to complete brushing with the grain.

Apply *light coats*. Two light coats are better than one heavy coat. Thick coats tend to drip. Work in the horizontal position whenever possible. This will reduce the chance of drips.

Varnish must dry completely before recoating. Drying time may vary between 2 and 24 hours. Check the manufacturer's instructions for drying time. Sand the surface lightly with 220 or 320 silicon carbide abrasive before recoating. This improves the bond between coats and makes the surface smoother.

It is important that the finishing area be dust free when applying varnish. This is because most varnishes dry slowly. Dust can become trapped in the varnish as it dries. The dust will make the finish rough. Removing dust from the finish is difficult and time-consuming. The entire finish may require sanding.

After the final coat has been allowed to dry completely, the surface may be rubbed. This is done with pumice and rottenstone or steel wool. The finish may then be waxed for protection.

Clean varnish brushes in mineral spirits after use. Store all rags in a covered container to eliminate the chance of fire.

QUESTIONS FOR REVIEW

1. What materials are combined to make varnish?
2. How do modified varnishes differ from natural varnishes?
3. What is the difference between a long oil and short oil varnish?
4. From what sources is the resin in varnish derived?
5. What solvents are commonly used to thin varnish?
6. What is stain varnish? How does it differ from other varnishes?
7. Why is it important to mix stain varnish well before application?
8. How is varnish applied?
9. What type of brush should be used to apply varnish? What type of brushing technique should you use?
10. Why is it best to apply light coats of varnish?
11. How will dust in the air affect a varnish finish?
12. Why is a varnish finish sanded lightly between coats?

SUGGESTED ACTIVITIES

1. Read the manufacturer's instructions on a can of varnish. List the type of oil and resin used in the varnish.

2. Read the manufacturer's instructions on a can of stain varnish. List the ingredients used to color the varnish.

3. Visit a paint store and list the types of varnish they sell. Are there any modified varnishes sold there?

CHAPTER 27

Lacquers and Acrylic Finishes

Lacquers and *acrylics* are clear finishes that will not yellow with age. They both dry quickly and are very popular furniture finishes. Lacquers dry by solvent evaporation. The solvent used for lacquer is *lacquer thinner*. It is a flammable liquid with a very strong odor. Lacquers should be applied only in ventilated spaces away from open flame. Lacquer thinner will soften a lacquer finish after it dries if it is allowed to contact it.

Acrylic finishes dry by chemical reaction. The most popular acrylic finishes use *water* as a solvent. Water is less expensive than petroleum solvents and it is not flammable. Acrylic finishes have no offensive odor.

KEY TERMS

lacquer	respirator
brushing lacquer	shading lacquer
acrylics	powdered stain
blushing	

LACQUER FINISHES

Lacquer finishes have become a favorite of the furniture industry. Lacquer is manufactured from wood pulp or cotton. The wood pulp or cotton is treated with acid, purified and then mixed with solvents.

Lacquer finishes dry very quickly. For this reason, most lacquer finishes are sprayed (Figure 27-1). There are some lacquers designed for brushing (Figure 27-2). These *brushing lacquers* dry much slower than spray lacquers. A *pure bristle brush* will work best with lacquer. Nylon bristles tend to soften in lacquer.

Figure 27-1. *Fast-drying lacquers are sprayed. This produces a very smooth finish.*

When brushing lacquer, dip only about one-third of the bristle length. Use long brush strokes and work with the grain. Do not over-brush the lacquer. Over brushing will cause brush marks. Avoid using spray lacquers for brushing. They dry too quickly for brush application. Clean equipment in lacquer thinner after use.

Lacquer must be applied in a well-ventilated space. Wear a *respirator* when spraying lacquer.

Figure 27-2. *Slow drying lacquers are applied with a brush. Use a pure bristle brush for best results.*

The respirator will protect you from breathing particles of overspray. Make sure no pilot light or other flame is burning while lacquer is being applied. An open flame could cause a fire or explosion. Lacquer is very flammable and will burn rapidly.

Lacquer finishes are very thin. You will need at least three coats. More coats must be applied to obtain a finish thick enough to rub or polish. Sand the finish with 320 grit abrasive between coats. This smoothes the surface and improves the bond between coats.

A lacquer finish can be rubbed out less than one hour after the final application. A surface will be dry enough to recoat 15 minutes after the lacquer is applied. Lacquer finishes may "blush" if they are applied on very humid days.

Blushing is a milky white patch that appears in the lacquer finish (Figure 27-3). It is caused by

moisture that has been trapped in the lacquer. Blushing can be eliminated if *retarder* is mixed with the lacquer. Retarder slows the drying process of the lacquer. This allows the moisture to escape.

Lacquer should be applied only over lacquer or a shellac washcoat. The lacquer solvents will dissolve most finishes applied beneath them. If lacquer dissolves the finish beneath it, the entire finish must be removed.

Lacquers may be mixed with *powdered stains* (alcohol based) to produce *shading lacquer* (Figure 27-4). Shading lacquers provide accent to moldings and carvings. Shading lacquers may also be used to hide glue blemishes. Shading lacquers are applied with an *airbrush* (Figure 27-5). Commercial shading lacquers are available in aerosol containers.

Figure 27-4. *Shading lacquers are made by mixing powdered stain with lacquer. They are used to provide accent to carvings and molding.*

Figure 27-3. *Blushing is caused by moisture trapped in the lacquer.*

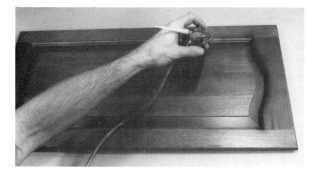

Figure 27-5. *Shading lacquer is applied with an airbrush. It is also available in aerosol form.*

211

ACRYLIC FINISHES

In the past decade clear *acrylic* finishes became a popular furniture finish. *Acrylics* have qualities similar to lacquers but none of the fire hazards. Acrylic finishes use water as a solvent. There is no danger of fire or explosion. After acrylic finishes dry, they do not soften when exposed to any solvent.

Because there is water in the acrylic finish, you must cover nails and screws with wood filler to prevent them from rusting.

Acrylic finishes may be brushed or sprayed. Wear a respirator when spraying acrylic finishes. Use a *nylon bristle brush* for brushing acrylic finishes. Pure bristles will soften in the acrylic finish. Use the same brushing procedures for acrylic finishes that you would use for lacquer finishes.

When acrylic finishes are applied, they will have a milky appearance. This will disappear as the finish dries. The milky appearance will help you see any spots that might have been missed.

Acrylic finish can be applied over almost any other finish. Drying time is about one hour. Surfaces can be recoated in two hours. It takes approximately three coats to obtain a fine acrylic finish. Sand the finish between coats with 320 grit silicon carbide abrasive. This will smooth the surface and improve the bond between coats.

Equipment may be cleaned with soap and water after use. Be sure to dry any metal equipment to avoid rust. Acrylic finishes should not be thinned. They are ready to apply from the can. Too much water in the finish will cause grain-raising problems.

QUESTIONS FOR REVIEW

1. How do lacquer and acrylic finishes dry? Can either of these finishes be softened after they dry?
2. What is brushing lacquer? How does it differ from other lacquers?
3. What causes blushing in a lacquer finish? How can it be avoided?
4. What precautions must be taken to apply lacquer safely?
5. What type of brushing techniques are used for applying lacquer and acrylic finishes? What type of brush should be used for each finish?
6. Why should lacquer and acrylic finishes be sanded between coats?
7. Should acrylic finishes be thinned?
8. How would you describe an acrylic finish? How does it differ from a lacquer finish?

SUGGESTED ACTIVITIES

1. Read the manufacturer's instructions on a can of lacquer. Make a list of the safety precautions recommended on the can.

2. Mix some shading lacquer using powdered alcohol stain. Check with your instructor before you begin. Your instructor can help you obtain the correct mix.

Paint is a general term that describes a colored opaque (not transparent) finish. All paints are surface coatings. They do not penetrate the wood. Paint can be used as a furniture finish on woods with little grain or color. It is more commonly used as a finish on houses and other wood products used outdoors.

The principle difference between paints and clear finishes such as varnish and lacquer is the presence of color. Color is provided by *pigments.* Pigments are finely ground solids that are dispersed in the paint. They can make up as much as 60 percent of the paint's ingredients. There are many kinds of paint such as *urethane, latex, enamel* and *lacquer.*

Urethane paints are much like clear polyurethane. The only difference is the presence of pigments. Enamel paint contains ingredients similar to varnish. *Lacquer paint* is a pigmented clear lacquer.

Paint may be applied in many different ways. Paint is most often applied by *brush. Roller* and *spray* applications are favored for larger jobs. This is because roller and spray applications are much faster than brush applications.

KEY TERMS

paint	semi-gloss
interior paint	gloss
exterior paint	primer
opaque	glaze
pigments	antiquing paint
urethane	roller
lacquer paint	brush
flat	spray

PAINT SELECTION

Paint is selected according to how it will be used. Paints may be classified for *interior* use or *exterior* use.

Interior paints are not tough enough to withstand severe weather. They will hold up well when used inside, but they break down rapidly outdoors. Exterior paints are much tougher. They resist fading, chipping and peeling. Good exterior paints will last five to seven years when applied correctly.

Paints may also be classified as a gloss, semi-gloss or flat paint.

Flat paints appear dull. They are commonly used as interior wall paints but may also be used as exterior house paints.

Semi-gloss paint is used as an interior paint. It is a tougher paint designed to withstand scrubbing. *Semi-gloss paint* may be used on wood trim or walls. It is commonly used as a wall paint in kitchens because it can be scrubbed.

Gloss paints are shiny. They are used for porches, decks and as exterior house paint. Gloss paint is very tough. It resists scrubbing and severe weather.

PRIMERS

Before new, unfinished wood is painted, a *primer* should be applied (Figure 28-1). A primer is a special type of paint. It is designed to improve the bond between paint and the wood. Each type of paint requires a different primer.

Figure 28-1. *New wood is coated with primer. Primer is a special type of paint. It improves the bond between paint and new wood.*

Read the manufacturer's instructions. They will tell you what type of primer is best for the job. Using thinned paint as a primer is not a substitute for commercial primer. Thinned paint does not have the same properties as a commercial primer.

GLAZES AND ANTIQUING PAINTS

Antiquing paints are interior paints that provide the base coat for an antiqued finish. Antiqued finishes make furniture appear to be older than it is. Antiquing is common on colonial furniture.

An *antiqued finish* has more than one color. After the base coat is applied, additional color is added by using *glaze.* Glaze makes moldings appear darker by providing accent. Glaze can also be used to suggest grain patterns on the painted surface.

Glaze is a thin paint. It is wiped on after the base coat dries (Figure 28-2). Glaze dries slowly. This provides enough time to wipe it into moldings and make grain-like patterns on the wood. Be sure to dispose of used rags safely.

Some antique finishes use a clear topcoat over the glaze. Follow the manufacturer's directions for applying the topcoat and for cleaning brushes.

GENERAL APPLICATION TECHNIQUES

Before you apply paint, read and follow the manufacturer's instructions. Make sure the paint is mixed well before you begin. When mixing a full can of paint, pour off some of the thin liquid on top first (Figure 28-3). This will eliminate spills. As the paint is stirred, pour back the thin liquid.

Protect any surface that will not be painted. Masking tape and newspaper or a dropcloth will protect surfaces well.

Pour some paint into the roller pan or small pail. Load your roller or brush and begin. When you apply paint with a brush, work with the grain. If a roller is used, you may also work across the

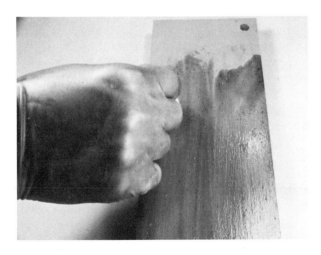

Figure 28-2. *Glaze is applied over antiquing paint for accent.*

Figure 28-3. *Pour off some of the liquid before mixing the paint. This reduces the chance of spills.*

Figure 28-4. *Rollers are often used to apply paint. Always finish with the grain.*

grain but always finish with the grain (Figure 28-4). This helps spread the paint uniformly.

Avoid thick coats of paint. Two thin coats of paint are much better than one thick coat. Thin coats dry faster and are less likely to wrinkle. When oil base paints are applied, the surfaces must be completely dry. Latex paints can be applied to damp surfaces without problems, but oil base paints will not adhere to a damp surface.

Use exterior oil paint only on a dry day. Humid (damp) weather slows drying. If rain is predicted, wait until the weather changes. Be sure the wood is dry before you paint.

Always clean painting equipment right after using. Use the solvents and cleaners recommended by the manufacturer. After the equipment is cleaned, be sure to store it properly.

QUESTIONS FOR REVIEW

1. How would you define the word *paint?*
2. How does paint differ from clear finishes such as lacquer and varnish?
3. How is paint usually applied? What other methods of application might be used on a large job?
4. How is paint selected? What type of paint would you buy for wooden siding?
5. What is the difference between a flat paint and a gloss paint?
6. For what purpose are primers used? How do you select the correct primer for the paint you are using?
7. Describe an antiqued finish. How does glaze provide accent to an antiqued finish?
8. How does glaze differ from other paints?
9. What precautions should be taken before paint is applied?
10. List some general techniques for applying paint correctly.

SUGGESTED ACTIVITIES

1. What applicators other than brushes and rollers may be used to apply paint. Visit a paint store and make a list of the types of applicators you find. Report your findings to the class.

2. Apply a coat of antiquing paint to a smooth scrap of hardboard. Apply glaze after the paint dries. Try to make the glaze look like a woodgrain pattern.

Special Finishing Effects

Often, special effects are used to enhance clear finishes. Two commonly used special effects are *distressing* and *decoupage.* Distressing includes a number of techniques that make a piece of furniture look used or older than it is. Making dark spots in the finish and dents in the molding or edges of furniture are common distressing techniques.

Decoupage is the process of embedding pictures, printed pages or small articles in a finish. Poems, souvenirs and letters of award are often used for decoupage plaques. These plaques can make a beautiful display. The clear finish looks like glass over the embedded article.

This chapter will help you learn distressing and decoupage techniques. You may want to practice these techniques on small scraps before you use them on a project. This will help you obtain good results.

KEY TERMS

distressing   glaze
decoupage   shading lacquer

DISTRESSING

Distressing may be done on the wood or as part of the finish. Distressing done on the wood includes denting, scarring or burning the wood. Distressing done in the finish includes scars and

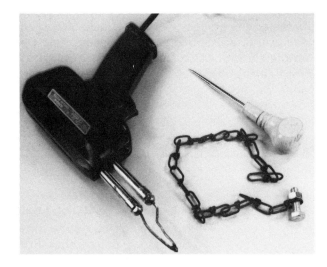

Figure 29-1. *Wood is distressed with tools like those pictured above.*

spots made in the finish with a glaze, shading lacquer or crayon.

Distressing of the wood is done with a hammer, chain, awl, woodburner or soldering iron (Figure 29-1). The wood is dented or scarred with these tools. The piece should appear worn but not destroyed. Distressing of the wood should be done before stain or finish is applied.

Plan your distressing before you begin. To look natural, there should be more wear on legs and lower molding than the sides and ends of a chest. Corners and edges of the top should appear more worn than the center. Small dents

Figure 29-2. *Lumber crayons can be used to distress the finish. Make small lines or spots on the finish.*

and scars will look more authentic than large ones. Avoid too much distressing because if the distressing is overdone, it will be distracting. Be sure to wear protective glasses when doing any type of distressing.

Distressing of the finish is done with glaze, shading lacquer and lumber crayons. Distressed finishes give the project an aged appearance. The glazes and shading lacquers are used to darken the moldings. This suggests a wax or dirt build-up. Lumber crayons can be used to make lines or spots on the wood (Figure 29-2). The lines and spots will appear as scars or dents in the wood.

Shading *lacquer* and *glaze* may also be used to speckle the finish with small dark spots. This is done with a toothbrush and a thin piece of wood. Dip the toothbrush into the glaze or shading lacquer. Then pull the piece of wood across the bristles. This will spatter the shading lacquer or

glaze onto the project in a random fashion (Figure 29-3). Be sure to pull the wood toward you to avoid spattering yourself.

Be careful not to drip shading lacquer or glaze onto the project. Too much speckling will become distracting. Some aerosol sprays are also designed to speckle a finish. Be sure to experiment on scraps of wood or poster board before finishing your project.

After the shading lacquer, glaze and lumber crayons have been used to distress the finish, apply a clear topcoat. This will make the finish appear uniform. It will also provide enough finish build-up for rubbing and polishing.

DECOUPAGE

Decoupage finishes are clear and quite thick. There are many types of commercial decoupage finishes available (Figure 29-4). Be sure to read the manufacturer's instructions before using any decoupage finish.

Figure 29-3. *Spots can be made by spattering shading lacquer with a toothbrush.*

Figure 29-4. *Decoupage materials.*

APPLY GLUE OR DECOUPAGE FINISH

CENTER PAPER AND BOND TO BOARD

SMOOTH OUT AIR BUBBLES

WORK YOUR WAY TO THE EDGES

APPLY DECOUPAGE FINISH. BE SURE THE SURFACE IS LEVEL OR THE LIQUID WILL RUN OFF

COAT EDGES

Figure 29-5. *Decoupage sequence. Two or three coats of decoupage finish may be needed. The paper should be embedded in the finish.*

ALLOW TO DRY

Figure 29-5. *Continued.*

FINISHED

The following steps for applying decoupage finishes are similar to those recommended by manufacturers (Figure 29-5).

1. Prepare the wood for a decoupage finish in the same way you would for any other finish.
2. Stain the wood if desired.
3. Seal the wood as recommended in the manufacturer's instructions.
4. Apply the decoupage finish and lay the paper or other article in the finish. Some decoupage finishes require glue to hold the paper to the wood. Allow the glue to dry before applying the decoupage finish. Be sure to smooth out wrinkles and air pockets.
5. Allow the finish to dry.
6. Apply additional coats to seal the article into the finish.
7. Rub and polish the finish in the same way you would any other finish.

QUESTIONS FOR REVIEW

1. How would you describe distressing? How is distressing done?
2. How would you describe decoupage? How is a decoupage finish applied?
3. How does distressing of the project, or wood, differ from distressing of the finish?
4. What tools are commonly used for distressing wood?
5. What materials are commonly used for distressing a finish?
6. How is speckling applied? What tools and materials are required to apply speckling?
7. Why should a topcoat be applied over a distressed finish?
8. How is a decoupage finish applied? Can you list the steps that should be followed when applying decoupage?

SUGGESTED ACTIVITIES

1. Make a plaque that can be used to decoupage some poem or souvenir.

2. Distress a scrap of stock using some of the processes discussed in this chapter.

Brushing a Finish

Even the best finishing materials will yield poor results if they are applied incorrectly. Incorrect application occurs when the brush you use is of poor quality or in poor condition. It will also occur when proper brushing techniques are not observed.

This chapter will help you identify a quality brush. It will also tell you how to use and maintain the brush correctly.

It will help you achieve good results when brushing any finishing material.

KEY TERMS

brush	wall brush
handle	flat varnish brush
plug	flat trim brush
ferrule	angular trim brush
setting compound	oval sash brush
bristles	

PARTS OF A BRUSH

There are five principal parts of a paint brush: the *handle, plug, ferrule, setting compound* and the *bristles* (Figure 30-1).

Handle

The *handle* may be made of wood or plastic. There are several handle shapes available (Figure 30-2). Choose a shape that fits your hand comfortably. A brush that is uncomfortable will cause fatigue.

Plug

The *plug* separates the bristles and forms an opening in the middle of the bristles. This opening holds paint and gives the brush a tapered shape. The plug can be made of wood or plastic. A plastic plug is best. Wood plugs absorb water and swell. This loosens the ferrule and causes bristles to fall out of the brush.

Ferrule

The *ferrule* holds the bristles and plug to the handle. It should be well attached to both the handle and the bristles. The metal used for the ferrule should be non-corrosive. Water and strong solvents used in finishing materials will cause rust.

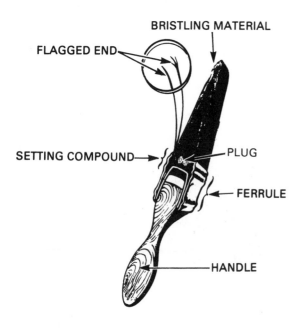

Figure 30-1. *The parts of a brush.*

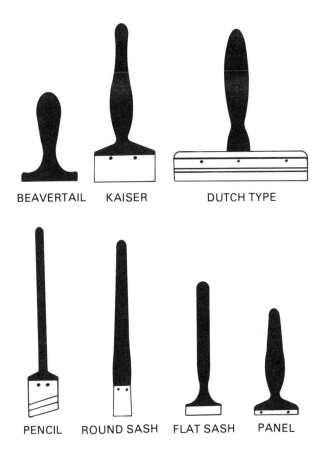

BEAVERTAIL   KAISER   DUTCH TYPE

PENCIL   ROUND SASH   FLAT SASH   PANEL

Figure 30-2. *Types of brush handles.*

Bristle

The *bristles* are the most important part of the brush. A low-quality bristle will produce a poor finish. High-quality bristles are tapered and have flagged ends (Figure 30-3). The taper causes the finishing material to flow downward and the flagged ends spread the finish evenly on the wood.

Nylon, polyester and Chinese hog bristles work best for wood finishes. Nylon and polyester bristles are synthetic, and they will not absorb water. This makes them suitable for use with water-soluble finishes. Nylon bristles tend to soften when in contact with alcohol or lacquer thinner. For this reason, they lose some snap or resilience when used to apply shellac and lacquer. Polyester bristles do not lose their snap in shellac or lacquer.

Chinese hog bristles are natural bristles. Natural bristles tend to absorb water. They lose their

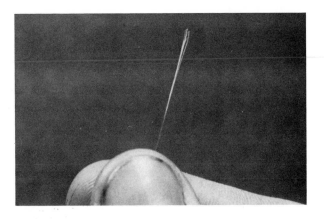

Figure 30-3. *Quality bristles have flagged ends.*

snap or resilience when used to apply water-soluble finishes.

Setting Compound

The *setting compound* holds the bristles together. Epoxy makes the best setting compound. This is because it will not dissolve when in contact with strong solvents. Inexpensive brushes with inferior setting compounds lose bristles while in use. This can damage the finish.

TYPES OF BRUSHES

The five most common brushes sold today are: the *wall brush, flat varnish brush, flat trim brush, angular trim brush* and *oval sash brush.*

Wall Brush

A *wall brush* (Figure 30-4) is used for painting walls or siding. It is usually 4" (100 mm) wide and has bristles 5" long (125 mm). The brush is large. It is able to carry a large load of paint. This is important when painting large surfaces.

WALL BRUSH

Figure 30-4. *This wall brush is used for painting large surfaces. Walls and siding are commonly painted with a wall brush.*

Flat Varnish Brush

Flat varnish brushes (Figure 30-5) are available in widths from 1" to 3" (25 to 75 mm). They are used to apply varnish and enamel to trim and furniture.

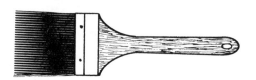

FLAT VARNISH BRUSH

Figure 30-5. *Flat varnish brushes are used to apply varnish and enamel.*

Flat Trim Brush

Flat trim brushes (Figure 30-6) are like flat varnish brushes except the bristles have chiseled ends. Flat trim brushes work very well for trimming window sashes. They are most often used by painters for precise trim work but may also be used to apply clear finishes.

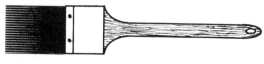

FLAT SASH AND TRIM BRUSH

Figure 30-6. *Flat trim brushes have a chiseled end. They work well for trimming windows.*

Angular Trim Brushes

The *angular trim brush* (Figure 30-7) has a chiseled and angular end. The angular bristles make it easier to trim corners. Angular trim

ANGULAR SASH AND TRIM BRUSH

Figure 30-7. *Angular trim brushes have a chisel shape and an angular end. They work well for trimming corners.*

brushes are seldom used for any job except trimming.

Oval Sash Brush

Oval sash brushes (Figure 30-8) are popular among some painters for trim work. They are available in diameters from ½" to 2" (12 mm to 50 mm). Oval sash brushes are seldom used for any job except trimming.

OVAL SASH BRUSH

Figure 30-8. *Oval sash brushes are used for trim work. The size is determined by diameter.*

SELECTING A BRUSH

When selecting a brush, you must consider the type of job being done and the type of finishing material being used (Figure 30-9). The brush you choose should fit the job. You would not want to apply varnish with a wall brush or apply paste wood filler with a high-quality brush.

SELECTING A BRUSH

BRISTLES
  TAPERED/DIFFERENT LENGTHS
  FLAGGED ENDS
  SUITED TO YOUR FINISH
  QUANTITY OF BRISTLES (FAN TEST)
  CORRECT WIDTH FOR THE JOB

PLUG AND SETTING COMPOUND
  SMALL PLUG
  PLASTIC OR RUBBER PLUG (WOOD SWELLS)
  EPOXY SETTING COMPOUND
  BRISTLES DO NOT SHED

FERRULE
  BONDED WELL TO HANDLE
  MADE OF NON-CORROSIVE METAL

HANDLE
  FEELS COMFORTABLE
  WELL BALANCED

Figure 30-9. *Brush selection.*

QUALITY BRUSH

INFERIOR BRUSH

Figure 30-10. *Bend the bristles into a fan shape. Quality brushes will have no gaps.*

Nylon bristles are best suited to water-soluble finishes. Polyester bristles work well in all finishes and Chinese hog bristles work best in finishes that do not contain water. Select bristles according to the type of finish being used.

Check the bristles when you buy the brush. Are they flagged? Are there enough bristles to do the job? Bend the bristles in your hand. They should form a fan with no gaps (Figure 30-10, *top*). A gap indicates that there are too few bristles to do a good job (Figure 30-10, *bottom*).

The ferrule should be anchored tightly to the handle. Make sure that it is made of a rust-resistant material. Check to see if the plug is

wood or plastic. Avoid brushes with wooden plugs. They will swell in water.

Also determine what type of setting compound was used to secure the bristles. Epoxy works best. Pull the bristles lightly through your thumb and forefinger. If the brush tends to shed, the setting compound may be weak.

Grip the brush. It should feel comfortable and balanced. Uncomfortable or poorly balanced brushes cause fatigue. Buy the best brush available. If well cared for, it will last a long time and produce quality finishes.

GOOD BRUSHING TECHNIQUES

When a brush is used correctly, it will last indefinitely and produce good results. The following techniques will help you use the brush correctly:

1. Remove any loose bristles from the brush before you begin.
2. Soak natural bristles in linseed oil for 24 hours before use. This will reduce water absorption.
3. Select a brush of the correct size. Use a small brush for trim work and a large brush for house painting. Painting small items with a large brush will cause the bristles to "fishtail" (Figure 30-11).

FISHTAIL

Figure 30-11. *Painting small items with a wide brush can cause fishtailing. A fishtailed brush works poorly.*

FINGERING

Figure 30-12. *Fingering is caused by poking a brush into corners or using it sideways.*

4. Avoid poking a brush into a corner or using a brush sideways. These practices break the bristles and cause "fingering" (Figure 30-12).
5. Load only ⅓ to ½ of the bristles with finishing material. If the brush is overloaded, paint will dry in the heel or spatter on the wood.
6. If the brush is overloaded, tap the bristles against the side of the can. Avoid dragging the bristles across the rim of the can. This can damage the bristles.
7. If you are right-handed, work from left to right. Left-handed persons should work from right to left. Keep the light between you and the surface. This helps you see any spots that are missed.
8. Take long strokes with your brush. Work from wet to dry areas. Apply the finishing material with the grain. Avoid overbrushing which leaves brush marks.
9. Work carefully along edges and ends. Watch for drips or runs. They can be removed easily when the finish is wet. When drips and runs harden, they are difficult to remove.
10. When the job is complete, clean and store your brush properly.

CLEANING A BRUSH

A brush must be cleaned immediately after use. If it is not, the finishing material will harden in

the brush and ruin it. Be sure to protect your hands and eyes when cleaning your brush. The following steps tell you how to clean a brush correctly:

1. Unload the brush. Brush excess finishing material in the bristles onto a piece of newspaper (Figure 30-13).
2. Rinse the brush in a small can of solvent (Figure 30-14). Make sure all finishing materi-

Figure 30-13. *Unload your brush on newspaper before cleaning. This reduces the amount of solvent needed to clean the brush.*

Figure 30-14. *Rinse the brush in solvent. Make sure all residue is removed from the brush.*

al is removed. Repeat this step if necessary. Figure 30-15 shows correct solvents for different jobs.

3. Remove excess solvent from the brush. Make sure all finishing material has been removed from the heel area of the brush.

4. Rinse the brush with soap and water (Figure 30-16).

5. Remove water from the brush and shape the bristles.

BRUSH CLEANING SOLVENTS	
MATERIAL	**SOLVENT**
STAINS	
WATER	WATER
OIL	TURPENTINE OR MINERAL SPIRITS
ALCOHOL	ALCOHOL
GELLED	TURPENTINE OR MINERAL SPIRITS
LATEX	WATER
NGR	SEE MANUFACTURER'S INSTRUCTIONS
CLEAR FINISHES	
SHELLAC	ALCOHOL
LACQUER	LACQUER THINNER
VARNISH	MINERAL SPIRITS OR TURPENTINE
POLYURETHANE	MINERAL SPIRITS OR TURPENTINE
ACRYLIC	WATER
PAINTS	
OIL BASE	TURPENTINE OR MINERAL SPIRITS
LATEX	WATER
ENAMEL	TURPENTINE OR MINERAL SPIRITS
OILS AND PASTE WOOD FILLER	
TUNG OIL	TURPENTINE OR MINERAL SPIRITS
LINSEED OIL	TURPENTINE OR MINERAL SPIRITS
PASTE WOOD FILLER	TURPENTINE OR MINERAL SPIRITS

Figure 30-15. *Brush cleaning solvents.*

Figure 30-16. *Rinsing the brush with soap and water removes solvent residue.*

6. Wrap the brush in newspaper (Figure 30-17). This will protect the bristles and hold them in the correct shape.

7. Hang the brushes or store them in a flat position. This will keep the bristles from bending.

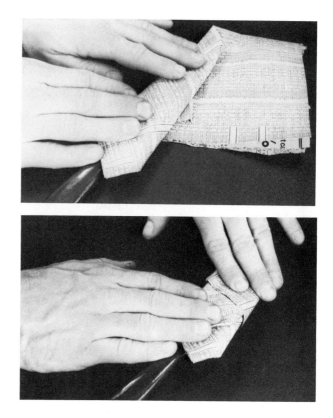

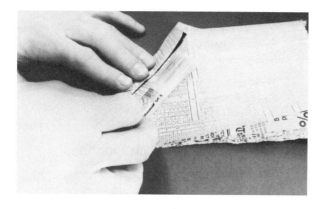

Figure 30-17. *Wrapping the bristles protects them. It also holds them in the correct shape.*

QUESTIONS FOR REVIEW

1. What are the five principal parts of a paint brush? What is the function of each?
2. Name the five most common types of paint brushes.
3. What considerations should be made when selecting a brush for any finishing job?
4. How do you identify a brush of high quality?
5. What brushing techniques can you recommend for obtaining a high-quality finish?
6. What brushing techniques can you recommend to prolong brush life?
7. What causes bristles to "finger"?
8. How do you unload too much paint?
9. Can you list the seven steps that must be performed to clean a brush properly?
10. Why should you wrap a brush in newspaper after cleaning it?

SUGGESTED ACTIVITIES

1. Visit a paint or hardware store and compare the quality of the paint brushes sold there. Use the chart in this chapter to select a high-quality brush. Describe the brushes and their qualities to your class.

2. Demonstrate the correct procedure for cleaning a brush.

3. Check the paint brushes in your home to be sure they are stored correctly. Make a list of the types of brushes you have.

CHAPTER 31

Spraying a finish is faster than brushing. Most industries prefer to spray their products because it is faster and less expensive. Spray systems are also set up in some woodworking shops. These systems speed the finishing process.

Shops that do not have a spray system may use *aerosol* finishes. Canned aerosol finishes can produce the same results as any other spray system. In order to use any spray equipment successfully, you must understand how the equipment works and know how it is adjusted.

KEY TERMS

siphon spray system	nozzle
air horns	test pattern
spray pattern	airbrush
transformer	aerosol
regulator	propellant

SIPHON SPRAY SYSTEMS

In a *siphon spray system,* air travels from a compressor to a *transformer* which regulates the pressure. The compressed air then runs to the spray gun. When you pull the trigger, the air travels through the gun and forms a vacuum at the nozzle. The vacuum lifts the finishing material from the cup and mixes it with compressed air as it leaves the nozzle (Figure 31-1). The compressed air that comes through the *air horns* forms the *spray pattern* into a cone or fan shape.

The amount of air going through the air horns is adjusted at the back of the gun (Figure 31-2). The pattern control knob regulates the amount of air going through the air horns.

The lower knob is the *fluid control knob* (Figure 31-2). It controls the amount of finishing material passing through the nozzle. Adjust the fluid

Figure 31-1. *Siphon guns used compressed air to lift finishing material from the cup.*

SPRAY GUN

AIR HOSE

CUP

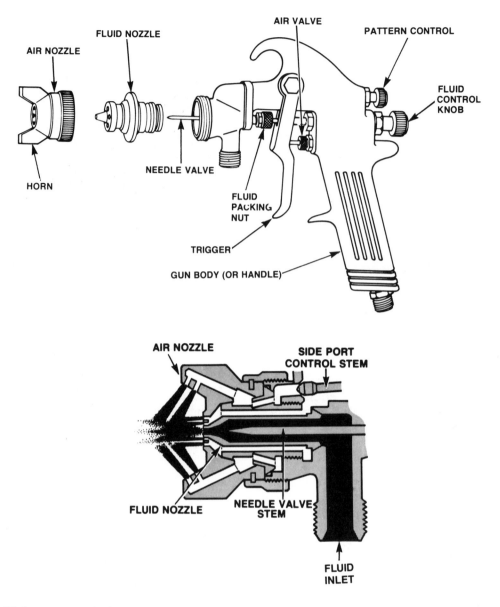

Figure 31-2. *Siphon gun controls.*

control knob so that the work looks wet when the finish is sprayed on.

The air pressure to the gun is adjusted at the transformer or regulator (Figure 31-3). As the handle on the transformer is turned clockwise, air pressure is increased. Adjust the air pressure between 25 and 40 psi (pounds per square inch). The transformer is located near the spray booth (usually on the wall) between the compressor and the gun.

Setting Up the Gun for Spraying
Before you set up the gun for spraying, make sure that you have a respirator and protective glasses. Check the ventilation through the booth to be sure it is working correctly. Observe all fire regulations during the entire spraying operation.

Thin the finishing material according to the manufacturer's instructions and fill the cup about two thirds. Attach the cup to the gun. Check the siphon hole on the gun to be sure it is

Figure 31-3. *Air pressure is adjusted at the transformer. Turn the handle clockwise to increase air pressure.*

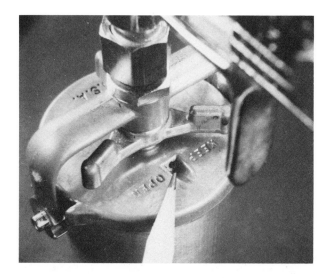

Figure 31-4. *Check the siphon hole before spraying. If it is blocked, the finishing material cannot be lifted.*

not blocked (Figure 31-4). If it is blocked, the finishing material cannot be lifted from the cup. Use a piece of wood to clear the hole. Never use

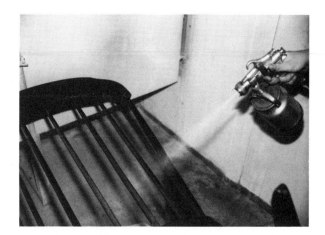

Figure 31-5. *Adjust the air horns to be parallel to the direction of gun travel.*

wire to clear holes on the spray gun because wire will change the hole diameter and damage the gun.

Install the air nozzle on the front of the gun. Turn the horns parallel to the direction of gun travel (Figure 31-5). Adjust the transformer to between 25 and 40 psi.

Spray a *test pattern* on paper or poster board to adjust the gun. Adjust the fan pattern and the fluid to the nozzle. The pattern should fit the part being finished. Use a wide fan pattern for large flat pieces. Use round patterns for table legs and other narrow pieces.

Adjust the fluid control so that a wet coat is applied. A wet coat flows on the wood and produces a smooth surface. If drips or runs appear, the coat is too wet. If the finishing material appears rough when it hits the wood, it is too dry.

If the finishing material tends to bounce off your test piece, lower the air pressure at the transformer.

After you have adjusted the gun, you are ready to begin spraying. For best results, you should spray at the lowest possible air pressure. This pressure will vary according to the thickness of the finishing material and the length of the air hose.

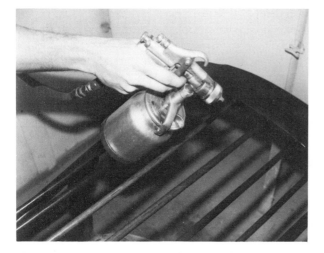

Figure 31-6. *Spray edges and corners before spraying large surfaces.*

Good Spraying Techniques

When a spray finish is applied correctly, it produces good results. The following spraying techniques will help you use the spray gun correctly.

1. Take a test pattern on a piece of paper or poster board to be sure the gun is adjusted correctly.
2. Spray edges and corners before spraying a large flat surface (Figure 31-6).
3. Keep the gun 10 to 12 inches from the work. Make sure the gun remains parallel to the work (Figure 31-7).
4. Trigger the gun off the work (Figure 31-8). Triggering the gun on the work will cause drips or runs.
5. Overlap strokes by 50 percent.
6. Clean gun thoroughly after use.

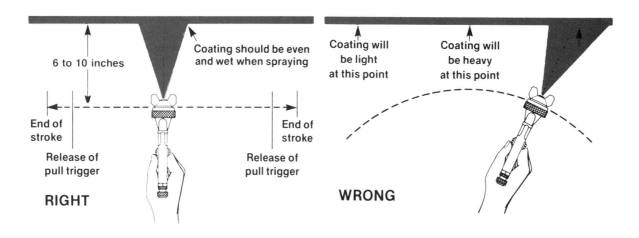

Figure 31-7. *Keep the gun parallel to the work when spraying.*

Figure 31-8. *Trigger the gun off the work. Be sure to overlap each stroke by 50%.*

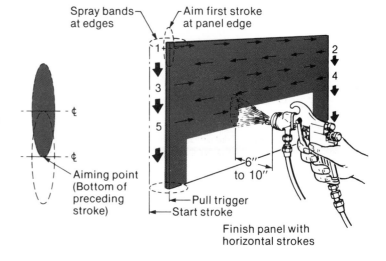

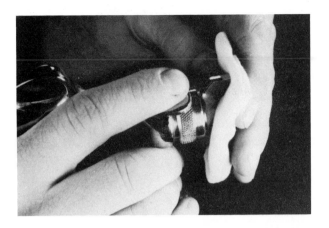

Figure 31-9. *Cover the air nozzle with a rag after the siphon tube is lifted out of the cup for backflushing. Then pull the trigger to flush the gun of finishing material.*

Figure 31-10. *The air brush is used for shading and touch-up work.*

Cleaning the Gun

After use, rinse the gun thoroughly with the solvent recommended by the manufacturer. If no solvent is specified, refer to Chapter 30, Figure 30-15, to determine the correct solvent.

Release the cup from the gun. Hold the siphon tube just above the cup and backflush the gun by covering the air nozzle with a rag and then triggering the gun. Any finishing material will be backflushed out the siphon tube. Figure 31-9 illustrates how to backflush a gun.

Remove the finishing material from the cup. Fill the cup one-third full of solvent and connect the cup to the gun. Spray the solvent through the gun. This will flush the gun.

Check the siphon hole to be sure it is clean. Wipe off the air nozzle and the outside of the gun. Make sure the holes in the air nozzle are clear. Return the gun to storage when it is clean.

THE AIRBRUSH

The *airbrush* is a small siphon gun. It is used for spraying small objects, for touch-up work, and for applying shading lacquer (Figure 31-10). The airbrush has two adjustments (Figure 31-11). Air pressure at the gun is controlled by turning the wheel below the trigger. The fan or spray pattern is controlled by turning a knurled ring located behind the spray nozzle.

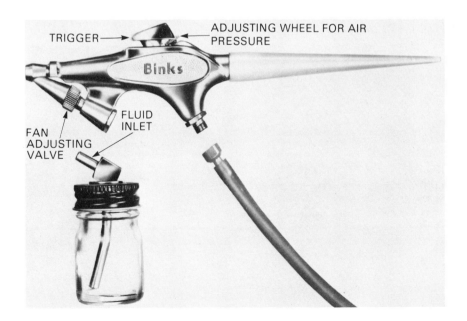

Figure 31-11. *Air brush controls.*

Air brushes use 8 to 20 psi air pressure for spraying. Adjust the fan pattern to suit the job. Check the siphon hole in the top of the cup to be sure it is clean. If the siphon hole is clogged, the gun will "spit" or spray in spurts. Use a wide pattern to spray a small object. The pattern should be smaller for applying shading lacquer. Always take a test pattern on paper or poster board before you begin. Air brushes are used in the same manner as other siphon spray guns.

Clean the air brush by rinsing it with solvent after use. It does not require backflushing. Be sure the airbrush has been cleaned thoroughly or it will work poorly the next time it is used. Check the siphon hole.

AEROSOL FINISHES

Aerosol finishes are stored in cans under pressure. The gas used for pressure is called a *propellant.* The propellant forces the finish through the nozzle when the nozzle is depressed. Aerosol finishes are used to spray small objects, touch up finishes or add accent to a finish.

Some aerosol finishes have two spray patterns. By turning the nozzle, the pattern can be changed. Always shake the aerosol can before starting to spray. Test the spray pattern or paper or poster board before you begin.

Trigger an aerosol spray like a spray gun (Figure 31-12). Apply light coats to avoid drips or runs. A 50 percent overlap works best with aerosol finishes. Work from a wet surface to a wet

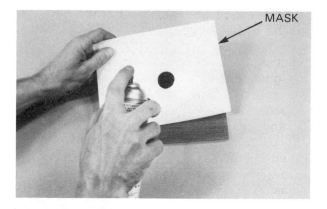

Figure 31-13. *When touching up a finish, the cardboard mask protects the rest of the finish from overspray.*

Figure 31-14. *Aerosol shading lacquers are used to accent the finish by darkening edges and moldings.*

Figure 31-12. *Trigger aerosol spray in the same way as a spray gun.*

Figure 31-15. *Clear the nozzle by inverting the can and depressing the nozzle. This forces all material out of the nozzle.*

surface whenever possible. This will make the finish appear smoother when dry.

Most aerosol finishes are flammable. Avoid using them near an open flame. Make sure that the space is well ventilated when applying aerosol finishes. Protect yourself with a respirator and glasses when applying aerosol finishes.

Avoid using aerosol finishes at temperatures below 68°F (20°C). Cool temperatures reduce the pressure of the propellant. This means that the finish will not be applied at the correct pressure. Reduced pressure can cause the spray to spit or spray unevenly.

Aerosol finishes work well for touching up a finish. The edges of a touch-up can be feathered by spraying through a cardboard mask (Figure 31-13). The mask protects the finish from spatter and yields a better touch-up finish.

Aerosol shading lacquers are also available. They are used for accent work on molding or edges (Figure 31-14). Apply shading lacquer in thin coats. Any drips or runs could ruin the entire finish. Be sure to test the color and spray pattern on a piece of scrap. If the color does not suit the wood, try a different color.

After you use an aerosol finish, clean the nozzle. Invert the can and depress the valve (Figure 31-15). This removes all finishing material from the nozzle. Store aerosol finish away from heat. Excess heat could cause the can to burst or explode.

QUESTIONS FOR REVIEW

1. How does a siphon spray gun lift the finishing material from the cup?
2. What function does the air nozzle serve? How are the horns on the air nozzle adjusted for spraying?
3. What function does the regulator or transformer serve? How is it adjusted?
4. Briefly describe the procedure for setting up a spray gun. What safety precautions must be observed?
5. How is the fan pattern on a spray gun adjusted?
6. What air pressure is suitable for applying a finish with a siphon gun?
7. What is the function of a test pattern? How is the test pattern made?
8. Why is a wet coat desirable when applying a spray finish?
9. List some spraying techniques for applying a finish.
10. How is the spray gun cleaned? Why is the gun backflushed?
11. How is the airbrush adjusted?
12. What forces the finishing material from an aerosol container?
13. What safety precautions must be observed when you apply spray finishes?
14. How does a cardboard mask improve touch-up jobs done with aerosol finishes?
15. How is the nozzle of an aerosol finish cleaned?
16. How should an aerosol can be stored when not in use?

SUGGESTED ACTIVITIES

1. Name the parts and controls on the spray gun found in your shop.

2. Demonstrate the correct way to clean the spray gun in your shop.

3. Ask your instructor if you can set up the spray gun. Practice spraying on a piece of cardboard. This will help you gain experience.

32 Rubbing and Polishing a Finish

Rubbing and *polishing* are the final steps in finishing your project. Rubbing is done with a fine abrasive. The rubbing operation levels the finish and increases the gloss or light-reflecting quality of the finish. For rubbing use abrasives such as pumice, rottenstone, steel wool and 320 to 600 grit silicon carbide abrasives.

Polishing is done after rubbing. Polish the finish for protection. Two common polishes are wax and lemon oil.

KEY TERMS

rubbing	steel wool
polishing	wool wax
pumice	flax soap
rottenstone	paste wax
silicon carbide	liquid polish

RUBBING A FINISH

Finishes can be *rubbed* in many different ways. Most methods use an abrasive and a lubricant. The lubricant reduces friction and keeps the finish from sticking to the abrasive. The three most common rubbing methods are: pumice or rottenstone with oil, silicon carbide abrasives with water, or steel wool with flax soap or wool wax.

Before using any rubbing technique, make sure the finish is dry. If less than three coats of finish have been applied, you may rub through the finish. Work slowly and carefully. Check your progress frequently. Rubbing through the finish can cause many extra hours of work.

Pumice and Rottenstone

Pumice and *rottenstone* (Figure 32-1) are very fine abrasives. Pumice is somewhat coarser than rottenstone. It is used before the rottenstone. There are three grades of pumice F, FF, and FFF. The finest pumice is FFF. Rubbing with pumice and rottenstone produces a very glossy finish. Mix pumice with rubbing oil to form a paste (Figure 32-2). Then dip a felt pad into the paste. Use the pad like a sanding block.

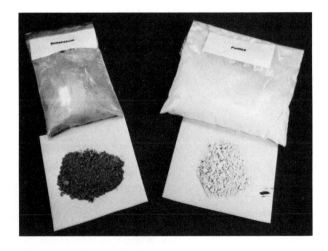

Figure 32-1. *These materials are used to rub a finish. Rubbing is done to level the finish and increase its gloss. Pumice and rottenstone are very fine abrasives. Pumice is used first because it is coarser.*

Figure 32-2. *Pumice or rottenstone is mixed with rubbing oil. When a paste is formed, rubbing can begin.*

Rub with the grain (Figure 32-3). Be careful when rubbing corners and edges. It is easy to rub through the finish at these points. Remove the pumice residue after it has been rubbed over the entire finish. Use a soft cloth.

Mix the rottenstone with rubbing oil and begin rubbing the finish. Use the same procedure for rottenstone as you used for pumice. The finish should appear smooth and glossy after the rottenstone has been rubbed onto the finish.

Clean all residue from the finish when the rubbing operation is completed. The finish is now ready for polishing. On some finishes, rottenstone may not be needed. The finish will be smooth enough after using pumice.

Figure 32-3. *The paste is rubbed on the finish with a felt block.*

Silicon Carbide Abrasives

Silicon carbide abrasives work well for rubbing a finish. Abrasive grits of 320 to 600 are most often used. Water is used as a lubricant with silicon carbide abrasives. Rubbing a finish with silicon carbide abrasives and water is commonly called *wet sanding.*

Wet sanding is one of the easiest ways to rub out a finish, but it may be used only on waterproof or water-resistant finishes. Wet sanding is not recommended for shellac finishes.

Wrap the abrasive around a felt or rubber block. Apply a few drops of water to the finish. Push the abrasive through the water and sand with the grain (Figure 32-4). The water will keep the finish

Figure 32-4. *Push the abrasive through the water. Keep the abrasive wet. Work with the grain.*

Figure 32-5. *Wool wax is pushed into a small piece of steel wool. Steel wool should be dampened before adding wool wax.*

Figure 32-6. *Rub the finish with the grain. Add wool wax to the pad when needed.*

from loading the abrasive. Keep the abrasive wet, but do not flood the surface. Check frequently so that you do not rub through the finish.

After all sanding has been done, remove any residue with a soft damp cloth. Wet sanding produces a low gloss or satin finish. Protect the finish with polish after rubbing.

Steel Wool
Steel wool works quite well for rubbing out a finish. The lubricant used with steel wool is *flax soap* or *wool wax.* Squeeze the paste-like lubricants into the steel wool before use (Figure 32-5).

Steel wool comes in the following grades: 3, 2, 1, 0, 00, 000, and 0000. Grades 000 and 0000 are very fine. They are well suited to rubbing a finish. Coarser grades such as 3 and 2 work well for removing old finishes.

Begin the rubbing operation by dampening a small pad of fine steel wool with water. Squeeze some flax soap or wool wax into the pad. Rub the finish with the grain (Figure 32-6). Be careful near corners and edges. It is easy to rub through the finish.

Remove the flax soap residue with a damp cloth. Allow the surface to dry before polishing.

POLISHES
Polishes are applied over wood finishes to protect them and increase their brilliance. Many products are sold for polishing wood finishes. The most common wood polishes include *paste wax, lemon oil* and *liquid polish* (Figure 32-7). Most polishes are combustible and should not be used near fire. Be sure to read the manufacturer's instructions before use.

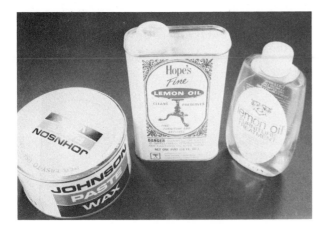

Figure 32-7. *These materials are used to polish a finish. Polish is applied to protect the finish.*

Figure 32-9. *Paste wax is applied with a soft cloth. Avoid thick coats. They tend to gather dust and streak.*

Figure 32-8. *Paste waxes.*

Paste Wax

Paste wax (Figure 32-8) is a combination of natural and synthetic waxes in a petroleum based solvent. It is a solid that softens when rubbed or heated. Some paste waxes are colored. They are used on dark finishes.

Paste wax is applied with a soft clean cloth (Figure 32-9). Avoid thick coats of wax. Thick coats cause streaks and tend to attract dust. Allow the wax to dry for 15 minutes after application. When the wax is dry, polish the surface with a lamb's wool buffer or with a soft cloth.

Lemon Oil

Lemon oil polishes usually contain oil extracted from lemon grass. These oils are mixed with petroleum based solvents. Lemon oil polishes are liquids. They are wiped onto the finish with a clean soft cloth.

Avoid thick applications of lemon oil finish. Thick applications will attract dust. Lemon oil polish does not require buffing after application. If a thick coat is applied, however, it will require buffing.

Some lemon oil polishes are sold in aerosol containers. Read and follow the manufacturer's instructions before using them.

Liquid Polish

Liquid polishes contain wax and other ingredients. Some contain cleaners. They remove dirt from the finish and protect it with a wax.

There are many types of liquid polish. Before using any of them, be sure to read the manufacturer's instructions. Most liquid polishes are wiped onto the finish with a clean soft cloth and allowed to dry. The polish is then buffed to remove any residue.

After a finish has been polished, it is difficult to refinish. This is because most waxes contain silicone. Any finishing material applied over silicone will cause a crater-like appearance on the surface. Always clean a finished surface before refinishing. Special cleaners are available for this job.

QUESTIONS FOR REVIEW

1. How would you define *rubbing?* How does rubbing differ from polishing?
2. What materials are used for rubbing out a finish?
3. Why is a lubricant used when rubbing out a finish?
4. How is pumice graded? Is pumice coarser than rottenstone?
5. Why must you be careful when rubbing out corners and edges?
6. What is wet sanding? Is wet sanding done to rub out a finish?
7. What grade of steel wool is used for rubbing out a finish? What lubricant is used with steel wool?
8. Why is a finish polished? What common polishes are used on wood finishes?
9. How is a paste wax polish applied?
10. How is a lemon oil polish applied?
11. Why is it difficult to refinish a polished surface?

SUGGESTED ACTIVITIES

1. Examine the rubbing and polishing materials used in your shop. Read the manufacturer's instructions. Make a list of the lubricants that may be used with each rubbing material.

2. Find out what type of polish is used on furniture in your home. Would you describe it as a paste wax, liquid polish or lemon oil?

SECTION 6

Power Tools

CHAPTER 33

Power Tool Safety

Power tools perform the same operations as hand woodworking tools, but power tools are faster than hand tools. The additional speed of power tools limits your reaction time if you make a mistake. This means that you will have to plan the job carefully to avoid mistakes or accidents.

Planning your work can be divided into four areas: *personal protection, material handling, power tool features,* and *power tool adjustment.* These four areas of knowledge will help you operate power tools safely and efficiently.

KEY TERMS

personal protection	push stick
protective glasses	push shoe
face shields	feather board
respirator	V block
ear plugs	ground
hearing protectors	double insulated
kickback	owner's manual

PERSONAL PROTECTION

When working with power tools there are many hazards from which you must protect yourself. The woodworking shop has dust, flying wood chips, noise, rotating shafts, sharp cutting tools and rough stock. All of these hazards can injure or harm you if you do not protect yourself.

Personal protective equipment has been designed to guard against injury. This equipment is used by athletes and workers where hazards exist. There are hazards in a woodworking shop. You should always wear personal protective equipment.

Figure 33-1. *Protective glasses should be worn at all times in a woodworking shop.*

Eye protection (Figure 33-1) is essential when you work in the wood shop. Flying wood chips and dust can cause eye discomfort and possible injury. *Protective glasses* eliminate any chance of chips striking your eyes.

In addition, you should wear a *face shield* (Figure 33-2) when you use bits or cutters with carbide tips. The face shield will protect your face and eyes if a carbide tip should shatter. A face shield also makes it easier to see what your tool is doing. No sawdust or chips strike your face or eyes when you wear a face shield. As a result, you can guide the tool or work better.

When performing sanding operations, be sure to use the dust collection system. If your shop does not have a dust collection system, wear a *respi-*

Figure 33-2. *A face shield will protect you from flying chips. Wear a face shield when using carbide cutters.*

Figure 33-3. *Respirators protect you from dust or vapor in the air. Wear a respirator when sanding or performing other dusty operations.*

Figure 33-4. *Hearing protectors and ear plugs protect your hearing from loud noises.*

rator (Figure 33-3). The respirator will filter dust particles from the air you breathe.

The noise level in some wood shops exceeds the 90-decibel level recommended by the Occupational Safety and Health Act (OSHA). Prolonged exposure to this noise can cause a hearing loss. You can protect your hearing with *ear plugs* or *hearing protectors* (Figure 33-4). Both ear plugs and hearing protectors seal out most noise and protect your hearing from damage.

Rotating blades, cutters and shafts may also present a hazard. A loose shirt sleeve can become wound into any rotating object and pull you toward it. Always roll your sleeves up above your elbow and tuck in your blouse or shirt. Remove rings, watches and neckties. These objects may catch on a rotating blade, cutter or shaft.

Some people wear gloves to protect their hands from slivers when moving rough stock. Gloves may be worn when moving rough stock, but they should not be worn when machining stock. A glove can become caught in a rotating blade or cutter and pull your hand into it. Do not wear gloves when you machine stock.

Long hair may also become entangled in a cutter or rotating shaft. Tie hair back or restrain it under a cap.

MATERIAL HANDLING

Handling material near power tools or feeding material into power tools requires your complete attention. There should be no distractions. Before you machine stock in the wood shop, plan your work. Allow plenty of time for the operation. Rushing a job may cause an accident or ruin the piece. Make sure the machining sequence allows safe handling of the stock.

Check your stock before you feed it into a machine. Make sure that the stock is large enough to be machined safely. Use hand tools to shape or cut small pieces. Check the piece to see if it has been planed. Certain machines, such as the table saw, cannot safely cut rough stock. Stock with knots and other defects should be cut into smaller pieces with the defects removed.

Do not stand behind stock when feeding it into a machine. The stock could kickback. A *kickback* pushes the stock back out of the machine with great force. A kickback is caused when stock is pinched between a cutter or blade and a stationary object like the fence. If you stand to the side of your work, you should be clear of any stock that kicks back. Feed stock into the cutter. Do not force the stock, let the cutter do the work.

If a piece of stock is too large or difficult to feed into a machine, get help. Sometimes you can clamp the piece and machine it with portable power tools. Small portable power tools will be easier to handle than large pieces of stock (Figure 33-5).

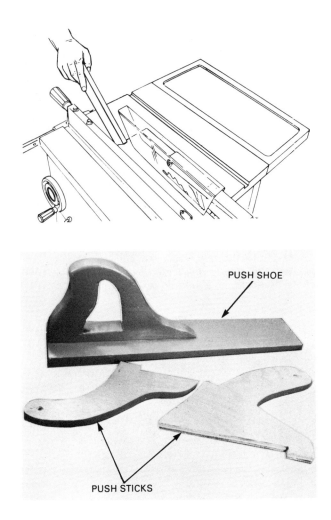

Figure 33-6. *Push sticks and push shoes protect your hands from blades and cutters.*

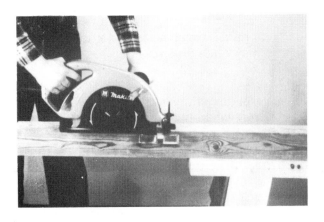

Figure 33-5. *Large pieces can be cut with portable power tools. It is easier to handle the tool than the work.*

Some pieces of stock should be fed with a *push stick* or *push shoe* (Figure 33-6). These are shop-made devices used to control stock. They keep your hands clear of the blade or cutter, but maintain complete control of the stock.

Another shop-made device that can be used to hold stock against a fence or table is the *feather board* (Figure 33-7). The feather board acts like a spring to hold stock against a surface while it is fed into the machine. A feather board should not be installed next to the blade or cutter because it may pinch the stock and cause a kickback.

Some material you handle will be irregular in shape. Irregularly shaped pieces require special holding devices. Round stock should be placed in a *V block* for most machining procedures

Figure 33-7. *The feather board acts like a spring. It holds stock against the fence or table. The guard has been removed for this photo. Always use the guard when sawing.*

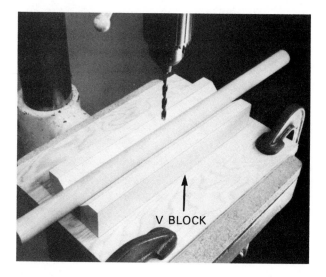

Figure 33-8. *Round stock should be held in a V block for machining.*

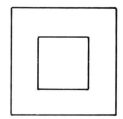

Figure 33-9. *This symbol means the handle of the tool is insulated. This type of tool does not need a three-prong plug.*

(Figure 33-8). Other shapes will require a special holding fixture. The type of fixture will vary with the job.

POWER TOOL FEATURES

The features of any power tool affect its safe operation. There are many features you should look for when you purchase or use a power tool. All tools should be *grounded* or *double-insulated* to protect you from electrical shock. Figure 33-9 shows the symbol for a double-insulated tool. Grounded plugs should be used only in grounded outlets (Figure 33-10). A grounded or double-insulated tool will protect you in normal conditions, but should not be used in damp or wet locations.

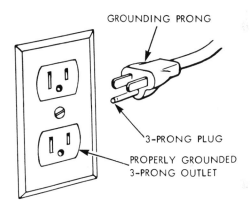

Figure 33-10. *Grounded plugs (three-prong) must be used in a grounded outlet.*

A power tool should also have enough horse-power to do the job without stalling or slowing down. Tools with too little power tend to chatter and are difficult to control. When they slow down, they burn and dull the cutting tool.

Power tools should also be equipped with appropriate guards to protect the operator. Figure 33-11 shows a plastic guard being used on a table saw. These guards should be strong, durable and easy to adjust. They should not make the tool difficult to use.

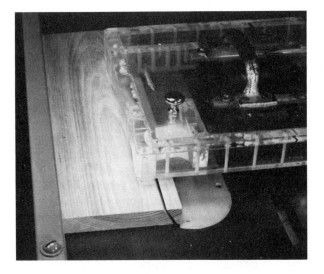

Figure 33-11. *This guard is strong and durable. Make sure all power tools have a guard. The guard should not make operation difficult.*

Power tools should feature quiet operation. Power tools that operate at a high noise level require that you wear hearing protectors or ear plugs. Failure to do so could cause a hearing loss. Check the owner's manual to determine the operating noise level of the tool.

Before you use any power tool, become familiar with its operating features. Study the *owner's manual* (Figure 33-12) and learn how to operate the power tool correctly and safely. Make sure that you know how to adjust it, maintain it and operate it.

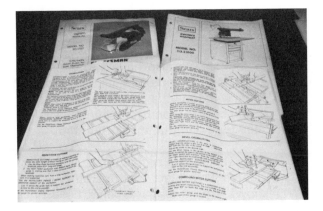

Figure 33-12. *Always study the owner's manual before using any power tool.*

POWER TOOL ADJUSTMENT

Power tool adjustment is very important. Improper or incorrect tool adjustment could affect operating safety. Tool adjustment is done with the power turned off or disconnected. Adjust the tool for a light cut. Do not overwork the tool or the cutter. Two light cuts are better than one heavy cut.

Check all adjustable parts of the power tool. Make sure they are locked or tightened securely. Make sure moving parts are lubricated and work easily. Keep machine tables and beds well waxed (Figure 33-13) so that the miter gage and other accessories move smoothly. A well-waxed bed or table also makes the stock easier to feed into the machine.

Figure 33-13. *Waxing machined surfaces makes it easier to feed stock and use accessories. It also protects those surfaces from rust.*

Follow maintenance procedures as recommended. If your power tool makes an unfamiliar noise, shut the machine off and find the cause before the tool is damaged. Beware of vibration problems. They can also be a danger signal.

Always adjust the machine with safety in mind. Use the guards for all operations. Let your stock cover the cutter whenever practical. The stock is then acting like a guard to protect you from the cutter.

Keep your bits or cutters sharp. A sharp tool requires less energy and yields a smoother cut.

There is less chance of a kickback when tools are sharp. Stock does not have to be forced into a sharp tool.

Remember, all power tools have limitations. Use a power tool to perform the operations for which it was designed. Avoid attempts to modify a power tool or its function.

WORKING SAFELY WITH OTHERS
When you work with power tools, you have an obligation to watch out for other students or workers. Whenever another student needs assistance, volunteer to help. Always use shop courtesy.

Stay clear of those using power tools. They should not be distracted. Avoid horseplay or running in the shop. This behavior is unsafe and is not tolerated in industry.

When you finish a job, return the machine to its normal operating position and clean up your mess. Scraps left on or near the machine could cause an injury.

QUESTIONS FOR REVIEW
1. Why is it important to plan the job carefully when you use power tools?
2. What are the four planning areas you must consider when performing a job with power tools?
3. What are some types of personal protective equipment you might wear when using power tools?
4. Why is hearing protection important when working with power tools?
5. Why are gloves a hazard when operating power tools?
6. What safe procedures would you recommend when handling material or feeding material into a power tool?
7. What is a kickback, and how is it caused? What can you do to avoid a kickback?
8. What are some shop-made devices that help you feed or guide material into a power tool?
9. Why must power tools be grounded? Does a grounded tool protect you in all conditions?
10. What is the purpose of a guard? How would you describe a well-designed guard?
11. How might the owner's manual help you operate a power tool safely and efficiently?
12. What are some procedures you would follow when adjusting a power tool?
13. What should be done when a power tool makes an unfamiliar noise or begins to vibrate?
14. Why are sharp bits or cutters safer than dull ones?

SUGGESTED ACTIVITIES
1. Make a list of the personal protective devices found in your wood shop.

2. With your instructor's help, make some protective devices for use in your shop. Sketch a design for a push stick, push shoe, feather board and V block.

3. Ask your instructor for a list of general safety rules that apply to your shop.

CHAPTER 34

Drill Press and Portable Drill

The *drill press* and *portable drill* both are power tools used to drill holes. They can also be used for other operations. The drill press is a stationary power tool found in most woodworking shops. The portable drill is found in the shop and on the job.

KEY TERMS

drill press	step pulley
twist drills	variable speed
spur machine bit	countersinking
Forstner bit	counterboring
multi-spur bit	sanding drum
spade bit	mortising attachment
hole saw	shaping attachment
fly cutter	router adapter
plug cutter	doweling jig

DRILL PRESS

The drill press (Figure 34-1) is used chiefly for *drilling, boring, counterboring* and *countersinking.* It may also be adapted to operations such as sanding, mortising, routing and shaping.

The size of the drill press is twice the distance from the center of the chuck to the column (Figure 34-1). A typical drill press has 7½" (190 mm) between the column and the center of the chuck. This is a 15" (380 mm) drill press. It can drill through the center of a 15" circle.

Parts Of The Drill Press

The base of the *drill press* supports the column (Figure 34-1). The table travels on the column and is held in position with the table locking clamp. When you remove the *index pin,* the table may be tilted and locked at any desired angle. The table may have a ¾" (18 mm) plywood pad attached to it. This protects the drill bit and table from striking each other.

At the top of the column is the drill head which holds the motor and the drilling mechanism (Figure 34-1). The motor drives a belt which turns the spindle. The spindle extends through the quill to turn the chuck. The quill controls the feed of the drill bit into the stock. When the universal feed lever is pulled downward, the quill moves into the work. The quill is spring-loaded and returns to the *up* position when the universal feed lever is released. The quill may be locked in any position with the quill lock.

The chuck holds the drill bit within three jaws. The jaws are tightened with a chuck key (Figure 34-2). Bits should be tightened securely before drilling stock.

Safe Operation Of The Drill Press

The drill press is a safe machine to operate when you observe the following practices:

1. Install drill bits. Make all adjustments with the power disconnected.
2. Always remove the chuck key from the chuck after installing a bit. If it is left in the chuck, it could be thrown at you when the drill press is turned on.
3. Wear protective glasses for all operations done on the drill press.
4. Use bits that are designed for power operation only. Make sure they are chucked securely.
5. Drill at the lowest practical speed. Feed the bit slowly. High feeds and speeds heat and dull the bit. They also burn the wood.

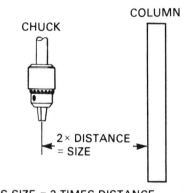

COLUMN

CHUCK

2× DISTANCE = SIZE

PRESS SIZE = 2 TIMES DISTANCE
BETWEEN CENTER OF CHUCK AND COLUMN

Figure 34-1. *Parts of the drill press.*

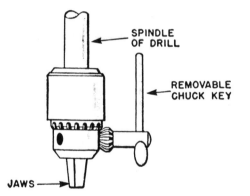

SPINDLE OF DRILL

REMOVABLE CHUCK KEY

JAWS

Figure 34-2. *Most chucks are tightened with a key. Be sure to remove the key before starting the drill press.*

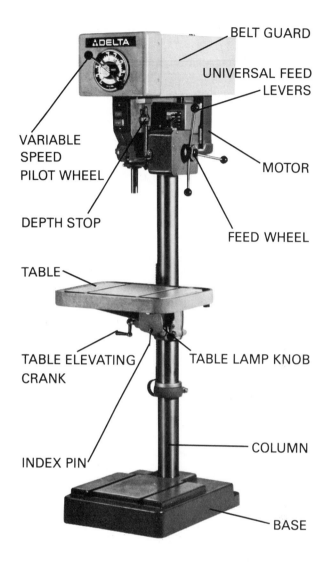

BELT GUARD
UNIVERSAL FEED LEVERS
MOTOR
VARIABLE SPEED PILOT WHEEL
DEPTH STOP
FEED WHEEL
TABLE
TABLE ELEVATING CRANK
TABLE LAMP KNOB
INDEX PIN
COLUMN
BASE

6. Use an awl to mark all work before drilling to ensure correct starting and accuracy.
7. When a large hole is to be drilled, it is a good practice to drill a pilot hole of a smaller diameter to guide the larger bit.
8. Clamp irregular pieces to the table while drilling. Round stock should be held in a V block. Be sure to clamp your work if you use a hole saw or fly cutter.
9. Make sure that the bit does not drill into the metal drill table. Use a plywood pad on the table and adjust the depth stop for additional protection.
10. Have your instructor check special setups or drilling operations on irregularly shaped stock.

11. When drilling, do not force the drill bit. Raise the bit frequently when drilling. This cools the bit and withdraws the chips.

Types Of Bits And Their Purpose
The most common type of bit used in the drill press is the *twist drill bit* (Figure 34-3). The twist drill bit is commonly used for holes from 1/64″ to 1/2″ diameter.

Figure 34-3. *Twist drill bit.*

A bit that is quite similar to the twist drill bit is the *spur machine bit* (Figure 34-4). The spur machine bit has a small point and two spurs. The spur machine bit drills a straighter, truer hole than the twist drill bit. There is also less grain tear out with the spur machine bit.

Spur machine bits are not available in sizes under ¼″ diameter. Twist drill bits are available in diameters from ¹⁄₆₄″ to over 1″ in ¹⁄₆₄″ increments.

Some auger bits are also used for power drilling in the drill press. These bits do not have a square tang or a feed screw. They are fed into the work with the universal feed lever.

Flat bottom holes are usually drilled with a *Forstner bit* (Figure 34-5) or a *multi-spur bit* (Figure 34-6). These bits cut on their outside edge as well as their center. They make an accurate hole and are well suited to drilling end grain.

Spade bits are inexpensive bits used for general drilling (Figure 34-7). They range in size from ¼″ to 1½″ diameter. Use a low drill press speed when drilling with a spade bit.

Figure 34-4. *Spur machine bit.*

Figure 34-5. *The forstner bit bores flat-bottomed holes.*

Figure 34-6. *The multi-spur bit bores flat bottomed holes.*

Figure 34-7. *Spade bits are used for general drilling.*

Holes with a diameter of 3" or greater are usually cut with a *hole saw* (Figure 34-8) or *fly cutter* (Figure 34-9). These cutters drill a small hole in the center and cut the outside of the hole. There are very few chips made with this process. The stock removed resembles a wheel.

When you use a hole saw or fly cutter use the slowest speed on your drill press. Keep your hands clear of the cutter. It is much larger than a conventional bit. Stock must be clamped when you use a hole saw or fly cutter. Have your instructor check any setup using the hole saw or fly cutter.

Plug cutters are frequently used on the drill press (Figure 34-10). They are fed into the stock like a drill bit, but do not make a hole. Instead, they cut a plug that may be used to fill a hole. The plug may be cut from wood of the same species and grain as the piece to be plugged. Plugs are usually driven into place with a mallet.

All bits must be sharp to cut efficiently. Protect cutting edges when the bit is not in use (Figure 34-11). Wipe the bits lightly with machine oil to

Figure 34-10. *The plug cutter cuts out a cylinder or plug. The plugs are used to fill holes in wood.*

Figure 34-8. *Carbide-tipped hole saw. The carbide tips are very hard. They stay sharp longer.*

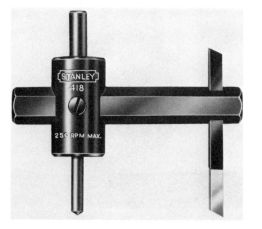

Figure 34-9. *The fly cutter is also called a circle cutter.*

Figure 34-11. *Store bits properly when not in use. Oil them lightly to prevent rust.*

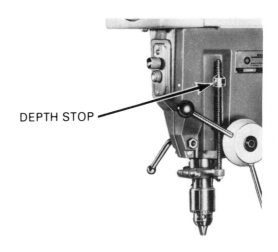

Figure 34-12. *The depth stop has an adjustable threaded ring that controls bit depth.*

DEPTH STOP

protect them from rust. Points on some bits may be sharpened with a file while others must be ground.

Setting Up The Drill Press
Any drill press setup requires that you perform the following operations: *chuck the bit, adjust table height, adjust table angle, adjust depth stop,* and *adjust drill speed.*

Chucking the Bit. After selecting the desired bit, insert it into the chuck between its three jaws. Tighten the jaws by turning the chuck ring. After hand-tightening the chuck, insert the chuck key and tighten it securely. Be sure to remove the chuck key after tightening the chuck. Turn the chuck by hand to make sure the bit is correctly aligned in the jaws.

Adjusting Table Height. Adjust the table height by releasing the table locking clamp and moving the table up or down on the column to the desired height. Then secure the table locking clamp. The height of the table should be adjusted so that the bit clears the work when the quill is up.

Adjusting Table Angle. The table has an index pin that holds the table perpendicular to the bit. By removing the pin and loosening the nut above it, you can tilt the table to any angle. After you adjust the table angle, tighten the nut to secure the table. Use a sliding T-bevel to check the angle. Some drill presses have an angle scale under the table.

Adjusting the Depth Stop. The depth stop limits travel of the quill and bit. If a blind hole (hole that does not go through the stock) is to be drilled,

the depth stop can be used to control the drilling depth. The depth stop has an adjustable threaded ring that stops the bit at the desired depth (Figure 34-12). The threaded ring is then locked in position. Make sure that the drill bit does not drill into the metal table.

Adjusting the Drill Speed. Drill speed adjustment varies with the drill press. There are two common systems for adjusting drill speeds: the *step pulley* and the *variable-speed* system.

On variable-speed drill presses, adjust the speed of the drill press while the motor is running. Start the motor and turn the variable speed pilot wheel on the front of the drill head (Figure 34-13). The indicator will tell you when you have reached the desired speed.

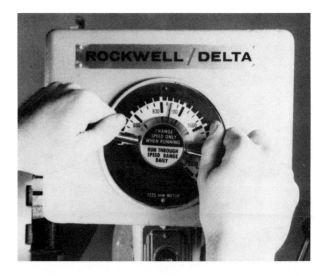

Figure 34-13. *Adjust a variable speed drill press while it is running. Turn the pilot wheel to change speeds.*

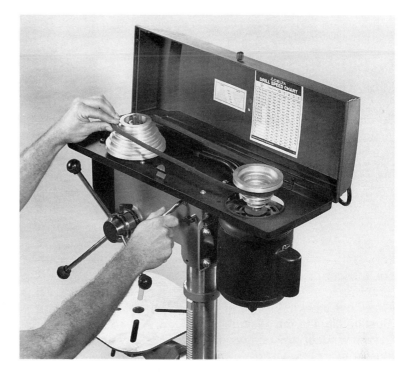

Figure 34-14. *The step pulleys control speed on some drill presses. Be sure the power is disconnected before moving the belt.*

On step pulley drill presses, the V belt is moved up or down on the pulleys. (Figure 34-14). The motor is loosened to simplify belt adjustment. When the smallest diameter on the motor pulley is used with the largest diameter on the spindle pulley, the drill is adjusted for its slowest speed. When you change the belt location on the pulleys, be sure the switch is off and the power is disconnected.

The speed of the drill press should be directly related to the size of the hole. The larger the hole, the slower the drill speed. Holes over ½" diameter should be drilled at the slowest possible speed.

Common Drilling Practices
Drilling is done in flat stock or irregular stock. The holes may be drilled straight into the work or at an angle. Each drilling operation requires a different procedure.

Before drilling, make sure you have center punched all the holes that you plan to drill. Use an awl to mark hole centers.

Drilling Holes in Flat Stock. Straight holes in flat stock are easy to drill. Set up the drill press as outlined above. Set your work on the table and line up the bit with the center mark. If you are using a hole saw or a fly cutter, clamp your work.

Turn on the motor and pull the feed lever down slowly. This will feed the bit into your work (Figure 34-15). Exert steady pressure, but do not force the bit into the work. Let the drill bit do the cutting. Back off on the feed lever occasionally. This will clear chips that have become packed into the flutes of the bit and cool the bit.

Figure 34-15. *Feed the bit into the work slowly. Use steady pressure, but do not force the bit.*

Figure 34-16. *Drilling flat stock at an angle requires tilting the table. Make sure the table is locked securely. Clamp your stock so it does not slip.*

When flat stock is drilled at an angle, the table must be tilted to the desired angle (Figure 34-16). Set the work on the table and line up the bit with the center mark. Clamp the stock to the table. Drill the hole using the same procedure you would use for a straight hole.

When you drill holes in the end of a long piece, turn the table 90° (Figure 34-17). The index pin can be inserted for accurate table location. The index pin can be used for 0° (flat) or 90° (Figure 34-18). Be sure to tighten the indexing nut.

When several identical pieces of flat stock are to be drilled, a *drilling fixture* can be built. A drilling fixture holds the stock in the desired position for

drilling. Using a drilling fixture increases accuracy and production rate.

Countersinking and Counterboring. Countersinking and counterboring are two common drilling operations performed on the drill press. They are usually drilled on flat stock, but may also be done on round or irregular stock.

Countersinking is a drilling operation needed for flat head screws. The chamfered hole made with

Figure 34-17. *The table is turned 90° for drilling into end grain.*

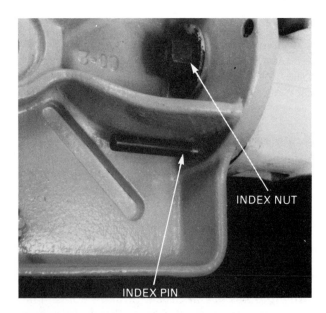

INDEX NUT

INDEX PIN

Figure 34-18. *Insert the index pin and tighten the indexing nut after turning the table 90°. For angles other than 0° and 90°, tighten only the indexing nut. The index pin is not used.*

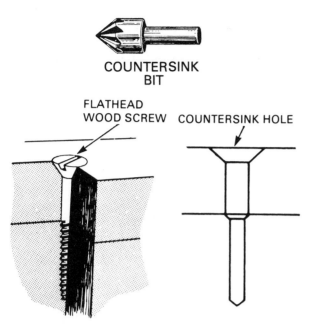

Figure 34-19. *Countersinking bits. The countersink produces a seat for a flat head wood screw. A standard countersinking bit drills only the seat. It can be used in a drill press or portable drill.*

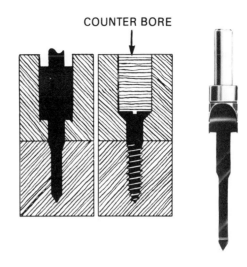

Figure 34-21. *The screw sink ® is designed for counterboring holes.*

Counterboring is done to drop a flat head screw below the surface of the wood. Counterbored screws are frequently covered with wood plugs or plastic wood. When counterboring, drill the larger hole first. Commercial bits are available for counterboring (Figure 34-21). They may be used in a drill press or portable drill.

Drilling Holes in Irregular Stock. Irregular stock requires careful setup before drilling. This is because pieces with an irregular shape will not lie flat on the table. Use clamps, fixtures or V blocks to secure stock with an irregular shape (Figure 34-22).

Before you drill stock with an irregular shape, have your instructor check your setup.

a countersink allows the wood screw to seat in the wood (Figure 34-19). The head of the screw is even with the surface of the wood when seated. Commercial bits (Figure 34-20) are available for drilling holes suited to wood screws. Some bits (Figure 34-20, *right*) may be used in a portable drill or drill press. They do three drilling operations at one time.

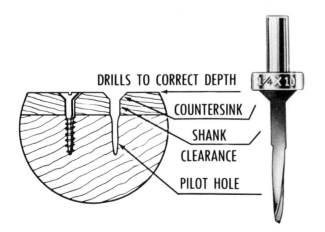

Figure 34-20. *A special bit,* right, *is both a drill and countersink. It does three drilling operations at once.*

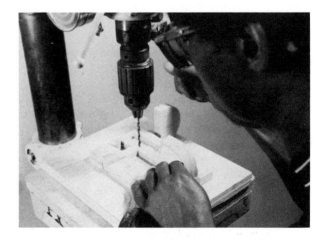

Figure 34-22. *This fixture holds a hook-shaped piece of wood. It also spaces the two holes.*

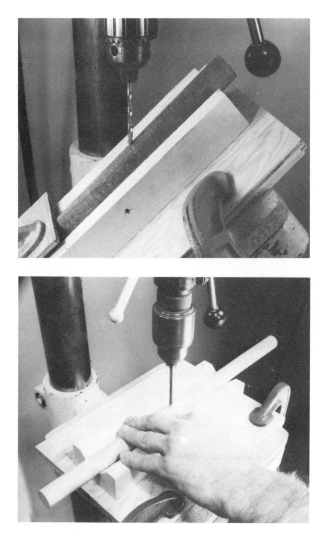

Figure 34-24. *An auxiliary table is used for sanding on the drill press. Use a very low spindle speed when sanding. Feed stock against cutter rotation.*

Figure 34-23. *A V block prevents round stock from turning. When drilling at an angle, clamp the V block and the work.*

By raising and lowering the table, you can use all of the abrasive on the drum. Do not lower the quill for this purpose. Pressure against the extended quill and spindle will cause them to wear abnormally.

Keep the spindle speed as low as possible when sanding. Be sure to feed stock against drum rotation.

Mortising With The Drill Press

Mortising attachments use the drill press to cut square holes. These attachments perform the same job as a mortiser, which is an industrial machine. Mortising attachments use a special drill. This drill is held in a hollow chisel (Figure 34-25). The hollow chisel cuts the square edges, and the special drill bit cuts the hole.

Mortising attachments come equipped with a fence. The fence holds the work perpendicular to the mortising bit. The holding devices keep the bit from sticking in the wood.

When you mortise your stock, do both ends of the mortise first. Then stagger your cuts. This will keep the chisel from bending. Take a second cut to clean out the completed mortise.

Drilling Holes in Round Stock. Round stock can be held securely with a V block (Figure 34-23). The stock will not turn in the block. Clamp the V block to the table. Make sure that the stock does not slip when drilled.

Sanding On The Drill Press

The drill press can be used as a spindle sander. To do this, chuck a special *sanding drum* in the drill press and clamp an auxiliary table in position (Figure 34-24). The auxiliary table has a hole to accommodate the sanding drum. By dropping the sanding drum into the auxiliary table hole, you can sand the entire edge of the stock.

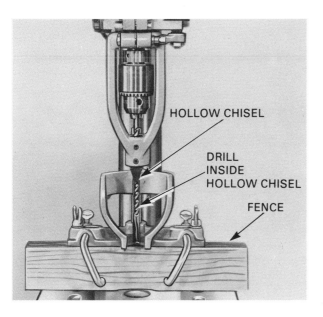

Figure 34-25. *Drill press set up for mortising. Hollow chisel and drill do the mortising.*

HOLLOW CHISEL

DRILL INSIDE HOLLOW CHISEL

FENCE

PORTABLE DRILLS

Portable drills (Figure 34-26) can be used in locations where a drill press cannot be used. With practice, you can drill holes with a portable drill as accurately as with a drill press. The size of a portable drill is determined by the chuck size. The most common portable drill sizes used are ¼" and ⅜".

Some portable drills have additional features such as: reversible chuck or spindle rotation, variable speed control and cordless operation. These features have no effect on drill size. The reversible chuck is used for installing and removing screws.

Portable drills are used frequently by woodworkers. Portable drills use the same bits for drilling as the drill press. These bits are chucked the same way in the drill press as in the portable drill.

Figure 34-26. *Portable drills can be used in places where a drill press could not be used. Drill size is determined by chuck size.*

Safe Operation Of The Portable Drill

The portable electric drill can be operated safely if you observe the following practices.

1. Chuck bits securely with the power disconnected.
2. Always remove the chuck key after installing the bit.
3. Wear protective glasses for all jobs performed with the portable drill.
4. Make sure the drill is grounded or double insulated.
5. Center punch your work before drilling. This will keep the bit from creeping.
6. Do not force the bit. Use moderate pressure and let the bit cut its way into the work.

Drilling With A Portable Drill

Before you begin, use a chuck key to chuck the bit securely. Make sure the cord is not in your way. Line up your bit with your center mark and turn on the motor. Let the bit do the cutting. Raise the bit occasionally to clear any chips packed in the hole.

A try square can help you drill a straight hole in your work (Figure 34-27). Use a sliding T-bevel for angled holes (Figure 34-28). For drilling dowel holes, use a *doweling jig* to guide the bit (Figure 34-29).

You can make a jig for drilling at an angle (Figure 34-30) or you may use a commercial drilling jig.

A sliding T-bevel can be used to provide the correct angle.

After you complete the drilling operation, remove the bit from the work and shut off the motor.

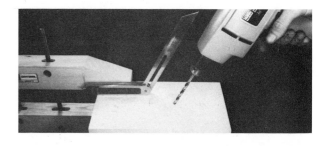

Figure 34-28. *A sliding T bevel can be used to guide the drill when drilling angled holes. When drilling through your work, back it up with scrap stock.*

Figure 34-29. *The dowelling jig guides the bit. This assures a straight hole.*

Figure 34-27. *When using a portable drill, let the bit do the cutting. A try square can be used to ensure a straight line. When drilling through your work, back it up with scrap stock.*

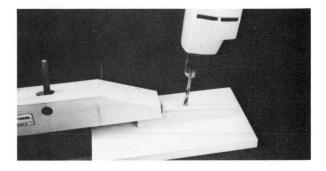

Figure 34-30. *You can make a jig for drilling holes at an angle. A sliding T bevel can also be used as a guide. When drilling through your work, back it up with scrap stock.*

QUESTIONS FOR REVIEW

1. How do you determine the size of a drill press?
2. Name the parts of the drill press and describe their function.
3. Why should a plywood pad be attached to the drill press table?
4. Discuss safe operating procedures that should be followed when using the drill press.
5. How do spur bits and twist drill bits differ in construction? Which bit will drill the straightest hole?
6. What bits are best for drilling a flat bottomed hole? How do these bits do their cutting?
7. What is an inexpensive bit used for general drilling called?
8. For what purpose is a plug cutter used?
9. List the five operations you must perform when setting up a drill press.
10. How is the speed of a drill press controlled on a step pulley drive system?
11. How is the speed of a drill press controlled on a variable-speed drive system?
12. When would you use a drill fixture? Of what help is a drill fixture?
13. Describe countersinking and counterboring. For what purpose are these drilling operations performed?
14. How would you set up the drill press for sanding? Why is an auxiliary table used when sanding?
15. Name the parts included in a mortising attachment used on the drill press. How is the mortising attachment used?
16. How do you determine the size of a portable drill? What are some additional features of a drill press?
17. Discuss safe operating procedures that should be followed when using a portable drill.
18. How can you control the drilling angle of a portable drill?
19. Discuss the correct procedure for drilling holes with a portable drill.

SUGGESTED ACTIVITIES

1. Make a list of the types of drill bits found in your shop. List one purpose for each of these bits.

2. Check the table on your drill press. Make sure the plywood pad is in good condition. If it needs to be replaced, check with your instructor to obtain the correct stock.

3. Set up the drill press for the following operations:
   a. Drilling a hole through a piece of flat stock.
   b. Drilling a hole through a piece of round stock.
   c. Drilling a hole to one-half of the depth of a piece of scrap stock.
   d. Drilling a hole at a 45° angle through a piece of stock.

Jigsaw And Saber Saw

The jigsaw and the saber saw are designed for cutting curves. Both machines have a *reciprocating* action that causes the blade to move up and down. Cutting occurs only on one stroke however. The jigsaw cuts on the *down stroke* and the saber saw cuts on the *up stroke.*

KEY TERMS

jigsaw	chuck
saber saw	internal cut
blade	rip fence
upper chuck	circle guide
lower chuck	pocket cut

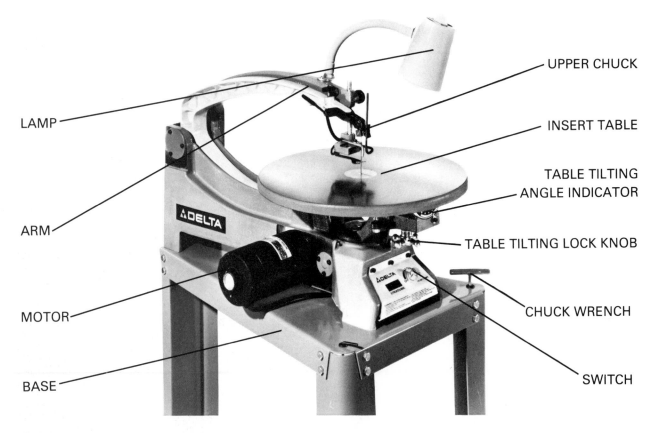

LAMP

ARM

MOTOR

BASE

UPPER CHUCK

INSERT TABLE

TABLE TILTING ANGLE INDICATOR

TABLE TILTING LOCK KNOB

CHUCK WRENCH

SWITCH

Figure 35-1. *The jig saw (or scroll saw) is a stationary machine with many parts. Study this illustration to learn the name of each part.*

JIG SAW

The *jigsaw* (also called a "scroll saw") is a stationary machine. It is usually attached to a bench or stand for operation (Figure 35-1). The distance from the back of the overarm to the blade is the size of the jigsaw. The most common size is 24″ (600 mm). Some jigsaws have a step pulley system to control the reciprocating speed (Figure 35-2). Other jigsaws have a fixed speed. Hard materials should be cut at slower speeds.

The jigsaw blade is held between the upper chuck and the lower chuck (Figure 35-3). Some blades are clamped in the chuck while other blades are held by spring tension. Blades held by spring tension have pins through them. These pins hook to the upper and lower chuck.

Figure 35-2. *Step pulleys control the cutting speed on some jig saws. Use slower speeds on hard materials. The guard has been removed for this illustration.*

Figure 35-3. *Blades are held between an upper and lower chuck. The upper chuck provides blade tension. The lower chuck drives the blade.*

The lower chuck drives the blade. The upper chuck is spring-loaded and provides blade tension. Blade tension is adjustable on some jigsaws but not on others.

Safe Operation Of The Jigsaw

The following rules will help you learn to operate the jigsaw safely and efficiently.

1. Install blades and make adjustments with the switch off and the power disconnected.
2. Make sure all guards are in position.
3. Make sure that the table is secured at the desired angle before you begin.
4. Make sure that the *hold-down* is contacting the stock before you begin.
5. Wear protective glasses when you use the jigsaw.
6. Keep your hands clear of the blade. Do not allow your fingers to line up with the blade when feeding stock into it.
7. Do not force your work. Let the blade cut the stock. Forcing your work will break the blade.

Installing Blades

Jigsaw blades are easily installed. Select a blade that is correct for the material you are cutting. A blade with 15 teeth per inch (25 mm) is suitable for general wood cutting. Use finer blades for hardwood and veneer. A coarser blade can be used for softwood and plywood. Before you install the blade, be sure to turn the switch off and disconnect the power.

Some jigsaws use blades that have pins through them. These blades are installed by hooking the

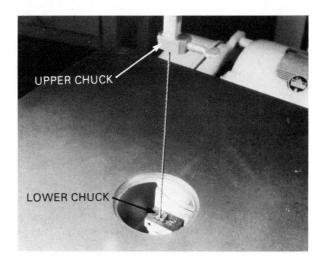

UPPER CHUCK

LOWER CHUCK

pins to the upper and lower chucks. (Figure 35-4). Make sure that the teeth are pointing downward toward the table and face the front of the saw.

Other jigsaws use longer blades that do not have pins. Begin by removing the table insert. Rotate the motor shaft or pulley until the lower chuck is at its highest point. Insert at least ½" (12 mm) of the blade into the chuck with the teeth pointing downward. Tighten the chuck securely.

Loosen the upper head. This will drop the *tension sleeve* and upper chuck. Place ½" (12 mm) of the blade into the upper chuck and tighten it. Raise the tension sleeve ¾" (18 mm) above the chuck and tighten the upper head (Figure 35-5). This must be done while the lower chuck is at the high point of its stroke. The tension sleeve keeps the blade rigid on its *up* stroke.

Replace the table insert and turn the pulley by hand. This will ensure that the blade has been installed correctly. Check the blade. Make sure that it does not bend or bind when you rotate the pulley. Be sure the blade is installed at a right angle to the table.

BOTTOM PINS HOOKED TO LOWER CHUCK

TOP PINS HOOKED TO UPPER CHUCK

TENSION APPLIED TO BLADE

TENSION SLEEVE

3/4"

Figure 35-4. *Blades with pins are hooked in the upper and lower chucks. Make sure the teeth point downward and toward the front.*

Figure 35-5. *Raise the tension sleeve ¾" (18 mm) above the upper chuck. This must be done while the lower chuck is at the high point of its stroke.*

Cutting Curves

When cutting curves, determine the path of the blade before cutting. Divide long complex cuts into parts. If the blade must make a tight turn while cutting, drill a *turning hole* at that point (Figure 35-6). The hole should be larger than the blade.

Adjust the hold-down so that it holds the work on the table during cutting (Figure 35-7). Turn on the saw and feed the stock under the hold-down. Do not force the stock. Use moderate feeding pressure. Follow your cutting sequence. When you cut a sharp curve, travel slowly. This will prevent the blade from bending, twisting or breaking. Do not let your fingers or thumbs line up with the blade while cutting. Figure 35-8 shows good cutting practice.

Remember to cut on the waste side of your line. This will leave some stock for edge sanding.

Figure 35-8. *Follow safety practices and good cutting procedures. Fingers or thumbs should never line up with the blade. Note that the table has been tilted for bevel cutting.*

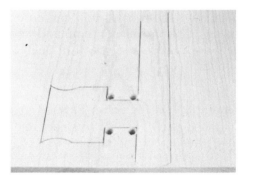

Figure 35-6. *Drill turning holes in tight corners. This allows the blade to turn easily. Make the hole slightly larger than the blade.*

Figure 35-7. *The hold-down should be in contact with the work. This holds the work firmly against the table.*

The table of the jigsaw can be tilted to cut bevels (Figure 35-8). Make sure the table is locked in position before you begin your cut. When your stock is tilted, the blade must cut through more stock. Travel slowly and try not to pinch the blade. Thicker stock requires slower feeding.

Internal Cuts

An *internal cut* is made inside the edges of the work. To make an internal cut, a hole must be drilled in the waste stock.

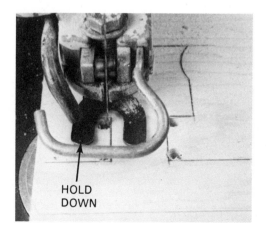

HOLD
DOWN

Install the jigsaw blade through this hole. After adjusting the hold-down, guide the blade along the layout line and complete the internal cut (Figure 35-9). To remove the work from the saw table, you must remove the blade.

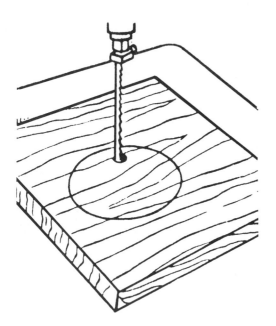

Figure 35-9. *Thread the blade through a hole in the waste stock for an internal cut.*

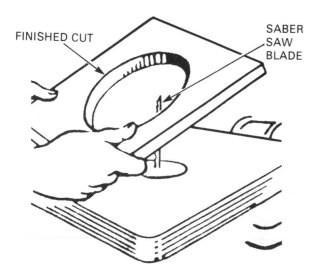

Figure 35-10. *Internal cuts are made easily on a jig saw with a saber saw blade. The upper chuck is not connected and it should be well out of the way. The work can be placed over the saber saw blade.*

A saber saw blade is sometimes mounted in the jigsaw for internal cuts. The saber saw blade is attached only to the lower chuck (Figure 35-10). The upper chuck is not connected. Internal cuts can now be made without removing the blade. A hole is drilled in the waste stock and the hole is placed over the blade.

SABER SAW

A *saber saw* is a portable tool used to rip and crosscut stock (Figure 35-11). It may also be used to cut irregular curves. The saber saw is a light-duty tool and it is not built to cut stock over 1 ½" (38 mm) thick. Heavier stock may be cut with a reciprocating saw. A reciprocating saw is a heavy-duty saber saw. It has more horsepower and uses larger blades.

The size of a saber saw is rated by the length of its blade stroke. This is usually ½" or ⅝" (12 to 15 mm). A longer stroke is more efficient. Horsepower ratings are also furnished for most saber saws. Some saber saws are variable-speed. With variable-speed saber saws you can control the number of blade strokes per minute. Other saber saws have a fixed blade speed of 3500 strokes per minute.

Safe Operation Of The Saber Saw
The following rules will help you learn to operate the saber saw safely and efficiently:

1. Install blades and make all adjustments with the switch off and the power disconnected.
2. Support your work. Clamp it to a bench or sawhorse. Do not hold your work by hand.
3. When you use the saber saw, keep both hands on the saw. This keeps them away from the blade.
4. Wear protective glasses when using the saber saw.
5. Do not force the blade. Let the blade do the cutting.
6. Keep the base and the shoe in contact with the work at all times.

Installing Blades
Select a *blade* for the job you are doing. A blade with about 10 teeth per inch (25 mm) is suitable for general cutting. Fine cuts require 12 teeth per inch and coarse cuts are made with 6 teeth per inch.

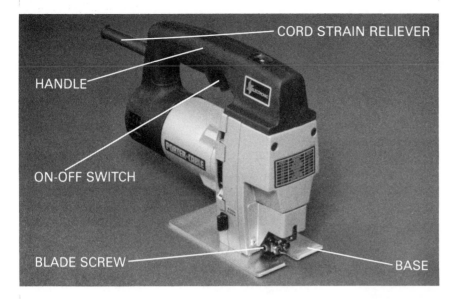

Figure 35-11. *The saber saw is a portable tool. It is used to cut irregular curves. Study this illustration to learn the name of each part.*

Blades are usually held in the *chuck* with a slotted screw or a socket screw (Figure 35-12). Disconnect the power and loosen the chuck. Insert the blade into the chuck about ½ inch (12 mm). Teeth should point forward and upward toward the base. Tighten the chuck securely after installing the blade.

Cutting With The Saber Saw

Before you make any cuts in your stock, lay it out carefully. Lay out the backside of paneling or plywood. The backside of your stock should be up when cutting. This is because the saber saw cuts on the upward stroke. Any splintering of the stock will be on the backside.

When you cut curves, number the cutting sequence. Make turning holes where needed.

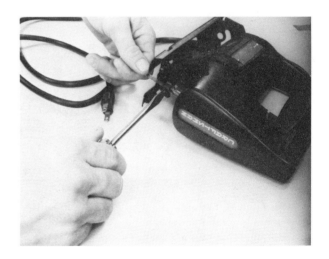

Figure 35-12. *Blades are held in the chuck with a screw. Be sure the power is disconnected when installing a blade.*

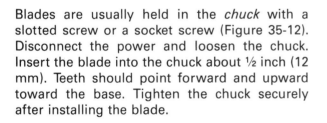

Guides are available for most saber saws. A *rip fence* will help you cut a line parallel to the edge of the stock (Figure 35-13). A *circle guide* allows the saber saw to pivot around a point to cut a circle (Figure 35-14). The guide can be adjusted to different lengths.

The saber saw blade should travel on the waste side of the layout line. Turn on the saw and feed the blade into the work. Do not force the blade. It will burn and dull quickly if you do. Turns that are too tight will also burn or break the blade.

Keep the base of the saber saw in contact with the work. If the saw bounces while cutting, the blade may break. If the saber saw bounces, check the blade. It may have been installed upside down.

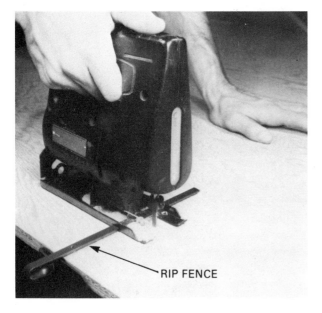

Figure 35-13. *The rip fence makes it easy to cut a line parallel to the edge.*

Figure 35-15. *Tilt the base to cut a bevel. Make sure the base is secure before cutting.*

Figure 35-14. *The circle guide will pivot around a point while the blade cuts a circle.*

Figure 35-16. *Pocket or plunge cuts do not require a hole for the blade. The blade cuts its own hole.*

Some saber saws have a base that will tilt. This makes it possible to cut a bevel. Make sure that the base is tightened securely before cutting a bevel (Figure 35-15).

When making an *internal cut* with the saber saw, drill a hole larger than the blade width in the scrap piece. Insert the blade in the hole and make the internal cut.

Sometimes it is not necessary to drill a hole when you make an internal cut. The blade can cut its own hole. This is known as a "plunge" or pocket cut (Figure 35-16). Hold the saber saw at an angle. The tip of the base is in contact with the stock. Turn on the saw and slowly lower the blade into the work. When the base rests on the stock, you can continue your cut.

QUESTIONS FOR REVIEW

1. For what purpose is a jigsaw used?
2. How do the blades on the jigsaws and saber saws move?
3. How would you determine the size of a jigsaw?
4. How are blades installed in a jigsaw?
5. In what direction should the teeth on a jigsaw blade point?
6. List the safe procedures you should follow when operating a jigsaw.
7. What is the function of the hold-down used on the jigsaw?
8. What is the function of the tension sleeve?
9. Why do you cut on the waste side of the layout line?
10. How does a turning hole help you when you cut a tight turn?
11. How is a bevel cut made on the jigsaw?
12. How does an internal cut differ from any other cut made with the jigsaw?
13. How is an internal cut made on a jigsaw?
14. Does an internal cut made with a jigsaw with a saber saw blade require blade removal?
15. Is the saber saw built to cut stock over 1 ½" thick?
16. How is the size of a saber saw rated?
17. List the safe procedures you should follow when operating a saber saw.
18. How are blades installed in a saber saw?
19. How should plywood be marked for saber saw cutting? How should it be cut?
20. What types of guides are available for use on the saber saw? How are they used?
21. What should be checked if the saber saw bounces during a cut?
22. How would you make a pocket or plunge cut with a saber saw?

SUGGESTED ACTIVITIES

1. Check the jigsaw in your shop to see if it has a fixed speed or a variable speed.

2. Measure the size of the jigsaw in your shop and record your measurement. Compare with other students.

3. Demonstrate the procedure for installing a blade in your jigsaw.

4. Demonstrate the procedure for installing a blade in your saber saw.

Band Saw

The band saw is a general-duty saw used in the woodworking shop. It is used to make *curved* or *irregular cuts, bevelled cuts* and *straight cuts.* The blade is one continuous piece of steel with a belt or band shape.

KEY TERMS

band saw	crosscut
blade guard	miter
blade guide	nibble cutting
fence	tangent cutting
miter gage	relief cutting
rip	compound curves

BAND SAW

The band saw (Figure 36-1) has a continuous blade and stroke. The blade runs over two wheels. One is at the top and one is at the bottom of the saw. The wheels are covered by guards. The wheels guide the blade. The diameter of the wheel indicates band saw size. If the wheel diameter is 20" (500 mm) then it is a 20" band saw.

The wheels have rubber tires that protect the blade while it turns. These tires are high or crowned in the middle (Figure 36-2). This shape keeps the blade in the middle of the tire. The blade travels on the highest part of the tire.

GUIDE POST

PUSH BUTTON
SWITCH

BALL BEARING
BLADE SUPPORT
ADJUSTING
SCREW

LOWER WHEEL
GUARD

BLADE GUIDE
ADJUSTING SCREW

BLADE TENSION KNOB

UPPER WHEEL GUARD

UPPER GUIDE HEIGHT
ADJUSTMENT KNOB

BLADE SUPPORT
ASSEMBLY

BLADE SLOT

MITER GROOVE

TABLE

TABLE CLAMP

ENCLOSED STAND

Figure 36-1. *The band saw and its parts. Study this picture to learn the name of each part.*

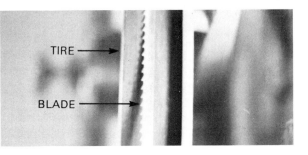

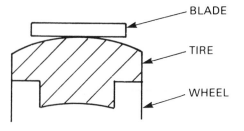

Figure 36-2. *The wheels have rubber tires that protect the blade. The tires are high in the center. The blade travels on the high spot.*

The upper wheel can be adjusted up or down to put tension on the blade. The upper wheel adjustment compensates for blades that are slightly longer or shorter than specified length. The upper wheel also tilts vertically. This adjustment centers the blade on the wheels. The lower wheel is not adjustable. It is attached to the motor and drives the blade.

The *blade guard* moves up and down above the table. It guards the non-cutting part of the blade and supports the *upper guide* (Figure 36-1).

The upper guide has a ball bearing blade support (Figure 36-3). It is located behind the blade. When stock is fed into the blade, the ball bearing blade support rests against the blade and holds it on the wheels. The blade is supported on the sides by the blade guides (Figure 36-3). The blade guides keep the blade from twisting when stock is cut.

The lower guide and the table tilting mechanism are below the table (Figure 36-4). The lower guide looks like the upper guide, but is not fastened to a guard. It is fastened to the band saw frame. The table tilting mechanism allows the table to be tilted. Some tables tilt both ways. Others tilt only one way.

Band saws often come equipped with a *fence* and *miter gage* (Figure 36-5). They can be used to guide the stock, but it is not necessary to use a fence or miter gage. There is no danger of a kickback with the band saw. The blade turns toward the table. The cutting action pulls the work downward and holds it against the table. Rough and warped stock can be cut on the band saw without danger of kickback. The band saw

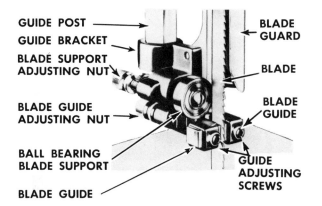

Figure 36-3. *The ball bearing blade support is mounted on the upper blade guide. Blade guides support the blade and keep it from twisting.*

Figure 36-4. *The table tilting mechanism is located below the table.*

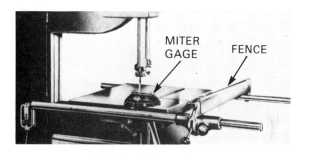

Figure 36-5. *Band saws often come equipped with a fence and a miter gage.*

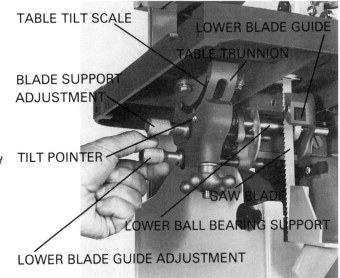

can be used to cut rough stock into smaller pieces before jointing or surfacing.

Safe Operation Of The Band Saw

The following rules will help you operate the band saw safely and efficiently:

1. Install blades and make all adjustments with the switch off and the power disconnected.
2. Make sure all guards are in place before operating the band saw.
3. Adjust the upper blade guide so that it is no more than ¼" (6 mm) above the work.
4. Do not allow your fingers to line up with the blade as you feed stock into it. Keep your hands at least 4" (100 mm) from the blade. Use a push stick if you must get closer.
5. Wear protective glasses when operating the band saw.
6. Allow the machine to come to full speed before cutting any stock. If the motor slows down while sawing, you are feeding the stock too fast.
7. When cutting tight curves, be sure to make relief cuts. Without relief cuts, the blade will become pinched in the work. This will dull or break the blade.
8. Do not remove cut-offs or scraps from the table while the blade is moving.
9. Do not back out of long cuts. This could pull the blade off its wheels. Plan your cutting sequence before you begin your work.
10. Before cutting round stock, such as dowels, clamp it securely or place it in a V block. This will keep it from rolling into the blade and jamming the teeth.

11. If a clicking sound appears while you are operating the band saw, turn off the machine and inspect the blade for cracks.
12. If the blade breaks while you are operating the band saw, turn off the machine and move away from it until it stops.
13. When sawing is completed, turn off the band saw. Allow the blade to stop turning before leaving the band saw. If the saw has a brake, apply it smoothly. Do not stand on the brake pedal.

Purchasing Blades

Band saw blades can be purchased in welded loops or in 100 foot lengths. Lengths of 100 feet are cut to the correct length and welded in the shop. Some band saws have a welding machine attached to them.

The owner's manual can tell you the correct blade length or you can compute blade length. Use this formula:

$$L = 2 H + \pi \times D$$

where H = Distance between wheel centers

L = Length of blade

D = Wheel diameter

pi = 3.14.

Blades are sold in various widths. The most common widths used in the school shop are ¼", ⅜" and ½". The tooth size and shape vary with blade type (Figure 36-6). Skip tooth blades have deep gullets and are popular for general wood cutting.

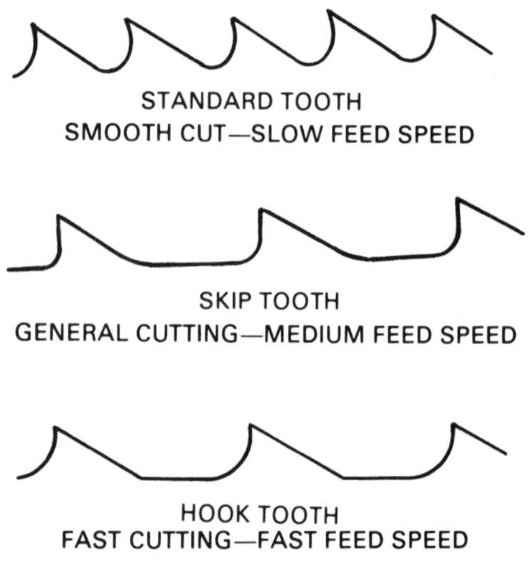

Figure 36-6. *Common blade types and their use.*

STANDARD TOOTH
SMOOTH CUT—SLOW FEED SPEED

SKIP TOOTH
GENERAL CUTTING—MEDIUM FEED SPEED

HOOK TOOTH
FAST CUTTING—FAST FEED SPEED

(A)

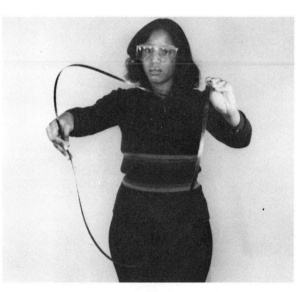

(B)

(C)

(D)

Figure 36-7. *Folding a small band saw blade. Make sure the teeth point away from you.*

Tooth size affects the number of teeth per inch. Coarse blades have four teeth per inch. These blades cut quickly. They remove large chips without clogging. Finer blades have more teeth per inch. Fine teeth yield a smoother cut. They remove small chips and require a slower feeding speed.

Welded band saw blades are coiled or folded for packaging. The large band saw blade is rolled into three or five smaller circles for shipping.

Figures 36-7 and 36-8 show the techniques for folding or coiling the blades. Figure 36-7 shows coiling for small blades (12″ to 14″ band saw).

(A)

(B)

(C)

(D)

(E)

Figure 36-8. *Folding a large band saw blade. Make sure the teeth point away from you.*

Figure 36-8 shows coiling for large blades (18" or larger band saw).

Installing Blades
Before installing a band saw blade, turn off the switch and disconnect the power. Remove the upper and lower wheel guards and remove the table insert if necessary. Push the upper and lower blade guides back so they will not touch the blade when it is mounted. Lower the upper wheel and place the blade over the wheels. The teeth always point downward toward the table and away from the ball bearing blade support (Figure 36-3).

Raise the upper wheel to put tension on the blade. When the blade is properly tensioned, turn the wheels by hand to check blade tracking.

If the blade is not riding in the center of the wheels, tilt the upper wheel.

The blade guides must now be adjusted. The ball bearing blade support is located 1/64" behind the blade and the blade guides are each 1/64" from the blade (Figure 36-3). Make sure that the teeth do not touch the blade guides. Check all adjustments. Replace the wheel guards and the table insert.

Turn the band saw on and off quickly. Watch the blade to be sure it is tracking correctly. Readjust the saw if the blade does not track correctly.

Cutting Stock With The Band Saw

Rough stock can be cut on the band saw. There is no danger of kickbacks with the band saw because the blade cuts with a downward force. Before making any cut on the band saw, adjust the upper blade guide. The upper blade guide should be no more than 1/4" above the work.

Cutting Warped Stock. Warped or rough stock can be cut on the band saw. Often it is impossible to machine a large piece of warped stock. If you cut warped stock into smaller pieces, machining will be simpler.

When you cut warped stock, the concave side should face the table (Figure 36-9). This provides better control of the stock because it cannot rock. The downward cutting force will force the stock toward the table.

Cutting Flat Stock. Flat stock may be *ripped, crosscut* or *mitered* on the band saw. You can use a fence or miter gage to guide your work, or you can guide it by hand to a layout line. A sharp band saw blade will cut a straight line. If the blade is dull, however, it will not cut a straight line. This condition is known as lead. If the band saw blade tends to lead, it is wise to cut close to your layout line and then plane or sand your piece to the line.

If you wish to square the miter gage to the blade, use the miter slot as a reference (Figure 36-10). The blade is too narrow to provide an accurate measure.

If you wish to cut a bevelled edge on your workpiece, the table may be tilted. Loosen the clamp and turn the table to the desired angle (Figure 36-11). Be sure to clamp the table securely after adjusting.

Figure 36-10. *Square the miter gage to the miter slot. The blade is too narrow to be accurate.*

Figure 36-9. *Cut warped stock with the concave side down. It is easier to control.*

Figure 36-11. *Cutting a bevel on the band saw. Make sure the table is clamped securely at the correct angle.*

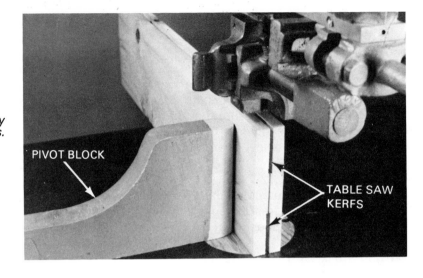

Figure 36-12. *The pivot block makes it easy to turn your stock if the blade leads. Kerfing the stock makes resawing easier.*

Resawing Stock

Resawing is similar to ripping. The purpose of resawing is to cut a thick piece of stock into two or more thinner pieces of stock. Resawn pieces have a similar grain pattern and provide an excellent grain match for table tops and drawer fronts.

Control stock while resawing. A fence or pivot block will control the stock, but a *pivot block* works best. The pivot block is a shop-made device that is clamped to the table. It controls the stock near the blade only (Figure 36-12). If the blade begins to lead, turn the stock to keep the blade cutting on the line. This is not possible when you use a fence.

The band saw blade will follow the path of least resistance. A knot could cause the blade to lead. If the stock is kerfed with a table saw before resawing, the blade will follow the kerf as it cuts. Make your kerfs ½″ to 1½″ (12 to 36 mm) deep on both edges of your work (Figure 36-12).

Feed the stock slowly when resawing. Forcing the stock will load the blade and cause it to lead. Do not allow your thumbs or fingers to line up with the blade. Feed the stock with a push stick.

Cutting Circles

Circular pieces may be cut on the band saw. There are special fixtures for this purpose (Figure 36-13). These fixtures may be built or pur-

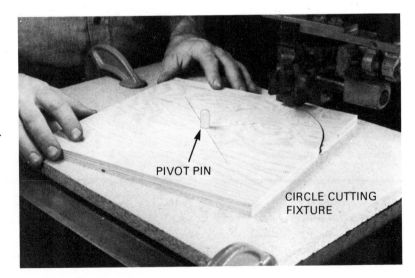

Figure 36-13. *Special fixtures are used for cutting circles on the band saw.*

chased. The circle cutting fixture provides a pivot point for the center of the circle. The stock turns around this point to cut a perfect circle.

Select a narrow blade (¼") for cutting a circle. Do not force the stock, or the blade will lead. Cut slowly to obtain a perfect circle.

Cutting Curves

The band saw cuts curves very well. When you cut a curve, make sure that you do not bend or twist the blade. The blade will become dull or break if you twist or bend it. Sharp curves can be made without bending the blade. You may use any of three cutting methods: *nibble cutting, tangent cutting* or *relief cutting* (Figure 36-14).

Nibble cuts actually nibble away stock in deep narrow curves. Tangent cuts are made tangent (at an angle) to the curve, but do not follow the

exact curve. Relief cuts are made perpendicular to the layout line at ⅜" to ½" (9mm to 12 mm) intervals. As the layout line is cut, small pieces break away because the curve cut meets the relief cut.

Blade width regulates the radius of the curve you cut. The narrower the blade, the sharper the curve. A blade ⅛" (3 mm) will cut a ¼" (6 mm) radius, a blade ¼" (6 mm) will cut a ¾" (18 mm) radius, a blade ⅜" (9 mm) will cut a 1" (25 mm) radius, and a blade ½" (12 mm) will cut a 1¼" (31 mm) radius without binding.

Before cutting a curve, plan your *cutting sequence* carefully. Number your cuts (Figure 36-15). Then make relief cuts and drill turning holes. Make these holes larger than the blade. Be sure that the cutting sequence does not cause your stock to hit the upper arm while cutting.

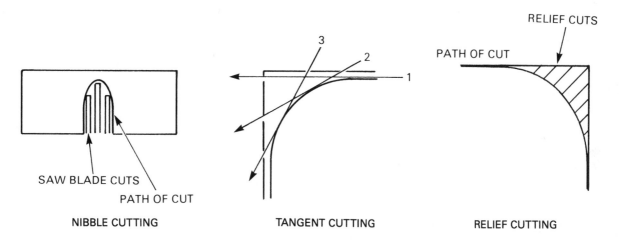

NIBBLE CUTTING   TANGENT CUTTING   RELIEF CUTTING

Figure 36-14. *Use these methods to cut curves.*

Figure 36-15. *Number your cuts before you begin. This will make your work easier.*

Stack Cutting

When several pieces are cut to the same shape, they can be stacked and fastened together by nailing in the waste stock. The stack is then cut as one piece (Figure 36-16).

Figure 36-16. *Several pieces can be stacked for cutting. They are fastened together in the waste stock.*

Cutting Compound Curves

Compound curves require two or more curved cuts in the stock. After the first curved cut is made in the stock, tape the waste stock to the work. This provides a flat surface for the other cuts that will be made (Figure 36-17).

Cutting Round Stock

If held securely, round stock, such as dowels, may be cut on the band saw. If round stock is not held securely, it may rotate into the blade as it is cut. This will jam the blade in the stock and break the blade. Round stock held in a parallel clamp (Figure 36-18) or V block may be cut without difficulty.

If you plan to split or rip round stock, use a V block to control your work (Figure 36-19).

Figure 36-18. *Round stock should be clamped for band sawing. The parallel clamp prevents the round stock from rotating.*

Figure 36-19. *When ripping round stock, use a V block to control it.*

Figure 36-17. *When making compound cuts, the waste stock (stock removed from the first cut) is taped to the work. This provides a flat surface for the second cut. The second cut shows all waste cut away from the work.*

QUESTIONS FOR REVIEW

1. What types of cuts will the band saw make?
2. How would you describe the band saw blade? How is it driven?
3. What function is performed by the upper guide and blade guard?
4. What two important band saw parts are located below the table?
5. Do band saws have a kickback hazard?
6. Discuss the procedures you should follow to operate the band saw safely and efficiently.
7. How are band saw blades sold? How do you determine the correct blade length for your machine?
8. Do coarse toothed blades cut quicker than fine toothed blades?
9. Describe the procedure for installing a blade on the band saw.
10. When you cut warped stock, which side should face the table?
11. Define resawing and discuss why stock is resawn. How would you set up the band saw for resawing?
12. Describe how to cut circles on the band saw.
13. Describe nibble, tangent and relief cuts. Why are they important to cutting curves?
14. What is the purpose of a cutting sequence? How does it help you locate turning holes?
15. How do compound curves differ from normal curves?
16. How is round stock cut on the band saw? Why must it be clamped?

SUGGESTED ACTIVITIES

1. Demonstrate the procedure for tilting the table on the band saw in your shop.

2. Demonstrate how to install a blade on the band saw in your shop.

3. Demonstrate the procedure for coiling or folding a band saw blade. Ask your instructor for a used blade to practice with.

4. Lay out some push sticks on scrap stock. Use the band saw to cut them to size.

The *rotary jointer surfacer* is designed to plane small pieces of stock. Pieces too small to be planed on the jointer may be planed on the rotary jointer surfacer. The rotary jointer surfacer is sold under the trade name of "Uniplane" by Rockwell International.

KEY TERMS

rotary jointer surfacer
cutterhead
bevel
chamfer

compound miters
infeed fence
outfeed fence

ROTARY JOINTER SURFACER

The rotary jointer surfacer (Figure 37-1) is a stationary machine found in many woodworking shops. The cutterhead in the rotary jointer surfacer is mounted vertically. It holds eight small cutters that plane the work (Figure 37-2). Stock is fed into the rotating *cutterhead* and is planed by the rapidly moving cutters.

The cutterhead rotates downward and forces the work toward the table. There is no danger of kickback. Warped stock under 12″ long (300 mm)

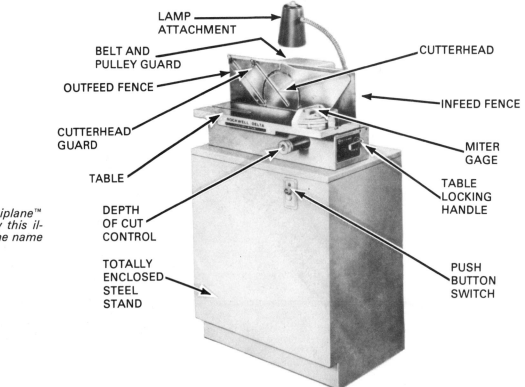

Figure 37-1. *The Uniplane™ and its parts. Study this illustration to learn the name of each part.*

LAMP ATTACHMENT
BELT AND PULLEY GUARD
OUTFEED FENCE
CUTTERHEAD GUARD
TABLE
DEPTH OF CUT CONTROL
TOTALLY ENCLOSED STEEL STAND
CUTTERHEAD
INFEED FENCE
MITER GAGE
TABLE LOCKING HANDLE
PUSH BUTTON SWITCH

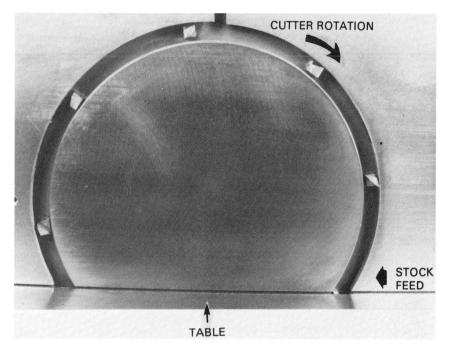

Figure 37-2. *The cutterhead holds eight small cutters. These cutters plane the work.*

and ⅜″ (9 mm) square may be planed safely. With practice, smaller pieces under 3″ long (75 mm) and ⅜″ (9 mm) square may be planed.

The table on the rotary jointer surfacer may be tilted to cut bevels and chamfers (Figure 37-3).

The table has a milled slot for a miter gage. The miter gage is used for planing miters and compound miters (Figure 37-4).

The depth of cut is adjusted with the control knob which moves the *infeed fence* in and out (Figure 37-1). The fence may be adjusted for cuts from ¹⁄₆₄″ to ⅛″ deep. The *outfeed fence* does not move. It is never adjusted.

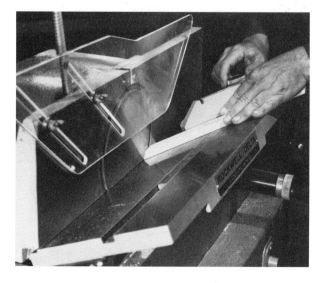

Figure 37-3. *Tilt the table to cut bevels and chamfers. Make sure the table is locked in position before use.*

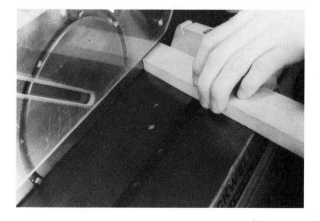

Figure 37-4. *Use the miter gage to plane miters and compound miters.*

Safe Operation Of The Rotary Jointer Surfacer

The following procedures and rules will help you learn to operate the rotary jointer surfacer safely and efficiently:

1. Make all adjustments with the switch off and the power disconnected.
2. Adjust the guard so that it is no more than 1/4" (6 mm) above your workpiece.
3. Wear protective glasses when operating the rotary jointer surfacer.
4. Allow the cutterhead to turn at full operating speed before feeding the work into it.
5. Use a push stick or push block to feed stock into the cutterhead. Keep your hands 4" away from the cutterhead.
6. Check stock for loose knots. If there are loose knots, do not plane the stock. The knot could shatter or jam the cutterhead and cause injury.
7. When other planing or sawing machines are operated at the same time as the rotary jointer surfacer, you should protect your hearing with ear plugs or hearing protectors.

PLANING STOCK ON THE ROTARY JOINTER SURFACER

When *face planing* stock, hold the face of the stock securely against the fence (Figure 37-5). If the stock is warped, place the concave face against the fence. Adjust the fence for a cut of no more than 1/16" (3 mm). Set the guard so that it clears the work by no more than 1/4" (6 mm).

If you are planing *end grain* or *edge grain,* check the table with a try square to see that it is square with the fence (Figure 37-6). If it is not, it can be adjusted by loosening the table clamps which are located at the table ends. Lock the table securely after adjusting it.

End grain planing is done with the miter gage (Figure 37-7). You can adjust the miter gage to an angle with a combination square or sliding T bevel. The miter gage is squared to the fence with a try square.

When all adjustments are made, turn on the rotary jointer surfacer. Allow the cutterhead to reach full speed. Feed your stock into the cutter-

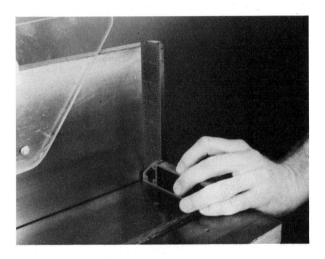

Figure 37-6. *Use a try square to check the angle between the table and the fence.*

Figure 37-5. *Hold the stock securely against the fence when face planing. Use a push stick to keep your hands clear of the cutter.*

Figure 37-7. *Use the miter gage when planing end grain.*

head. Use a push stick or push block to feed your stock. If the stock chatters, take a lighter cut.

Dull cutters will chatter even with a light cut. Dull cutters sometimes make a convex cut. Both conditions mean the cutters need grinding.

PLANING BEVELS AND CHAMFERS

The table on the rotary jointer surfacer can be adjusted to cut *bevels* and *chamfers.* Loosen the table clamps located on both table ends and adjust the table to the desired angle. Adjust the guard no more than ¼" (6 mm) above your work. If you plane end grain, place the miter gage in the table slot. Your infeed fence should be adjusted for a cut of ¹⁄₁₆" or less.

Turn on the machine. Allow it to come up to full speed. Feed your stock into the cutter (Figure 37-3). Use the miter gage or a push stick to feed your stock. Do not force the work into the cutterhead. Let each cutter do the work.

PLANING COMPOUND MITERS

Compound miters require two adjustments. First adjust the miter gage to the desired angle. Set this angle between the miter gage and infeed fence. Then adjust the table to the desired angle. This angle is set between the infeed fence and the table.

The guard should then be adjusted to no more than ¼" (6 mm) above your work. Adjust the infeed table for a cut of ¹⁄₁₆" (2 mm) or less. Place your work against the miter gage and feed it into the cutterhead (Figure 37-4). Hold your work firmly against the miter gage to keep your angles true.

QUESTIONS FOR REVIEW

1. Is the size of your workpiece important when using the rotary jointer surfacer?
2. How many cutters are in the cutterhead?
3. Does the rotary jointer surfacer have a kickback hazard?
4. How is the depth of cut adjusted on the rotary jointer surfacer?
5. List the procedures that you should follow to operate the rotary jointer surfacer safely and efficiently.
6. Discuss the procedure for face planing stock on the rotary jointer surfacer.
7. How would you cut a compound miter on the rotary jointer surfacer?

SUGGESTED ACTIVITIES

1. Demonstrate adjustment of the infeed fence on the rotary jointer surfacer.

2. Demonstrate adjustment of the table for cutting chamfers and bevels.

Jointers and Power Planes

The *jointer* is a stationary machine. It is used for smoothing rough stock and planing stock edges or ends. The *power plane* is a portable, hand-held machine. It does the same operations as the jointer.

Jointers may also be used to bevel or chamfer stock, cut tapers, and rabbet stock edges. With practice, these operations can also be done with a power plane.

KEY TERMS

jointer	push stick
cutterhead	snipe
chipbreaker	rabbet
infeed table	power plane
outfeed table	power block plane
push shoe	

JOINTER

The *jointer* (Figure 38-1) is used in the woodshop for planing stock. Before you operate a jointer, you should know the names of all its principal parts, what they do and how they are adjusted.

The *cutterhead* (Figure 38-2) is mounted horizontally between the infeed and outfeed tables. The cutterhead is driven by a motor through a V belt and pulley system. The motor is located in the base of the jointer below the cutterhead. The cutterhead turns at approximately 4500 rpm.

The cutterhead usually has three knives wedged into place with a *chipbreaker* (Figure 38-2). The knives remove material as the work is fed across the rotating cutterhead. The knives are all adjusted to the same height when they are installed in the cutterhead. They are not moved after instal-

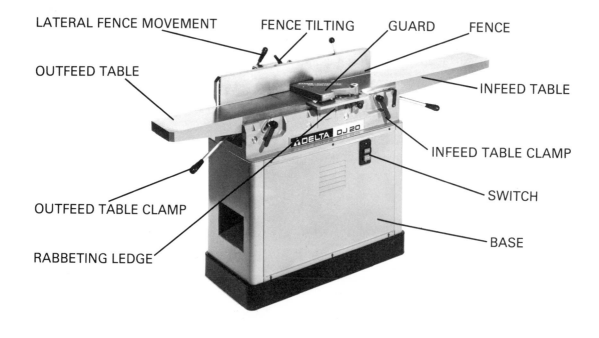

Figure 38-1. *The parts of a jointer. Study this illustration to learn their names.*

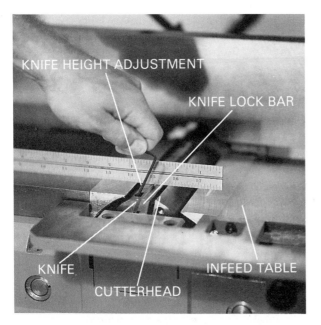

Figure 38-2. *The cutterhead is mounted between the infeed and outfeed table. The knives are wedged into the cutterhead by the hex head set (gib) screws.*

lation except for sharpening. The *length of the knives* indicates jointer size. If the knives are 8" (200 mm) long, it is an 8" jointer.

The *infeed* and *outfeed* tables (Figure 38-1) are both adjusted for jointer operation. Under each table is a handwheel or crank to control table height. Each table has a locking device which locks the table after adjustment. Some tables have a locking device on the handwheel; others

are located on the table ways beneath the table. This locking device must be loose to adjust table height.

The *infeed table* is adjusted more often than the outfeed table. Infeed table height controls the amount of stock removed. The infeed table supports the work as it is fed into the cutterhead. It is adjusted 1⁄32" (1 mm) to 1⁄8" (3 mm) below the height of the knives (Figure 38-3). Depth of cut can be read on the indicator located on the side of the jointer.

The *outfeed table* supports the work after it is planed. It is adjusted to the same height as the knives in the cutterhead (Figure 38-3). If the outfeed table is too high, the jointer will cut a *taper* (Figure 38-4). If the outfeed table is too low, it will cut a *snipe* (Figure 38-4). A snipe is a

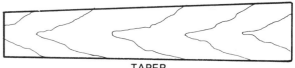
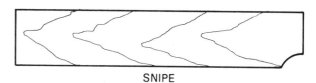
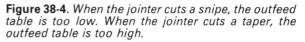

Figure 38-4. *When the jointer cuts a snipe, the outfeed table is too low. When the jointer cuts a taper, the outfeed table is too high.*

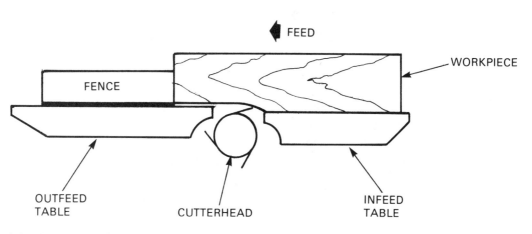

Figure 38-3. *The infeed table is set for the depth of cut. The outfeed table is even with knives. It supports the work after it is planed.*

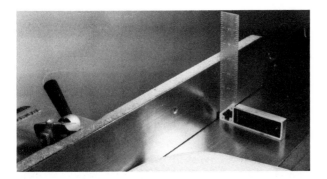

Figure 38-5. *Squaring the fence to the table. Be sure the fence is locked in position before use.*

gouge at the rear edge of your work. The outfeed table is adjusted only to correct a taper or snipe condition.

The *fence* controls the angle at which the work is fed across the jointer. It is squared with the table for most operations (Figure 38-5). The fence can be adjusted to an angle for cutting chamfers or bevels. The fence has a locking device to secure it at the desired angle. Most fences tilt toward and away from the cutterhead.

Accessories

Two accessories that should be available at every jointer are the *push shoe* (Figure 38-6) and the *push stick*. These accessories are used to

Figure 38-6. *Feed stock across the knives. Do not force the stock. Stand to the side of the jointer—not behind it.*

feed stock across the jointer. They help you control the stock and keep your hands more than 4″ (about 100 mm) away from the cutterhead.

Safe Operation Of The Jointer

The following procedures will help you become a safe and efficient operator of the jointer:

1. Make all adjustments to the jointer while it is off.
2. Make sure that the depth of cut is correct for your work. Edge cuts should not exceed ⅛″ (3 mm) and face cuts and end cuts should not exceed ⅟₁₆″ (2 mm).
3. Make sure the guard is in position and operating correctly. Always use the guard when planing stock.
4. Short stock and thin stock cannot be planed safely. For face and edge grain planing, your piece should be at least 12″ long (300 mm), ⅜″ (9 mm) thick and ⅜″ (9 mm) wide. For end grain planing, your piece should be at least ⅜″ (9 mm) thick, 12″ (300 mm) wide and 6″ (150 mm) long.
5. Plane new and clean stock only. Stock with knots or defects should not be planed. Never plane stock containing nails, wire, dirt or grit.
6. Protect yourself when you operate the jointer. Wear protective glasses. If the jointer is operated in a noisy area, wear ear plugs or hearing protectors.
7. When operating the jointer, stand to the side of the machine. This will protect you in case of a kickback.
8. Feed your stock with a push stick or push shoe. This will keep your hands clear of the cutterhead (Figure 38-6).
9. Never place your hands directly over the cutterhead. Always keep your hands 4″ to 6″ (100 to 150 mm) away from the cutterhead.
10. If stock vibrates when planed, take a lighter cut. If the stock still vibrates, the knives may need sharpening.

Face Planing On The Jointer

Face planing is done to smooth rough stock and prepare it for the surfacer. Make sure the piece is at least 12″ (300 mm) long and ⅜″ (9 mm) square. Lay the work on the infeed table. The concave side of the stock should face the table. Make sure there are no defects in the stock.

Adjust the infeed table for no more than a 1/16″ (2 mm) cut. Make sure the fence is square to the table and securely fastened.

With the work clear of the cutterhead, turn on the jointer. Feed your stock across the cutterhead with the push shoe (Figure 38-6). Stand to the side of the jointer as you feed your stock. Make sure that your work is completely clear of the cutterhead before you release it.

Inspect the jointed face. If the grain has a chipped or torn appearance, you are planing against the grain. Reverse the direction of feed to eliminate chipped grain. Continue planing until the face is smooth. Your stock may now be edge planed on the jointer or the other face may be planed in the surfacer.

Edge Planing On The Jointer
Edges are planed to make them even and remove saw marks. Plane the stock edge so it is square (90° angle) to the face. This allows the stock to be easily ripped or glued edge-to-edge. Edge planing is sometimes called jointing.

When you plane an edge, make sure the fence is perpendicular to the table. Adjust the infeed table for a cut of no more than 1/8″ (3 mm). Check the grain direction on your work. Try to plane with the grain (Figure 38-7).

Place the concave edge of rough stock downward on the infeed table. With the work clear of the cutterhead, turn on the jointer. Feed your stock across the cutterhead with a push stick. If the stock is wider than 6″ (150 mm), you do not

need a push stick. You may push it by hand. Stand to the side of the jointer as you feed the work across the cutterhead. Make sure your work is clear of the cutterhead before you release it. If chipped grain appears, reverse the direction of feed. Continue planing until the edge is smooth.

Planing End Grain And Plywood Edges
End grain and plywood edges are difficult to plane. This is because they tend to break or chip at the end of the cut (Figure 38-8). To eliminate

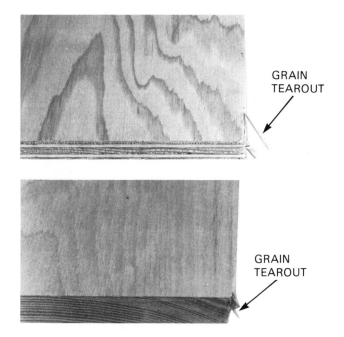

GRAIN TEAROUT

GRAIN TEAROUT

Figure 38-8. *End grain and plywood will chip if they are planed like edge grain.*

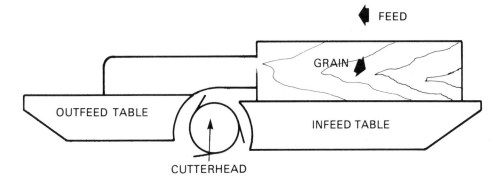

Figure 38-7. *Plane stock with the grain. This will avoid torn or chipped grain.*

this problem, plane in two steps. Set the fence at the desired angle and adjust the infeed table for a cut of no more than 1/16" (2 mm).

The first step is to feed your piece into the cutterhead about one inch (25 mm) and lift it straight up off the table (Figure 38-9). The second step is to feed the other end into the cutterhead and complete the cut (Figure 38-10). The first cut eliminates any chipping of the grain. Remember stock should be 12" (300 mm) wide and 6" (150 mm) long for end grain planing.

Never face plane plywood. The veneers and glue may damage the knives. Hardboard and particle-board should not be jointed.

Cutting Bevels And Chamfers On The Jointer

When stock is edge jointed with the fence tilted, a chamfer is cut. Additional cuts make the chamfer a bevel. The fence can be tilted toward the table or away from it (Figure 38-11). Make sure the table is locked securely. The face of the stock must be firmly against the fence (Figure 38-12). You may need several cuts to complete the bevel.

Chamfers or bevels on end grain should be cut on the table saw or rotary jointer surfacer. They are too difficult to cut on the jointer.

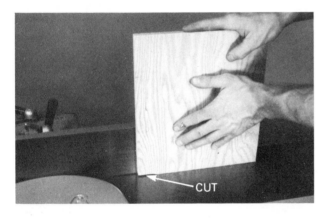

Figure 38-9. *Plane about one inch (25 mm) of the end and lift the piece off the cutter.*

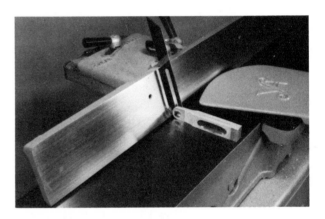

Figure 38-11. *Adjusting the fence with a sliding T bevel. Make sure the fence is locked securely before you begin.*

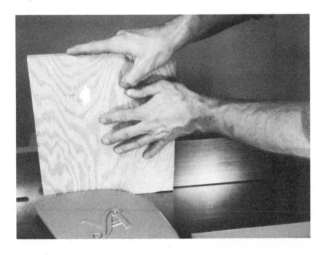

Figure 38-10. *Turn the piece around and feed it across the cutterhead. Make sure that solid stock is at least 12" (300 mm) wide and 6" (150 mm) long when you plane end grain.*

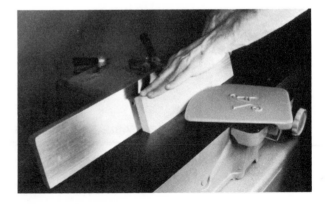

Figure 38-12. *Planing a bevel. Keep the face of the stock against the fence.*

Planing A Taper On The Jointer

After the *taper* is laid out, measure the end where the largest amount of stock is to be removed. If ⅛″ (3 mm) or less is to be removed, set the infeed table to remove that amount. If the amount of stock to be removed is greater than ⅛″, divide it into two or more cuts and set the infeed table to that dimension. For instance, if ⅜″ (9 mm) is to be removed, you could set the infeed table for a ⅛″ (3 mm) cut and make three cuts (Figure 38-13).

Place the work on the jointer with the beginning of the taper resting on the outfeed table. Clamp a *stop block* to the jointer behind the work (Figure 38-14). Butt the end of the work against the stop block and lift the front of the work until it clears the knives. Turn on the jointer and slowly lower the work onto the knives (Figure 38-15). The stop block will prevent a kickback. Feed the stock across the knives with a push stick. Repeat the process until you reach your layout line. Be sure to have your instructor help you set up the jointer for tapering.

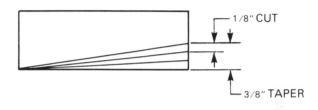

Figure 38-13. *Take a series of cuts to make a taper. Each cut should be ⅛″ (3 mm) or less.*

Figure 38-14. *Clamp a stop block to the jointer. The beginning of the taper should rest on the outfeed table.*

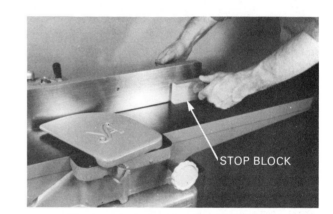

Figure 38-15. *Slowly lower the work onto the jointer knives. Then, push the work across the knives.*

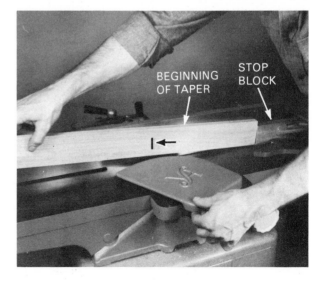

Planing Rabbets On The Jointer

Planing *rabbets* on the jointer may require removal of the guard. It should be done cautiously. When the jointer is set up, the fence

Figure 38-16. *The fence covers the unused portion of the blade when cutting a rabbet. Be very careful if the guard must be removed to plane a rabbet.*

Figure 38-17. *Power plane,* top, *and power block plane,* bottom. *Study this illustration to learn the names of their parts.*

covers the unused portion of the blade (Figure 38-16). Be sure to feed the work with a push stick. It is safer to cut rabbets with a router or table saw whenever possible.

Determine the dimensions of the rabbet. Adjust the distance from the end of the jointer knife to the fence for the rabbet width. Set the infeed table to a fraction of the rabbet depth. If the rabbet depth is ½" (12 mm) set the infeed table for a ⅛" (3 mm) depth of cut. After each cut, lower the jointer table ⅛" (3 mm) until the entire ½" (12 mm) depth is cut. Have your instructor help you set up the jointer for rabbeting.

POWER PLANE

The *power plane* (Figure 38-17) is a portable tool that operates like a jointer turned upside down. The power plane is held like a hand plane. Since the power plane is hand-held, it will take practice to work with the same accuracy as the jointer.

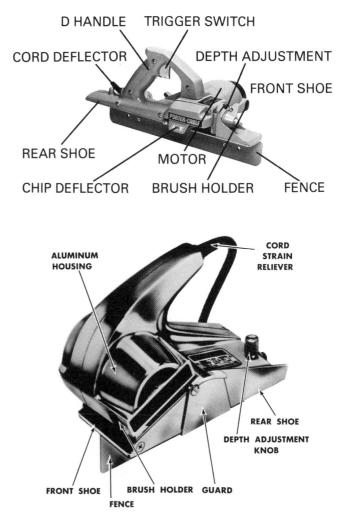

Stock that is too heavy to be controlled on the jointer can be planed successfully with a portable power plane.

Power planes come in two general sizes. The larger plane (Figure 38-17, *top*) is like a hand jointer plane. The smaller *power block plane* (Figure 38-17, *bottom*) is like a hand block plane.

Power planes have an adjustable *front shoe* which controls the depth of cut. It is adjusted by a *control knob* on the top of the jointer. The *cutterhead* may have spiral knives or straight knives. Some power planes have a *fence* or edge guide permanently attached to the side while others have a fence that is mounted only when needed.

Power planes vary in design. It is important to read manufacturer's instructions before using the power plane.

Safe Operation Of The Power Plane
The following procedures will help you operate the power plane safely and efficiently.

1. Make all adjustments with the power disconnected. Be sure all guards are in place.
2. Plane new and clean stock only. Stock with knots or defects should not be planed. Never plane stock containing nails, wire, dirt or grit.
3. Clamp your work securely before planing. Do not attempt to hand hold stock you are planing. If pieces are too small to clamp safely, use a hand plane.

4. Protect yourself when you operate the power plane. Wear protective glasses. If the power plane is operated in a noisy area, wear ear plugs or hearing protectors.
5. Take light cuts. It is better to make two or three light cuts than to make one heavy cut.
6. Keep your hands clear of the knives. If the power plane has two handles, use them. This will keep your hands clear of the knives.
7. Keep the power cord clear of the power plane.
8. Never face plane plywood. Hardboard and particleboard should not be planed.

Planing Flat Surfaces
Adjust the power plane for a cut of no more than 1⁄16″ (2 mm). Some power planes may require a smaller cut. Check manufacturer's instructions. Adjust the fence or edge guide to the desired angle and secure it. If you are planing a wide surface, you will not need the edge guide. Place the front shoe on the work. Make sure the knives are not touching the work. Turn on the power plane and feed it across your work (Figure 38-18). Keep the power cord away from the power plane.

Handle the power plane in the same way as a hand plane. Press downward on the front shoe as you begin the cut and downward on the rear shoe as you end the cut.

Keep your hands on the grips as you operate the power plane. Do not force the power plane. Let the knives cut the stock.

Figure 38-18. *Planing with a power plane. Feed the power plane slowly. Do not force it. Keep the power cord clear of the cutter.*

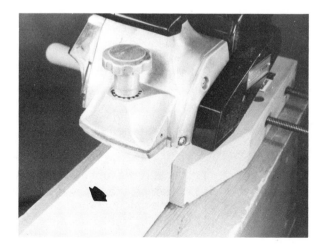

Cutting Chamfers And Bevels With The Power Plane

Bevels and chamfers can be cut by adjusting the fence or edge guide to the desired angle. Hold the fence or edge guide against the work, and the power plane will cut a chamfer or bevel.

Bevels can be cut on doors with a power plane. Some power planes are sold with an edge guide adjusted for a five-degree bevel.

On some power planes, the front shoe is grooved (Figure 38-19). This groove will ride on the corner of the work while the knives cut a chamfer behind it. Practice on scrap stock before you bevel or chamfer your work.

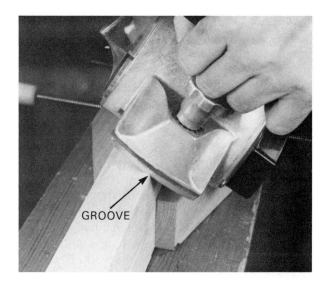

GROOVE

Figure 38-19. *This power plane has a grooved front shoe. The groove rides on the corner while the knives cut a chamfer behind it.*

QUESTIONS FOR REVIEW

1. Name the principal parts of the jointer and describe their function.
2. Is the infeed table adjusted more often than the outfeed table?
3. What causes tapers and snipes to be cut by the jointer? How are they eliminated?
4. Describe the procedures you should follow to operate the jointer safely and efficiently.
5. What is the minimum size a piece should be for face and edge jointing? For end jointing?
6. How do you know when you are planing against the grain?
7. When you are planing rough stock, which side should face the table?
8. Why is end grain difficult to plane?
9. Describe the procedure for cutting chamfers or bevels on the jointer.
10. How is a taper cut on the jointer? Why is a stop block clamped to the jointer when tapering?
11. Why must rabbets be cut cautiously? Why is the infeed table lowered after each cut during rabbeting?
12. What is the function of a power plane? What are its principal parts?
13. Describe the procedures you should follow to operate the power plane safely and efficiently.
14. Describe the procedure for planing flat surfaces with the power plane.

SUGGESTED ACTIVITIES

1. Check the fence on the jointer in your shop. Make sure it is at a right angle (square) to the table.

2. Ask your instructor for some scrap stock with a taper layout on it. Set the jointer up to cut this taper. Ask your instructor to check your setup.

3. Adjust the front shoe on the power plane in your shop for a 1/16" cut.

CHAPTER 39 Surfacer

The surfacer is also known as a *planer* or *thickness planer*. It is designed to plane one face or edge of a board parallel to the other face or edge. Stock is sometimes planed true on one face and edge using the jointer before planing the opposite face or edge in the surfacer. Rough stock that is true can be planed in the surfacer without first being jointed. The jointed face or edge is on the table when stock is fed into the surfacer. The surfacer is designed to plane solid stock only. It should not be used to plane any other material.

KEY TERMS

surfacer	gib assembly
cutterhead	elevating handwheel
pressure bar	bed rollers
chipbreaker	carrier board
corrugated infeed roller	

SURFACER

The *surfacer* (Figure 39-1) is used in most woodworking shops. The surfacer is designed to take light cuts. Be sure you know surfacer terminology and safe operation before you use the machine.

The size of the surfacer is determined by the *length of the cutterhead* and the maximum thickness of stock that can be planed. For example, a 24″ × 9″ surfacer has a 24″ (600 mm) cutterhead and will plane stock that is up to 9″ (225 mm) thick.

Once stock is in the surfacer, feed is automatic. The *corrugated infeed roller* pushes the stock into the rotating *cutterhead* (Figure 39-2). Sur-

facers usually have an anti-kickback device. The knives in the cutterhead remove stock as the piece is fed under them. As the piece leaves the cutterhead, the outfeed roller pulls the stock out of the surfacer (Figure 39-2).

The *chipbreaker* is located in front of the cutterhead and the pressure bar is located behind the cutterhead (Figure 39-2). The chipbreaker helps control grain tearout. As the knives remove chips, the chipbreaker breaks them before they lift the grain or tear the wood. The *pressure bar* pushes the stock toward the table as it passes through the surfacer. The pressure bar keeps the stock from vibrating as it is planed. This reduces the number of machine marks on the stock.

The knives are held in the cutterhead in the same way as the knives on the jointer. The *gib assembly* wedges each knife into the cutterhead. Most surfacers have three or four knives spaced equally in the cutterhead. Some cutterheads have small cutters that spiral around the cutterhead.

Surfacer Controls

Surfacers have a *power switch,* a *feed control,* an *elevating handwheel* and a *bed roller adjustment* (Figure 39-1). On some machines, there is also a *power table control* and a *feed lever.* The power table control moves the table up and down with electric power. The feed lever engages and disengages the feed mechanism.

The *power switch* turns the machine on and off. All adjustments should be made with the power switch off. The elevating handwheel raises and lowers the bed or table. One revolution of the elevating handwheel raises or lowers the table a

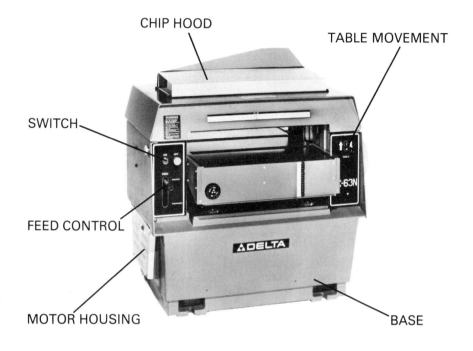

CHIP HOOD

TABLE MOVEMENT

SWITCH

FEED CONTROL

MOTOR HOUSING

BASE

Figure 39-1. *The controls and parts of the surfacer. Study this illustration to learn their names and function.*

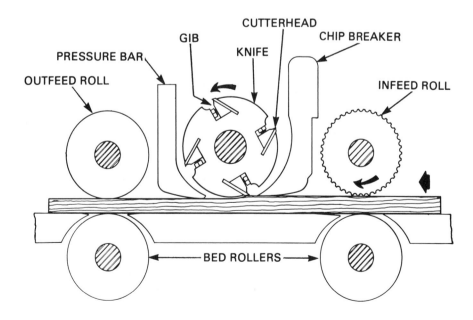

CUTTERHEAD

GIB

KNIFE

CHIP BREAKER

PRESSURE BAR

OUTFEED ROLL

INFEED ROLL

BED ROLLERS

Figure 39-2. *Cutaway view of the surfacer planing a piece of stock.*

given amount. An indicator (a depth of cut gage) next to the table gives the thickness of the stock after it is machined (Figure 39-1).

The feed control wheel regulates the rate at which stock is fed through the surfacer. Slower feed speeds are used for hardwoods. They produce fewer machine marks. The *bed roller* adjustment controls the height of the bed or table rollers. Rollers are adjusted to maximum height for stock that is rough on one face (Figure 39-2). The rollers raise the stock slightly off the bed to reduce friction. This allows the rough stock to cross the bed easily.

Safe Operation Of The Surfacer

The following procedures will help you operate the planer safely and efficiently:

1. Make all adjustments with the power switch off. Adjust the planer to take a cut of no more than 1/16″ (about 2 mm).
2. Surface new stock that has a true face or edge. Stock with loose knots or other defects should not be planed.
3. Stock should be at least 12″ (about 300 mm) long and 3/8″ (about 9 mm) square to be surfaced normally. Smaller pieces require special procedures.
4. Protect yourself when surfacing stock. Wear protective glasses. If the surfacer is noisy, wear earplugs or hearing protectors (Figure 39-3).

5. Stand to the side of your work as you feed it into the surfacer. Keep your hands on the edges or top of the work as it is fed into the surfacer. If your hand is under the stock, it could get pinched between the table and work.
6. Make sure that the dust collection system is in operation when you operate the surfacer.
7. Plane stock with the grain. The surfacer is not designed to plane across the grain. Sheet stock such as particle board and plywood cannot be planed in the surfacer.
8. Plane only one thickness at a time. If you have several pieces of different thickness, plane the thickest piece first. All the pieces should be about the same thickness if you are going to plane them together.
9. If the work becomes stuck, turn the surfacer off. After the cutterhead comes to a complete stop, lower the table and investigate.
10. Have a helper receive the work as it comes through the surfacer.

SURFACING STOCK

Rough stock with a true surface or stock which has been jointed to a true surface can be surfaced. Measure your stock in the center and at all four corners to determine its thickness. Set the depth of cut. About 1/16″ (2mm) should be removed from the work. For example, if the stock measured 13/16″ (about 19 mm) at its thickest point, then the surfacer bed or table would

Figure 39-3. *Protect yourself when surfacing stock. Wear hearing protectors to guard against loud noises.*

Figure 39-4. *Place stock true face down on bed. Thin end should be toward the surfacer. Stand to the side with your fingers on the edges or top of the stock.*

be adjusted to ¾″ (18 mm). This would remove ¹⁄₁₆″ from the work. If the piece is tapered, feed the thin end first. If the stock is rough on both sides, raise the bed rollers to their highest position.

Turn the surfacer on and allow it to come to full speed. Place the stock on the bed with the thin end toward the surfacer and the smoothest face down (Figure 39-4). Push the stock forward until the infeed roller begins to feed it into the cutterhead. Be sure to stand to the side of the stock and keep your fingers on the edges or top of the stock.

As the board is being surfaced, go to the rear of the machine and support your stock as it leaves the machine. A helper may also do this. This will keep the end of the piece from raising up into the cutterhead. Do not allow stock to accumulate on the outfeed end of the machine. Pieces could become jammed as they leave the surfacer.

Continue taking cuts of no more than ¹⁄₁₆″ (about 2 mm) until your stock has been surfaced to the desired thickness.

Surfacing Short Stock
When pieces of stock are less than 12″ (300 mm) long they will not reach from the infeed roller to the outfeed roller. This means that they can be fed into the surfacer, but the outfeed rollers cannot pull them out of the surfacer. Pieces under 12″ long will become stuck inside the

Figure 39-5. *Short stock can be followed by a piece 12″ (300 mm) long or longer. This will push the short piece through. Make sure both pieces are the same thickness.*

surfacer. To surface short pieces, push them through with other pieces of the same thickness. Feed the short pieces one behind the other through the surfacer. The last piece fed through the surfacer must be longer than 12″ (Figure 39-5). It pushes the short piece into the outfeed roller and is then pulled through by the outfeed roller. This procedure prevents stock from getting stuck inside the machine.

If stock is shorter than 6″ (150 mm) long, it is best to surface it with the rotary jointer surfacer or a hand plane.

Surfacing Thin Stock

Stock that is ⅜″ thick or less is considered thin stock. Thin stock must be placed on a *carrier board* to be surfaced. The carrier board supports the stock and minimizes vibration that could shatter the stock. Sheet stock such as ¾″ plywood or particle board makes a good carrier board (Figure 39-6).

Adjust the table for stock thickness. Remember, if you are planing stock to ¼″ (about 6 mm) on a ¾″ (about 18 mm) carrier board, the table must be set at 1″ (about 24 mm) to compensate for the carrier board. Feed stock on the carrier board in the same way you would feed any other pieces. Make sure pieces are 12″ (about 300 mm) long or longer or they will become stuck in the surfacer.

Carrier boards are sometimes designed to hold stock at an angle. This type of carrier board is used to make molding with an angular shape (Figure 39-7).

Squaring Stock On The Surfacer

Stock used for table legs or turnings can be squared on the surfacer. Once stock has been jointed, with two perpendicular surfaces, the stock may be squared by removing stock from the two rough surfaces (Figure 39-8). Adjust the table to the desired height and feed the stock through the surfacer. The stock is then turned 90° and surfaced again at the same table adjustment. You may have to take additional cuts to obtain the desired dimension.

Figure 39-6. *Thin stock (under ⅜″ or 9 mm) is surfaced on a carrier board. Thin stock must be at least 12″ (300 mm) long when surfaced on a carrier board.*

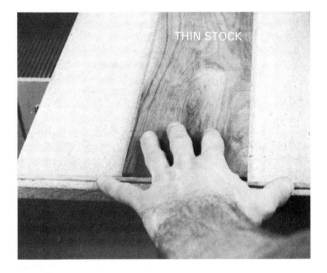

Figure 39-7. *Making picture frame molding with an angular carrier board. The rabbet was cut before the stock was planed.*

Figure 39-8. *Stock with two perpendicular surfaces jointed can be surfaced square.*

QUESTIONS FOR REVIEW

1. What is the function of a surfacer? How does the surfacer operate?
2. How do the chipbreaker and pressure bar improve the quality of stock planed in the surfacer?
3. How would you determine the size of the surfacer?
4. Name the controls found on the surfacer and describe their function.
5. List the procedure that you should follow to operate the surfacer safely and efficiently.
6. How do you determine the first table or bed adjustment when you are surfacing stock?
7. Why is it important to support your stock as it leaves the surfacer?
8. Why is a carrier board used to surface thin stock? What materials make good carrier boards?
9. Discuss the procedure for surfacing short stock. Why must the last piece be 12″ long or longer when surfacing short stock?
10. How can turning stock and table legs be squared with the surfacer? How is turning done?

SUGGESTED ACTIVITIES

1. Adjust the table on the surfacer to remove ¹⁄₁₆″ (about 2 mm) from a piece of stock. Ask your instructor to give you a piece of stock.

2. Locate the adjustment lever for the bed rollers on your surfacer.

Table Saw

The table saw is used to make accurate cuts in surfaced stock. It may also be used to cut a taper, bevel, chamfer or dado. The table saw is one of the most common power tools found in the woodworking shop.

Before operating the table saw (Figure 40-1) it is important to know the correct terminology. You should also be familiar with table saw accessories and controls.

KEY TERMS

table saw	carbide-tipped blade
fence	pitch
miter gage	arbor
dado head	miter
push stick	dado
feather board	groove
rip blade	rabbet
crosscut blade	taper
combination blade	tenon

TABLE SAW

The largest blade that can be used on a table saw determines its size. A table saw with a 10″ (250 mm) diameter blade is a 10″ (250 mm) table saw.

Table Saw Accessories And Devices

The three most important accessories used on the table saw are the *fence,* the *miter gage* and the *dado head.* You may also use devices like the *push stick* and *feather board* for some table saw setups.

Fence. The *fence* (Figures 40-1 and 40-2) is used for ripping stock to width. It is attached to guide bars or rails mounted on the table. This allows

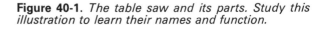

ELECTRICAL OVERLOAD PROTECTION
SPLITTER   GUARD   TABLE   FENCE
BLADE
MITER SLOT
MITER GAGE
LOCK KNOB
BLADE TILT HANDWHEEL
COCK KNOB
BLADE TILT SCALE
MOTOR HOUSING
PUSH BUTTON SWITCH
BLADE ELEVATING HANDWHEEL
CABINET
BASE

Figure 40-1. *The table saw and its parts. Study this illustration to learn their names and function.*

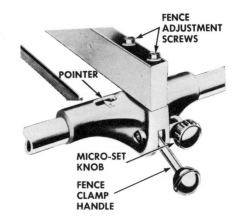

FENCE ADJUSTMENT SCREWS
POINTER
MICRO-SET KNOB
FENCE CLAMP HANDLE

Figure 40-2. *The fence travels on a rail or guide bar. It is locked in place with a clamp or threaded fastener.*

the fence to slide and be adjusted easily. The fence is held to the rails or guide bars by clamping pressure after adjustment.

Miter Gage. The *miter gage* (Figure 40-3) is used for crosscutting stock to length. There are two slots in the table top. The miter gage slides in these slots. The miter gage may be adjusted to cut stock at an angle. The knob on the miter gage locks it at the angle you select. Use a try square to square the blade to the miter gage. Raise the blade to full height for an accurate adjustment. Do not let tooth set give you a false reading (Figure 40-4).

The miter gage may be equipped with a stop rod for cutting several pieces of equal length (Figure 40-5). The stop rod is attached to the miter gage.

Some miter gages have clamping devices attached to them. They help control stock during cutting (Figure 40-6).

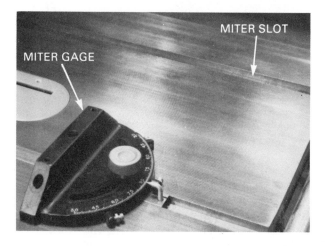

Figure 40–3. *The miter gage is used for crosscutting. It travels in a slot. There are usually two slots cut in the table.*

Figure 40-5. *The stop rod is used to cut several pieces to the same length.*

Figure 40-4. *Use a try square to set the angle between the blade and miter gage. Do not let tooth set give you a false reading. The head of the square may be placed against the blade or miter gage.*

Figure 40-6. *Some miter gages have a clamping device. This provides better control of your work.*

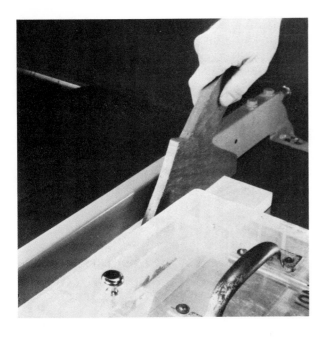

Figure 40-7. *Push sticks are used to feed narrow strips between the blade and fence.*

FEATHERBOARD

Figure 40-8. *The feather board holds stock against the fence or table. Do not allow the feather board to pinch stock between the blade and fence. The guard has been removed for clarity. Always use a guard when sawing.*

Push stick. *Push sticks* are shop-made devices used to feed narrow strips between the blade and the fence (Figure 40-7). The push stick keeps your fingers clear of the blade when ripping narrow strips. All table saws (and other power machines) should be equipped with a push stick.

Feather Boards. *Feather boards* are shop-made devices that hold stock against the table or fence (Figure 40-8). They are used for setups that require extra support. Feather boards may be clamped to the table or fence, but they should not pinch stock between the blade and fence. The feather board may be set up in front of or behind the blade.

Table Saw Controls
The table saw has three important controls that regulate the saw blade: *blade height, blade tilt* and electrical power (on-off) *switch.*

Blade Height. The *blade height* control is located on the front of the table saw. Blade height is regulated with a handwheel or crank and is adjusted to no more than ¼″ above the stock being cut (Figure 40-1). Blade height controls have a locking device which holds the blade at the adjusted height.

Blade Tilt. The *blade tilt* control is also regulated with a handwheel or crank. The tilt control is found on the side of the table saw. Blade tilt can be adjusted and locked at any adjusted angle (Figure 40-1).

On-Off Switch. The table saw is turned on and off by an electrical *switch*. The switch may be on the front or side of the table saw. Be sure you know where the switch is located before using the table saw (Figure 40-1).

Safe Operation Of The Table Saw
The table saw can be operated safely. The rules listed here will help you become a safe table saw operator:

1. Saw only smooth stock. Twisted stock should not be cut on the table saw.
2. Use a push stick for ripping strips narrower than 5″ (125 mm).
3. Rip narrow strips (under ¾″ or 18 mm) on the band saw and then plane them to thickness.
4. Adjust the blade height no more than ¼″ (6 mm) above stock thickness.
5. Use sharp blades. Make sure that you have the right blade for the job.

6. Use the guard. If you cannot use the guard, ask your teacher for help.
7. Control your work with the fence. Never cut freehand (without using the fence or miter gage).
8. Stand to the side of your work. Do not stand behind it.
9. Use a stop block or stop rod when you crosscut. Do not pinch stock between the fence and blade.
10. Wear protective glasses when using the table saw. Wear a face shield when using a carbide-tipped blade.
11. Make all adjustments with the switch off. Disconnect the saw while changing blades.
12. When making special cuts, have your teacher check your setup.

Saw Blades

There are many types of blades used on the table saw. These blades are also used on radial arm saws, portable circular saws and motorized miter boxes. When you select a blade, you must know its qualities and its purpose. You must also know when a blade is dull or has pitch on it. Dull blades or blades with pitch are unsafe.

Most saw blades are either *rip, crosscut* or *combination.* These blades differ in tooth shape and purpose (Figure 40-9).

Rip Blades. *Rip* blades have chisel-shaped teeth with round gullets (Figure 40-9). The tooth is designed to cut wood with the grain. Rip blades should not be used to crosscut wood.

Crosscut Blades. *Crosscut* blades have triangular shaped teeth that come to a point (Figure 40-9). The tooth is designed to cut wood fibers that go along the grain.

Combination Blades. Combination blades have both rip and crosscut teeth (Figure 40-9). They are designed to rip, crosscut and cut miters. Combination blades also cut plywood.

Some combination blades are hollow ground (Figure 40-9). Hollow ground blades are also called planer blades because the wood looks like it was planed after cutting.

Some combination blades are *carbide-tipped.* Carbide-tipped blades have small pieces of carbide brazed to each tooth (Figure 40-9). These blades stay sharp much longer than regular blades. Carbide-tipped blades should be used to cut hard board or particleboard. Occasionally the teeth on a carbide blade break loose; so wear a faceshield for extra protection.

Dull Blades. Dull blades are unsafe. They can cause the stock to kick back. A kickback throws the stock toward you while sawing.

Hard materials such as particleboard and hard board will dull regular blades quickly. A dull blade has round cutting edges. The cutting edges do not come together but look rounded.

Some blades bind because they have no *set.* Set makes the saw *kerf* wider than the blade. Each tooth on the blade is bent to provide set (Figure 40-9). Alternate teeth are bent in opposite directions. This provides clearance in the kerf.

RIP   CROSSCUT

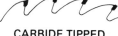

COMBINATION   CARBIDE TIPPED

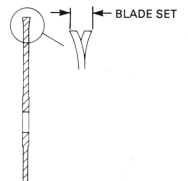

← BLADE SET

HOLLOW GROUND BLADE

Figure 40-9. *The most common circular saw blades: rip, crosscut and combination.*

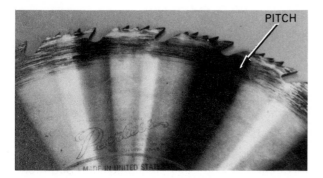

Figure 40-10. *Pitch is wood resin that builds up on the blade. Pitch buildup is caused by heat.*

Pitch. *Pitch* is wood resin that builds up on the blade. This build-up is caused by heat. Pitch build-up increases the chance of kickback (Figure 40-10). Keep blades clean with pitch remover.

CHANGING BLADES

When you change blades, be sure to disconnect the power. Lift the throat plate (Figure 40-3) to expose the arbor. The table saw *arbor* may have right-hand or left-hand threads. Inspect the threads to determine which type the saw has. Tighten the arbor nut on right-hand threads by turning it clockwise. Tighten a left-hand arbor nut by turning it counterclockwise.

Remove the nut and arbor washer from the arbor. Install the new blade with the teeth pointing toward you as you stand in front of the machine (Figure 40-11). Replace the washer and tighten the arbor nut.

Figure 40-11. *The teeth should point toward you when you stand in front of the saw. Inspect the arbor before you begin. This will help you decide whether it has left- or right-hand threads.*

RIPPING TO WIDTH

The *fence* is used for ripping stock. Adjust the fence for ripping stock to desired width. Measure the distance from the fence to a tooth on the saw blade. Use a tooth that is set toward the fence. This will give you an accurate cut.

Be sure that the fence is locked to the rail. Adjust the blade to no more than ¼″ (6 mm) above the stock height. Replace the guard and turn the machine on. Begin ripping the stock. If the stock is narrower than 5″ (125 mm) use a push stick.

CROSSCUTTING TO LENGTH

Crosscutting to length is done with the *miter gage*. A single piece of stock may be marked with a pencil and then cut. When several pieces are to be cut, a stop block or stop rod should be used. The stop block is clamped to the fence to keep the stock from being pinched (Figure 40-12). The distance between the blade and the stop block will be the stock length.

The stop rod (Figure 40-5) can be attached to the miter gage for cutting stock to length. Stock length is the distance from the blade to the stop rod. Make sure that the stop rod is attached securely.

CUTTING PLYWOOD

A *combination* or *carbide-tipped* blade should be used for plywood. Crosscut blades may also be used. Carbide blades are best for plywood. Apply masking tape where the plywood will be cut. This prevents the veneer face from splinter-

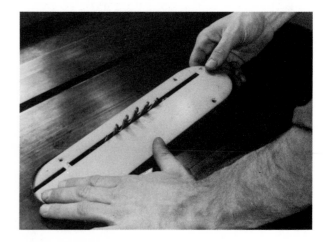

Figure 40-12. *A stop block is clamped to the fence. It prevents stock from being pinched between the fence and the blade.*

ing (Figure 40-13). You then saw through the tape. Scoring stock along the cutting line with a utility knife also reduces splintering.

When you cut plywood on the table saw, make sure that the visible or good side is up. Most splintering occurs on the underside. This is natural because the cutting blades are turned downward. Use the fence or the miter gage to control the plywood. Help is needed when cutting full sheets of plywood or particle board.

CUTTING PARTICLEBOARD

Particleboard cuts like plywood. It is cut with a *carbide-tipped* blade. No other blade cuts efficiently. Since there is no grain in particleboard, it seldom splinters. Particleboard must be controlled with the fence or miter gage during cutting (Figure 40-14). Large sheets may be cut with a portable circular saw first. This makes it easier to handle.

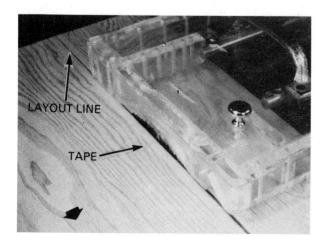

Figure 40-13. *Apply masking tape along the cutting line. This will keep the veneer face from splintering.*

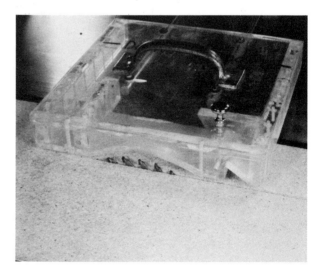

Figure 40-14. *Control particleboard with the fence or miter gage. Use a carbide-tipped blade when cutting particleboard.*

CUTTING MITERS

The table saw will cut *miters* and *compound miters*. Compound miters are cuts made by tilting both the miter gage and saw blade. All miter cuts use the miter gage for control. When you cut a frame, the stop rod may be used to make all four sides the same length.

Adjust the miter gage to the desired angle with a sliding T bevel (Figure 40-15). The sliding T bevel or combination square must contact the flat of the blade and not the teeth. The tooth set affects angle measurement. You can use a combination square to set an angle of 45°.

When cutting compound miters, set the blade angle with a sliding T bevel (Figure 40-16). Do not let tooth set give you a false measure. Check your miter setup on scrap stock before you cut your work.

CUTTING CHAMFERS AND BEVELS

Chamfers and *bevels* are cut by tilting the blade to the desired angle (Figure 40-17). Control stock with a *fence* or *miter gage.* Lay out stock and adjust the fence or miter gage for cutting. Be sure that the fence does not hit the saw blade.

Figure 40-15. *Use a sliding T bevel to set the angle of the miter gage. Do not let the blade set give you a false reading.*

Figure 40-17. *Cutting a bevel on the table saw. Make sure the stock removed does not get pinched between the fence and blade. This could cause a kickback.*

Stock that is removed should not be pinched between the fence and blade. This will cause a kickback. When you use the miter gage to cut chamfers or bevels, hold the work securely. If you use the fence, be sure to use a push stick. Use the guard for all chamfer and bevel cuts.

CUTTING DADOES AND GROOVES

Dadoes and *grooves* are cut using the dado head. The dado head includes two cutters ⅛" (about 3 mm) thick and one or more chippers ¹⁄₁₆"

Figure 40-16. *Use a sliding T bevel to set the angle of the blade. Do not let blade set give you a false reading. Check your setup on scrap stock.*

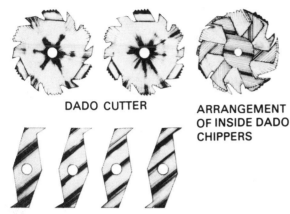

DADO CUTTER

ARRANGEMENT OF INSIDE DADO CHIPPERS

DADO HEAD SET

Figure 40-18. *Dado cutters and chippers.*

or ⅛" (about 1 to 3 mm) thick (Figure 40-18). The dado head will cut dadoes and grooves ¼" to ¹³⁄₁₆" (about 6 to 20 mm) wide. The two ⅛" cutters are used for ¼" dadoes. Chippers are added for larger dadoes (Figure 40-18).

INSTALLING THE DADO HEAD

The *dado head* is installed like any other blade. Disconnect the power before you begin. Stand in front of the saw. Place the cutter on the arbor with the teeth pointing toward you. Then place chippers on the arbor. The chippers should also point toward you. Place the other cutter on the arbor and replace the washer and nut as shown in Figure 40-19.

Before you tighten the dado head, make sure the chippers are staggered. This balances the dado head. The cutting edge of the chippers should be in the gullets of the dado cutters. Tighten the

Figure 40-19. *Dado head mounted on the arbor. Notice how the chippers fit in the gullets between the cutters.*

Figure 40-20. *Replace the throat plate before you begin. A special throat plate is used with the dado head.*

dado head and install the special dado throat plate (Figure 40-20).

Check your setup on scrap stock. The width of the cut can be changed by adding or removing chippers. Use the fence for cutting grooves and the miter gage for cutting dadoes. Control the depth of cut by raising or lowering the dado head.

CUTTING RABBETS

Rabbets can be cut using the dado head (Figure 40-21). Be sure that the dado head does not touch the fence when cutting rabbets.

Figure 40-21. *Cutting a rabbet with the dado head. Make sure the dado head does not touch the fence when cutting a rabbet.*

Rabbets may also be cut with a regular saw blade. This requires two cuts. Lay out stock and adjust blade height. Set the fence and make the first cut. Readjust the fence and blade for the second cut. Make sure the stock being removed is not pinched between the blade and the fence (Figure 40-22).

CUTTING TAPERS

Tapers are cut with a tapering jig. It is used to rip tapered pieces. There are many types of tapering jigs. Some jigs are adjustable and others are not. Figure 40-23 shows a common non-adjustable tapering jig.

Each tapering jig is set for a specific taper. The fence is then locked into place. The tapering jig is controlled by the fence.

CUTTING TENONS

Tenons may be cut using the dado head (Figure 40-24). Use the miter gage to hold the stock. The fence or stop rod can control tenon length.

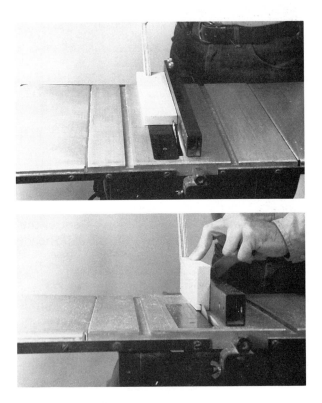

Figure 40-22. *Cutting a rabbet with a saw blade. Make sure the stock removed does not get pinched between the fence and blade. This could cause a kickback.*

Figure 40-24. *Tenons may be cut with the dado head. A miter gage is used to control the stock.*

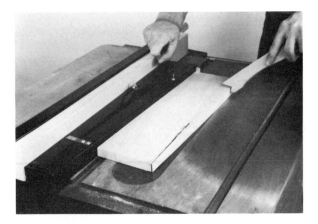

Figure 40-23. *Tapering jigs are used to rip tapered pieces. The tapering jig is controlled by the fence.*

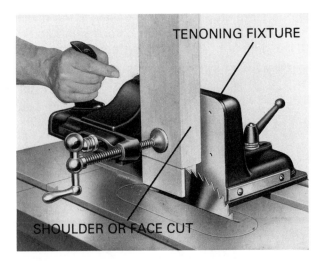

TENONING FIXTURE

SHOULDER OR FACE CUT

Figure 40-25. *Cutting a tenon with the tenoning jig. Make shoulder cuts first. Then make cheek cuts using the tenoning fixture. The cheek cut has just been made. Never attempt cheek cuts without a fixture.*

Tenons may also be cut with a saw blade. Two cuts are required. The face of the stock is cut first to mark tenon length. The stock is then clamped in a tenoning fixture to make the "cheek cuts".

Cheek cuts require a fixture for control (Figure 40-25). Never attempt cheek cuts without a fixture.

QUESTIONS FOR REVIEW

1. How do you know the size of a table saw?
2. Name and describe the three most important accessories on the table saw.
3. Name and describe two shop-made devices used with the table saw.
4. How is the miter gage squared with the blade?
5. What controls are important to table saw operations? Where are they found?
6. List some safe practices that should be followed when operating the table saw.
7. What are the principle types of circular saw blades? Sketch the tooth shape of each.
8. What is blade set? What is the purpose of blade set?
9. What is the advantage of carbide-tipped blades?
10. How do you identify a dull blade? Is pitch harmful to a saw blade?
11. Outline the steps you would follow to change a table saw blade?
12. What type of blade is best for plywood? How do you keep plywood from splintering when it is cut?
13. Describe the process for cutting chamfers and bevels.
14. Name the parts of a dado head. Discuss the procedure for mounting the dado head.
15. Discuss the procedure for cutting tenons. Why is a tenoning jig needed?
16. Describe the two methods for cutting rabbets on the table saw.
17. How are tapers cut?

SUGGESTED ACTIVITIES

1. Make a list of the types of circular saw blades found in your shop.

2. Adjust the rip fence on your table saw for ripping stock to a width specified by your instructor.

3. Demonstrate the procedure for installing a saw blade or dado head on your table saw. Make sure you have checked with your instructor and disconnected the power before you begin.

Radial Arm Saw

The *radial arm saw* is used chiefly for cutting stock to length. It may also be used to rip stock to width and cut dadoes or grooves.

KEY TERMS

radial arm saw	miter
yoke	dado
crosscutting	groove
ripping	tenon
arbor	

RADIAL ARM SAW

Radial arm saw (Figure 41-1) terminology will help you learn how to operate the saw safely and efficiently. You should also become familiar with radial arm saw controls before operating the saw.

The largest blade that can be used on the radial arm saw determines its size. For example, a radial arm saw with a 10″ diameter blade is a 10″ radial arm saw.

RADIAL ARM SAW CONTROLS

The radial arm saw has five important controls that are related to the blade. The five controls are *blade height, blade tilt, yoke rotation, radial arm pivoting* and electrical power (on-off) *switch* (Figure 41-1). These controls differ on various saws. Check manufacturer's instructions for your saw before making adjustments.

Blade Height. An elevation crank controls blade height. This handle may be on the column or on the base of the radial arm saw (Figure 41-1). Adjust the blade height to cut a ¹⁄₁₆″ kerf into the wooden table.

Blade Tilt. Tilt the blade on the radial arm saw by releasing the latch pin mechanism on the *yoke* and the bevel latch. (Figure 41-1). A scale and indicator are located on the yoke. This will help you adjust the blade to the desired angle. Be sure to clamp the locking mechanism after adjusting the blade.

Yoke Rotation. The yoke must be rotated for *ripping.* To rotate the yoke, release the clamping mechanism and the swivel latching pin (Figure 41-1). Turn the yoke 90°. The latching pin will engage when the yoke is in the correct position. You may have to raise the blade slightly to turn the yoke. The blade must cut into the table about ¹⁄₁₆″ after rotating the yoke. This enables the blade to rip through the stock it is cutting.

Radial Arm Pivoting. Pivot the radial arm for cutting miters or making angular cuts. To pivot the radial arm, release the arm latch lever and turn the arm (Figure 41-1). The arm latch lever will engage at 45° left or 45° right. If you are cutting miters, engage the arm latch lever. If you want a different angle, secure the radial arm with the arm clamping mechanism. The latch lever will not be engaged.

On-off Switch. The radial arm saw is turned on and off with an electrical *switch.* The switch is either on the front of the saw or on the column (Figure 41-1). Be sure you know how to turn the machine on and off before you operate it.

PRINCIPLE OF OPERATION

The radial arm saw uses the same blades and accessories as a table saw. The blade on the radial arm saw is pulled through the work while

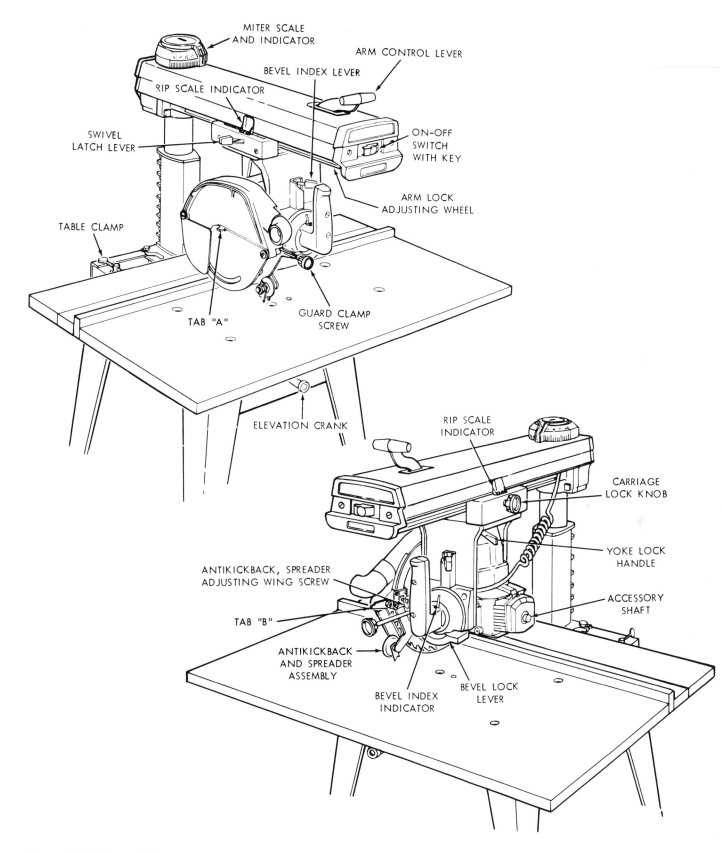

MITER SCALE
AND INDICATOR

ARM CONTROL LEVER

BEVEL INDEX LEVER

RIP SCALE INDICATOR

SWIVEL
LATCH LEVER

ON-OFF
SWITCH
WITH KEY

ARM LOCK
ADJUSTING WHEEL

TABLE CLAMP

TAB "A"

GUARD CLAMP
SCREW

ELEVATION CRANK

RIP SCALE
INDICATOR

CARRIAGE
LOCK KNOB

YOKE LOCK
HANDLE

ANTIKICKBACK, SPREADER
ADJUSTING WING SCREW

ACCESSORY
SHAFT

TAB "B"

ANTIKICKBACK
AND SPREADER
ASSEMBLY

BEVEL INDEX
INDICATOR

BEVEL LOCK
LEVER

Figure 41-1. *The radial arm saw and its parts. Study this illustration to learn their names and functions.*

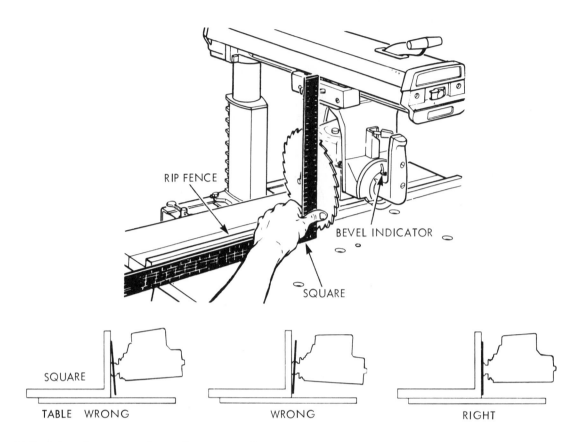

RIP FENCE

BEVEL INDICATOR

SQUARE

SQUARE

TABLE WRONG

WRONG

RIGHT

Figure 41-2. *A framing square is used to square the blade to the table.*

crosscutting. It is important that you keep your hands clear of the blade's path when crosscutting. Ripping on the radial arm saw is similar to ripping on the table saw.

SAFE OPERATION OF THE RADIAL ARM SAW

The radial arm saw can be operated safely. The rules listed here will help you safely operate the radial arm saw:

1. Do not try to cut warped stock. Stock that is to be ripped must have a true edge in contact with the fence.
2. Keep your work in contact with the fence at all times.
3. Before you use the radial arm saw be sure all controls and latches are clamped securely.
4. Use the guard for all operations.
5. Adjust the blade guard so that it clears the stock by no more than ¼".

6. Keep your hands clear of the blade's path. Hands should be 4" away from the blade at all times.
7. Wear protective glasses when using the radial arm saw. Wear a face shield when using a carbide-tipped blade.
8. Use sharp blades. Make sure that you have the right blade for the job.
9. Make all adjustments with the power off. Disconnect the power before you change blades.
10. Use a block or a jig to cut round stock.
11. When crosscutting, pull the saw into the work. When the cut is complete, return the yoke to the back of the table and clamp it in position. Clamping keeps the yoke from creeping.
12. When crosscutting, do not allow the blade to climb the workpiece. This can stall the motor and may throw the saw out of adjustment.
13. When ripping stock, feed it against the blade's rotation.

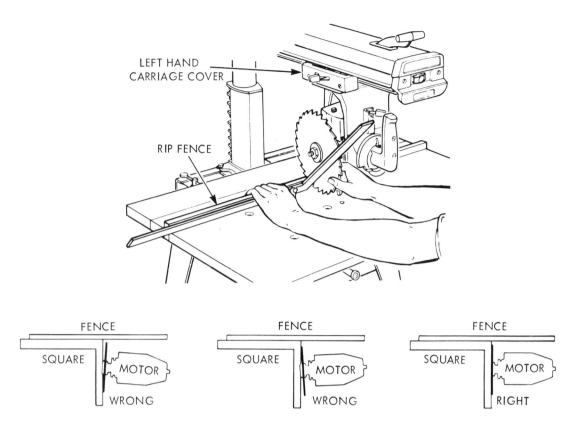

Figure 41-3. *A framing square is used to square the blade to the fence.*

14. Use a push stick for ripping strips under 5″ wide.
15. Avoid ripping narrow strips (under ¾″) (about 18 mm) on the radial arm saw. Use the band saw or table saw. Narrow strips may also be planed to thickness.
16. Do not rip stock shorter than 12 inches (about 300 mm) long. Use the table saw or band saw.
17. Do not stand directly behind the stock when you are ripping it.

CHANGING BLADES

On most radial arm saws, it is necessary to remove the guard when changing blades. Be sure to disconnect the power before removing the guard. The *arbor* may have left- or right-hand threads. Inspect the threads to determine which type the saw has.

Remove the nut and arbor washer from the arbor. Install the new blade with the teeth pointing toward the fence. Replace the washer and tighten the arbor nut. Adjust the blade to correct height with the elevating handle.

CROSSCUTTING TO LENGTH

Adjusting the Saw

The saw must be adjusted carefully to make square cuts. The blade must be perpendicular to the fence and the table for a square cut.

Blade Perpendicular to the Table. Place a try square or framing square on the table and against the blade. If the square butts against the table and blade, the blade is perpendicular to the table. (Figure 41-2).

Blade Perpendicular to the Fence. Place a square against the fence and pull the yoke toward you (Figure 41-3). The blade should follow the other leg of the square if the leg is perpendicular to the table.

Figure 41-4. *Grasp the yoke and pull the blade into your work. Do not allow the blade to climb your work.*

Crosscutting Procedure

After squaring the blade or adjusting it to the desired angle, place your stock against the fence. Line up your mark with the blade by adjusting the stock. Remember to keep the saw kerf in the waste stock. Turn on the power and release the clamp. Pull the blade into your work, but do not allow it to climb your work (Figure 41-4). Remember to keep your work against the fence. Keep your hands 4" away from the blade at all times. Return the yoke to the back of the table, secure the clamp, and turn off the power.

Cutting Duplicate Parts

Secure a clamp to the fence when cutting duplicate parts to length. Be sure to allow for blade set when measuring the distance from the clamp to the blade.

Square one end of all pieces that are to be cut. Place the square end against the clamp. Before you begin, cut a piece of scrap stock to check your setup. Be sure that the saw is making a square cut (Figure 41-5). Make any needed adjustments and follow the crosscutting procedure. Keep the table clear of sawdust. This will increase accuracy.

Figure 41-5. *Cutting duplicate parts to length. Be sure the square end is butted against the clamp.*

RIPPING STOCK TO WIDTH

Ripping stock requires rotating the yoke so that the blade is parallel to the fence. After the yoke is rotated, adjust the saw for ripping. Be sure to install a rip or combination blade before you rip

Figure 41-6. *Ripping stock to width. Be sure to use a push stick when ripping stock less than 5" (125 mm) wide. Never stand behind the piece you are ripping.*

stock. The blade must be sharp. Sharp blades reduce the chance of kickbacks.

Adjusting The Saw For Ripping

Adjust the guard so that it clears the stock by ¼" (6 mm). The anti-kickback mechanism should contact the stock and the spreader (splitter) should be in line with the blade. Measure the desired rip distance from the blade to the fence and tighten the clamp. If you wish to rip with a bevel edge, you must tilt the blade to the desired angle.

Ripping Procedure

Stock to be ripped should be at least 12" (300 mm) long. A true edge should be in contact with the fence and the stock should not be warped. Feed the stock against the blade's rotation. Keep the true edge against the fence and push the pieces clear of the blade. If the stock is less than 5" (125 mm) wide, use a push stick to feed it into the blade. Do not stand directly behind your work when ripping (Figure 41-6). There is always a chance that the stock could kick back.

CUTTING PLYWOOD

Full size sheets of plywood cannot be handled efficiently on the radial arm saw. Cut the sheets into smaller pieces with a table saw, a portable circular saw or a saber saw. The smaller pieces may then be cut on the radial arm saw. A crosscut or combination blade may be used to cut plywood. Carbide-tipped blades work best.

Plywood is normally cut with the good side or exposed side down. This limits splintering to the back or unexposed surface. Splintering can be eliminated by applying masking tape to the cutting line before cutting. Scoring along the cutting line with a utility knife will also eliminate splintering.

CUTTING MITERS

A *miter* is a crosscutting operation done with the radial arm pivoted (Figure 41-7). Adjust the radial arm to the correct angle. Pull the saw.

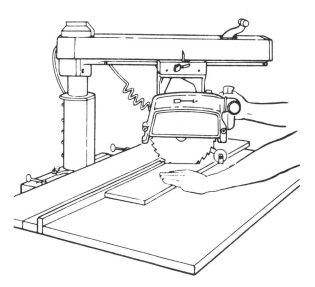

Figure 41-7. *Cutting a miter. Pivot the radial arm to the correct angle. Pull the saw through your work.*

There are positive stops at 45° to ensure accurate miters. Make a trial cut in scrap stock and check the angle with a combination square or sliding T bevel. Compound miters are made by tilting the blade and pivoting the radial arm.

CUTTING DADOES, GROOVES AND TENONS

Dadoes, grooves and *tenons* are cut with a dado head using crosscutting or rip cutting procedures.

Installing The Dado Head

Install the dado head like any other blade. Disconnect the power before you begin. Place the cutter on the arbor with the teeth pointing toward the fence. "Chippers" are then placed on the arbor. The chippers should also point toward the fence. Place the other cutter on the arbor and replace the washer and nut.

Before you tighten the dado head, make sure the chippers are staggered. This balances the dado head. The cutting edge of the chippers should be in the gullets of the dado cutters. Tighten the dado head and adjust it to the correct depth. Replace the guard.

Check your setup on scrap stock. If the dado is too narrow, you can space the cutters and chippers using another chipper.

Dadoes And Tenons

A *tenon* is made with a series of *dado* cuts (Figure 41-8). It is cut in the same way as a dado. When cutting dadoes, the work remains stationary and the dado head is pulled into it. Some

Figure 41-8. *Cutting a tenon using the dado head. Use the same procedure for cutting rabbets.*

dadoes and tenons are cut at an angle. Obtain the angle by tilting the *dado head* or pivoting the radial arm. You may make rabbets along the end of your work with this operation.

Grooves

When cutting *grooves,* the dado head is turned parallel to the fence and the stock is fed into the dado head. Cutting grooves is like ripping. Be sure to lower the guard to within ¼" (6 mm) of the work and feed into cutter rotation. Keep the work in contact with the fence while performing the grooving operation. Do not stand directly behind the workpiece when grooving stock because of possible kickbacks.

Grooves may be cut at an angle by tilting the dado head. Rabbets along the edge of your work may also be cut using this grooving operation.

QUESTIONS FOR REVIEW

1. List the principal uses of the radial arm saw.
2. How can you tell the size of a radial arm saw?
3. Discuss the procedure for adjusting blade height on the radial arm saw.
4. How is the blade on the radial arm saw tilted?
5. For what purpose is the yoke on the radial arm saw rotated?
6. When is it necessary to pivot the radial arm? What operation requires tilting the blade and pivoting the radial arm?
7. How is the radial arm saw like the table saw? How does it differ?
8. List some safe practices that should be followed when operating the radial arm saw.
9. Discuss the procedure for changing blades or installing the dado head on the radial arm saw.
10. Describe the technique you would use to determine if the blade on the radial arm saw was perpendicular with the table or fence.
11. When you cut duplicate parts to length, how do you control their length?
12. Discuss the steps that must be followed when ripping stock to width.
13. Can a full sheet of plywood be cut in a half with the grain or across the grain on the radial arm saw? Why?
14. Differentiate between a groove, dado and tenon. Describe how each is cut.
15. How is a rabbet cut with a radial arm saw?

SUGGESTED ACTIVITIES

1. Demonstrate the procedure for installing a saw blade on the radial arm saw. Make sure that you have checked with your instructor and disconnected the power before you begin.

2. Demonstrate the procedure for tilting the saw blade on the radial arm saw to an angle named by your instructor.

3. Adjust the arm on the radial arm saw for a miter cut. Check with your instructor before making any adjustment.

CHAPTER 42

Portable Circular Saw and Motorized Miter Box

The *portable circular saw* and the *motorized miter box* are versatile machines. Both are portable and both cut while the stock remains stationary. Each machine is fed into the work. The portable circular saw is often used by carpenters to frame houses, but it may also be used in the shop when the stock is too large for a table saw or radial arm saw. The motorized miter box is a high-speed circular saw that is mounted to a spring-loaded arm. The motorized miter box can be used for cut-off work, but it is best suited to miter work on trim or molding.

KEY TERMS

portable circular saw	crosscutting
motorized miter box	ripping
arbor locking button	pocket cut
telescoping guard	miter
rip guide	compound miter
arbor bolt	spacer block

PORTABLE CIRCULAR SAW

The *portable circular saw* is the most common circular saw in use today. It is important that you know correct terminology and correct operating procedure (Figure 42-1).

The size of a circular saw is determined by the *largest blade* that it will accommodate. The most common size sold today is the 7¼" (about 180 mm) saw. The blade is protected by two guards (Figure 42-1). The guard above the blade is a *stationary guard* and the guard below the blade is a *telescoping or retractable guard.* The guard retracts into the stationary guard when the blade is cutting. When the saw is cutting, the *base* or *shoe* rides on the work. The base can be adjusted to cut bevels by loosening the angle adjusting nut. The base also has a rip slot where the *rip guide* may be attached for ripping operations. The rip guide is an accessory that comes with most saws. The switch is in the handle.

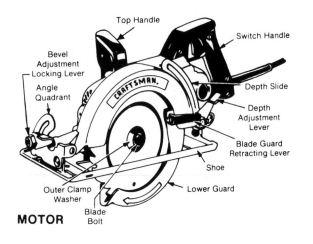

Figure 42-1. *The circular saw and its parts. Study this illustration to learn their names and function.*

Safe Operation Of The Portable Circular Saw

The following rules will help you safely operate the portable circular saw:

1. Make certain that the saw is grounded correctly.
2. Make sure that the guard is working correctly. Never remove the guard when operating the saw.
3. Use the correct blade for the job.
4. Wear protective glasses when operating the portable circular saw. If you use a carbide-tipped blade, be sure to wear a face shield.
5. Make all adjustments with the power disconnected.
6. Set the blade exposure to no more than ¼" (6 mm) greater than stock thickness.
7. Always support the stock on a bench or saw horse. Clamp short stock to the bench or saw horse.
8. Do not allow the stock to pinch the blade while cutting.
9. If the saw has two handles, use them. You cannot contact the blade if you use the handles.
10. Keep yourself balanced while sawing. Do not reach out too far.

Changing Blades

Before changing blades, be sure to disconnect the power. Wedge a piece of stock between the blade and the shoe to hold the blade stationary (Figure 42-2). Some saws have an *arbor locking button* or device that will do this (Figure 42-3).

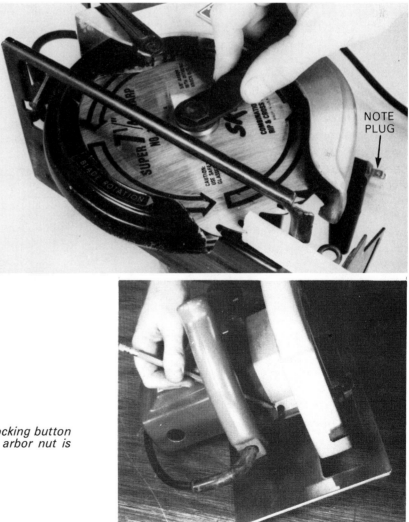

Figure 42-2. *Hold the blade with a piece of stock while loosening the arbor nut.*

Figure 42-3. *Some saws have an arbor locking button or device. It holds the arbor while the arbor nut is loosened.*

Figure 42-4. *Install a sharp blade. Replace the arbor washer and bolt. Teeth should point in the direction of blade rotation.*

The *arbor bolt* may have right or left-hand threads. Inspect the threads to determine which type the saw has. Remove the arbor bolt and washer. Retract the *telescoping guard* and remove the blade. Install the correct blade and replace the arbor washer and bolt (Figure 42-4). The teeth should point in the direction of blade rotation.

Crosscutting Stock To Length

Mark your stock and support it on a bench or sawhorse. Clamp it in position if necessary. Set the blade exposure to no more than ¼″ (6 mm) greater than stock thickness.

Set the shoe on your work. The blade should be clear of the stock and on the waste side of your mark. Turn on the power and allow the saw to gain full speed. Push the saw slowly into your work (Figure 42-5). Let the blade do the cutting—do not force it. Keep the blade on the waste side of your mark. Follow through with the cut allowing the scrap stock to fall. Do not allow the stock to pinch the blade or the blade will burn and become dull.

To control the saw, a straightedge may be clamped to the work as a fence. This will give a straight uniform cut. Do not clamp the straightedge to the scrap stock.

If the crosscut requires a beveled edge, you can adjust the shoe to the correct angle (Figure 42-6).

Ripping Stock To Width

Mark your stock and support it on a bench or sawhorse. Clamp it in position if necessary. Set the blade exposure to no more than ¼″ (6 mm)

Figure 42-5. *Start the saw and wait for it to gain full speed. Push the saw slowly into the work. Do not force the saw. Let the blade do the cutting.*

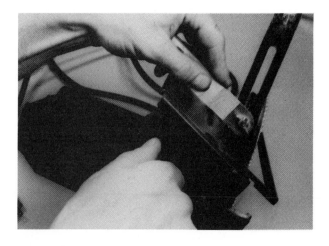

Figure 42-6. *For bevel cuts, adjust the shoe to the correct angle. Make sure the shoe is locked securely in position.*

Figure 42-7. *The rip guide rides along the edge of your work. It controls the width of the cut.*

greater than stock thickness. You may want to install the rip guide for control. The rip guide rides along the edge of your work (Figure 42-7). When making a bevel rip, adjust the shoe to the correct angle.

Line up the saw and turn on the power. When the saw gains full speed, push it slowly into your work. Let the blade do the cutting. If the blade binds, back up to free the blade and then turn the saw off. Open the kerf with wedges or a holder and begin sawing again (Figure 42-8).

Cutting Plywood

Plywood should be cut with a *combination* blade or a *crosscut* blade. *Carbide-tipped* blades work best. The good side or finish side of the sheet should be down during cutting.

Cutting plywood and other sheet stock is like cutting solid stock. The sheet must be well-supported and adjusted so that it does not pinch the stock as it is cut (Figure 42-8). The rip guide or a straightedge may be used to control the saw.

Use the same cutting procedures on plywood and sheet stock that you would use on solid stock. It may be necessary to seek help when cutting plywood. Your helper or helpers can support a large piece as it is cut. This will eliminate any pinching of the blade. Remember to keep your balance when cutting sheet stock or solid stock.

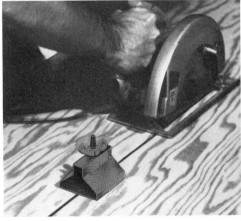

Figure 42-8. *Keep the kerf open with a special holder or wedges. This keeps the stock from pinching the blade.*

Figure 42-9. *Line the blade up with the waste side of your mark for a pocket cut. The blade should not touch the work.*

Pocket Cuts

When it is necessary to cut a hole in a piece of stock, a *pocket cut* may be used. Mark the stock and adjust the blade exposure to no more than ¼" (6 mm) greater than stock thickness. Retract the blade guard and rest the front of the shoe on your work. The blade should be lined up with the waste side of your mark, but should not touch the work (Figure 42-9).

Turn on the power. When the saw gains full speed, slowly lower the blade into the stock (Figure 42-10). When the shoe is in total contact with the stock, cut to the end of the mark. This

Figure 42-10. *Start the blade and slowly lower it into the work. When the shoe contacts the work, cut to the end of your mark.*

procedure must be followed on each line. You may have to cut the waste stock free at the corners with a handsaw.

Do not allow the saw to twist during the cut. This will cause the blade to bind, burn and get dull. Keep your hands clear of the blade during this operation. If you are unsure of the correct procedure, ask your instructor for help.

MOTORIZED MITER BOX

The *motorized miter box* (Figure 42-11) is used to cut *miters* on trim and molding. It is like a portable circular saw on a spring-loaded arm. A *crosscut* blade is used on the motorized miter box. This blade is designed for smooth cutting at higher rpm's than the blades used on other circular saws. The size of the motorized miter box is determined by the largest diameter blade that it will accommodate. The most common sizes are 9" and 10" (225 to 250 mm).

Understanding the terminology related to the motorized miter box will help you learn to operate it efficiently and safely. The motor arm contains the *handle* and *switch* (Figure 42-11). The motor arm is spring-loaded so it returns to the UP position after cutting. The *carrying lock* can be used to hold the motor arm to the table during transportation (Figure 42-11).

The angle of cut is adjusted with the *miter latch* and *miter clamp*. The fence and table remain stationary.

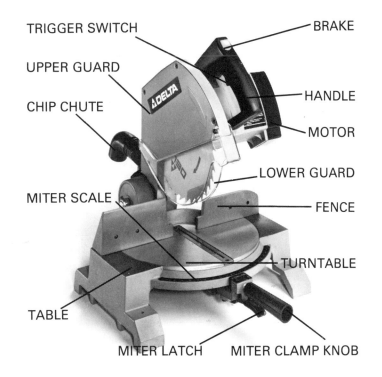

Figure 42-11. *The motorized miter box and its parts. Study this illustration to learn their names and function.*

Changing Blades

The blade is secured to the arbor by the arbor collars and nut. The guard must be removed when you change the blade. Make sure that the power is disconnected. Blades on the motorized miter box are changed in the same way as blades on a portable circular saw (Figure 42-12).

Figure 42-12. *Remove the guard when changing the blade. Be sure the power is disconnected. Use the correct wrenches to remove the arbor nut.*

Safe Operation Of The Motorized Miter Box

The following rules will help you safely operate the motorized miter box:

1. Make certain that the saw is grounded correctly.
2. Make sure that the guard is working correctly.
3. Use a blade of the correct diameter that is rated for high rpm operation.
4. Wear protective glasses when using the motorized miter box. When you use a carbide-tipped blade, wear a face shield.
5. Make all adjustments while the saw is disconnected.
6. Never attempt to hold pieces less than 12" (300 mm) long. Clamp short pieces to the fence. This will keep your hands away from the blade.
7. Keep the stock in contact with the fence and table when cutting.
8. Do not force the tool; let it cut through the stock.
9. Make sure that the motorized box is anchored securely.
10. Clamp round stock when cutting it.

Cutting Miters

Cutting miters requires correct adjustment of the motorized miter box and proper cutting procedures.

Adjusting the Angle. The blade angle is adjusted by loosening the miter clamp knob and squeezing the miter latch. The entire motor arm will then move to the desired angle. The miter latch has positive stops at 0°, 22½° and 45° but may be set at any angle. After the desired angle is set, tighten the miter clamp knob (Figure 42-13).

Cutting Procedure. Place the stock against the fence and table. Line up your mark with the

Figure 42-14. *Grasp the motor arm. Turn on the power. Pull the blade into the stock slowly.*

blade. Remember to keep the kerf in the waste stock. Grasp the motor arm. Turn on the power and let the blade gain full speed. Pull the blade into the stock slowly (Figure 42-14). Let the blade cut the stock. Raise the motor arm out of the work and release the trigger.

Compound Miters

Cove molding and picture frames require *compound miters* in the corners. To cut compound miters, use a *spacer block* cut at 45° to back up the work. Adjust the blade angle and cut the compound miters (Figure 42-15).

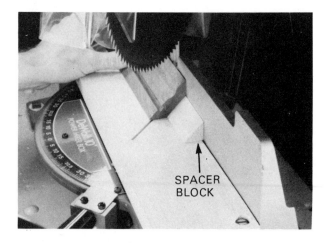

Figure 42-15. *Use a spacer to back the work when cutting compound miters.*

Figure 42-13. *Set the motor arm to the desired miter angle. Be sure to tighten the miter clamp knob.*

QUESTIONS FOR REVIEW

1. How is the size of a portable circular saw or motorized miter box determined?
2. How is the blade on the circular saw adjusted for cutting bevels?
3. List some safe practices that should be followed when operating a portable circular saw.
4. Describe the procedure for changing blades on a portable circular saw or motorized miter box.
5. Describe the procedure for crosscutting and ripping with a portable circular saw.
6. What blade is used for cutting plywood?
7. What type of blade is used on the motorized miter box?
8. List some safe practices to follow when you use the motorized miter box.
9. How is the blade angle adjusted on the motorized miter box?
10. Describe the cutting procedure that should be followed when using the motorized miter box.
11. How are compound miters cut on the motorized miter box?

SUGGESTED ACTIVITIES

1. Measure the blade on your portable circular saw to determine its size. Be sure the power is disconnected before you begin.

2. Demonstrate the procedure for installing a blade on your portable circular saw. Make sure the power is disconnected and you have checked with your instructor before you begin.

3. Adjust the angle of cut on the motorized miter box to an angle specified by your instructor.

The *lathe* is a machine designed to transform stock into cylindrical objects. A tool much like a woodcarving chisel is used to cut the stock as it is turned. The tool is controlled by the operator while being held on the tool support or tool rest.

LATHE

Working on a lathe (Figure 43-1) is called *turning*. There are many parts on a lathe. Become familiar with the parts and their safe use before starting work.

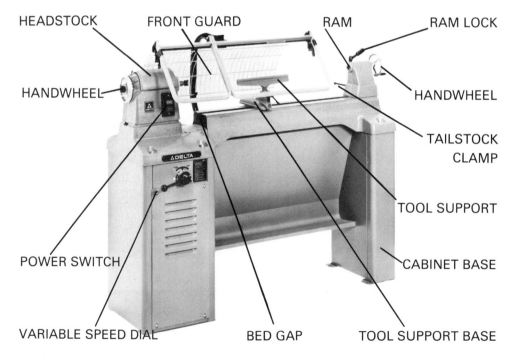

Figure 43-1. *The lathe and its parts. Study this picture to learn their names and function.*

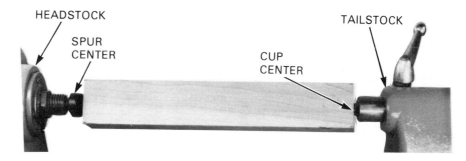

Figure 43-2. *Turning stock is clamped between the headstock and tailstock. Clamping pressure comes from the tailstock.*

KEY TERMS

lathe	knockout bar
headstock	tool support
tailstock	cutting
bed	scraping
spur center	turning
live center	split turning
cup center	taper
dead center	shoulder
spindle	bead
faceplate	cove
turning chisels	duplicator
outboard side	backing stock

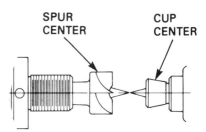

Figure 43-3. *The spur center and cup center are both tapered. The spur center (or live center) fits into the spindle on the headstock. The cup center fits into the tailstock. A tapered fit holds them securely.*

Stock may be turned between centers or on a faceplate. Stock turned between centers is clamped between the *headstock* and *tailstock* (Figure 43-2). Clamping pressure is applied by turning the *handwheel* on the tailstock. Stock is turned by the headstock through the *spur center* (Figure 43-3). Because the spur center drives the stock it is called the *live center*. The tailstock holds the *cup center* (Figure 43-3). It does not turn and is called the *dead center.*

When stock is turned on a *faceplate,* the faceplate is held to the headstock by the threaded *spindle* (Figure 43-4). The stock is held to the faceplate with wood screws.

The size of the lathe is determined by its *swing.* Swing is twice the distance from the bed to the center of the headstock spindle. A 10″ to 12″ (250 to 300 mm) lathe is common.

Principal Lathe Parts
The three principal parts of the lathe are the *headstock, tailstock,* and *tool support* (Figure

Figure 43-4. *The faceplate is held to the headstock by the threaded spindle.*

43-1). If you know how to operate the lathe, the quality of your lathe work or turnings will improve.

Headstock. The headstock usually contains a motor control switch. The motor turns the spindle. Some controls are *variable-speed.* The spindle speed is regulated by turning the control switch. On variable-speed lathes, spindle speed should be adjusted only while the motor is in operation.

Spindle speed on other lathes is regulated by *step pulleys.* The power is disconnected when changing the speed on lathes equipped with step pulleys.

The headstock spindle has external threads which hold a faceplate. It also has an internal taper to hold the spur center, also called the *live center.*

Tailstock. The *tailstock* is used to clamp the work between centers. It slides on the bed of the lathe and is locked in place with the tailstock locking clamp (Figure 43-1). The handwheel exerts pressure on the workpiece through the *cup center,* also called the *dead center.* It can be locked in position with the indexing pin or *spindle lock* (Figure 43-1). Backing off on the handwheel releases the cup center from its taper fit. The cup center requires lubrication before turning. This reduces heat build-up. The cup center remains stationary while the work is turning. Without lubrication, heat would build up in the cup center. Wax works well as a lubricant (Figure 43-5). When you turn stock, be sure the tailstock is tightened securely.

Tool Support. The *tool support* (or tool rest) holds the lathe tools at the correct height when turning stock (Figure 43-1). The tool support can be raised, lowered or swiveled in its base. The base slides on the lathe bed and is held in position with the clamp lever. The tool rest should be about 1/8" (3 mm) above the centerline of your workpiece and no more than 1/8" (3 mm) away from it (Figure 43-6). Be certain that the tool support and its base are clamped securely in position.

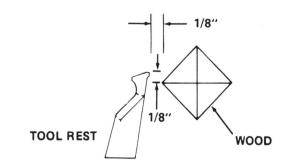

Figure 43-6. *The tool rest should be 1/8" (3 mm) above center and no more than 1/4" (6 mm) away from the work.*

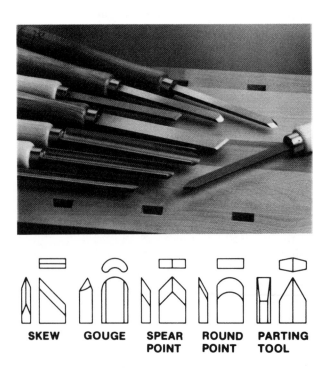

Figure 43-7. *Lathe tools or turning chisels.*

Figure 43-5. *Waxing the cup center reduces friction and heat. The cup center would burn the work if not lubricated. Push the wax into the cup.*

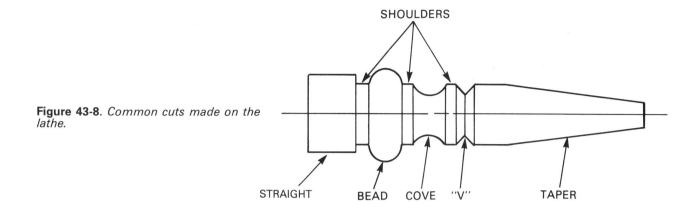

Figure 43-8. *Common cuts made on the lathe.*

SHOULDERS

STRAIGHT BEAD COVE "V" TAPER

Lathe Tools

Lathe tools or *turning chisels* are designed for cutting and shaping stock turned on the lathe. Each tool is designed for a specific job and is sharpened accordingly. The most common lathe tools are: *skew, gouge, round point, spear point* and *parting tool* (Figure 43-7).

Figure 43-8 shows the common cuts made with lathe tools. Use the correct tool for the job.

The *gouge* is used for rough work and cutting coves. The rough shaping of square stock into round stock is done with the gouge. The gouge is never used on faceplate turning because it could tear the work from the faceplate. The *skew* is used to smooth the rough turning. When the skew is turned on edge, it can be used to cut decorative lines or mark the stock for other cuts.

The *round nose* is used to smooth round stock or cut coves. The *spear point* is used to make decorative cuts such as beads. The *parting tool* can be used to cut shoulders next to beads and coves, but it is used chiefly to cut the turned piece away from the waste stock.

Sharpening Lathe Tools. Lathe tools are ground to the desired cutting angle (Figure 43-7) with a grinding wheel. Always wear eye protection when grinding. When you grind lathe tools, it is important to frequently quench them with water. Dip the tool in the water cup attached to the grinder. This will keep it cool and preserve its temper.

After you have ground the tool to the desired angle, hone it on a stone. Frequent honing keeps

Figure 43-9. *Tools with more than one cutting angle must be honed on both faces.*

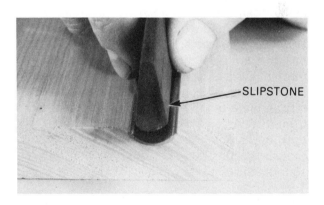

SLIPSTONE

Figure 43-10. *Use a slipstone to remove the wire edge from the gouge.*

the tool sharp. Hone a lathe tool as you would hone a plane blade or chisel. Tools with more than one cutting angle such as the spear point and skew must be honed on both faces (Figure 43-9). Remove the wire edge inside the gouge by honing with a slipstone (Figure 43-10).

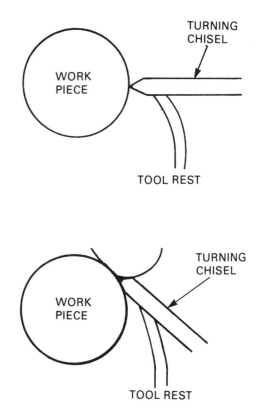

Figure 43-11. *The scraping method removes stock with an abrasive action. Scraping is easier to learn than cutting.*

Figure 43-12. *The cutting method removes stock with a paring action. The cutting method requires less sanding.*

After a lathe tool has been sharpened, it can be honed many times before regrinding.

Lathe Speeds
Lathe speed is determined by revolutions per minute (rpm) and workpiece diameter. A piece 6″ (150 mm) in diameter turning at 600 rpms travels past the tool rest 3 times as fast as a piece 2″ (50 mm) in diameter turning at 600 rpms. The larger the diameter of your work, the slower it must turn. A piece 6″ (150 mm) in diameter should be turned at the lowest possible speed. Stock 2″ (50 mm) in diameter may be turned at 2000 rpms. Slower speeds are necessary when turning square stock into a cylinder.

Turning Methods
There are two methods for removing stock when turning: *cutting* and *scraping*.

The scraping method removes stock with an abrasive action (Figure 43-11). The turning chisel is held on the tool rest and against the work. The cutting edge on the tool scrapes the work and removes stock. The turning chisel is easy to control when scraping, but the cutting edge becomes dull more quickly. You should master

the scraping method before attempting the cutting method.

When the cutting method is used (Figure 43-12), stock is removed with a paring action. This requires the turning chisel to be on the tool rest and laid against the work. The cutting method is more difficult than the scraping method.

The key difference between scraping and cutting is the angle at which the turning chisel is held.

Safe Operation Of The Lathe
Successful turning requires a knowledge of safe practices. Study the following safety rules before operating the lathe:

1. Roll sleeves up above your elbows and restrain long hair. Long hair or loose sleeves can wrap around the turning and pull you into the lathe. Remove neckties and jewelry.
2. Always wear a face shield to protect you from flying chips.
3. If your lathe has a guard, use it at all times.
4. Keep your tool rest ⅛″ (3 mm) above the center of the work. This will allow greater tool control.

5. Keep your tool rest within ¼″ (6 mm) of your work at all times. This provides additional leverage for tool control.
6. Lubricate the dead center with wax. This will eliminate stock burning.
7. Keep tools sharp and in good condition for best turning results.
8. Turning stock should have straight grain and be free from defects. Defective stock may break or disintegrate during turning.
9. Turning stock 3″ square or greater should have the corners chamfered before turning.
10. If you glue up stock for turning, allow the glue to cure for 24 hours and be sure that all joints are tight.
11. Be sure that your stock is mounted securely before you begin turning. Stock must be clamped securely between centers or screwed tightly to the faceplate.
12. Have your instructor check your setup before you begin turning.
13. Rough out stock at slow speeds. Turn large pieces at slower speeds.
14. If stock chatters or seems to be out of balance while turning, shut off the lathe and check the workpiece. It may not be securely screwed to the faceplate or clamped correctly between centers.
15. When doing a faceplate turning, remove the dead center if it is not in use. The dead center is sharp and could cut you.
16. Do not use the gouge on bowls or faceplate turnings. The gouge can dig into the work and may cause it to shatter.
17. When turning bowls turn the outside first and use the scraping method. This will minimize any chance of breakage.
18. When sanding or French polishing stock, remove the tool rest. Your fingers could be pinched between the tool rest and the workpiece.
19. When using the parting tool, be sure to make a clearance cut so the tool will not bind in the work.
20. If your lathe is equipped with a brake, use it. Do not attempt to stop the lathe by gripping the turning workpiece.

Selection Of Turning Stock

Stock that is to be turned on the lathe is subjected to extreme centrifugal (spinning) force. This force can cause defective stock to burst or disintegrate. Using defective stock may cause injury.

Stock with knots or twisted grain should *not* be used for lathe work. Select stock that has straight grain and no defects.

Gluing Lathe Stock. After selecting the stock, if it is necessary to glue it up for lathe work, be sure that all joints fit tightly. Use a good grade of polyvinyl (white) or aliphatic (cream yellow) glue to join your pieces (Figure 43-13). Do not use contact cement to join your pieces.

Allow the stock you have glued to cure at least 24 hours before turning. Check all joints to be sure they are tight. Do not turn stock with loose joints.

When stock is glued up for a *split turning,* brown paper is glued between the pieces. The paper makes the turning easy to split. Each part of the

Figure 43-13. *Use polyvinyl (white) or aliphatic (yellow) glue for gluing stock that will be turned. Never use defective stock for lathe work.*

A. STOCK READY FOR GLUING

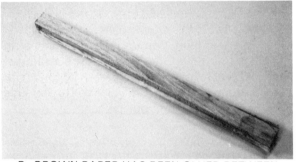

B. BROWN PAPER HAS BEEN GLUED BETWEEN
PIECES

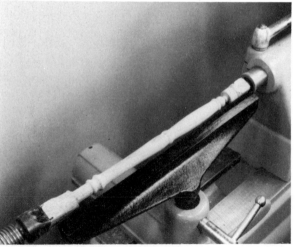

C. STOCK IS TURNED TO SHAPE

Figure 43-14. *Split turning.*

D. TURNING IS SPLIT WITH A UTILITY KNIFE

E. TWO SPLIT PIECES READY FOR USE

F. HEAD AND HANDLE HAVE BEEN SPLIT

FINAL PROJECT SEE FIG. 54-55

split turning is applied to a woodworking project for decorative effect.

Figure 43-14 shows how a split turning is done. You glue the split turning to the woodworking piece or project.

Mounting Stock On The Lathe
Faceplate Turning. After your stock has been securely screwed to the faceplate (Figure 43-15)

it can be attached to the headstock spindle. If the work is too large to be attached over the lathe bed, it can be attached on the outboard side of the headstock (Figure 43-16). Generally, only large bowls are turned on the outboard side.

When the faceplate is attached *over* the lathe bed, the spur center must be removed. The spur center is removed with a *knockout bar* (Figure 43-17). The knockout bar is inserted from the outboard side. Tap the spur center with the knockout bar to release it.

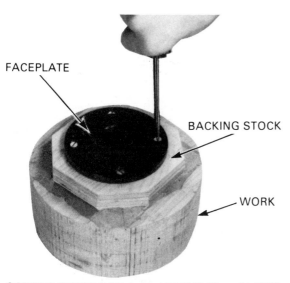

SCREWS SHOULD BE 1 1/4" (ABOUT 31 mm) LONG OR LONGER

Figure 43-15. *Use screws 1¼" (31 mm) to 1½" (37 mm) long to secure stock to the faceplate. After all screws are tight, the faceplate may be mounted on the spindle.*

Figure 43-17. *Tap the spur center with the knockout bar to release it. Hold the spur center so it does not fly out of the spindle.*

Figure 43-16. *A faceplate may be mounted on the outboard side of the headstock. This is done when the work is too large for the lathe bed.*

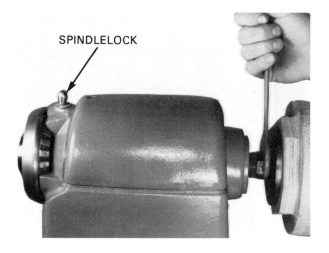

SPINDLELOCK

Figure 43-18. *Lock the spindle, then use a wrench to remove the faceplate from the spindle. Release the spindle after removing the faceplate.*

The faceplate is then screwed to the spindle. Make sure that the threads are aligned correctly. When turning over the bed, remove the cup center from the tailstock before turning. This is done by backing off the handwheel. Adjust the tool rest and have your instructor check your setup.

To remove the faceplate, lock the spindle and use a wrench to turn the faceplate (Figure 43-18).

Turning Between Centers. For stock to turn between centers, it must be driven by the spur center. Kerfs are cut into the ends of the stock so that they engage with the spur center. The centers of the stock are drilled so that the points on the cup and spur center may be correctly located (Figure 43-19). Stock not kerfed or drilled may split when mounted between centers.

Insert the spur center into the headstock spindle and the cup center into the tailstock. Engage your work on the spur center. On large turnings you may have to drive the spur center into the work with a mallet. Move the tailstock about 1" (25 mm) away from the end of your work. Secure the tailstock with the locking clamp. Lubricate the cup center with wax. Turn the handwheel until the cup center has cut into the work. Secure the spindle lock and adjust the tool rest. Have your instructor check your setup.

Turning A Cylinder. When roughing out square stock, turn at a slow speed. When turning between centers, you can use a gouge for roughing out the work. Be sure to adjust your tool rest as stock is removed. When the piece becomes round, the skew may be used to smooth the work.

Check the diameter of your work with a caliper (Figure 43-20). Never use the caliper to check the diameter of a piece that is in motion. After the stock is turned to the correct diameter, you may lay out the piece for additional cuts such as coves and tapers.

Figure 43-19. *Stock should be kerfed and the centers should be drilled for turning between centers. The kerfs engage with the spur center to turn the work.*

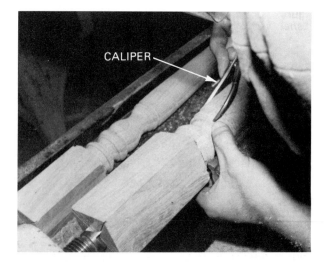

CALIPER

Figure 43-20. *A caliper can be used to check the diameter of your turning. Never check your stock while it is moving.*

Laying Out Round Stock
Round stock should be measured and marked carefully before making additional cuts. Make all layout lines with a sharp pencil while the lathe is off (Figure 43-21).

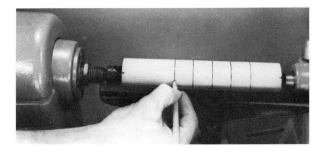

Figure 43-21. *After stock has been turned into a cylinder you can lay out other cuts. Use a pencil to make your layout.*

Figure 43-22. *The toe of the skew makes a small V-shaped cut. This cut eliminates grain chipping.*

The toe of the skew may also be used to cut the layout lines. This is done while the lathe is running. The toe of the skew makes a small V-shaped cut that breaks the wood fibers and eliminates grain chipping (Figure 43-22).

Templates may also be used to lay out or check your turning. A layout template uses sharp points to score the turning at the correct points (Figure 43-23). Some templates follow the shape of your work and may be placed against or around your work to check the shape or diameter (Figure 43-24).

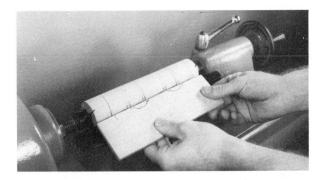

Figure 43-23. *A layout template may be used to mark duplicate parts rapidly. Sharp points are driven into the edge of the template. The sharp points scribe the stock at the correct spots.*

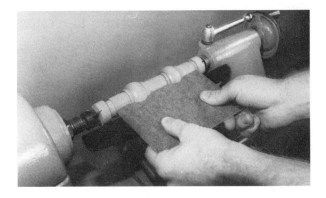

Figure 43-24. *A template can be used to check the shape of your turning.*

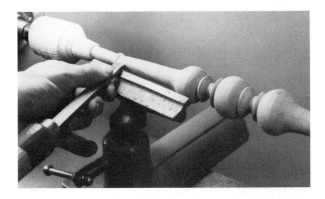

Figure 43-25. *Work toward the small end of the taper. The diameter at the small end should be slightly oversize. This will allow for sanding.*

Cutting Tapers
Tapers (Figure 43-25) are usually cut from the larger diameter to the smaller diameter. The smaller diameter should be first cut with a

parting tool. This kerf gives you a guide. Cut the taper with a skew or square nose. Work toward the smaller end, checking the diameter with a caliper. The diameter should be slightly oversize so it can be sanded.

Cutting Shoulders

Shoulders look like steps. They are formed between different diameters on the turning. When a round section of a turning meets a square section, a shoulder is also formed. Shoulders are often found on table legs (Figure 43-26).

When cutting a shoulder, make the first cut with the toe of the *skew*. A shoulder between a square and round section requires that the corners be nicked with the toe of the skew (Figure 43-27). Failure to do so may cause chipping at the corners.

After the corners are nicked, the shoulder may be cut with the *parting* tool. Be sure to make a clearance cut for the parting tool (Figure 43-28).

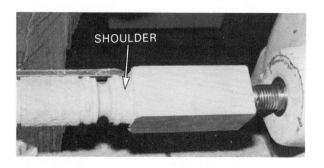

Figure 43-26. *Shoulders look like steps in the turning. When a square section joins a round section, a shoulder is formed.*

Figure 43-27. *Nicking the stock with the toe of the skew when forming a shoulder. The nick prevents tear out at the corners.*

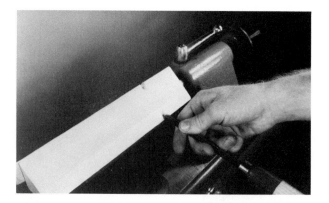

Figure 43-28. *The parting tool separates the shoulder. Notice the clearance cut. This prevents the parting tool from binding.*

Cutting Beads

Beads are cut with a spear point or skew (Figure 43-29). They may be separated with a parting tool or spear point.

Cutting Coves

Coves are usually cut with a *round nose* (Figure 43-30). The round nose is fed into the stock and moved from side to side to obtain the desired arc. Use a round nose that is slightly smaller than the cove. Cuts with a V shape are made with a *spear point.* Move the tool from side to side to obtain the correct shape.

Lathe Duplicators

Many lathes have *duplicators* attached to them (Figure 43-31). The duplicator enables you to make identical parts. Usually a follower traces the original part or a template. The follower controls the cutting tool so that all parts are cut the same size and shape. Duplicators vary in design and operation. Read the manufacturer's instructions on how to set up and use the duplicator correctly.

Faceplate Turning

Faceplate work often involves turning of thin sections and end grain. Tools must be kept sharp for this work because too much tool pressure might cause the work to disintegrate.

Large faceplate turnings should be cut to a cylindrical shape on the band saw before they are mounted on the lathe. Screws that secure the faceplate to the work or backing stock should be

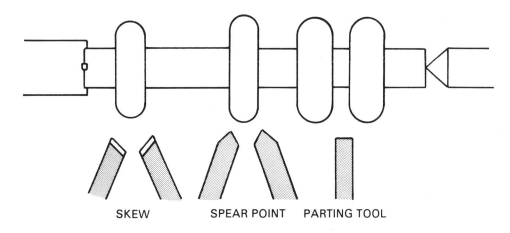

SKEW   SPEAR POINT   PARTING TOOL

Figure 43-29. *Using the skew, spear point and parting tool for cutting beads.*

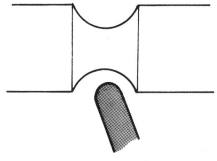

ROUND NOSE

Figure 43-30. *The round nose is used to cut a cove. Choose a round nose that is slightly smaller than the cove. This will prevent binding.*

Figure 43-31. *Duplicators are used to make identical parts. Be sure to read the owner's manual before using the duplicator.*

GUARD

NEW PART

FOLLOWER   ORIGINAL PART

1 ¼″ (31 mm) to 1 ½″ (37 mm) long. Brown paper is used when you glue backing stock to the work. Figure 43-32 shows the turning and finish sequence for a bowl.

Many special chucks and attachments are used for turning faceplate work. Before using the attachments, have your instructor check your setup.

Take light cuts when doing faceplate work. When turning bowls, shape the exterior profile of the bowl first. If the bowl has a lid, the lid is made before the inside of the bowl is turned. The lid is cut from the end of the turning.

3. TURN OUTSIDE FIRST

1. ATTACH FACEPLATE TO BACKING STOCK WITH WOOD SCREWS

4. KEEP YOUR TOOL REST CLOSE TO YOUR WORK

2. BROWN PAPER MAKES IT EASY TO SPLIT THE WORK AWAY FROM BACKING STOCK

Figure 43-32. *Turning and finishing a bowl.*

5. BEGIN TURNING THE INSIDE DO NOT FORCE THE TOOL

6. TAKE LIGHT CUTS

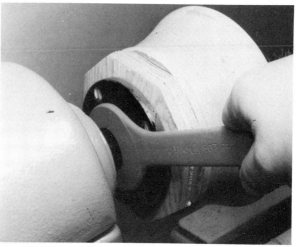

8. REMOVE THE FACE PLATE

7. SAND THE BOWL

BROWN PAPER

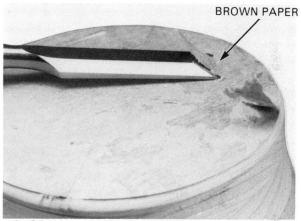

9. SEPARATE THE BACKING SHEET AND THE BOWL

10. APPLY THE FINISH

Sanding Lathe Work

Select abrasives with C or D weight paper for sanding turnings. Be sure to remove the tool rest before sanding. Garnet abrasives with 60, 80 or 100 grit will smooth most turnings. Cut the abrasive into strips and hold it against the work as it turns (Figure 43-33). When the piece is smooth, stop the lathe and sand with the grain. This will remove crossgrain scratches.

Finishing Turned Pieces

Turned pieces may be finished on or off the lathe. Legs to a table or other assembly should be finished off the lathe to match the other parts.

Figure 43-33. *Use thin strips of abrasive to sand work on the lathe. Be sure to remove the tool rest before sanding.*

Bowls used for foods are finished off the lathe with non-toxic materials such as salad bowl finish.

Other turnings may be finished on the lathe. French polish is often used. Dip a rag into the French polish and apply it to the turning workpiece (Figure 43-34). The friction of the rag against the work causes the finish to dry.

Apply enough French polish to obtain the desired gloss. Be sure to remove the tool rest before applying French polish.

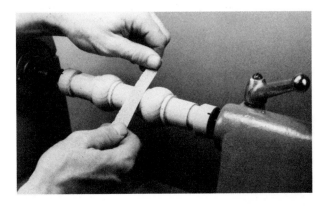

Figure 43-34. *French polish is applied to the piece while it is turning. The friction of the rag against the work causes the finish to dry.*

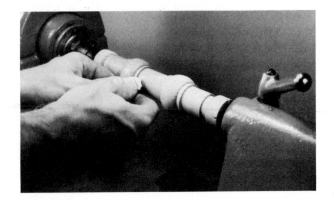

QUESTIONS FOR REVIEW

1. What are the three principal parts of the lathe? What is the function of each?
2. Does the tailstock slide on the bed of the lathe?
3. Name and describe the common types of turning tools used on the lathe.
4. Are gouges used for rough cutting square turning stock?
5. How are lathe tools sharpened?
6. How fast (rpms) should a piece 6″ in diameter be turned on the lathe?
7. When roughing out stock, at what speed should the piece be turned.
8. List safety precautions you should follow when operating the lathe.
9. Should the tool rest be ¼″ above the center of your workpiece?
10. May gouges be used on faceplate turnings?
11. Can stock with knots or twisted grain be safely turned on the lathe?
12. What glues work well for gluing up turning stock? How long must the glue cure before the piece is turned?
13. Describe the procedure for mounting faceplate on the lathe. How does this differ from mounting stock between centers?
14. Describe the procedure for cutting a shoulder on a turning.
15. Describe how faceplate turning differs from turning between centers. What special precautions should be taken when using a faceplate?

SUGGESTED ACTIVITIES

1. Use the knockout bar to remove the spur center from the headstock.

2. Make a list of the lathe tools found in your shop. Name one common cut made by each.

3. Check the lathe tools in your shop for sharpness. Hone any lathe tool that is dull.

4. Prepare a piece of stock for spindle turning. Mount the piece in the lathe and adjust the tool support. Have your instructor check your setup.

CHAPTER 44

Router and Laminate Trimmer

The router is a portable power tool used for shaping and cutting wood or plastic. The size of the router is determined by its horsepower rating. The *laminate trimmer* is a portable power tool used for trimming plastic laminates.

KEY TERMS

router

base

motor

collet chuck

shaft

shaper table

edge guide

router bit

pilot tip

router guide

dado

groove

laminate trimmer

ROUTER

All routers have a *base* and a *motor* (Figure 44-1). The motor is moved up and down in the base. This travel determines the depth of cut. The base has a locking device to hold it at the desired setting.

The router has control handles or knobs connected to the base (Figure 44-1). The handles may contain the control switch on the motor. Other routers have the control switch on the motor.

The motor has a *collet chuck* on its *shaft.* This chuck holds the router bit. Most routers hold bits with a ¼″ shank. The motor also has a locking

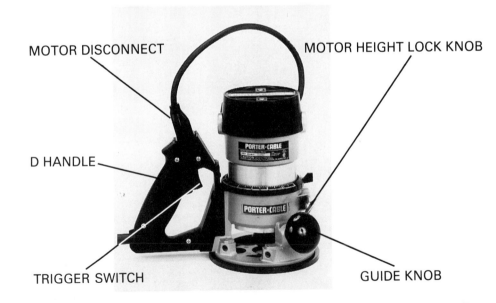

MOTOR DISCONNECT

MOTOR HEIGHT LOCK KNOB

D HANDLE

TRIGGER SWITCH

GUIDE KNOB

Figure 44-1. *The router and its parts. Study this illustration to learn their names and function.*

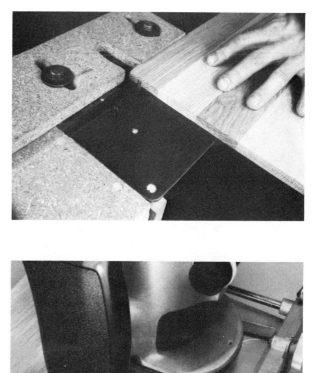

Figure 44-2. *The shaper table holds a router. The router is mounted under the table. It can be used like a shaper. Safer routing of small pieces can be done on the shaper table.*

Figure 44-3. *The edge guide controls the path of the router. The router cuts parallel to the edge of the work.*

device. It holds the shaft stationary so the collet chuck can be loosened or tightened.

The router may be used with accessories such as a *shaper table* (Figure 44-2) or *edge guide* (Figure 44-3). The shaper table enables you to use the router as a small shaper. The edge guide is used to control the path of the router.

Safe Operation Of The Router

Before you operate the router, it is important that you study the safe operating procedures. These rules will help you to operate the router safely and efficiently:

1. Always wear protective glasses and a face shield when operating the router.
2. Some routers operate at high noise levels. Protect your hearing with ear plugs or ear protectors when operating one.
3. Change bits and make all adjustments with the power disconnected. Make sure that the bit is sharp.

4. Before operating the router, restrain long hair. Remove jewelry and neckties. Loose sleeves should be rolled above the elbows and shirttails should be tucked in.
5. Make sure stock is clamped securely before routing. Never attempt to hand hold the stock you plan to route.
6. Do not start the router while the bit is in contact with the workpiece. The bit must be fed into the work at full speed.
7. When you use a shaping table or edge guide with the router, make sure that they are attached securely.
8. Feed the router from left to right as you face the work. On curved edges feed the router in a counterclockwise direction.
9. Take light cuts. Heavy cuts slow the router, burn and tear the wood, and dull the bit. Limit cuts to a maximum depth of ⅛″ to ³⁄₁₆″ (3 to 5 mm).
10. Use only carbide-tipped router bits to cut plywood or particle board. These materials will dull steel bits rapidly.

339

Types Of Router Bits

Router bits are named for the cut they make. Figure 44-4 shows router bits commonly used for woodworking.

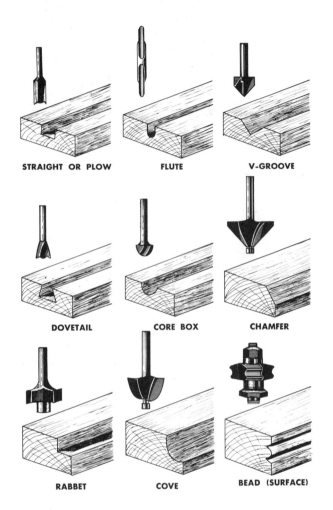

STRAIGHT OR PLOW   FLUTE   V-GROOVE

DOVETAIL   CORE BOX   CHAMFER

RABBET   COVE   BEAD (SURFACE)

Figure 44-4. *Common router bits and their function.*

Figure 44-6. *High-speed steel bits can be sharpened by honing. Hone only the flat faces of the bit.*

Bits are also classified as *high-speed steel* or *carbide-tipped.* High-speed steel bits do not cut plywood or particle board well because those materials are very hard. Carbide-tipped bits have a carbide insert brazed to the cutting edge. The carbide is very hard and will cut plywood, particle board and plastic laminates. Carbide bits stay sharp longer than high-speed steel bits.

Some router bits are in one piece and others are assembled (Figure 44-5). One-piece bits are made from a single piece of steel. Assembled bits may have two or more pieces.

High-speed steel router bits cut efficiently when they are sharp. You may keep them sharp by honing the flat face of the bit on a sharpening stone (Figure 44-6). Sharpen only the flat faces of the bit.

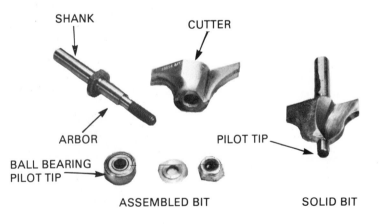

SHANK   CUTTER

ARBOR

BALL BEARING PILOT TIP

PILOT TIP

ASSEMBLED BIT   SOLID BIT

Figure 44-5. *An assembled bit and a solid bit. Many cutters will work on the arbor of the assembled bit.*

Carbide-tipped router bits are very hard. They cannot be honed. They are sharpened with a special grinder.

Pilot Tips. A *pilot tip* is the non-cutting portion of a router bit. It is always located at the tip (Figure 44-5). The pilot tip controls the depth of cut made by the bit. It rides along the edge of the stock while the bit is cutting.

Some router bits have ball bearing pilot tips (Figure 44-5). The bearing turns freely and will not burn the edge of the work. Solid steel pilot tips often burn the edge when they become hot. Keep solid steel pilot tips clean to avoid burning.

Installing Router Bits

Router bits are held in a collet chuck. Before installing a router bit, be sure that the power is disconnected. Insert the bit into the chuck. At least ½" (12 mm) of the bit shank should be inserted into the chuck.

Lock the shaft on the router and tighten the collet with a wrench (Figure 44-7). *Be sure to release the lock on the shaft before operating the router.*

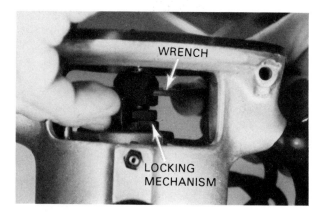

Figure 44-7. *Lock the shaft to chuck the bit. At least ½" (12 mm) of the bit shank should be inserted in the chuck. Tighten the collet with a wrench.*

Adjusting The Router

After the router bit is installed in the collet chuck, adjust the router for the depth of cut. Loosen the clamping mechanism and move the motor up or down in the base of the router to obtain the desired depth of cut. The distance from the end of the cutting edge to the router base determines the depth of cut (Figure 44-8).

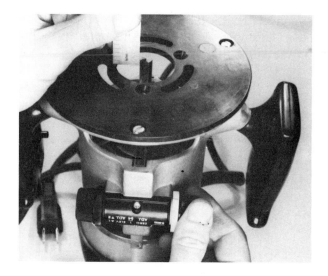

Figure 44-8. *Measuring the distance from the cutting edge to the router base to determine the depth of cut. This bit is set for a cut of 3/16" (about 5 mm).*

After you adjust the depth of cut, lock the base to the motor with the locking mechanism. Make all adjustments with the power off.

Router Guides

Router guides control the direction of travel. Their design may be simple or complex. Router guides include straightedges, edge guides, box guides, router fixtures, and follower guides.

Straightedge. A *straightedge* is any piece of stock with a true edge. It should be at least 3/8" (9 mm) thick. The straightedge is clamped to the work (Figure 44-9). Measure the distance be-

Figure 44-9. *Routing along a straight edge. Be sure the bit pulls the router toward the straight edge. Clamp the straight edge securely before you begin.*

tween the router bit and the edge of the router base. Use this measurement to determine the clamping position for the straightedge.

Be sure to clamp the straightedge securely. Feed the router so that the bit pulls the router *towards* the straightedge.

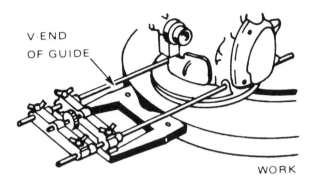

Figure 44-10. *Using an edge guide on circular stock. Check your set up on scrap stock before you begin.*

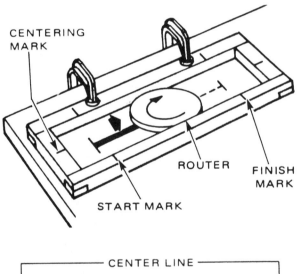

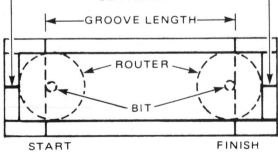

Figure 44-11. *The box guide limits movement of the router. The box opening is the same size as the base of the router.*

Edge Guide. An *edge guide* is an accessory for the router (Figure 44-3). It has two metal rods that are screwed to the router base. The guide slides on these rods. The distance between the edge guide and the router bit is the same as the distance from the edge of the work to the cut.

Some edge guides can be used to control the router on circular stock (Figure 44-10). An edge guide used for circular work contacts the work at two points. A circular edge guide should be adjusted on scrap stock for best results.

When you use an edge guide, be sure that all adjustments are made with the power disconnected. Tighten all adjusting screws securely to ensure the accuracy of your setup.

Box Guide. A *box guide* controls the travel of a router between two straight edges. The two ends of the box control the length of the cut. A box guide must be very accurate. If you make a box guide, lay it out carefully. Align the box guide and clamp it to the work (Figure 44-11). Then set the router into the box while it is running.

Move the router from one end of the box to the other. Do not shut off the router until it is removed from the box guide. If you shut the router off while it is in the box guide, the bit will burn the workpiece and dull the cutter by burning. Burn marks are very difficult to remove.

Router Jig. *Router jigs* are usually shop-built devices. The design will vary according to the size and purpose of the work, but most are designed for straight cuts (Figure 44-12). The

Figure 44-12. *Shop made router jigs are usually designed to make straight cuts.*

Figure 44-13. *Follower guides are attached to the router base. The bit goes through the follower guide.*

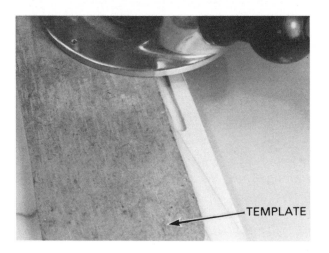

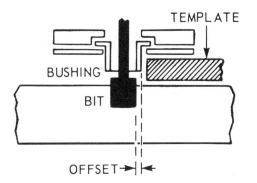

Figure 44-14. *The follower guide rubs against the template. It cuts a shape like that of the template.*

router usually travels in the router jig while the work is clamped below it.

Follower Guide. Follower guides are attached to the router base (Figure 44-13). The bit goes through the follower guide and acts like a pilot tip. It rubs against a template to control the path of the bit (Figure 44-14). The template is clamped over the work and the follower guide follows the edge of the template (Figure 44-15).

Follower guides are always used with the dovetail jig (Figure 44-16). The follower guide rides along the edge of the template on the dovetail jig.

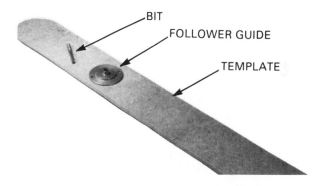

Figure 44-15. *A router template and follower guide. The follower guide rubs against the template.*

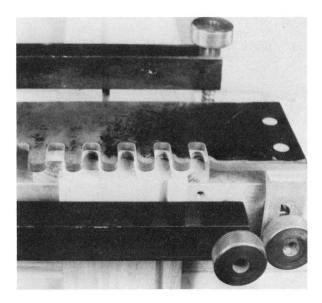

Figure 44-16. *A follower guide rubs against the dovetail template when cutting dovetails.*

Shaping An Edge

When you shape with the router, you must begin on the end grain. Start on one end and feed the router from left to right around your work. Grain tear-out will usually occur (Figure 44-17). Any grain tear-out will be removed as the router travels along the edge of the work (Figure 44-17).

When shaping an edge, control the bit with a router guide or by using a bit that has a pilot tip. Some edge shapes may require the use of two router bits (Figure 44-18). Be sure to shape all edges and ends before you change the bits or setup.

Cutting Dadoes And Grooves

Dadoes and *grooves* are cut with a straight bit. The router is controlled with a router guide. A pilot tip cannot be used. A blind groove or dado is made by *plunge cutting*. A plunge cut is made by lowering the moving bit into the work at the starting point. Then feed the router to the other end of the cut and lift from the work (Figure 44-19).

Figure 44-17. *Route end grain first. Feed from left to right. When you route the edge grain, the tear-out will be removed.*

GRAIN TEAROUT

Figure 44-18. *Two different bits were used to shape this edge. Make all cuts with the first bit before changing bits.*

Figure 44-19. *Blind cuts are made using a plunge cut. The moving bit is lowered into the wood and fed to the end of the cut. Take light cuts (about ⅛" or 3 mm) when plunge cutting.*

The end points of a blind groove or dado may also be drilled to the correct diameter. This procedure enables you to set the bit into the hole before starting the cut. The drilled ends help you make the groove or dado the correct length.

Freehand Routing

Freehand routing is done without any form of guide. The router is controlled only by the operator. Freehand routing requires skill for a quality job. If you plan to do freehand routing, be sure to practice on scrap stock. Check with your instructor before freehand routing.

It is easier to control the router during freehand routing if you take light cuts. Heavy cuts will cause the router to chatter or bounce during operation. Lay out the design on your wood before you begin.

Routing With The Shaper Table

The *shaper table* holds the router in an inverted position (Figure 44-2). The router remains sta-

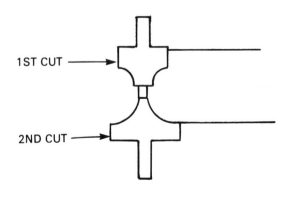

1ST CUT

2ND CUT

tionary while stock is fed into it. The shaper table works well on small pieces which are difficult to clamp.

Installing the Router. On some routers, the base is removed and the motor is inserted in the shaper table. Other routers are installed with the base attached. Be sure the correct router bit is in the chuck before placing the motor in the shaper table.

Adjust the router motor in the shaper table for the correct depth of cut. Lock the router securely into position after adjustment.

Adjusting the Shaper Table. Adjust the fence to the correct position and tighten it securely (Figure 44-20). If a ring guard is used, place it over the bit and lock it in position.

Figure 44-21. *The laminate trimmer is a portable power tool. It is used to trim plastic laminates.*

Figure 44-20. *Adjust fences and tighten them securely. Use the ring guard with the shaper table if available.*

Shaping Stock. Do not stand behind your workpiece when using the shaper table. Keep your hands clear of the bit. You may need a push stick to control pieces shorter than 12″ (300 mm). Do not shape pieces shorter than 6″ (150 mm). Always feed your work against the cutter rotation. This will force the work against the fence for greater control.

LAMINATE TRIMMER

The laminate trimmer is a portable power tool. It is used for trimming plastic laminates (Figure 44-21). The laminate trimmer is smaller than a router. It may be controlled with one hand. The smaller size enables the laminate trimmer to fit

in tight spaces. A router equipped with a laminate trimming bit may also be used to trim plastic laminates.

The laminate trimmer has a collet chuck like the router. Bits are installed in the same way. Laminate trimmer bits look like router bits, but they are all carbide-tipped.

The laminate trimmer has three principal parts: the *motor unit,* the *edge guide* and the *base* (Figure 44-21). The edge guide is adjustable and controls the distance between the bit and the edge of the counter.

The trimmer base controls the angle of cut made by the bit. By setting the trimmer base at an angle, trimming in a corner is possible.

Some laminate trimmers have a router base that may be used instead of the trimmer base. This converts the laminate trimmer into a small router.

Safe Operation Of The Laminate Trimmer

When using the laminate trimmer, you should follow the safe operating procedures listed for the router. These rules will help you operate the laminate trimmer correctly.

Trimming Laminates

Two adjustments are made before using the laminate trimmer. Adjust the base to the correct height and secure it in position. Then adjust the edge guide so that the carbide bit trims the work correctly. Test the trimmer on scrap stock before trimming the plastic laminate (Figure 44-22).

Figure 44-22. *Test your set-up on scrap stock before you begin. This laminate trimmer is set up correctly.*

QUESTIONS FOR REVIEW

1. Is the size of a router determined by its horsepower?
2. How is the router bit held in the router?
3. List the safe operating procedures you must follow to operate the router or laminate trimmer.
4. How is the router adjusted for cutting depth?
5. List some types of router bits and sketch their shape.
6. Do carbide-tipped router bits become dull faster than high-speed steel router bits?
7. What is an assembled router bit? How does it differ from a one-piece or solid bit?
8. What is the purpose of a pilot tip? How does the pilot tip work?
9. What causes a pilot tip to burn the edge of your work?
10. List some of the router guides used to control the router's travel. What is the purpose of each?
11. Should a router bit with a pilot tip be used to cut grooves and dadoes?
12. Describe the procedure for cutting a blind groove or dado.
13. How is a shaper table used with a router?
14. What is a laminate trimmer? How does it differ from a router?

SUGGESTED ACTIVITIES

1. Make a list of the types of router bits you have in your shop. Describe them by the cut they make. Also describe them as one-piece or assembled bits.

2. Demonstrate the procedure for installing a bit in your router. Have your instructor check your work. Be sure the router is disconnected before you begin.

3. Compare the laminate trimmer and router in your shop. How are these tools similar and different? Make a list of your observations.

The *shaper* is a stationary power tool. It is used to cut joints and shape stock. Before you use the shaper, you should know the parts of the shaper, what they do, and how they are maintained. It is also important to know safe operation procedures before you use the shaper.

KEY TERMS

shaper	depth collar
fence	assembled cutter
miter gage	solid cutter
ring guard	starting pin
spindle	

SHAPER

The shaper (Figure 45-1) has a *fence* with two parts. The fence controls and regulates the depth of cut. The fence is locked into position with a clamping device. The table of the shaper is slotted to accommodate a *miter gage*. The miter gage is used when shaping end grain.

A *ring guard* covers the *spindle* and *cutter* when in use. The ring guard prevents contact with the cutter. The spindle is driven by the motor through a series of V belts. The height of the spindle is controlled by the elevating handwheel on the front of the machine.

The control switch is mounted on the base or under the table. It controls the *motor*. On some shapers, the control switch may also control the direction in which the spindle rotates (clockwise or counterclockwise).

The spindle turns the cutter. The cutter is fastened to the spindle with a washer and two nuts. Place the washer over the cutter and tighten the

Figure 45-1. *The shaper and its parts. Study this illustration to learn their names and function. The ring guard and cutter have been removed for clarity.*

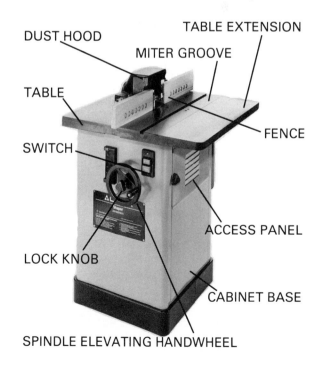

DUST HOOD

TABLE EXTENSION

MITER GROOVE

TABLE

FENCE

SWITCH

ACCESS PANEL

LOCK KNOB

CABINET BASE

SPINDLE ELEVATING HANDWHEEL

Figure 45-2. *A washer and two nuts hold the cutter in place. Make sure the nuts are tightened securely.*

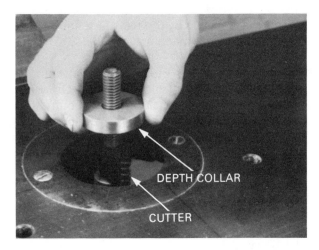

Figure 45-3. *A depth collar may be placed over the cutter. The depth collar controls the depth of cut.*

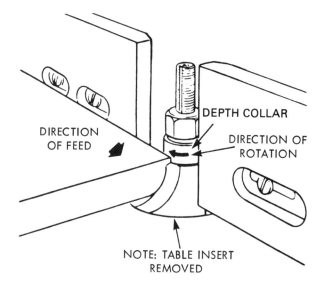

Figure 45-4. *The depth collar controls the depth of cut. It acts like the pilot top on a router bit. Always install the cutter to shape the underside of your work. The stock then acts as a guard. It covers the cutter.*

nuts securely (Figure 45-2). This prevents the cutter from coming loose during operation.

Depth collars may also be attached to the spindle (Figure 45-3). Depth collars control the depth of cut. At least ¼″ (6 mm) of the depth collar should be in contact with the stock during the shaping operation. This limits the amount of stock removed. It acts like the pilot tip on a router bit (Figure 45-4).

Shaper Cutters
There are two types of shaper cutters: solid and assembled.

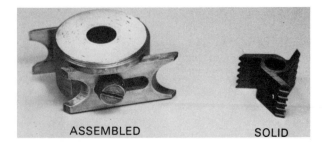

Figure 45-5. *Solid cutters are made from a single piece of steel. Assembled cutters have several parts. They are not as safe as solid cutters.*

Solid cutters have three cutting edges or wings and are made from a single piece of steel (Figure 45-5). Solid cutters require no adjustment, they are ready to use. There are many types of solid cutters available. Keep these cutters sharp by honing the flat faces of the wings on a sharpening stone.

Assembled cutters use straight cutters. The straight cutters are held in a head which clamps the cutters in place (Figure 45-5). The head is fastened to the spindle. Assembled cutters are difficult to adjust and are not usually found in the school shop. They are not as safe as solid cutters.

Many different cutter shapes are used with the shaper. The shapes made by shaper cutters are similar to the shapes made by router bits.

Safe Operation Of The Shaper

The shaper can be operated safely. The rules listed here will help you become a safe shaper operator:

1. Install shaper cutters with the switch off and the power disconnected. Make all adjustments with the switch off.
2. Make sure that fences are tightened securely after adjustment.
3. Do all shaping on the underside of your stock. This enables the stock to act as a guard and eliminates kickbacks caused by the stock being pinched between the table and cutter (Figure 45-4).
4. Use the ring guard for all shaping operations.
5. Take light cuts. Cuts should be ⅛" to ¼" (3 to 6 mm). Two light cuts are better than one heavy cut.

6. Stock that is to be shaped should be flat and true. Twisted or defective stock should not be shaped. Do not shape pieces shorter than 12" (300 mm) long.
7. Wear protective glasses *and* a face shield when shaping stock. Both are necessary.
8. Your work should always be controlled by the fence, miter gage or depth collar. Never work freehand.
9. Stand to the side of your work. Do not stand behind it because of a possible kickback.
10. Feed the stock against cutter rotation. Use a push stick to feed stock into the shaper. Keep your hands at least 6" (150 mm) from the cutter at all times.
11. When shaping irregular edges, ask your instructor for help.
12. Always have your instructor check the setup before you begin.

Installing Cutters

Turn the switch off and disconnect power before installing the cutter. Remove the two nuts and the lock washer from the spindle. Place the shaper cutter and any depth collars on the spindle. Install the cutter so that the underside of the stock is shaped (Figure 45-4).

Replace the lock washer and tighten one of the nuts securely to the washer. Tighten the second nut securely against the first. Adjust the cutter height with the elevating handwheel.

Straightedge Shaping

Straightedge shaping uses the fence for stock control (Figure 45-6). When shaping end grain,

Figure 45-6. *The fence controls the stock when shaping an edge.*

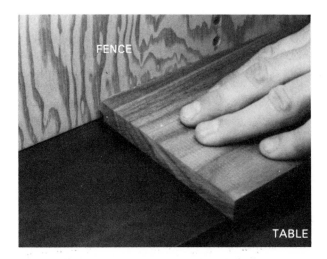

Figure 45-7. *The miter gage and fence are used to shape end grain.*

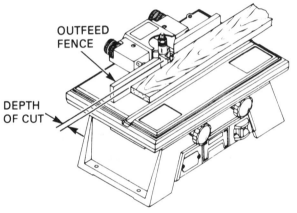

COUNTERCLOCKWISE CUTTER ROTATION

Figure 45-8. *When stock is removed from the entire edge, the fences must be offset. Check your set up on scrap stock.*

the miter gage is also used (Figure 45-7). When stock is removed from the entire edge, the fences must be offset (Figure 45-8). The outfeed fence must be moved toward the work to compensate for the stock that is removed. When the entire edge is not shaped, the fences form a straight line. The stock follows the line made by the fences.

After the fences are adjusted and the ring guard has been positioned, you are ready to edge shape your stock. Make sure the fences are securely tightened. Begin by shaping the end grain. Hold the stock against the fence and miter gage. Be sure to feed the stock against cutter rotation. Any end grain tear-out will be removed when the edge grain is shaped.

Edge grain shaping does not require a miter gage. If the pieces you are shaping are less than 6″ (150 mm) wide, use a push stick to feed them into the cutter.

Shaping A Rabbet

Shaping a rabbet is a form of straight edge shaping. A straight cutter is used. The spindle is adjusted for rabbet height and the fences are adjusted for rabbet depth.

Shape end grain rabbets first. Use a fence and miter gage for end grain rabbets. Edge grain rabbets use only the fence for control (Figure 45-9). If the stock is less than 6″ (150 mm) wide, use a push stick to feed your work into the cutter.

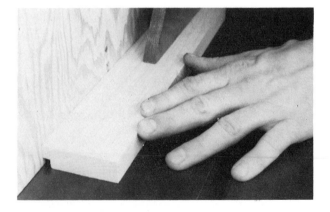

Figure 45-9. *Edge grain rabbets are controlled by the fence.*

Irregular Edge Shaping

Irregular or curved edges do not use the fence or miter gage for control (Figure 45-10). Curved or

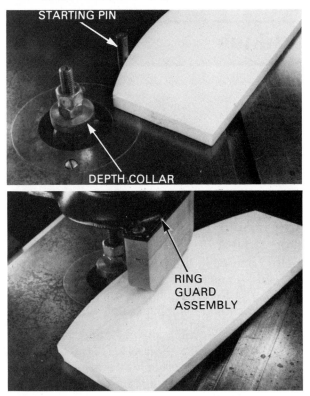

STARTING PIN

DEPTH COLLAR

RING GUARD ASSEMBLY

Figure 45-10. *Irregular or curved edges can be shaped by using a depth collar and a starting pin. This operation can be done more safely with a portable router. Be sure to put the ring guard in position before making the cut.*

irregular stock is controlled with a *depth collar.* A depth collar rides on the edge of the stock and controls the depth of cut. At least ¼" (6 mm) of the depth collar must contact the work.

A *starting pin* is also used with the depth collar. The pin is inserted in a tapered hole on the shaper table. The work rests on the starting pin as it is fed into the cutter and depth collar.

Some irregularly-shaped pieces are fastened to a template. The template rides on the depth collar while the work is shaped by the cutter. Always use a ring guard or protective collar over the cutter and depth collar.

Keep your hands at least 6" (150 mm) away from the cutter. A kickback can pull your hand into the cutter.

Place the stock against the starting pin and ease the work into the rotating cutter. Start with edge grain and work your way into end grain. Always feed against cutter rotation. After beginning the cut, you do not have to use the starting pin, but it may be helpful for controlling stock at corners or deep curves.

Heavy cuts should be made in two consecutive passes. Take about one half of the cut with the first pass and then readjust the shaper for the complete cut.

QUESTIONS FOR REVIEW

1. For what purpose is the shaper used?
2. What is the function of the fences?
3. How do you control the height of the spindle?
4. Does the spindle on some shapers turn in two directions?
5. Name two types of shaper cutters.
6. Discuss the rules that must be followed for safe operation of the shaper.
7. Why must the power be disconnected when installing shaper cutters?
8. How do depth collars control your stock? How does the starting pin help you control your stock?

SUGGESTED ACTIVITIES

1. Make a list of the shaper cutters found in your shop. Does their name describe the cut they make?

2. Set the shaper up for a cut specified by your instructor. Be sure to observe all safety rules while you work.

CHAPTER 46

Sanding Machines

Sanding machines smooth a surface by removing stock. Stock is removed with coated *abrasives*. Sanding machines are either stationary or portable.

Stationary sanders are mounted on a bench or attached to the floor. Stock is fed into the sander.

Portable sanders are hand held. With a portable sander, the stock is secured and the sander moves. Sanders should not be used to do the work of saws or planing machines. Sanding machines are not designed to remove large amounts of stock.

Abrasives are expensive. You can make them last longer if you do not force the abrasive against the work or hold the work in one place. Forcing dulls the abrasive and gouges the work. The wood and abrasive may also become burned when the abrasive is forced against the work. By feeding work slowly and keeping the abrasive or work moving, you can make the abrasive last much longer. Avoid wasteful practices.

KEY TERMS

stationary sander	tracking mechanism
portable sander	spindle sander
abrasive	finishing sander
disc sander	orbital
belt sander	oscillating
brush backed sanding wheel	

SAFE OPERATION OF SANDING MACHINES

Before operating a portable or stationary sander, you should know the safe operating procedures. The following safety rules will help you operate sanding machines safely and efficiently:

1. Turn off the switch and disconnect the power when changing abrasives.
2. Make sure the abrasives are installed correctly and that all guards are in place. Do not operate the machine if the abrasive is loose.
3. Make all adjustments with the switch off and the power disconnected.
4. Be sure to wear protective glasses during all sanding operations.
5. If the sander does not have a dust collection system, wear a dust mask.
6. Keep your hands clear of abrasive discs and belts. Your fingers could be pinched between the abrasive and the sanding table.
7. When belt sanding or disc sanding on stationary machines, hold the work securely on the table. Do all sanding on the side of the disc or belt that travels downward toward the table.
8. Use push sticks and other accessories to control small pieces that you sand on the disc or belt sander. If the piece is smaller than 2″ (50 mm) square and ½″ (12 mm) thick, it should be clamped in a special fixture or sanded by hand.
9. When you use a portable sander, keep the cord well away from the abrasive. The abrasive can break or fray the cord.
10. Always clamp stock securely before sanding with a portable sander.

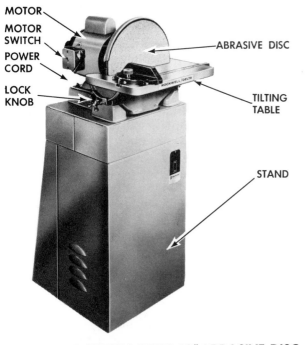

MOTOR
MOTOR SWITCH
POWER CORD
LOCK KNOB
ABRASIVE DISC
TILTING TABLE
STAND

ROCKWELL DELTA 12″ ABRASIVE DISC FINISHING MACHINE

Figure 46-1. *Stationary disc sanders sand straight pieces and outside curves. They are often used to smooth stock after rough sawing.*

DISC SANDERS

Disc sanders may be portable or stationary. Stationary models are used to sand straight pieces and outside curves to a layout line after rough sawing (Figure 46-1). Portable disc sanders are used for sanding large surfaces. They are frequently used to prepare floors and wood siding for finishing (Figure 46-2).

Both portable and stationary disc sanders use a circular piece of abrasive. The abrasive is held against a steel or rubber disc with glue or a threaded fastener. The diameter of the disc indicates the size of the sander.

Stationary Disc Sanding

Stationary disc sanders are used chiefly to sand the edges and ends of stock. The table on the disc sander may be adjusted for sanding chamfers or bevels. A miter gage may be used to sand stock at any desired angle (Figure 46-3).

Sanding is always done on the side of the disc that travels toward the table. The downward force holds the stock against the table and makes it easier to control.

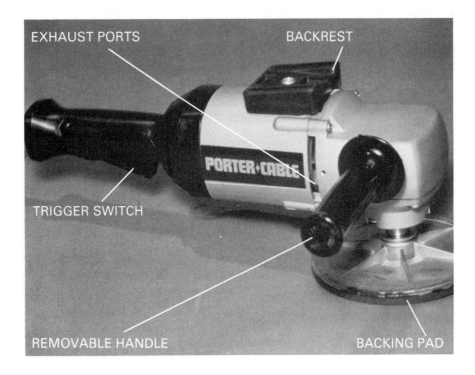

EXHAUST PORTS
BACKREST
TRIGGER SWITCH
PORTER+CABLE
REMOVABLE HANDLE
BACKING PAD

Figure 46-2. *Portable disc sanders are used to prepare wood floors and siding for finishing.*

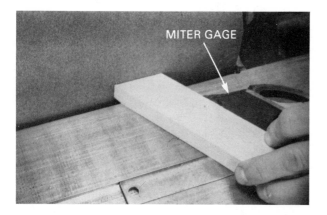

Figure 46-3. *The miter gage is used when sanding stock at an angle.*

Figure 46-4. *When sanding small pieces use a fixture or a push stick. Pieces smaller than 2″ (50 mm) square and ½″ (12 mm) thick should be hand sanded.*

Figure 46-5. *When disc sanding, about one-third of the disc should contact the work. Keep the sander moving. This will prevent gouging.*

If you are sanding small pieces, clamp them to a fixture or use a push stick (Figure 46-4). Pieces smaller than 2″ (50 mm) square and ½″ (12 mm) thick should be hand sanded.

Portable Disc Sanding

Portable disc sanders are used chiefly for face sanding stock. With a portable disc sander, about ⅓ of the disc should contact the work (Figure 46-5).

Place the running disc sander on the work. Keep the sander moving constantly. If the sander remains in one place, it will gouge the work. It will also dull the abrasive and burn the stock. Be sure to wear protective glasses when you are disc sanding.

BELT SANDERS

Belt sanders may be stationary or portable. Stationary models (Figure 46-6) are used for sanding stock edges, ends and faces. Portable

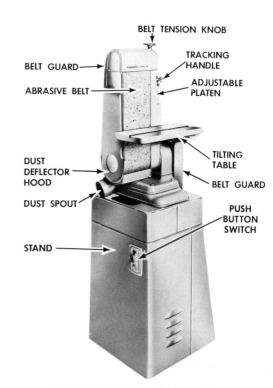

ROCKWELL DELTA 6″ ABRASIVE BELT FINISHING MACHINE

Figure 46-6. *Stationary belt sanders are used for sanding stock edges, ends and faces.*

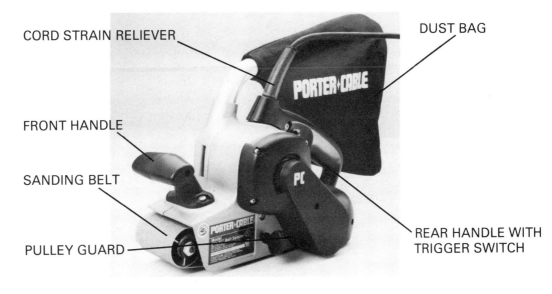

CORD STRAIN RELIEVER

DUST BAG

FRONT HANDLE

SANDING BELT

PULLEY GUARD

REAR HANDLE WITH
TRIGGER SWITCH

Figure 46-7. *Portable belt sanders are commonly used to sand face grain surfaces. They may also be used to sand end and edge grain.*

belt sanders (Figure 46-7) are used chiefly for face sanding stock, but may be used for end and edge grain sanding.

The size of the belt used on the sander indicates belt sander size. There are two dimensions to this size: the width and the circumference of the belt. A 3 x 24 belt sander uses a 3″ wide belt with a 24″ circumference.

All belt sanders have a *tracking mechanism*. A tracking mechanism centers the belt on the

drums of the belt sander (Figure 46-8). If the belt is not centered on the drums, adjust it with the tracking mechanism.

Stationary Belt Sanding
Stationary belt sanders have a table which supports the work during sanding. The table tilts for sanding bevels and chamfers. A miter gage may be used to set the stock for sanding at any desired angle.

Figure 46-8. *The tracking mechanism centers the belt on its wheels.*

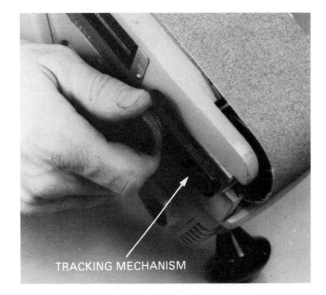

TRACKING MECHANISM

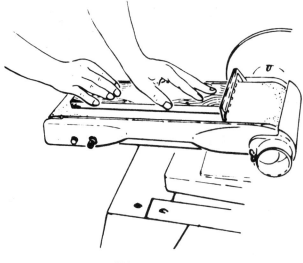

HORIZONTAL

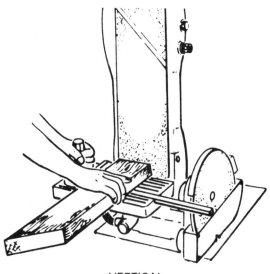

VERTICAL

Figure 46-9. *Stationary belt sanders can be operated in the horizontal or vertical position.*

Stationary belt sanders may be operated in the horizontal or vertical position (Figure 46-9). Be sure the machine is fastened securely in position before you begin sanding.

Portable Belt Sanders

Portable belt sanders must be running before they contact the work. Be sure your work is clamped securely (Figure 46-10). Set the back of

the belt sander onto the work first. The moving belt will pull the sander onto the work. Keep the sander moving at all times. Take overlapping strokes with the grain. Make sure that the cord is out of the way while you are sanding. Lift the belt sander off the work before you shut it off.

Be careful not to round corners or edges while belt sanding. When you sand narrow edges, you may clamp scrap stock to your work to help

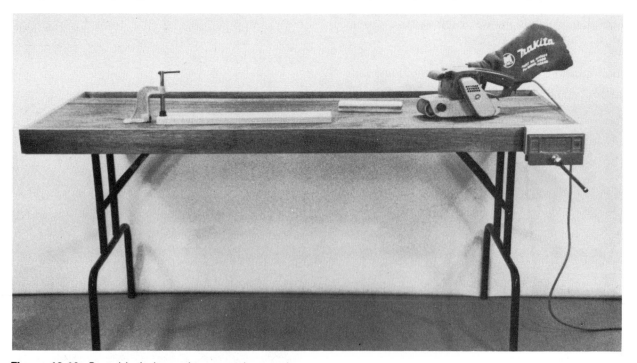

Figure 46-10. *Portable belt sanders must be running before they contact the work. Be sure your work is clamped securely.*

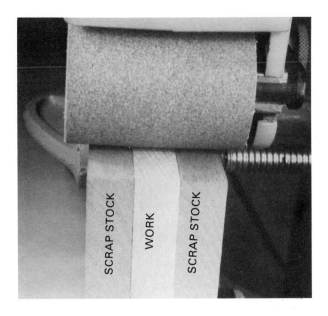

Figure 46-11. *Scrap stock can protect the edges of your work from rounding.*

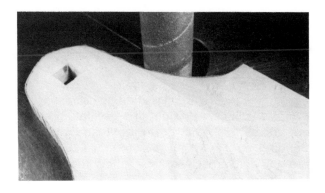

Figure 46-13. *Use the correct drum for the job. The size of the curve determines drum size.*

guide the belt sander (Figure 46-11). Smaller belt sanders are easier to control than large, heavy machines.

SPINDLE SANDERS

Spindle sanders are stationary machines. They are designed to sand curves (Figure 46-12). Spindle sanders may use drums of different diameters. The drums have abrasives glued to them. The size of the curve you are sanding will determine the correct drum for the job (Figure 46-13). The drum is mounted on the spindle. Be sure to disconnect the power when you change drums.

The spindle on some sanders oscillates up and down while the spindle turns. This oscillating motion increases abrasive life by spreading wear over a larger area.

The table on the spindle sander may be tilted for angular work. Make sure the table is fastened securely before you begin sanding. Be sure to feed your work against spindle rotation.

BRUSH BACKED SANDING WHEELS

Brush backed sanding wheels are used on irregular surfaces. The abrasive is backed with bristles similar to those found in a toothbrush. The bristles bend with the abrasive to follow an irregular surface.

Brush backed wheels may be part of a stationary machine or may be attached to another machine such as the lathe. The wheel should be driven at speeds from 600 to 1800 rpm depending on wheel diameter. Larger wheels should turn at a slower rpm.

Figure 46-12. *Spindle sanders are stationary machines. They are designed to sand curves.*

FINISHING SANDERS

Finishing sanders are portable machines (Figure 46-14). They are used for the final machine sanding before finishing.

Finishing sanders are classified as *oscillating* or *orbital* machines. Straight line oscillating sanders travel back and forth in a straight line. Sanding marks left by the straight line sander are not visible because they follow the grain of the wood.

Rotary oscillating sanders and orbital sanders travel in a circular path. This path leaves sanding marks that go against the grain of the work. The sanding marks left by these machines may detract from the finish if they are not removed by hand sanding.

Finishing sanders are rated by the number of orbits or oscillations they make in a minute. The higher the number of rpm's (oscillations or orbits per minute), the more efficient the sander is. It is a good practice to hand sand surfaces lightly after the final machine sanding. This eliminates any swirl marks left by the sander.

Finishing sanders use ¼ to ½ of an abrasive sheet. A clamp holds the abrasive to the sander (Figure 46-15). Both ends of the sheet are

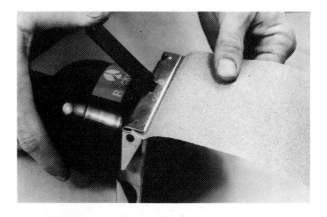

Figure 46-15. *Abrasives are held on the sander with a clamping device.*

clamped to the sander. Use abrasives with C-weight or heavier paper. A-weight paper is too light for machine sanding.

Lay out the abrasive sheet carefully before cutting it. This will help you make the most of each sheet. Flexing the abrasive before you cut it will increase abrasive life (Figure 46-16).

Some orbital finishing sanders are quite small (Figure 46-17). Because of their size, they may be

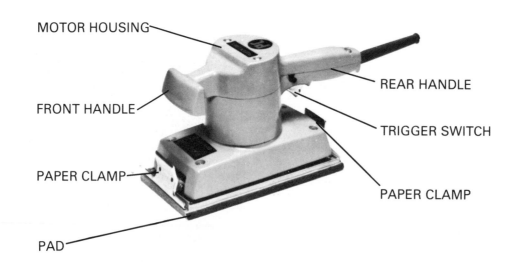

MOTOR HOUSING
REAR HANDLE
FRONT HANDLE
TRIGGER SWITCH
PAPER CLAMP
PAPER CLAMP
PAD

Figure 46-14. *Finishing sanders are portable machines. They are used for the final machine sanding before finishing. Hand sanding follows finish sanding by machine. This eliminates swirl marks.*

Figure 46-16. *Flexing the abrasive will increase its sanding life. Use* C *or* D *weight paper for best results. Lighter paper tears too easily.*

used in cramped spaces. These motorized sanders (sometimes called *block sanders*) are very efficient for small areas. They remove stock rapidly and are easy to control.

Orbital and oscillating finishing sanders are placed on the work with the motor running. Travel is with the grain (Figure 46-18). Take overlapping strokes as you sand your work. Do not lean on the sander. Let the weight of the sander do the work. Keep the cord clear of the sander.

Figure 46-17. *Some finishing sanders are small. They work well in tight spaces. They are also easy to control.*

Figure 46-18. *When using a finishing sander, travel with the grain. Overlap your strokes. Never lean on the sander. Let the weight of the sander do the work.*

QUESTIONS FOR REVIEW

1. How does a stationary sander differ from a portable sander?
2. List some of the safe practices you should follow when operating portable or stationary sanding machines.
3. How do you determine the size of a disc sander?
4. How are abrasives held to the disc sander?
5. How would you operate the portable or stationary disc sander? What procedures should you follow?
6. If sanding machines do not have a dust collecting system, what precaution should you take?
7. How do you determine the size of a belt sander?
8. For what purpose is the tracking mechanism on the belt sander used?
9. Can the stationary belt sander be used to sand bevels or chamfers?
10. What is the procedure for sanding a surface with a portable belt sander?
11. What is the principal function of the spindle sander? How is it used?
12. Do spindle sanders have only one drum that fits the spindle?
13. How does the brush backed sander remove stock? What shapes are most often sanded with the brush backed sander?
14. For what purpose are finishing sanders used? What is the difference between orbiting and oscillating sanders?

SUGGESTED ACTIVITIES

1. Make a list of all sanding machines found in your shop. Divide them into two groups: portable and stationary.
2. Demonstrate to your instructor the procedure for installing a belt on a sander in your shop.
3. Cut some coated abrasive sheets the correct size for the portable sanders in your shop.

SECTION 7

Specialized Woodworking Topics

Carpentry is a specialized area of woodworking. A *carpenter* builds houses and commercial structures. The work of some carpenters is specialized. Form carpenters erect concrete forms for large buildings, bridges and highways. Roofing carpenters install roofs and related trim.

The work of other carpenters is not as specialized. A general carpenter may build a room addition, remodel the kitchen of a house, or build houses and apartments.

KEY TERMS

apprenticeship	scaffolds
carpentry	subfloor
carpenter	siding
footing	trim
foundation	brick veneer
sill plate	roof
joists	stairs
bridging	drywall

THE CARPENTER'S JOB

Carpenters learn skills on the job. They also learn related knowledge such as math and blueprint reading in school. When a carpenter belongs to a union, the training period is known as an *apprenticeship.* The apprenticeship for a carpenter lasts about four years. A carpenter must have a high school education. An understanding of math and English is very important.

Carpenters work in all types of weather. Carpenters may work on ladders, scaffolds and roofs. This work can be hazardous. The carpenter must be able to lift heavy boards and work in awkward positions.

There is satisfaction in working as a carpenter. When a building is completed, there is pride in a job well done. The work of the carpenter is challenging. Each job provides the carpenter with new skills and knowledge. Learning and growing on the job provides a good feeling.

Carpenters buy all of their own hand tools (Figure 47-1). In addition, some purchase their own portable power tools. It is important to store tools correctly and keep them sharp. Figure 47-2 shows a common type of tool box.

Figure 47-1. *Carpenters buy their own hand tools. This is a basic set of carpentry tools. These tools will help you do most jobs.*

Figure 47-2. *Storing tools correctly keeps them sharp and free of rust. You may want to build a tool box. This tool box is a type commonly used by carpenters.*

HOUSE CONSTRUCTION

House construction is one of the most common carpentry jobs. It is divided into the following areas: footing and foundation, sill and joists, subfloor, exterior walls, exterior finish, roof and interior finish. The carpenter is involved in all of these areas.

Footing And Foundation

A *footing* is the concrete base on which a foundation is built (Figure 47-3). The footing supports the entire building. The footing is buried to protect it from frost in cold weather. Frost could crack the footing or cause part of the building to settle. In cold climates, footings must be deeper. This is because the ground freezes much deeper in cold climates.

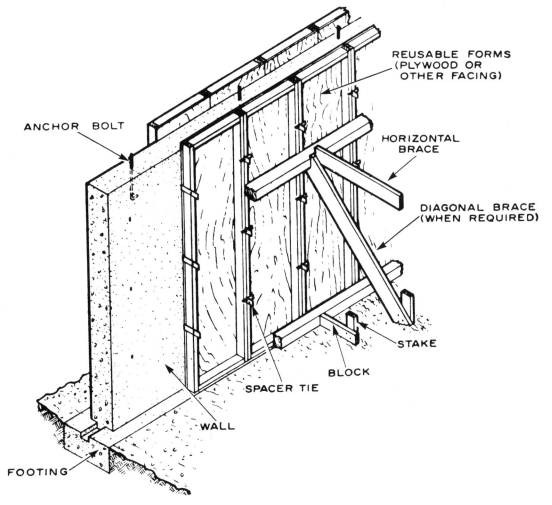

Figure 47-3. *The footing is the base of a house. The walls are then built on the footing. The concrete forms are built by the carpenter.*

The *foundation* may be made of concrete, block or wood. Concrete and block foundations are most common. The foundation walls (Figure 47-3) form the basement or crawl space. The top of the foundation holds the sill and subfloor.

Some houses do not have a foundation. They are constructed on a slab. A slab (Figure 47-4) is made of concrete. It makes up the footings and floor of the house.

Sill and Joists

A *sill plate* is bolted to the foundation (Figure 47-5). Between the footing and the plate is a *sealer* for insulation.

Joists are nailed to the sill plate (Figure 47-5). When joists cross a large span, a girder is used (Figure 47-5). The girder may be made of wood or steel.

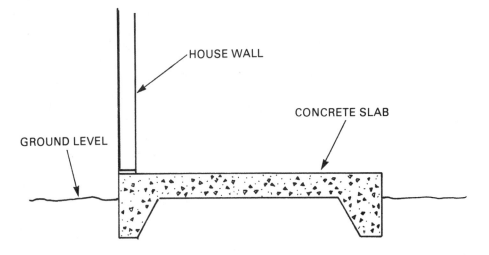

Figure 47-4. *A slab is made of concrete. It makes up the footing and floor of the house.*

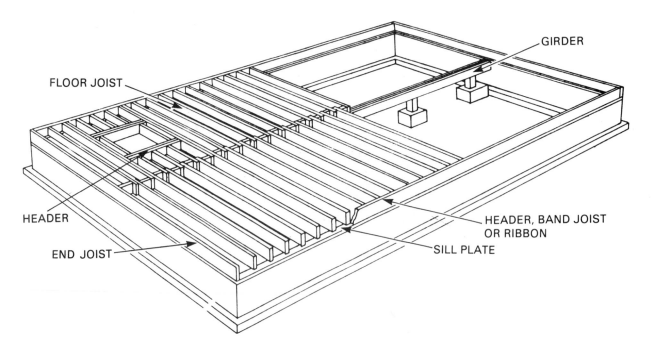

Figure 47-5. *The sill plate is bolted to the foundation. The joists are then nailed to the sill plate and girder.*

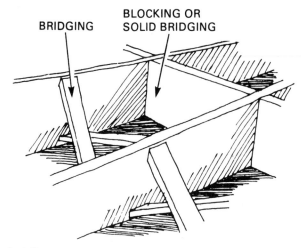

Figure 47-6. *Solid and diagonal bridging makes the floor more rigid and spreads the load more evenly.*

Bridging (Figure 47-6) is installed between the floor joists. The bridging makes the joists more rigid and spreads the load. Bridging may be solid or diagonal. Some diagonal bridging is made of metal.

Framing members must be doubled around openings in the floor (Figure 47-5). This strengthens the floor around the opening.

Subfloor

The *subfloor* is nailed to the floor joists. Plywood subfloor is normally used (Figure 47-7).

The subfloor is nailed to every joist to reduce the chance of squeaks. On some houses, the subfloor is glued and nailed (Figure 47-8). The glue also helps reduce squeaking. If the nails loosen,

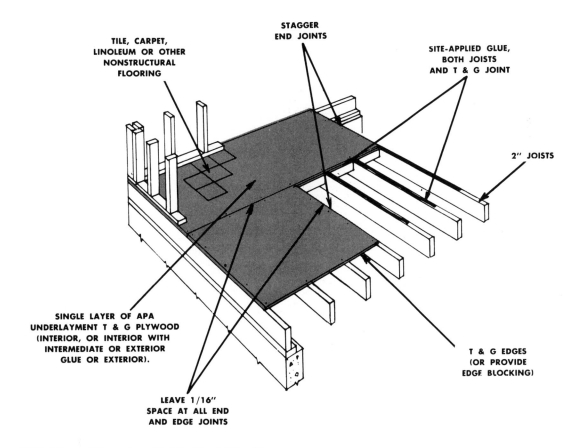

Figure 47-7. *The subfloor is nailed to the joists. The walls are then built on the subfloor.*

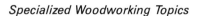

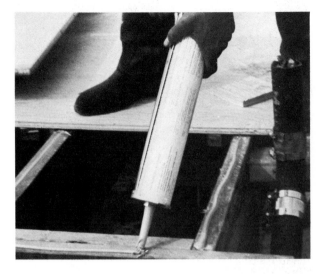

Figure 47-8. *Gluing the subfloor to the joists helps reduce squeaking. Mastic adhesives are used for this job.*

the glue still holds. Mastic adhesives are used to glue the subfloor to the joists.

Exterior Walls

The exterior walls are built on the subfloor (Figure 47-9). The wall framing is made of the sole plate, studs, and top plate. The entire wall assembly is nailed to the subfloor. Openings for doors and windows need extra framing. When all walls are in place, the top plate is doubled (Figure 47-10). The double top plate ties the walls together. It laps over each corner.

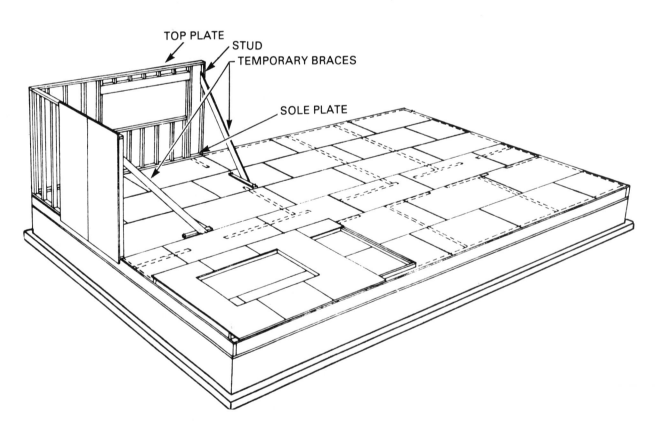

Figure 47-9. *Exterior walls are built on the subfloor. Openings for doors and windows need extra framing.*

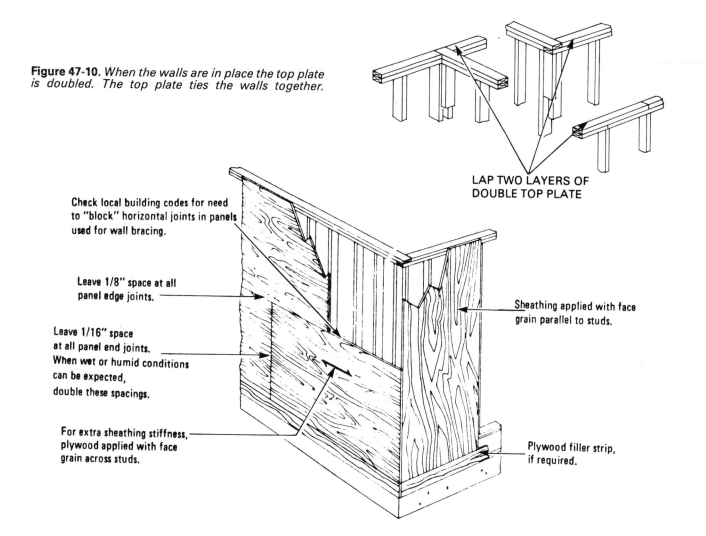

Figure 47-10. *When the walls are in place the top plate is doubled. The top plate ties the walls together.*

LAP TWO LAYERS OF DOUBLE TOP PLATE

Check local building codes for need to "block" horizontal joints in panels used for wall bracing.

Leave 1/8" space at all panel edge joints.

Leave 1/16" space at all panel end joints. When wet or humid conditions can be expected, double these spacings.

For extra sheathing stiffness, plywood applied with face grain across studs.

Sheathing applied with face grain parallel to studs.

Plywood filler strip, if required.

Figure 47-11. *Sheathing is nailed to the walls. This gives the walls extra strength. It makes them rigid. (American Plywood Association)*

Plywood sheathing (Figure 47-11) or insulation board is nailed over the wall framing. This makes a strong wall. *Let-in braces* are needed (Figure 47-12) when insulation board is used. Let-in braces are cut into the studs. They form a diagonal. Let-in braces strengthen the walls. Exterior doors and windows are installed after sheathing.

Exterior Finish

Siding and *trim* cover the sheathing. Siding adds protection and decoration to the house. There

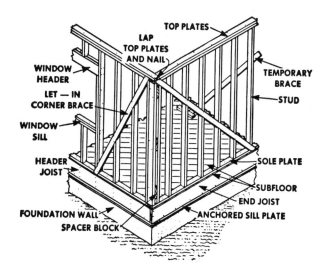

TOP PLATES
LAP TOP PLATES AND NAIL
WINDOW HEADER
LET — IN CORNER BRACE
WINDOW SILL
HEADER JOIST
FOUNDATION WALL
SPACER BLOCK
TEMPORARY BRACE
STUD
SOLE PLATE
SUBFLOOR
END JOIST
ANCHORED SILL PLATE

Figure 47-12. *Let-in braces are cut into the studs. They are needed when insulation board is used. They make the walls strong and rigid.*

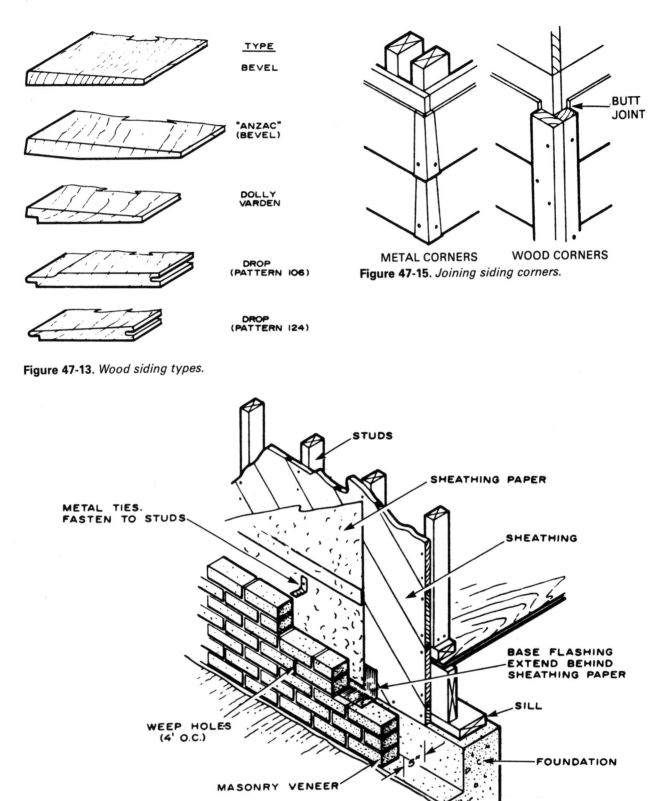

TYPE

BEVEL

"ANZAC" (BEVEL)

DOLLY VARDEN

DROP (PATTERN 106)

DROP (PATTERN 124)

Figure 47-13. *Wood siding types.*

BUTT JOINT

METAL CORNERS   WOOD CORNERS

Figure 47-15. *Joining siding corners.*

STUDS

SHEATHING PAPER

SHEATHING

METAL TIES. FASTEN TO STUDS

BASE FLASHING EXTEND BEHIND SHEATHING PAPER

SILL

WEEP HOLES (4' O.C.)

5"

FOUNDATION

MASONRY VENEER

Figure 47-14. *Brick veneer is installed by masons. It covers the sheathing. It is used instead of siding.*

Figure 47-16. *Trim around windows and doors makes the house look finished. Trim is installed both outside and inside.*

are many types of siding (Figure 47-13). Vinyl or metal siding is available, too. Sometimes brick veneer (Figure 47-14) is used for siding. Solid brick houses are also built. Masons perform most cement and concrete jobs. Metal or wood corners (Figure 47-15) are used.

Trim is used to frame windows and doors (Figure 47-16). It makes the house look finished. Wooden trim is usually clear dimensional lumber. On some houses, trim has a decorative shape.

Roof

A *roof* may be built from *trusses* (Figure 47-17). It may also be built from individual *rafters* (Figure 47-18). Trusses span longer distances without

support. They do not need a supporting wall inside the house.

The parts of an assembled rafter roof include rafters, ceiling joists and a ridge. Some carpenters brace rafters with collar ties (Figure 47-18). This keeps the rafters from spreading under load.

Rafters are laid out with a framing square. The carpenter uses the *rise* and *run* to step off a rafter (Figure 47-19). The rise is the number of inches per foot that the roof slopes. The run is always measured in a one foot unit. In metric measure, the rise and run are in millimeters.

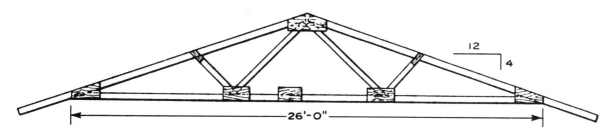

Figure 47-17. *Roof trusses are designed to span a large area without center support.*

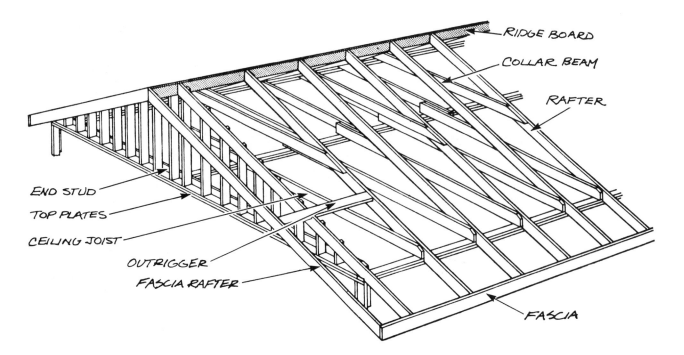

Figure 47-18. *A roof may be built from individual rafters. Collar ties or beams keep the rafters from spreading under load.*

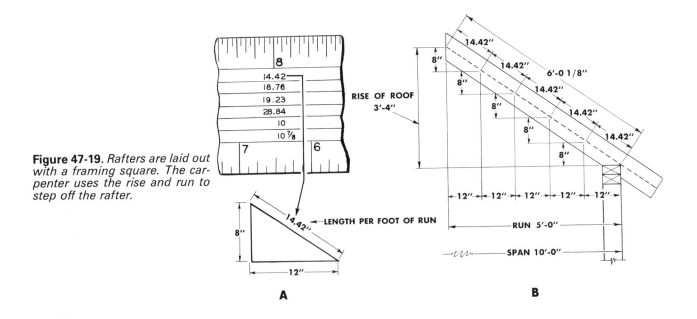

Figure 47-19. *Rafters are laid out with a framing square. The carpenter uses the rise and run to step off the rafter.*

Sheathing is nailed to the trusses or rafters (Figure 47-20). Plywood is commonly used for sheathing a roof. Roofing felt covers the sheathing, and shingles are then nailed over the felt (Figure 47-21). Shingles may be made of wood or asphalt.

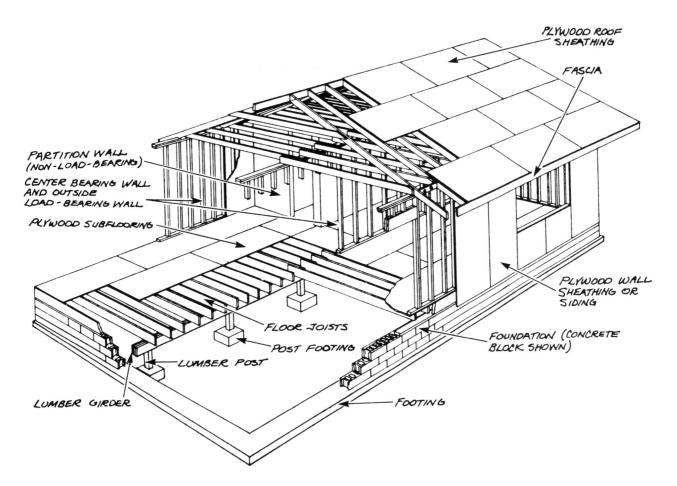

PLYWOOD ROOF SHEATHING

FASCIA

PARTITION WALL (NON-LOAD-BEARING)

CENTER BEARING WALL AND OUTSIDE LOAD-BEARING WALL

PLYWOOD SUBFLOORING

PLYWOOD WALL SHEATHING OR SIDING

FLOOR JOISTS

POST FOOTING

LUMBER POST

FOUNDATION (CONCRETE BLOCK SHOWN)

LUMBER GIRDER

FOOTING

Figure 47-20. *Sheathing is nailed to the trusses or rafters. The roofing felt and shingles are nailed to the sheathing.*

Figure 47-21. *Roofing felt and shingles cover the sheathing. Shingles are nailed over the roofing felt.*

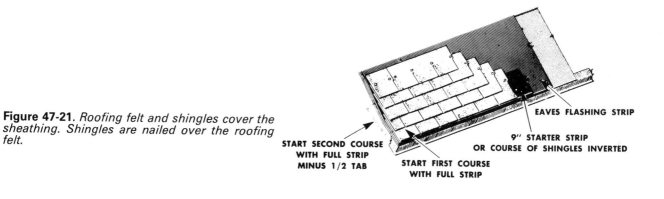

EAVES FLASHING STRIP

9" STARTER STRIP OR COURSE OF SHINGLES INVERTED

START SECOND COURSE WITH FULL STRIP MINUS 1/2 TAB

START FIRST COURSE WITH FULL STRIP

Asphalt shingles (Figure 47-22) are made of felt and asphalt. The exposed surface appears sandy. This surface resists wear. The most common asphalt shingles measure 12" x 36" (300 mm x 900 mm). Asphalt shingles are less expen-sive than wooden shingles. They are more commonly used for house construction.

The roof must be trimmed after it is shingled. A soffit and fascia (Figure 47-23) are added. The

	SHINGLE TYPE	SHIPPING WEIGHT PER SQUARE	PACKAGES PER SQUARE	LENGTH	WIDTH	UNITS PER SQUARE	HEADLAP	EXPOSURE
STRIP SHINGLES	2 AND 3 TAB SQUARE BUTT	235 LB	3	36"	12"	80	2"	5"
STRIP SHINGLES	2 AND 3 TAB HEXAGONAL	195 LB	3	36"	11 1/3"	86	2"	5"

Figure 47-22. *Asphalt roof shingles have a sandy surface that resists wear. They come in different shapes.*

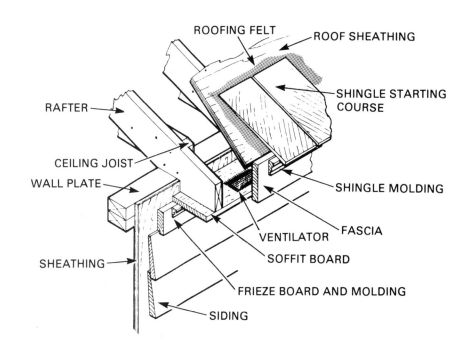

Figure 47-23. *The soffit and fascia hide rafter tails. They give the roof a finished look.*

soffit and fascia hide the rafter tails to give the roof a finished look.

Interior Finish

Interior finishing of a house is very important. The buyer wants a quality job. If the quality is poor, the house will be difficult to sell.

Interior finishing includes jobs such as: building stairs, covering walls, trimming windows and doors, laying floors and carpet and installing baseboard.

Building Stairs. *Stairs* have to be built between floors. They are also built from a porch to ground level. It takes an experienced carpenter to lay out stairs correctly. All treads must be the same size and all risers must be the same height (Figure 47-24). The wood used for treads should be dense. Quarter-sawn stock works best.

Figure 47-24. *Stairs are built between floors. It takes an experienced carpenter to lay out stairs.*

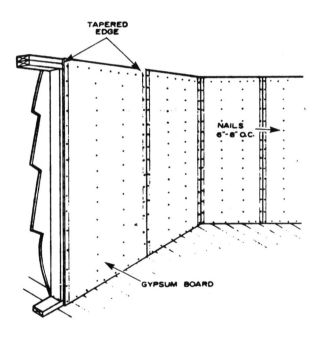

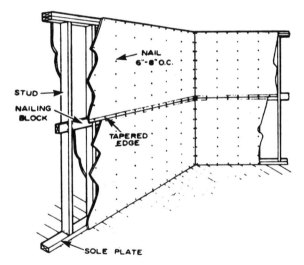

Figure 47-25. *Drywall or gypsum board is used to finish interior walls.*

Covering Walls. Walls are usually covered with 4' x 8' drywall panels (Figure 47-25). The drywall joints are then taped. Joint compound is used to smooth the joints (Figure 47-26). Smooth drywall is ready for paint or other covering. Sheet stock is also used for interior wall covering.

Trimming Windows and Doors. Most windows and doors are pre-hung (Figure 47-27). Pre-hung windows and doors are installed as a unit. All trim is attached after installation and the window or door is ready to work.

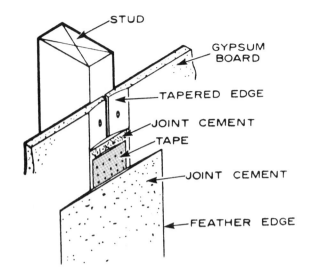

Figure 47-26. *Tape and joint compound (cement) are used to smooth the joints. Nail dimples are smoothed with joint compound.*

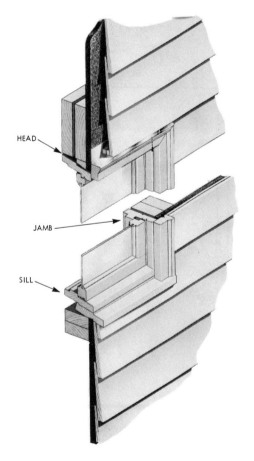

Figure 47-27. *Pre-hung windows are installed as a unit. Accuracy is very important when installing pre-hung windows.*

When windows or doors are installed, accuracy is important. The units must sit level and square. Units that are not level or square may not work.

Windows and doors must fit snugly. Loose doors or windows will raise heating and cooling costs. The carpenter repairs any window or door leaks before leaving the job.

Laying Floors and Carpet. A plywood or particle board subfloor is covered with some type of flooring. Some floors are covered with tile or hardwood. Living areas are usually covered with carpet. Carpet insulates and deadens sound. This adds to the comfort of the living area. Carpet also adds beauty to the floors of a house. Flooring is installed by people who specialize in floor covering.

Baseboard. Baseboard is used to make the corner joint between the floor and the wall look finished (Figure 47-28). Baseboard comes in many shapes and many different materials. Some are wood while others are made of vinyl or plastic.

Baseboard is nailed in place. Nails go through the drywall into the studs and sole plate. The nails are covered with colored wax or plastic wood.

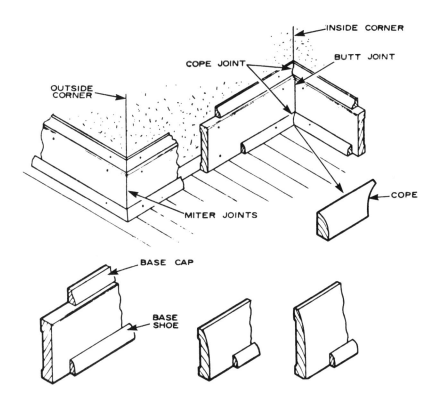

Figure 47-28. *Baseboard makes interior walls look finished. It covers the joint between the floor and wall.*

LEARNING CARPENTRY

If you are interested in learning carpentry, you may want to build a scale model house (Figure 47-29). Building a model house will help you learn how a house fits together.

Building a garden shed (Figure 47-30) or a dog house (Figure 47-31) will also help you learn carpentry. Smaller buildings have plans like

Figure 47-29. *Building a scale model house will help you learn how a house fits together.*

Figure 47-30. *A garden shed is built the same way as a house. You can learn carpentry skills by building a garden shed.*

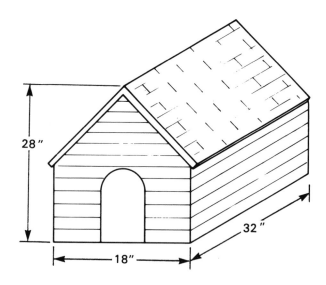

Figure 47-31. *A doghouse uses the same carpentry skills as a house.*

those of a house. They also require the same carpentry skills. When you complete a dog house or garden shed, you will have gained many carpentry skills.

QUESTIONS FOR REVIEW

1. How would you define carpentry?
2. Can you describe some of the jobs done by carpenters?
3. What is the difference between a special and a general carpenter?
4. What education must a person have to become a carpenter?
5. Into what areas would you divide the work of building a house?
6. How is a sill attached to a foundation? Why is sill sealer used?
7. Why is the subfloor sometimes glued to the joists?
8. What is the function of let-in braces in wall sheathing?
9. What material can be used in place of siding over the sheathing?
10. How is the frame of a rafter roof assembled? What are the principal parts of an assembled roof frame?
11. How does a truss roof differ from an assembled roof? What advantage does a truss roof have?
12. What are some common roofing materials? Which material is most often used?
13. What jobs would a carpenter do to finish the interior of a house?

SUGGESTED ACTIVITIES

1. Make a list of the common hand tools a carpenter must have for work.

2. Build a scale model house. Label all parts such as the studs, and joists.

3. Check with your apprenticeship board to determine how to begin a carpentry apprenticeship.

Furniture and Cabinetry

CHAPTER 48

Cabinetmaking is a specialized woodworking trade. Cabinetmakers usually build *fixtures* and *cabinets* for stores and houses. Some cabinetmakers build fixtures for churches, banks, and medical buildings.

People who build *furniture* are also called cabinetmakers. Furniture and cabinets have a similar appearance and use the same construction methods. Cabinet and furniture construction requires skill and accuracy.

The difference between furniture and cabinets is that cabinets are installed or *mounted* while furniture is movable. It is not mounted or installed.

KEY TERMS

cabinetmaking	lipped door
fixtures	flush door
furniture	hardware
plastic laminates	box
mullions	case
rails	carcass
stiles	frame and panel
overlay door	

THE CABINETMAKER'S JOB

The cabinetmaker does not usually work at the construction site. Cabinetwork is done in a shop (Figure 48-1). The cabinetmaker works from blueprints and drawings. A cabinetmaker learns cabinetmaking in school and on the job. The beginning cabinetmaker may attend a trade school during non-working hours.

Cabinetmakers who belong to a union must complete a four-year apprenticeship. An appren-

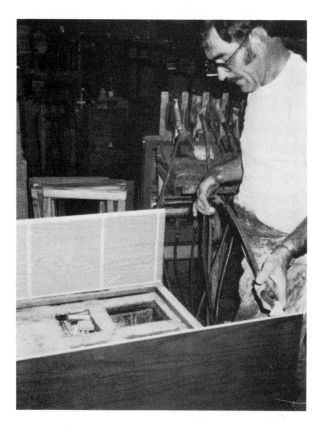

Figure 48-1. *Cabinetmakers usually work in a shop. They must know how to read blueprints and lay out stock. The work requires skill and accuracy.*

ticeship combines classroom knowledge and work experience. To become a cabinetmaker you should have a high school education. You should also have a technical background. High school courses in drafting, architecture, woodworking and carpentry are very important.

The cabinetmaker works indoors. Some of the materials are heavy. The cabinetmaker must lift

Figure 48-2. *Cabinetmakers must do accurate work. Cabinet materials are expensive. A mistake can be very costly.*

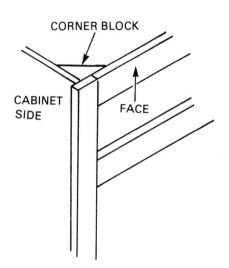

Figure 48-4. *Corner blocks strengthen cabinets. They are glued in place. Nails or staples hold the glue blocks while the glue dries.*

and handle these materials. Cabinet shops are often dusty and noisy. The work requires accuracy (Figure 48-2). Cabinet materials are expensive. A mistake can be costly. Cabinetmakers must buy and maintain their own hand tools.

They are also responsible for the power tools in the shop. Routine maintenance and sharpening are part of a cabinetmaker's work.

CABINET ASSEMBLY

Most cabinets have common parts (Figure 48-3) such as *sides, top, front* or *face, back, doors* and *drawers.* Cabinets differ in the way the parts are

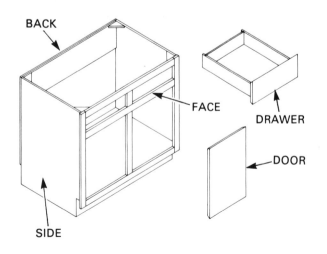

Figure 48-3. *Common cabinet parts.*

joined. Some use simple joints such as the butt joint. Some use complex joinery such as mortise and tenon or double dowel joints.

Corner blocks are used to strengthen cabinets (Figure 48-4). They are glued and fastened in place. Corner blocks can be fastened with staples, nails or screws.

Cabinet Sides

Cabinet sides are cut from sheet stock. Hardwood plywood is sometimes used for decorative sides. Decorative sides can also be made by paneling over particle board or plywood.

When a solid stock frame is used for a cabinet side, it can be covered with thin sheet stock. Plywood or hardboard can be used for this purpose. Most kitchen base cabinet sides are 23¼" (590 mm) wide and 34½" (876 mm) high. This makes the base cabinet 24 inches (610 mm) deep and 36 inches (914 mm) high when assembled. Wall cabinets vary in height. They are usually 12" (300 mm) deep.

Cabinet Tops

Cabinet tops or counter tops are usually made of *particle board* and covered with a *plastic laminate.* Veneer may also be used to cover the particle board top. (Application of plastic laminates and veneers is covered in Chapter 49).

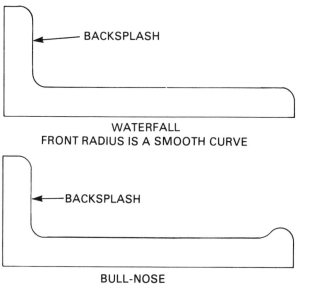

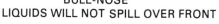

Figure 48-5. *Two types of postformed tops.*

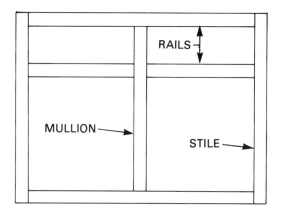

Figure 48-6. *Parts of a cabinet front.*

A nailing strip (Figure 48-3) is part of the cabinet back. The cabinet is attached to the wall through the nailing strip. The nailing strip is usually ⅝" to ¾" (15 mm to 18 mm) thick. It is attached to the cabinet sides and glued to the cabinet back.

Cabinet Doors

Cabinet doors are made of sheet stock or solid wood. Hardwood veneer on particle board or plywood is most common. There are three common types of doors: *overlay, lipped* and *flush.* (Figure 48-7). Most kitchen cabinets use *overlay* doors because they are easy to fit.

Some counter tops come already formed with a "backsplash" (Figure 48-5). They are covered with a plastic laminate. These counter tops are called "postformed". They are commonly used for kitchen cabinets. They may also be used on other types of cabinets.

Cabinet Fronts

The cabinet front or face is made of *hardwood.* The three parts of the front are the *mullions, rails* and *stiles* (Figure 48-6). These parts are usually ¾" (18 mm) thick and I ¾" to 2" (43 mm to 50 mm) wide. The parts are usually assembled with dowel or mortise and tenon joints. Drawer openings vary in width. Their height is usually 4½" to 5" (112 mm to 125 mm).

The cabinet face is glued to the cabinet ends and base. Nails or staples are used for added strength. The cabinet face is usually butted to the ends and bottom. Some faces are joined to the bottom and ends with a rabbet or dado joint.

Cabinet Back

Cabinet backs are made of sheet stock. *Plywood* and *hardboard* are most commonly used. Standard thickness for cabinet backs is ¼" (6 mm).

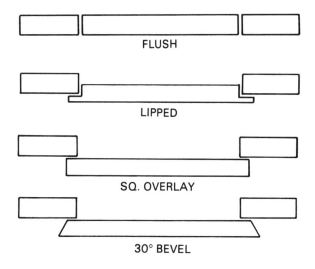

Figure 48-7. *Cabinet door types.*

Lipped doors can be cut on the shaper. A special bit is used for shaping lipped doors. Be sure to allow 1/16" (2 mm) clearance between the cabinet face and each rabbet edge.

Flush doors fit inside the rails and stiles. These doors require 1/16" (2 mm) clearance at each edge. Flush doors must be beveled on the hinge side. The bevel keeps the door from rubbing the stile when opened.

Drawers

Cabinet and furniture drawers are similar. They may be simple or complex (Figure 48-8). *Simple* drawers are easy to build. But they are not as strong as *complex* drawers. Complex drawers use locking joints. These joints remain strong after years of use. All drawers have a bottom that fits into grooved sides, front and back (Figure 48-9).

A *guide* assures smooth drawer movement. On some drawers, two guides are used (Figure 48-10). Drawer guides keep the drawer from sticking when opened or closed.

Some commercial guides use metal rails and nylon rollers (Figure 48-11). Others use a single metal rail and a nylon roller (Figure 48-12). Nylon guides may also be attached to drawer backs

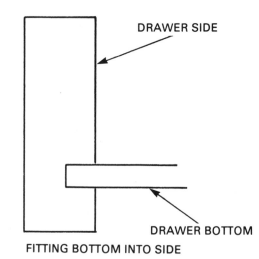

FITTING BOTTOM INTO SIDE

Figure 48-9. *The drawer bottom fits into a groove cut in the drawer parts.*

Figure 48-10. *Commercial two-track drawer guide.*

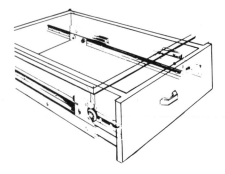

Figure 48-11. *Nylon rollers and steel guides provide smooth drawer movement.*

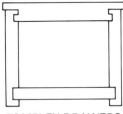
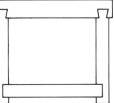

COMPLEX DRAWERS
LOCKING JOINERY

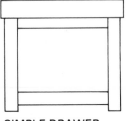
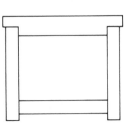

SIMPLE DRAWER
BUTT AND RABBET JOINTS

Figure 48-8. *Complex drawers last longer than simple drawers. This is because all parts are locked together.*

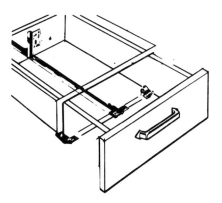

Figure 48-12. *Single steel guide with nylon rollers.*

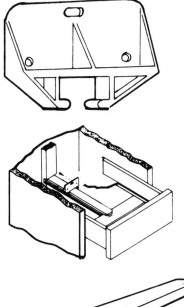

Figure 48-13. *Nylon guides slide over a T-shaped piece of wood.*

(Figure 48-13). They slide on a T-shaped piece of wood.

Shop-built guides can be used on the drawer sides or the drawer bottom (Figure 48-14). These guides should be finished and well waxed to ensure smooth drawer movement.

HARDWARE

The *hardware* used on cabinets and furniture is

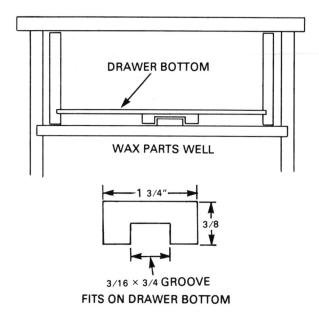

DRAWER BOTTOM

WAX PARTS WELL

3/16 × 3/4 GROOVE
FITS ON DRAWER BOTTOM

Figure 48-14. *Shop-made drawer guide.*

similar. There are many hardware items. Some common hardware items include *pulls, latches, hinges* and *locks.*

Pulls

Pulls or handles (Figure 48-15) are used to open doors and drawers. Pulls are usually fastened with wood screws or machine screws. Measure and lay out holes carefully before drilling.

Latches and Catches

Latches and *catches* are used to hold doors in the open or closed position. Latches are usually

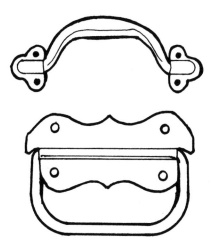

Figure 48-15. *Cabinet and furniture pulls. These pulls are attached with wood screws or machine screws.*

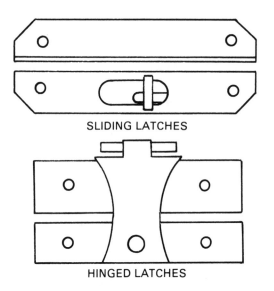

SLIDING LATCHES

HINGED LATCHES

Figure 48-16. *Latches are used to hold doors or lids open or shut.*

CATCH → ← KEEPER

BULLET CATCHES

Figure 48-18. *A bullet catch is used to hold a drawer shut.*

mounted to the door front and stile (Figure 48-16). Door catches are usually mounted to the door back and shelf bottom (Figure 48-17). Some catches (Figure 48-18) can also be used to hold drawers shut.

Hinges

Hinges (Figure 48-19) allow the door to swing from the stile. There are many types of hinges such as *butt, semi-concealed, pivot* and *wrap-*

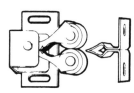

DOUBLE ROLLER CATCH WITH SPRING

ELBOW CATCH

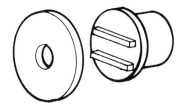

ROUND MAGNETIC CATCH

TITAN MAGNETIC CATCH

SPIRAL GRIP CATCH

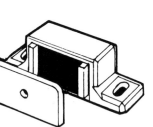

MAGNETIC CATCH

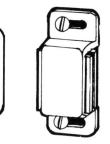

MAGNETIC CATCH

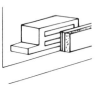 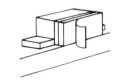 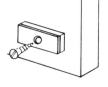

SELF-ADHERING MAGNET CATCH

Figure 48-17. *Door catches are usually mounted to the door back and shelf bottom.*

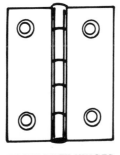

BRASS BUTT HINGES

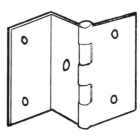

WRAP AROUND HINGE

Figure 48-19. *Hinges allow a door to swing from the stile or frame.*

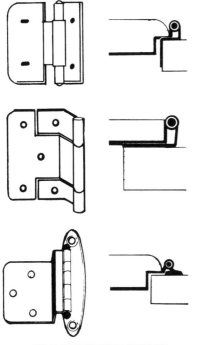

SEMI-CONCEALED HINGES

Figure 48-20. *Common types of hinges.*

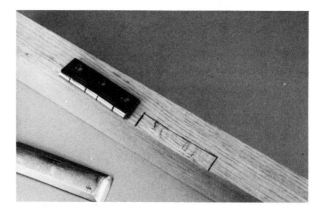

Figure 48-21. *The dado cut for a butt hinge is sometimes call a* gain.

Lay out the dado or gain carefully. The hinge must fit snugly. This distributes the door weight.

Semi-concealed hinges are used with *lipped doors* (Figure 48-20). One leaf of the hinge is bent. This allows it to be screwed to the door back. Screws in the faces of sheet stock are stronger than screws in the edges.

Pivot hinges are also screwed to the back of the door (Figure 48-22). They are commonly used with *overlay doors.* Heavy doors use a third pivot hinge (Figure 48-23) located in the center of the door.

Wrap-around hinges are screwed to the door back. The other leaf wraps around the stile (Figure 48-20). It is held in place with a wood screw. The wrap-around hinge resists stress when the door is opened.

around (Figure 48-20). Some of these hinges are self-closing. A self-closing hinge is spring loaded. It will close the door when released in the open position.

Butt hinges are commonly used on *flush doors.* A small dado is cut in the door and stile (Figure 48-21). The dado holds the butt hinge. A dado that is used for setting a hinge is sometimes called a *gain.*

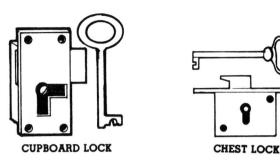

CUPBOARD LOCK **CHEST LOCK**

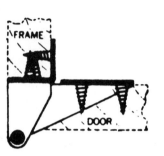

Figure 48-22. *Pivot hinges are screwed to the back of the door.*

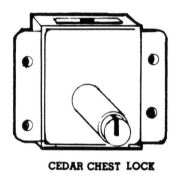

CEDAR CHEST LOCK

Figure 48-24. *Locks are used to secure doors, drawers or lids.*

Locks

Locks (Figure 48-24) are used to secure doors, drawers and lids. Locks are sometimes fastened to a wooden part or assembly. Other locks are fitted into a mortise. Some locks have a bolt that locks the door to the stile. The bolt is moved by turning the key.

Installing Hardware

Before you install any hardware *read the directions.* Be sure you know how it works. When in doubt, attach the hardware to a piece of scrap. This will reduce the chance of damage to your work.

Templates (Figure 48-25) are sometimes included with the hardware. These templates simplify layout and installation. Handle these templates carefully. If they are torn, they will not be accurate.

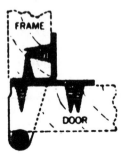

Figure 48-23. *A center pivot hinge must be used on heavy doors.*

Some hardware comes with decorative screws or nails. These fasteners must be driven careful-

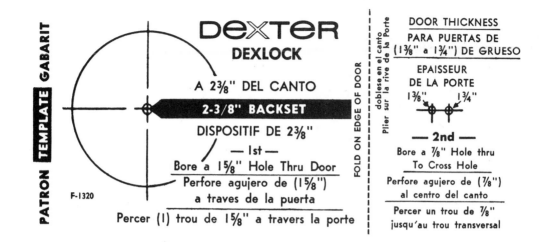

Figure 48-25. *Some hardware comes with a template. The template will simplify layout. Handle the template carefully.*

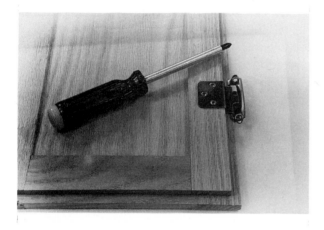

Figure 48-26. *Drive decorative screws carefully. Remember, brass screws need a larger pilot hole than steel screws.*

Figure 48-27. *This dart board was made using case construction.*

ly (Figure 48-26). If the heads are damaged, the hardware will lose some of its beauty. Make sure your pilot holes are larger for brass screws than steel screws. Brass screws tend to break easily.

FURNITURE ASSEMBLY

There are many types of furniture assembly. Each type has a name. The most common types include *box, case, frame and panel* and *carcass.*

Box

Box construction uses simple joinery. Glued panels or solid stock are most commonly used for box assembly, such as the pencil box. One common piece of box furniture is the cedar chest.

Case

Case construction is box construction turned on end (Figure 48-27). Joinery in case construction is more complex than in box construction. This is because drawers are commonly found in case construction.

Frame And Panel

Frame and panel construction uses complex

Figure 48-28. *This blanket chest was made using frame and panel construction.*

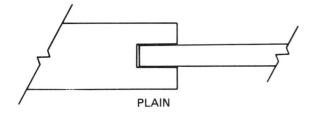

PLAIN

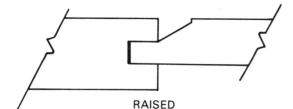

RAISED

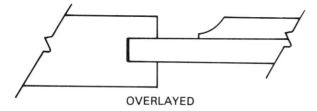

OVERLAYED

Figure 48-29. *Frame and panel construction may be plain, raised or overlayed.*

joinery (Figure 48-28). Solid stock is used to frame sheet stock or thin panels of solid stock. The panels may be plain, raised or overlayed (Figure 48-29).

Panels are held in the grooves of the frame. They are not glued. This allows expansion and con-

traction of the panel. Many types of furniture use frame and panel construction.

Carcass

Carcass construction is usually a combination of case construction and frame and panel construction (Figure 48-30). Frame assembly may be used for webs. If a panel is added, the web becomes a dust panel (Figure 48-31). Dust panels are used to keep dust from dropping into a drawer below it.

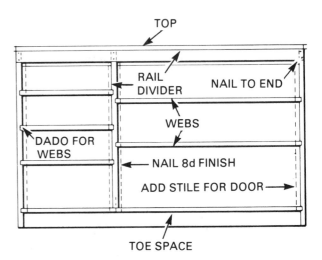

Figure 48-30. *This dresser was built using carcass construction.*

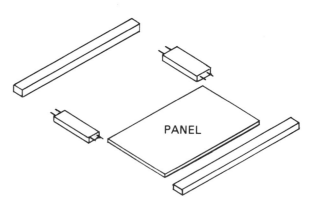

Figure 48-31. *Placing a panel in the web makes it a dust panel. The panel is locked in a groove joint. The panel keeps dust from dropping in the drawer below.*

Desks and dressers are common examples of carcass construction. Carcass construction requires accurate layout and measure. An error on any part could cause assembly problems.

QUESTIONS FOR REVIEW

1. What type of work is commonly done by a cabinetmaker?
2. How would you describe the difference between cabinets and furniture?
3. What are the common parts of a cabinet? From what materials are these parts made?
4. What three types of doors are used on cabinets? Can you draw a sketch of each?
5. How does a simple drawer differ from a complex drawer? Which drawer is stronger?
6. What is the purpose of a drawer guide? From what materials are drawer guides made?
7. What common types of hardware are used on furniture and cabinets? What is the purpose of each?
8. What should you do before installing any hardware on a cabinet?
9. Why must decorative fasteners be driven carefully?
10. How would you describe box assembly of furniture? How does box assembly differ from case construction?
11. How would you describe frame and panel furniture assembly? How are panels held in the frame?
12. How would you describe carcass construction? How would you classify dust panels used in carcass construction?

SUGGESTED ACTIVITIES

1. Inspect some cabinets found in your home. Make an isometric assembly sketch of the cabinet showing joinery details.
2. Visit a home improvement center that sells kitchen cabinets. Compare high and low priced units. Make a list of the differences between high and low priced units.

Veneers and Plastic Laminates

Veneers and *plastic laminates* are thin sheets of material. They must be glued to a backing sheet for support. The veneers and plastic laminates break easily and cannot be used without a backing sheet.

KEY TERMS

veneer	backing sheet
plastic laminate	contact cement
laminating	roller
veneer knife	router
form	laminate trimmer
mold	panel bit
caul	

VENEERS

Veneers are sheets of wood (Figure 49-1) under ⅛" (about 3 mm) thick. They are usually glued to backing sheets of plywood or particle board. When the *backing sheet* is covered with veneer, it looks like a piece of expensive hardwood. This process is sometimes called *laminating.*

Veneers shrink and swell less than solid stock. When glued to a backing sheet, they do not shrink or swell. There is a little chance of warpage.

Common veneers are usually ¹⁄₂₈" (less than 1 mm) thick. They are *sliced* or *peeled* from high quality logs (Figure 49-2). Softwood veneers are usually peeled from logs (Figure 49-2). Because veneers are sliced or peeled from logs, they vary in length and width.

Veneers are often bent to irregular shapes. They can be bent easily. Several layers of veneers can be bent and glued into an irregular shape. Figure 49-3 shows forks that have been bent into

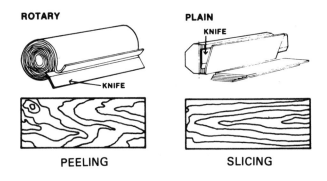

Figure 49-2. *Methods of producing veneers. Hardwood veneers are usually sliced. Softwood veneers are usually peeled.*

Figure 49-3. *Several layers of veneer have been glued together to make this salad fork. A mold holds the veneers in place until the glue cures.*

Figure 49-1. *Veneers are less than ⅛" (about 3 mm) thick. Common veneers are ¹⁄₂₈" (less than 1 mm) thick.*

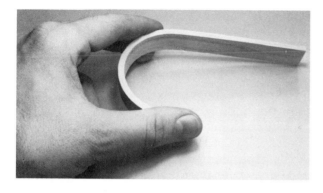

Figure 49-4. *These hooks were made from five layers of veneer. A band clamp held them to the form while the glue cured.*

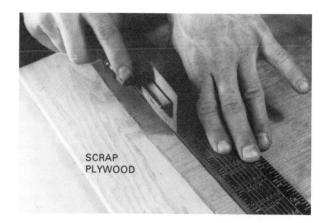

SCRAP PLYWOOD

Figure 49-6. *The veneer knife or saw is pushed and pulled toward the center of the piece. Protect the bench with a piece of scrap plywood.*

irregular shapes. A mold is used for bending the wood. The glue makes the veneers hold their bent shape. The hooks in Figure 49-4 were also bent to shape and glued.

Working With Veneer

Veneers can be cut and joined like other pieces of solid stock. Because they are thin, they tend to split and splinter. Special cutting tools will reduce splitting.

Cutting Veneers. A *veneer knife* (Figure 49-5, *right*) or veneer saw will cut veneer well. Although it is sometimes called a knife, it has fine teeth. These teeth cut well with or across the grain. The blade is curved for crosscutting. It is pushed toward the center on the forward stroke. On the return stroke it is pulled toward the

center. Sawing toward the center (Figure 49-6) reduces the chance of splintering at the edges.

The veneer knife should be guided with a straightedge. A piece of hardwood or a framing square will work. Be sure to protect the workbench when cutting veneers. Place a scrap piece of softwood or plywood under the veneer being cut (Figure 49-6). Avoid using particle board or hardboard to protect the workbench. Their hardness dulls the veneer knife quickly.

Veneers may also be cut with shears or a utility knife (Figure 49-5, *left*). These tools do not cut as well as a veneer knife. They are good for cutting veneers to rough size.

Joining Veneers. Veneers are joined together to make wider pieces. They are also joined together to make decorative patterns (Figure 49-7) and

UTILITY KNIFE   VENEER KNIFE

Figure 49-5. *A veneer knife or veneer saw,* right, *has very small teeth. These teeth cut well with or across the grain. The utility knife,* left, *may also be used to cut veneers to rough size.*

Figure 49-7. *Veneers can be cut to make decorative patterns like these.*

Figure 49-8. *Marquetry uses veneers to make pictures or designs.*

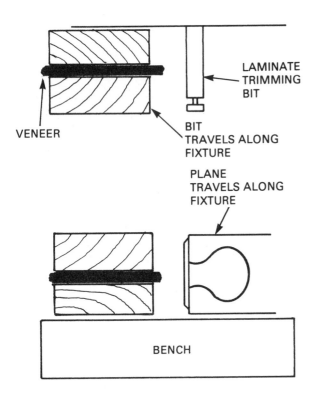

Figure 49-9. *Trimming veneer edge.*

marquetry (Figure 49-8). Edges of veneers must fit together well for joining.

The veneer edges are smoothed with a plane or a laminate-trimming router bit. The veneer is clamped in a fixture with the edge exposed about 1/16" (about 2 mm). See Figure 49-9. The plane or router bit travels along the edge of the fixture. The exposed veneer is removed leaving the edge smooth.

To join the veneers, place them on the bench with the good side up. Line up the edges and tape them together (Figure 49-10). Apply tape across the joint every 4" to 6" (100 to 150 mm). Apply tape along the joint (Figure 49-11). The tape goes over the other pieces of tape.

Figure 49-10. *Tape the edges together every 4 to 6 inches (100 to 150 mm).*

Figure 49-11. *Apply tape along the joint. Apply it over the other pieces of tape.*

Turn the veneers over and fold them back (Figure 49-12). Apply glue along the edges. Lay the veneers down and tape over the glue joint (Figure 49-13).

Figure 49-12. *Fold the veneers back and apply glue to the edges.*

Figure 49-13. *Tape over the glue joint. The tape will hold the veneers while the glue cures.*

After the glue dries remove the tape. The veneer may now be glued to a backing sheet.

Gluing Veneer to a Backing Sheet. Veneer can be glued to a backing sheet with *contact cement.* It may also be glued with a powder or liquid glue such as plastic resin or polyvinyl. If these glues are used, the veneer must be clamped in place for 12 to 16 hours.

Contact cement sticks to itself. Veneers glued with contact cement do not require clamping. (See the section in this chapter on plastic laminates for contact cement gluing techniques.)

Powder glues must be mixed carefully for veneer work. If they are too thick, they are difficult to apply. If they are too thin, the excess water will curl the veneers. Liquid glues must be specially made for large veneer jobs. All general-duty liquid glues are too thick.

Spread the glue over the entire backing sheet. A *brush* or *roller* will work well. Make sure that a thin coat covers the entire sheet. Lay the veneer on the backing sheet good side up. Make sure the veneer is lined up correctly. About three thicknesses of newspaper should cover the exposed veneer face. This helps to spread the clamping pressure over the veneer. Place a piece of sheet stock over the newspaper and veneer and clamp all layers to the backing stock (Figure 49-14).

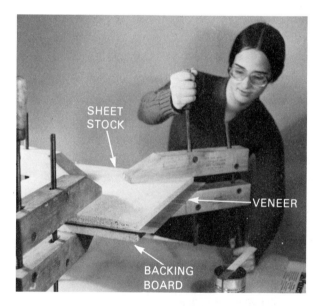

Figure 49-14. *Clamping veneer to a backing sheet. Make sure the veneer is lined up correctly.*

Gluing Small Pieces of Veneer. Veneers less than 6" (150 mm) wide and 8" (200 mm) long can be glued with common liquid glues. Both polyvinyl and aliphatic glues work well. Thin the glue slightly with water. Mix one part water to five parts glue and spread it onto the backing stock. Put the veneer in place and place an iron on the veneer to heat the glue (Figure 49-15). This speeds curing. Use a medium heat. The glue will tend to bubble or boil slightly. Move the iron slowly to assure a uniform bond. If the veneer

Figure 49-15. *Heat will make the glue cure quicker. Use an iron on small pieces only. Keep the iron moving. Be sure to use a medium heat.*

Apply glue between veneer layers. Line up the pieces and wrap them in waxed paper (Figure 49-16). The waxed paper keeps the veneers from sticking to the form. Then clamp the veneers to a form or press them between the caul parts. The lamination should dry for around 16 hours. The waxed paper slows down drying. Remove the lamination and trim to final shape.

PLASTIC LAMINATES

Plastic laminates are made from a combination of melamine and phenolic plastic. These plastics will not melt when heated. Plastic laminates are easy to clean. They also resist stains and burns. Plastic laminates are used for furniture, kitchen counters and table tops. Some plastic laminates are colored or have a decorative pattern (Figure

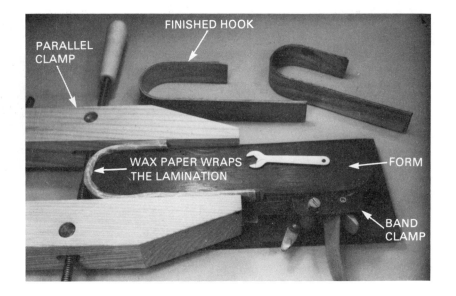

Figure 49-16. *Wax paper keeps the veneers from sticking to the caul or mold.*

darkens, the iron is too hot. Remove the dark areas with light sanding.

Laminating Veneers. Veneers are bent to an irregular shape with a *form* or a *caul.* A form (Figure 49-16) has veneers clamped to it. A caul (Figure 49-3) is a two-part mold. It presses the veneers into the desired shape. After the glue dries, remove the laminated veneers from the form or caul.

49-17). Others have a woodgrain pattern. They are used for furniture tops on dressers or tables. A few plastic laminates have a metallic look. They are used for special jobs.

There are three kinds of laminates: *standard, backing* and *postformed.* Standard laminates are used for most laminate jobs. Backing laminates are used for door backs and other light-duty uses. Postforming laminates are used to

Figure 49-17. *Plastic laminates are sold in colors and patterns. Metallic and woodgrain laminates are also available.*

Figure 49-18. *Cutting plastic laminates on the table saw. Be sure the good side is up.*

make formed countertops. They are also used to edgeband curved countertops. Postformed laminates look like other plastic laminates, but they are different. Although postformed laminates are almost as thick as standard laminates, they will bend when heated. Common plastic laminates come in two thicknesses. Standard laminates are 1/16" (about 2 mm) and backing laminates are 1/32" (about 1 mm) thick.

Working With Plastic Laminates

Plastic laminates require *cutting, gluing* and *trimming.* All of these operations use common woodworking tools and practices.

Cutting Plastic Laminates. Plastic laminates can be cut with power tools such as the table saw, router and saber saw. They may also be scored and broken or cut with shears. Power tools should have carbide blades for cutting plastic laminates. Plastic laminates are hard. They will dull other tools rapidly.

Plastic laminates are always cut 1/2" to 1" (12 to 25 mm) oversize. This is to allow for slight error and for trimming. It is difficult to work with a plastic laminate that is cut to exact size. Be sure to wear eye protection when you work with plastic laminates.

Attach a wood strip to the fence when using a table saw. This will keep the laminate from creeping under the fence. Feed the laminate slowly into the blade. Be sure the good side is up (Figure 49-18).

Figure 49-19. *Place the good side down when using the saber saw. Laminates will break if not supported.*

Place the good side down if you use a saber saw (Figure 49-19). Be sure to support the plastic laminate. It is brittle and will break or chip easily. A fine tooth blade is needed. Coarse blades will chip or break the plastic laminate.

Before you use any power tools for cutting plastic laminates, be sure you know how to operate them safely.

Clamp the plastic laminate between two pieces of stock for scoring (Figure 49-20). The good side should be up. Use a sharp scratch awl to score

Figure 49-20. *Scoring a laminate sheet. Make sure that it is clamped securely.*

Figure 49-21. *If the laminate is scored well, it will snap along the line. Bend the laminate toward the straightedge.*

the laminate. Score the laminate well. Then lift the laminate toward the straightedge. It will snap along the line (Figure 49-21).

Gluing Plastic Laminates. Contact cement is commonly used to glue plastic laminates to a backing sheet. Be sure to follow the manufacturer's instructions when using contact cement. Some are flammable. They cannot be used near an open flame.

The correct order for gluing plastic laminates to the backing sheet is sides, front, top. This order makes the least number of joints visible from the front or top.

Apply contact cement to the front edge, back edge and both ends of the backing sheet. Apply it also to the edge and end strips. A *brush* or *roller* may be used to spread the contact cement. Let the contact cement dry. Test dryness with a piece of brown paper (Figure 49-22). If it does not stick, the surfaces are ready.

Place the ends in position. Be sure to align them correctly before bonding. Once the surfaces touch they cannot be moved. Then align and bond the front and back. On kitchen cabinets, the back edge is not visible. It does not need to be laminated.

Figure 49-22. *Test the contact with brown paper. If the contact cement does not stick to the paper, it is ready.*

Trim the front, back and ends so the top can be glued in position. Contact cement is now applied to the top and the top laminate. After the cement dries, align the two surfaces. Sticks are placed between the laminate and backing sheet (Figure 49-23). This prevents surfaces from sticking before they are aligned.

Figure 49-23. *The sticks allow the laminate to be aligned with the backing sheet.*

Figure 49-24. *Remove the center stick and push the laminate onto the backing sheet. Work from the center toward the ends.*

Remove the center stick. Push the laminate into contact with the backing sheet (Figure 49-24). The laminate is worked from the center. Remove the sticks and push the surfaces together. Use a roller to press the pieces together (Figure 49-25). Then trim the top.

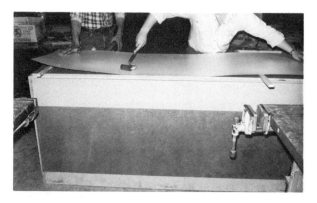

Figure 49-25. *Use a roller to bond the laminate to the backing sheet.*

Note: Use the same techniques for gluing veneer with contact cement.

Trimming Plastic Laminates. Plastic laminates are trimmed with a router or *laminate trimmer.* A router with a laminate trimming bit or *panel bit* can be used (Figure 49-26). The laminate trimming bit works best because it has a ball bearing pilot tip.

The panel bit works best for cutting holes in plastic laminates. These holes are commonly cut for sinks. The panel bit will drill a hole with its point (Figure 49-26). The pilot tip will then control the cut. (When using a router be sure to follow the safety rules in Chapter 44.)

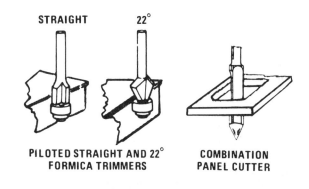

Figure 49-26. *These router bits will trim plastic laminates. The panel bit will drill through the laminate and cut holes for sinks and ranges.*

Figure 49-27. *The laminate trimmer is designed for working with plastic laminates. Be sure you know how to operate it safely before you begin.*

The laminate trimmer is a specialized power tool (Figure 49-27). It was designed for laminate work. Because it is smaller than a router, it is

395

easier to work in corners. It is also lighter and easier to handle. The bit used in a laminate trimmer will cut straight or at an angle. This is changed by raising or lowering the base. (When using the laminate trimmer, be sure to follow the safety rules in Chapter 44.)

Some hand tools may also be used for trimming plastic laminates. There is a hand-held laminate trimmer. It is made of plastic with a carbide cutter (Figure 49-28).

Files may also be used to remove small amounts of stock. A medium cut file removes stock quickly. A fine cut file removes less stock but leaves a smoother edge.

A hand scraper will also trim plastic laminates. It removes a small amount of stock. The hand scraper leaves the plastic laminate very smooth. Scrapers and files are often used to break sharp corners.

Figure 49-28. *This laminate trimmer is a hand tool. It has a carbide cutter. The cutter scores the plastic laminate.*

QUESTIONS FOR REVIEW

1. Define veneer.
2. Are all veneers the same thickness?
3. What is the difference between veneer peeling and veneer slicing?
4. Define veneer laminating.
5. How are veneers cut? What tools do the best job?
6. For what purpose are veneers joined? What is the procedure for joining them?
7. What types of glue are used for joining veneer to a backing sheet? Which glues require clamping?
8. Describe plastic laminates. What are the qualities of plastic laminates?
9. What is the difference between standard, backing and postformed plastic laminates?
10. How are plastic laminates cut? Which tools work best?
11. Why are plastic laminates cut larger than the surface they will cover?
12. Describe the procedure for gluing plastic laminates or veneers to a backing sheet with contact cement.
13. How do you know when the contact cement is ready for bonding?
14. What type of router bits may be used for trimming plastic laminates?
15. How does a laminate trimmer differ from a router? What are its advantages?
16. What hand tools can be used to trim plastic laminates?

SUGGESTED ACTIVITES

1. Use a veneer knife to cut a scrap of veneer. Work carefully so that you do not tear the end grain.

2. Check with your instructor to see what type of glue is used for gluing veneers to backing stock in your shop.

3. Try gluing a scrap of veneer or plastic laminate to scrap backing stock. Use the glue recommended by your instructor.

Manufacturing is the process of building a product in large quantities. Some commonly manufactured wood products are picture frames, stereo speakers and kitchen cabinets. A manufactured product always follows a basic design. The product may look different by changing small parts, color or dimensions. Figure 50-1 shows different designs for the same basic product. This clock project is studied throughout the chapter. These and other clocks, as well as many other interesting projects, are presented in Chapter 54 "Building Woodworking Projects."

THE GAME ROOM CLOCK

THE 24-HOUR CLOCK

THE KITCHEN CLOCK

THE EXECUTIVE CLOCK

BASIC DEN CLOCK

ROMAN DEN CLOCK

ARABIC DEN CLOCK

NAUTICAL CLOCK

Figure 50-1. *These clocks have the same basic frame. Each clock has the same basic design. Changing faces and numerals makes them look different.*

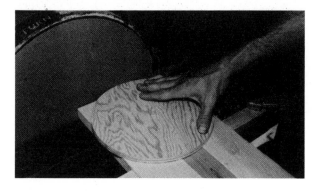

Figure 50-2. *Clock faces can be sanded quickly using this fixture. Building and setting up the fixture takes time but it saves production time.*

Manufactured products can be built faster than a single product. Ten chairs can be built faster if one person makes all the legs while others build the seats and backs. This is because the worker becomes skilled at making one part. If one person built the entire chair it would take longer to build. Each task would be unfamiliar. Progress would be slow. Also, ten parts can be cut almost as fast as two parts. This is because machine setup can take more time than the actual cutting (Figure 50-2).

Less labor is needed to build a manufactured product. Each unit costs less. Also, time and money are saved. This savings is passed on to the buyer. Some manufactured products cost less to buy than a single unit would cost to build.

The manufacturer buys raw materials such as wood and glue in large quantities. This lowers the cost of the raw materials. Figure 50-3 is a raw material order sheet. This order sheet lists the raw materials needed to manufacture 25 clocks.

Parts used in a manufactured product are machined with the aid of *jigs* and *fixtures.* A jig guides the tool into the work. A fixture holds or guides the work while it is machined.

Jigs and fixtures reduce the time needed to make each part. They must be very accurate. Jigs and fixtures help make parts uniform in size and shape. This makes the parts interchangeable. They will fit on any assembly.

RAW MATERIAL ORDER SHEET

HARDWOOD (NOTE: ALL HARDWOOD MUST BE THE SAME SPECIES)

185 LINEAL FEET	3/4" x 25/8" x 18" 18mm x 67mm x 450mm
2 SHEETS PLYWOOD	1/4" x 4' x 8' 6mm x 1200mm x 2400mm
1 SHEET PLYWOOD	1/2" x 4' x 8' 12mm x 1200mm x 2400mm

MOTORS (CLOCK MOTORS POWERED BY A "D" CELL BATTERY)

25 MOTORS WITH HANDS GUARANTEED FOR ONE YEAR AGAINST DEFECTS.

SUPPLIES

1 QUART (1 LITER) WHITE OR YELLOW GLUE
1 GALLON (4 LITERS) PENETRATING OIL FINISH

NOTE: ORDER NUMERALS AND CLOCK FACES SUITED TO YOUR CLOCK DESIGN.

Figure 50-3. *This order sheet would be used to build twenty-five clocks like those pictured in Figures 51-1.*

KEY TERMS

manufacturing	safety
prototype	packaging
route sheet	shipping
flow chart	advertising
quality control	sales

THE MANUFACTURING SEQUENCE

Products are designed to serve a need. They are only manufactured when surveys indicate enough sales to make a profit. The manufacturer must make a profit to stay in business.

A study is made before a product is manufactured. The product must:

1. Serve a need,
2. Compete with existing products,
3. Be manufactured safely,
4. Work reliably and safely,
5. Produce a profit.

THE MANUFACTURING SEQUENCE

PRODUCT DESIGN

DESIGN DEPARTMENT

**DESIGNS A NEW PRODUCT
IMPROVE A PRODUCT DESIGN**

ENGINEERING DEPARTMENT
BUILDS THE FULL SIZE WORKING MODEL
  (PROTOTYPE)
DECIDES HOW TO MANUFACTURE THE
  PRODUCT
FINDS STANDARD SIZE PARTS
REDUCES WASTE IN THE DESIGN

MARKETING DEPARTMENT
USES PROTOTYPE TO PROJECT SALES
  (MARKET ANALYSIS)
SETS RETAIL PRICE

SALES DEPARTMENT
HELPS ADVERTISING DESIGN SALES
  BROCHURE
DEVELOPS ADVERTISING AND SALES
  PLAN

PROTOTYPE

PERSONNEL DEPARTMENT
HIRES NEW WORKERS
PROVIDES NEEDED TRAINING

SAFETY DEPARTMENT
INSPECTS THE PRODUCT FOR SAFETY
FINDS HAZARDOUS OR DANGEROUS
  CONDITIONS

ENGINEERING DEPARTMENT
DEVELOPS ALL DRAWINGS
DEVELOPS ROUTE SHEETS
BUILDS NEEDED JIGS & FIXTURES

**WORKING,
DRAW-
INGS AND
ROUTE
SHEETS**

PURCHASING DEPARTMENT
STUDIES DRAWINGS, THEN SEEK BIDS
BUYS RAW MATERIALS AND STAN-
  DARD PARTS

QUALITY CONTROL
STUDIES DRAWINGS TO DETERMINE
  TOLERANCES

**FLOW
CHART**

ENGINEERING DEPARTMENT

USES THE FLOW CHART AS A TIME-
  TABLE
TRACES THE PROGRESS OF ALL PARTS
SCHEDULES MACHINES BY USING THE
  FLOW CHART

**MANU-
FACTURED
PRODUCT**

ENGINEERING DEPARTMENT
MACHINES ALL PARTS
ASSEMBLES PRODUCT
HELPS DESIGN OWNER'S MANUAL

QUALITY CONTROL
INSPECTS ALL PARTS
INSPECTS FINISHED PRODUCT

SAFETY DEPARTMENT
CHECKS ALL OPERATIONS FOR SAFETY
HELPS DESIGN OWNER'S MANUAL

PACKAGING DEPARTMENT
DESIGNS PACKAGE
HELPS DESIGN OWNER'S MANUAL
PACKS ALL INSPECTED PRODUCTS

SHIPPING DEPARTMENT
SHIPS PRODUCTS BY AIR, MAIL, TRUCK
  AND RAIL
SEEKS FAST PRODUCT DELIVERY

SALES DEPARTMENT
DEVELOPS SALES BROCHURES WITH
  MARKETING AND ADVERTISING
EXPLAINS PRODUCT'S FEATURES
ASSISTS UNSATISFIED CUSTOMERS
BILLING AND COLLECTING

Figure 50-4. *The manufacturing sequence.*

Figure 50-4 shows the manufacturing sequence for a product. This sequence is a plan of procedure for manufacture and sales of a product.

Product Design
The first step in the manufacturing sequence is *product design.* A product is designed to fill a consumer need. It may also be designed to compete with a product already being sold. A design which is a copy usually has improvements or additional features.

Most designs consider appearance first. The designer usually does not decide how the product will be built. Building the product is the job of the *engineering department.* The engineering department decides how the parts will be made and how the product will be assembled.

Prototype
A *prototype* is a full-size working model. It is *custom-made* to match the designer's specifications. A custom-made product is not manufac-

---

MARKET ANALYSIS

---

1. WHICH CLOCK DO YOU LIKE BEST?
   (CHECK ONE)

   24 HOUR CLOCK __   KITCHEN CLOCK __
   GAME ROOM CLOCK __   EXECUTIVE CLOCK __
   BASIC DEN CLOCK __   NAUTICAL CLOCK __
   ROMAN DEN CLOCK __   ARABIC DEN CLOCK __

2. WHAT DO YOU THINK THE RETAIL PRICE OF THIS
   CLOCK WOULD BE? (CHECK ONE)

   $15.00 to $20.00 __ $20.00 to $25.00 __
   $25.00 to $30.00 __ $30.00 to $35.00 __

3. WOULD YOU BUY THIS CLOCK AT THE PRICE
   CHECKED ABOVE? (CHECK ONE)

   YES __   NO __   UNCERTAIN __

4. IF YOUR ANSWER TO QUESTION 3 IS NO OR
   UNCERTAIN, PLEASE EXPLAIN.

Figure 50-5. *This market analysis helps a company determine retail price. It also helps them determine sales.*

tured; it is built as a single unit. The *engineering department* usually builds the prototype.

A prototype serves many uses. It helps the *marketing department* project potential sales and retail price. This is known as a market analysis (Figure 50-5). The marketing department then works with the *advertising* and *sales department* to develop an advertising plan. including catalog descriptions and sales brochures.

Advertisements are developed through an analysis of the basic product or prototype. An analysis of the clock shown in Figure 50-1 would give the following key points or sales features:
  Battery operated;
  Easy to install;
  Movement guaranteed for one year;
  Quality hardwood construction;
  Needs no winding;
  Available in many styles;
  Easy to maintain;
   Oil finish easily cleaned or repaired;
   Replace battery yearly.

These key points are used to develop advertisements and sales brochures.

The prototype helps the engineering department decide what machines should be used to make each part. The prototype also helps decide how the product should be assembled. The *personnel department* discusses manpower needs with the engineering department. They can then decide if workers need to be hired. They will also decide if training programs are needed.

The engineering department studies the prototype. It decides if the product can be changed in any way. Their changes are made to reduce waste or use standard-sized parts. Standard sized parts are manufactured or processed. This makes them cheaper to buy and easier to obtain.

The *safety department* also inspects the prototype. They make sure that it cannot injure the buyer. A dangerous product should never be sold. The safety department protects the worker and buyer from danger. If the safety department finds a hazard, the design is changed. The engineering department and safety department review all changes in design.

All departments within the manufacturing plant work together. They interact on manufacturing decisions. No decision is made by a single

ROUTE SHEET FOR A CLOCK FACE

OPERATION	EQUIPMENT USED
1. CUT TO SIZE 11 7/8" SQUARE	TABLE SAW
2. DRILL 1/2" HOLE IN CENTER	DRILL PRESS
3. CUT TO SHAPE 11 7/8" DIA	BAND SAW (USE CIRCLE CUTTING JIG)
4. SAND EDGES OF FACE TO 11 3/4" DIA	DISC SANDER (USE CIRCLE SANDING JIG)
5. EDGE BAND CLOCK FACE	PORTABLE SANDER
6. SAND CLOCK FACE	
7. ATTACH NUMERALS OR CLOCK FACE	
8. STORE UNTIL NEEDED	

Figure 50-6. *This is a route sheet for a clock face.*

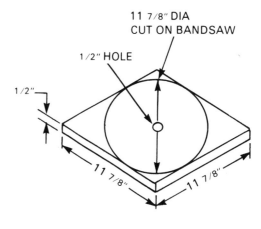

department. Interaction between departments reduces manufacturing problems.

Working Drawings

Working drawings are the drawings needed to manufacture the product. The drawings are made from the prototype. The engineering department makes the working drawings.

An assembly drawing describes all the parts and how they fit together. There is also a drawing of each part. This drawing also appears on the route sheet.

The *route sheet* (Figure 50-6) describes how the part is machined. The drawing on the route sheet makes it easy to understand. The route sheet is used by the people who make the part. It helps them do the job correctly. The route sheet lists any jigs or fixtures needed to make the part.

This reduces setup time. Workers know what is needed by reading the route sheet.

The purchasing department studies the working drawings. They decide what raw materials need to be purchased. They check with suppliers to get their best price. The supplier's best price is called a *bid*. The purchasing department decides which bids to accept. The orders for raw materials are then made.

Flow Chart

A *flow chart* (Figure 50-7) is a plan of procedure for all the parts in the product. It is also a time-table. The engineering department can trace the progress of any part. If a part is behind schedule, extra workers or machines may be added. Each part follows a path. The symbols on this path represent production steps.

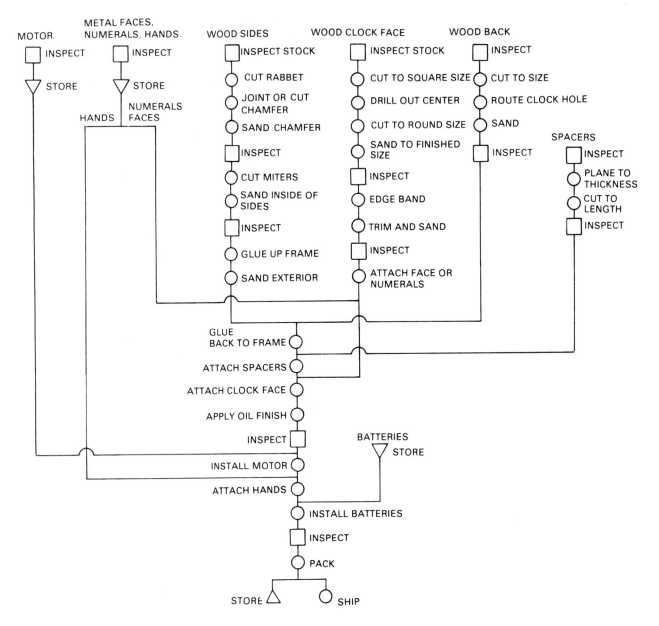

Figure 50-7. *The flow chart is a plan of procedure. It plots all the parts in the product.*

The engineering department can find machines that will be overworked. Operations can be moved from busy machines. This keeps production on schedule.

Quality Control

Accuracy is important in manufacturing. If one part is machined incorrectly, the entire assembly may not fit together. Parts must be accurate to be interchanged. Accuracy is checked by the quality control department.

The *quality control* department has three jobs.

1. To inspect incoming raw materials and parts (Figure 50-8). This is done to be sure that raw materials are of the correct quality. Parts are

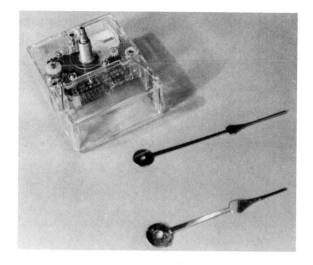

Figure 50-8. *These motors must be inspected as raw materials. The motors must meet manufacturing standards. Inspection is the job of quality control.*

also checked. They must meet manufacturing standards.

2. To check parts machined in the shop for accuracy. They are checked often. If an error is found, very few parts will be wasted.
3. To inspect the assembled product. This is done before packaging. This inspection keeps product quality high. Products with flaws are rejected. These products may be repaired or used for parts.

Quality control is important: poor quality control can mean a loss of sales and reputation.

Safety
The safety department checks product safety and manufacturing safety. The safety department judges all prototypes for safety. The prototype must be safe before the product is mass produced.

When a product is mass produced the safety department checks all operations. They look for possible hazards and remove them. The safety department works closely with the engineering department. They look at all operations for possible hazards.

Safety is important. An accident could cause an employee to be out of work. It could also damage equipment. Accidents are expensive. The safety department can save money for the manufacturer.

Packaging And Shipping
A manufactured product is *packaged* for two reasons. First, the package protects it from damage. Second, it makes the product look more attractive. Both reasons for packaging are related to sales. People want to buy attractive products. They also want the product undamaged when they open the package.

An *owner's manual* is sometimes printed in the packaging department. The owner's manual helps the buyer use and maintain the product correctly. The owner's manual may also give information about the warranty, repair or safe operation. The owner's manual is an important link between the manufacturer and the buyer. Figure 50-9 is an owner's manual for a clock.

Shipping of the product is very important. If stores do not have the product in stock, sales may drop. Products have to be shipped promptly. Buyers rarely wait for a product. They will buy a competing product instead.

Workers in the shipping department have to know how fast shippers deliver. They compare truck, rail, air and postal systems. They select the best system for the buyer.

CONGRATULATIONS:

YOU HAVE JUST PURCHASED A **TIMEWORKS** KITCHEN CLOCK. WE HOPE THAT YOU WILL BE PLEASED WITH YOUR NEW CLOCK.

WHEN MOUNTING YOUR CLOCK, BE SURE IT IS LEVEL. THE CLOCK MOTOR WORKS BEST IN A LEVEL POSITION. THE MOTOR CAN BE ADJUSTED TO KEEP ACCURATE TIME. THERE IS A SCREW ON THE BACK OF THE MOTOR. TURNING THIS SCREW WILL CHANGE THE SPEED OF THE CLOCK.

CHANGE THE BATTERY YEARLY. FOR BEST RESULTS, USE AN ALKALINE BATTERY. THE HARDWOOD HAS AN OIL FINISH. WAX IT OCCASIONALLY AND IT WILL RETAIN ITS LUSTER.

THE CLOCK MOTOR IS GUARANTEED FOR ONE YEAR. IF THE MOTOR OR CLOCK IS DEFECTIVE, PLEASE RETURN IT TO THE ADDRESS BELOW FOR ADJUSTMENT OR REPAIR.

THANKS FOR BUYING A **TIMEWORKS** CLOCK.

Figure 50-9. *Owner's manual. This is an important link between the buyer and manufacturer.*

Personnel

The personnel department hires and trains employees. Special training is needed to perform certain jobs (Figure 50-10). Employees must work safely and accurately. Accidents and errors can reduce profits.

LAYING OUT CLOCK FACES WITH A TEMPLATE

CUTTING THE MOTOR HOLE IN THE BACK

SANDING THE CLOCK FACE TO EXACT SIZE ON THE DISC SANDER

PANEL CUTTING BIT IS USED TO CUT OUT THE MOTOR HOLE. THE BIT TRAVELS ALONG THE TEMPLATE

ATTACHING NUMERALS TO THE CLOCK FACE

GLUING THE CLOCK FRAME TOGETHER

Figure 50-10. *The jobs pictured above require special training. The personnel department trains employees to do these jobs safely and accurately.*

INSTALLING A CLOCK FACE.
THE TEMPLATE IN THE LEFT CORNER HELPS CENTER THE FACE

ATTACHING A METAL FACE TO THE WOODEN CLOCK FACE

Figure 50-10. *Continued.*

ATTACHING THE HANDS TO THE MOTOR

Sales

The *sales* department educates the buyer. Sales people tell stores and buyers why they need their product. They explain all the features of their product. This helps a buyer choose the best product for the money.

The sales department is also the manufacturer's representative. When a buyer is unhappy, the sales department meets the buyer. It is their job to do everything possible to make the buyer happy.

Sales people also work with the marketing and advertising department. Together they develop advertisements, sales brochures and a catalog description. The product has to look good in the catalog. A good looking product appeals to the buyer.

QUESTIONS FOR REVIEW

1. How would you describe manufacturing? What are some wood products that are commonly manufactured?
2. Why is a manufactured product less expensive than a custom made product?
3. How would you describe a jig? How does this differ from a fixture?
4. How do jigs and fixtures help in the manufacture of a product?
5. List the steps in the manufacturing sequence. Discuss the importance of each step.
6. What is a prototype? For what purpose is it used?
7. Why would the engineering department want to change the prototype?
8. Of what importance are working drawings and route sheets? How are they used?
9. How does the engineering department use the flow chart to keep production on schedule?
10. Why is quality control so important when manufacturing a product?
11. What are the three jobs of the quality control department?
12. What is the function of the safety department in the manufacturing sequence.
13. Why is safety so important to manufacturing?

14. Why are manufactured products packaged?
15. Why is an owner's manual often included in the packaging?
16. Why is the shipping department important to the manufacturer?
17. In addition to selling the manufactured product, what other functions does the sales department perform?

SUGGESTED ACTIVITIES

1. Select a project for manufacture. Sketch at least three jigs or fixtures that would speed construction.

2. Select a project for manufacture. Develop a flow chart for the project. Use your school shop as the factory.

3. Inspect any wooden product that has been manufactured. See if you can estimate the cost of the raw materials and labor. What is the margin of profit on each unit?

SECTION 8

Wood Technology

The Parts of a Tree

Trees are plants. They have common growing patterns. You should know how a tree grows and be able to name its parts. This knowledge will help you use wood wisely.

KEY TERMS

seedling	springwood
root system	summerwood
sapwood	pith
xylem	grain
phloem	quarter-sawn
cambium	flat-sawn
sapling	hardwood (deciduous)
heartwood	softwood (coniferous)
annual rings	

TREE GROWTH

A tree begins as a seed. The seed sprouts and growth begins (Figure 51-1). Roots begin to draw water and minerals from the ground. The

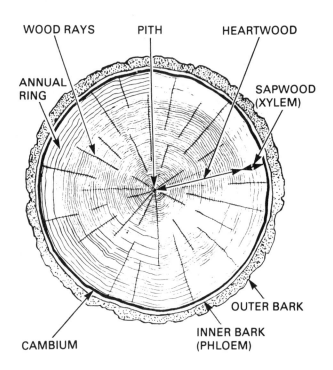

Figure 51-2. *Cross section of a tree trunk.*

Figure 51-1. *A tree begins as a seed. The seed sprouts and growth begins.*

small tree is called a *seedling*. It begins to grow leaves and strengthen its stem. The stem grows around the pith. The *pith* (Figure 51-2) is the hollow tube in the center of the stem.

The *root system* develops in three different sections. The *taproot* forms first. It anchors the tree and draws minerals and water from the ground. As the tree grows, *side roots* extend out from the tree. Side (or lateral) roots are not deep. They grow smaller roots called *feeder roots.* The feeder roots catch rainwater and minerals from the ground. The lateral and feeder roots also anchor the tree.

The roots send minerals and water to the *sapwood* or *xylem* (Figure 51-2). The xylem is the woody part of the tree. The water and minerals travel upward to the leaves. The *leaves* change minerals and water into food. They need sunlight and carbon dioxide to change minerals and water into food.

The food made by the leaves travels down through the *phloem.* The phloem (Figure 51-2) is the inner part of the bark. It brings food to the other wood cells in the tree (Figure 51-2) through the rays.

With food, the tree produces more cells. The cambium divides and makes the tree larger. The *cambium* (Figure 51-2) is located below the bark. It divides and produces bark and xylem cells.

As the tree forms a trunk, it is called a *sapling.* It is called a sapling until it forms heartwood. As the tree matures, the xylem cells in the center of the tree become plugged. It is then called the *heartwood* (Figure 51-2).

The heartwood is usually darker than the *sapwood.* This is caused by plugging of the cells. Heartwood is not an active part of the tree. Its only job is to help support the tree. The sapling is considered a full grown tree when some of the sapwood turns into heartwood.

Growth rings can be seen in the end view of a log (Figure 51-2). These rings are called the *annular* (or "annual") *rings.* This is because the tree grows one complete ring each year. The annular ring is divided into two parts: the springwood and the summerwood.

The *springwood* or early wood is grown in the spring (Figure 51-3). The cells are porous. This is because early growth is rapid. The springwood is light in weight. It is not as tough as the summerwood.

The *summerwood* (Figure 51-3) grows slowly. It is dense and hard. It is usually darker than the springwood. Summerwood resists wear better than springwood.

Hardwood trees have leaves that drop off each fall. These trees are called "deciduous" or leaf-bearing trees. Deciduous leaves are broad leaves.

Softwood trees have leaves shaped like needles. The needles stay on the tree in all seasons. Softwood trees are called "coniferous" or cone-bearing.

Figure 51-4 shows leaves for common hardwood and softwood trees. Trees with broad leaves, such as the American elm or the sugar maple,

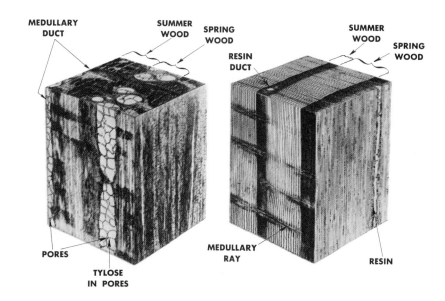

Figure 51-3. *Springwood is porous. This is because it grows rapidly. Summerwood is dense and hard. It grows slower than springwood.*

Figure 51-4. *Hardwood trees have broad leaves that drop off each fall. Softwood trees have needle-shaped leaves. They stay on the tree in all seasons.*

are *hardwoods*. Trees with needles, such as the Douglas fir or the redwood are *softwoods*.

WOOD CHARACTERISTICS

When a tree is harvested, it is cut into boards and dried. The lumber is then processed for many uses. Using the lumber wisely requires a knowledge of how a tree grows. The parts of a tree can affect the quality and stability of the wood.

Pith. Wood around the *pith* tends to warp. This is because it has not grown in a uniform way. The small seedling is twisted and blown around while it is growing into a sapling. All the twisting puts stresses in the wood. These stresses cause wood near the pith to warp.

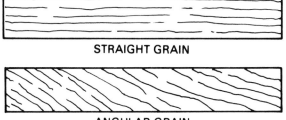

STRAIGHT GRAIN

ANGULAR GRAIN

Figure 51-5. *The face grain of a piece of wood may be straight or angled.*

Figure 51-6. *A straight grain post can support more weight. This is because angular grain is weaker. The strength is parallel to the grain.*

Sapwood and Heartwood. The strength in *sapwood* and *heartwood* is about the same. Both are used for structural lumber. Heartwood is harder than sapwood. It is also more resistant to decay. The heartwood of certain woods (redwood or cypress, for example) is favored for its decay resistance.

Grain. Wood *grain* may be straight or angled (Figure 51-5). Grain is affected by the way the tree is sawed. It is also affected by the way the tree grows. Knots caused by branches can cause angular grain in stock.

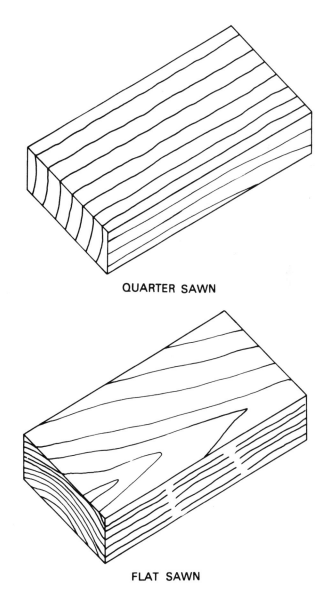

QUARTER SAWN

FLAT SAWN

Figure 51-7. *There is more grain slant in flat-sawn lumber.*

Angular grain is not as strong as straight grain. Wood usually breaks along the grain. Straight grain is less likely to break (Figure 51-6).

Annular Rings. *Annular rings* are related to the grain. If the tree is *flat-sawn* (Figure 51-7) the grain tends to be angular. If the tree is quarter-sawn (Figure 51-7) there is less grain slant.

The annular rings also affect strength and shock resistance. Notice the way the annular rings travel in the hammer handle (Figure 51-8).

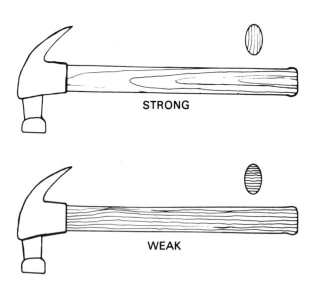

Figure 51-8. *The annular rings should be parallel to the hammer's swing. This provides the greatest strength.*

Springwood and Summerwood. Quarter-sawn wood wears better than flat-sawn wood. This is because the *summerwood* protects the *springwood* from wear (Figure 51-9). The summerwood is dense. It resists wear. This keeps the springwood from wearing.

In flat-sawn wood, the springwood wears quickly because the bands of springwood are wider than the summerwood (Figure 51-9). The summerwood cannot protect the springwood.

Springwood does not hold paint as well as summerwood. Paint is less likely to fail on quarter-sawn wood. Many types of siding are quarter-sawn for this reason.

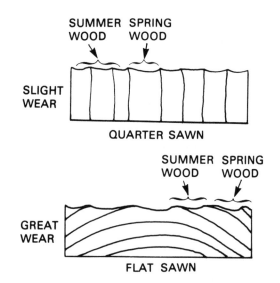

Figure 51-9. *Flat-sawn wood wears quickly. This is because the faces have wide bands of springwood.*

Wood Shrinkage and Swelling. Wood swells and shrinks least along the grain (Figure 51-10). The greatest shrinkage is tangent to the annular rings (Figure 51-10). Shrinkage and swelling perpendicular to the annular rings is about one half of that tangent to the annular rings (Figure 51-10).

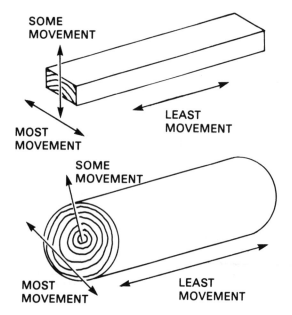

Figure 51-10. *Movement (shrinkage and swelling) in wood varies in relation to the annular rings and grain.*

412

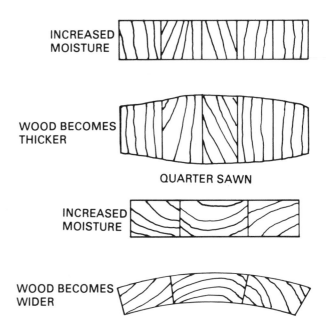

INCREASED
MOISTURE

WOOD BECOMES
THICKER

QUARTER SAWN

INCREASED
MOISTURE

WOOD BECOMES
WIDER

FLAT SAWN

Figure 51-11. *Movement in flat-sawn lumber can damage a table top or other wide piece. This is why many floors are made from quarter-sawn stock.*

If wood stays at one moisture level, it will not shrink or swell. If it gains moisture, it will swell. If it loses moisture, it will shrink.

Table tops and flooring are often made of quar-ter-sawn stock. Quarter-sawn stock will change thickness, not width, if it shrinks or swells (Figure 51-11). This will not damage a table top or floor. If the width changed, the table top or floor could be ruined (Figure 51-11).

QUESTIONS FOR REVIEW

1. How does tree growth begin? How does a seedling become a sapling?
2. What are the three types of roots in a tree's root system?
3. What is the xylem? What is the phloem? What is their function in tree growth?
4. How do leaves help tree growth?
5. What is the difference between hardwood and softwood trees?
6. Where is the cambium? How does it affect tree growth?
7. How does sapwood differ from heartwood? Would heartwood be found in a sapling?
8. What purpose does the heartwood serve?
9. What are the two parts of an annular ring? How do they differ?
10. Why does wood containing pith tend to warp?
11. Which is more decay-resistant—sapwood or heartwood?
12. How does the grain angle affect strength in wood?
13. How do annular rings affect wood strength?
14. Which has greater wear resistance—springwood or summerwood? Why?
15. How is wood shrinkage related to the annular rings? Does quarter-sawn wood shrink or swell with a change in moisture?

SUGGESTED ACTIVITIES

1. Examine the end grain in a log. Identify the sapwood, heartwood and annular ring.

2. Examine the end grain of some wood samples. Tell whether they were flat-sawn or quarter-sawn.

CHAPTER 52

Forestry

Forestry management is the practice of caring for forests. Without forestry management, a large amount of valuable lumber would be lost each year. Forestry management attempts to control fire, disease, insects and natural competition among trees. The work includes replanting and cutting trees.

When forestry practices are used, the forest is called a *managed forest.* If no forestry practices are used, the forest is called a *natural forest.* This chapter will discuss differences between natural and managed forests.

This chapter will also describe the six forest regions found in the United States. The qualities of each region and the species of wood grown will also be described.

KEY TERMS

forestry	air drying
managed forest	kiln drying
natural forest	stickers
forest regions	solar drying
clear cut harvesting	

Forest Regions

The United States has about eight percent of the world's forests. This is about 750 million acres or 34 percent of our land. There are many different tree species in our forests. Each species favors one or more of our forest regions.

There are six forest regions in the United States (Figure 52-1): the West Coast or Pacific Coast Forest, Western Forest, Southern Forest, Northern Forest, Central Hardwood Forest and Tropical Forests.

West Coast Forest. The *West Coast Forest* produces most trees from which plywood is produced. Douglas fir is one of the major softwood trees in the West Coast Forest. Framing lumber and plywood are both made of Douglas fir.

The *coast redwood* grows only in the West Coast Forest. It is one of the largest trees in the United States. Redwood is very resistant to decay. It is often used in damp places for this reason.

Red alder is a common hardwood of the West Coast Forest. In recent years, red alder has become favored for furniture and upholstery frames.

Western Forest. The *Western Forest* is chiefly a softwood forest. Some of the most common species include *pine, fir,* and *spruce.*

The Western Forest produces dimensional stock and factory lumber. The clear stock is often shaped into molding, window parts and other decorative pieces.

Southern Forest. The *Southern Forest* is located in the southeastern part of the United States. One-fourth of all plywood used in the United States comes from the Southern Forest. One-third of our lumber is also produced there.

The Southern Forest produces a mix of hardwoods and softwoods. Most softwoods are a species of pine or cypress. Hardwoods include: *gum, oak, cottonwood, yellow poplar, ash* and *pecan.*

Northern Forest. The *Northern Forest* produces a small amount of lumber. This is because the

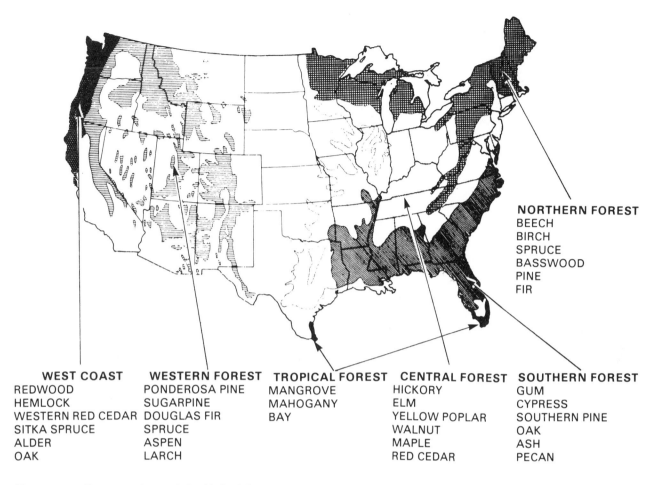

WEST COAST
REDWOOD
HEMLOCK
WESTERN RED CEDAR
SITKA SPRUCE
ALDER
OAK

WESTERN FOREST
PONDEROSA PINE
SUGARPINE
DOUGLAS FIR
SPRUCE
ASPEN
LARCH

TROPICAL FOREST
MANGROVE
MAHOGANY
BAY

CENTRAL FOREST
HICKORY
ELM
YELLOW POPLAR
WALNUT
MAPLE
RED CEDAR

SOUTHERN FOREST
GUM
CYPRESS
SOUTHERN PINE
OAK
ASH
PECAN

NORTHERN FOREST
BEECH
BIRCH
SPRUCE
BASSWOOD
PINE
FIR

Figure 52-1. *Forest regions of the United States.*

growing season in the northern states is short. Trees grow slowly in colder climates.

The *Northern Forest* contains a mix of softwoods and hardwoods. Softwoods include: *pine, fir, tamarack* and *hemlock.* Hardwoods include: *oak, birch, walnut, maple, cherry* and *basswood.*

Central Hardwood Forest. The *Central Hardwood Forest* produces most of our domestic hardwoods. Many of these hardwoods are called "Appalachian hardwoods." This is because they are produced in the Appalachian mountain states.

Common hardwoods in the Central Hardwood Forest include *oak, hickory, elm, ash, walnut, gum, cottonwood* and *yellow poplar.*

Tropical Forests. *Tropical Forests* in the United States are limited. The southern tip of Florida and Texas are both Tropical Forests. These forests account for a very small part of the United States' lumber production. The principal species of the Tropical Forest is *mahogany.*

Managed and Natural Forests
A forest region may have both *natural* and *managed* forests. The highest quality lumber will usually come from the managed forest. This is because forestry practices speed growth and ensures the health of all trees in the forest.

It is easy to see the difference between a natural forest and a managed forest. The floor of a managed forest is free of decaying trees and limbs. The trees grow straight and tall. The lowest branches are often twenty feet (about 6 meters) from the forest floor (Figure 52-2).

A natural forest is full of decaying branches and trees. Tree branches are usually quite low. There are many saplings fighting for light. These saplings grow slowly because the natural forest is very shady. Often these saplings will have a crooked trunk. The trunk has bent to find sunlight.

Lumber from a natural forest is low in quality. The trunk is usually full of knots. The knots are caused by low branches on the tree. Often trees from the natural forest will have twisted grain. This is caused by a bent trunk.

Lumber from a managed forest is of higher quality. Small or diseased trees are removed. This lets healthy trees grow faster. Foresters trim low branches from trees in a managed forest. This reduces the number of knots in the wood. Waste is reduced (Figure 52-3). High quality lumber will sell for a higher price.

Foresters also trim the crowns (tops) of some trees. This lets sunlight hit all trees in the forest. Sunlight speeds growth. It also ensures that all trees grow straight.

The floor of a managed florest is kept clean. This reduces the amount of wood decay. Bacteria and insects live on debris of the forest (Figure 52-4). By removing debris, there is less chance of decay in trees. Healthy trees produce more wood.

Trimmings from the managed forest are sold for pulpwood or firewood. This increases wood

Figure 52-2. *These southern pine trees are growing in a managed forest. The forest floor is free of decaying trees. The first branch on many of these trees is 20 feet or 6 meters (6000 mm) from the ground.*

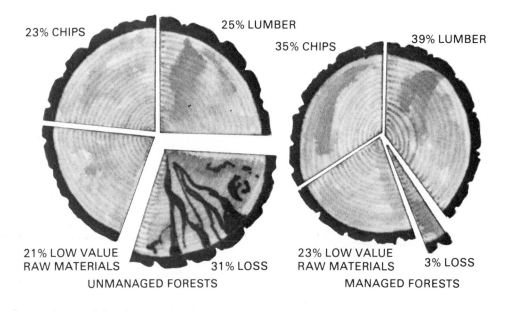

23% CHIPS 25% LUMBER

21% LOW VALUE RAW MATERIALS 31% LOSS

UNMANAGED FORESTS

35% CHIPS 39% LUMBER

23% LOW VALUE RAW MATERIALS 3% LOSS

MANAGED FORESTS

Figure 52-3. *Comparison of lumber production in natural (unmanaged) and managed forests.*

Figure 52-4. *Bark beetles and other insects live on forest debris. This increases decay in living trees.*

production. Trees are removed as they reach maturity. This allows the fast growing trees to reach maximum size before they are cut.

Some people feel that managed forests are not in harmony with the environment. These people feel that managed forests are a threat to ecology. When managed forests are handled correctly this is not true.

Ecologists dislike *clear cut harvesting* in the managed forest (Figure 52-5). Clear cut harvesting is the process of cutting all trees in a section of the forest. The area is then seeded or planted with seedings. Foresters defend clear cut harvesting. Both ecologists and foresters present some important arguments.

Figure 52-5. *Clear cutting removes all trees in a section of forest. It takes many years for the trees to grow back.*

ADVANTAGES OF CLEAR CUT HARVESTING
Trees are easy to remove.
No damage to other trees.
New seedlings have plenty of sun and water.
 This means faster growth.
More vegetation for wildlife such as deer.

DISADVANTAGES OF CLEAR CUT HARVESTING
Replanting is expensive.
Replanting can fail. The seedlings could die.
Bare soil can erode with rainfall.
Scenic beauty of the forest is lost while seed-
 lings grow into saplings.
Birds and other tree inhabitants are driven
 away.

Figure 52-6. *Logs are first debarked at the mill.*

Harvesting Timber
Timber harvesting follows an orderly sequence. Trees are cut at the base of the trunk. This is called *felling.* The logs are then trimmed. All limbs are removed. The limbs are used for pulpwood and firewood.

The tree trunk is then cut into two or more lengths. This is known as *bucking.* The lengths are loaded onto trucks. Logs are then taken to the mill.

Cutting Logs Into Lumber
When logs reach the mill, they are debarked (Figure 52-6). Bark is removed because it contains dirt. The dirt will dull saw blades quickly. Bark is collected and sold. Bark is favored for landscaping and gardening.

The logs are then cut into boards or slabs (Figure 52-7). After cutting, they are ready for drying.

Drying Lumber
Lumber must be dried before it is used. Wet wood is likely to decay if it is not dried. Wood will not glue or hold nails well when wet. Most lumber is either *kiln* dried or *air* dried.

Kiln drying is done with heat and steam. The wood is placed inside a kiln (Figure 52-8).

The kiln is sealed and steam is piped in. The steam begins drying the wood. As it dries, heat

Figure 52-7. *Logs are next cut into boards. They are now ready for drying.*

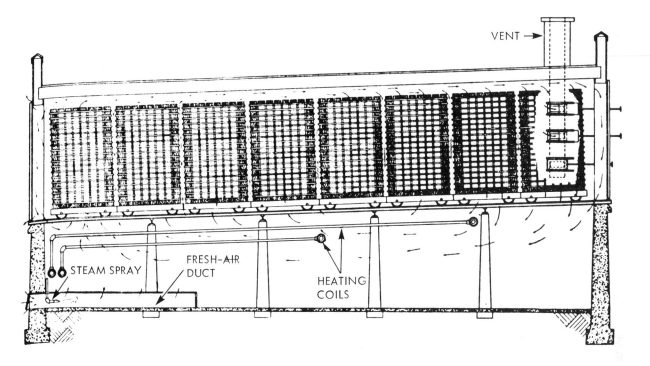

Figure 52-8. *This is a natural circulation dry kiln. Wood travels from the right end to the left end. Heat and steam are used to dry the lumber.*

Figure 52-9. *Air circulates through the lumber to dry it. Air dried lumber is protected from the weather by a roof. Stickers provide space between layers.*

is added. The heat removes additional water. Dry heat continues to remove water.

Drying removes most of the water. Construction wood is dried to 19 percent moisture or less. Furniture wood is dried to 6 to 8 percent moisture content.

Air drying is done outdoors. Wood is cut and stacked. "Stickers" (small strips of wood) are

placed between each layer of wood (Figure 52-9). This allows air to circulate between the layers. The wood is protected from sun and rain by a roof (Figure 52-9). There are no sides on the building. Air is free to travel through the lumber.

Air drying takes longer than kiln drying. But air drying uses less energy. Air dried lumber is usually used for construction. It is seldom used for furniture.

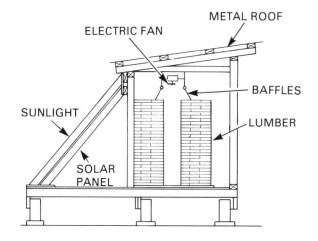

ELECTRIC FAN

METAL ROOF

SUNLIGHT

BAFFLES

LUMBER

SOLAR PANEL

Figure 52-10. *This kiln uses sunlight to dry the wood. This process does not use fossil fuel.*

Solar Wood Drying

Solar wood drying is faster than air drying. It does not use fossil fuel so it is less expensive than kiln drying. The process uses sunlight to heat a solar kiln (Figure 52-10). The heat dries the wood even in cold winter climates.

Solar wood drying is not used widely. Experiments have proven its value. It will probably become more widely used in the future.

QUESTIONS FOR REVIEW

1. What is forestry management? Of what importance is forestry management?
2. How much land in the United States is forested?
3. What are the six forest regions of the United States?
4. What are the most common trees in each forest region?
5. The Northern Forest covers many acres. Why is the amount of lumber produced so small?
6. Is the lumber production from our Tropical Forests very large? Why?
7. What is the difference between a managed forest and a natural forest?
8. Does a natural forest or a managed forest produce the best quality lumber?
9. What is clear cut harvesting?
10. What are advantages and disadvantages of clear cut harvesting?
11. How are trees harvested? What is felling? Bucking?
12. What is the difference between kiln drying and air drying? Which is faster?
13. What is solar drying? Why is it important?

SUGGESTED ACTIVITIES

1. Visit a forest or park. Can you tell whether tree growth is natural or managed? Why?

2. Look at the trees in the forest or park you visit. Decide which trees should be removed to allow others to grow larger.

New Research for Woodworking

CHAPTER 53

Research is any form of study that tries to identify new knowledge. New knowledge in woodworking is very valuable. This knowledge helps you use wood correctly. It can also reduce the expense of using wood.

There are many areas of woodworking research. Much of this research is done by Forest Products Laboratory. The Forest Products Laboratory is part of the United States Department of Agriculture. It is located in Madison, Wisconsin. The Forest Products Laboratory helps woodworkers solve problems by providing information and help to those who need it.

Today's research has been related to wood use and wood production. The demand for wood is growing. This demand can be answered in only two ways, by increasing our wood supply and by making better use of our wood supply.

KEY TERMS

research
hybrid seeds
forest residue
computerized sawing
best opening face (BOF)
fuel plantations
laser beam cutting
sliced lumber

INCREASING OUR WOOD SUPPLY

Our wood supply can be increased by faster tree growth. It can also be increased by reducing waste during harvest or processing. Some research now underway is aimed at increasing our wood supply.

Faster Tree Growth

Fast growing trees can increase our yearly lumber yield. Researchers have found that seeds from fast growing trees usually produce fast growing trees. Researchers have developed faster growing trees by developing *hybrid seeds.* These seeds are produced in a laboratory.

The seeds are planted under special conditions. A greenhouse protects the seedlings from wind and weather. It also provides sunlight and warm growing conditions. A greenhouse seedling grows much faster than one grown outdoors. A greenhouse seedling will develop to two-year maturity in nine months. The seedling is then planted in the field. It grows rapidly. This rapid development helps increase our wood supply.

Reducing Waste

Waste during tree harvest can be reduced. It can be further reduced when the tree is cut into lumber. Research has helped reduce waste. Smaller logs can be used for lumber. Branches and wood residue have become important for use in particle board. New sawing techniques have been computerized for greater efficiency. Thin kerf and kerfless machining of wood has reduced waste caused by the saw kerf.

Using Smaller Logs. Until recent years small logs and limbs were sold for pulpwood or firewood. This is because small logs were hard to machine. Research has shown that small logs are valuable. New machining methods cut small logs into usable shapes (Figure 53-1). The chips are used for paper production. The shaped log is

Figure 53-1. *New machining methods cut small logs into usable shapes.*

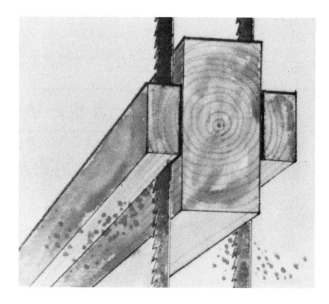

then cut into lumber. Some of these machines can handle trees as small as 4″ (100 mm) in diameter.

New veneer cutting techniques have also been developed for small logs. Until now only large diameter logs were used for plywood veneer. Today, logs as small as 10″ (250 mm) in diameter can be peeled for veneer. The log is peeled down to a 4⅞″ (about 122 mm) diameter. The log is then processed into construction lumber.

Computerized Sawing. *Computerized sawing* reduces waste when the log is cut into lumber. The computer receives data from the log scanner (Figure 53-2). The log scanner tells the computer where defects exist in the log. The computer then develops a cutting plan. This plan finds the largest boards with the fewest defects.

Computerized sawing is also called *Best Opening Face (BOF).* This is because the opening cuts determine the best lumber. Researchers have found that computerized sawing can increase production by as much as 14 percent.

Laser Beam Cutting. Research in *laser beam cutting* has been conducted by Forest Products Laboratory. The laser produces a kerf smaller than a saw blade. This reduces waste.

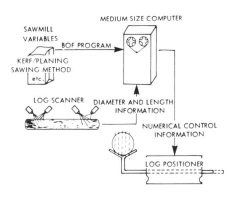

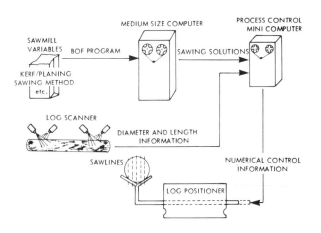

Figure 53-2. *Computers are used to decide the best way to cut logs. The computer selects a cutting method that reduces waste.*

In addition, laser cutting produces little noise and no sawdust. The cuts are smooth (Figure 53-3). Lasers will cut at angles with or against the grain.

Figure 53-3. *Laser cutting produces a kerf smaller than a saw blade. There is no sawdust with laser cutting.*

Right now, lasers are only experimental. They cut too slowly for commercial use. As more powerful lasers are developed, they may become useful for cutting wood.

Slicing Lumber. When lumber is sliced, there is no kerf. No kerf means less waste. *Sliced lumber* does not require planing. This also means less waste. Veneers have been sliced successfully for a long time. Research is now being done to see if lumber can be sliced. Logs sliced and then glued into lumber would produce better lumber.

Lumber is sliced in the same way as veneer. Wood slices best when it is hot. Lumber up to 1" (25 mm) thick has been sliced. There is some fracturing of the wood on the knife side of the cut. Deep fractures can reduce the strength of

Residue Fuel Flow Concepts

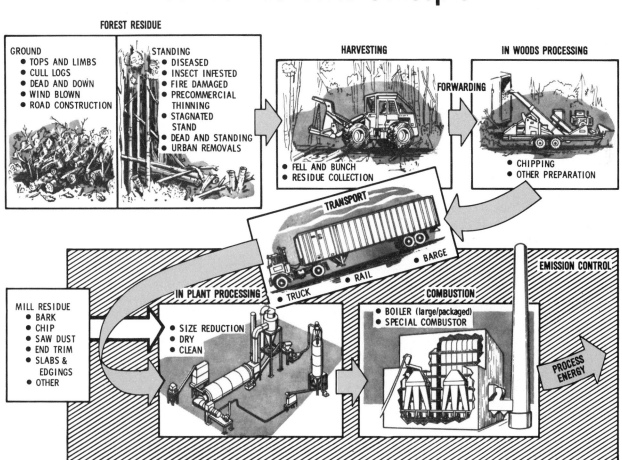

Figure 53-4. *Transforming wood residue into energy.*

the wood. More research is needed in the area of wood slicing.

Using Residue

Forest residue such as limbs and branches were of little value in years past. Today, this residue is used for pulpwood and particle board. Chippers are brought to the forest. They process the residue into chips of the right size and shape.

Research developed the machinery that processes the chips. It also helped paper manufacturers develop ways of breaking down certain woods into paper. This has increased the amount of wood that can be made into paper. Today, the worldwide demand for paper is increasing five percent per year.

The demand for fossil fuel has also increased rapidly in the past decade. This has made wood residue a valuable source of energy. Forest research estimates wood residue to be 500 million tons. One-half of this residue could easily be utilized for energy (Figure 53-4). This amounts to seven percent of our nation's energy needs. It is equal to almost 900 million barrels of oil.

Reasearch of wood residue for energy continues. Researchers will determine the best ways of using this residue. They will investigate conversion of wood residue into liquid and solid fuel. They will also consider the growth of *fuel plantations.*

USING WOOD WISELY

Wise use of our wood supply will make it go farther. Researchers want to find ways of reducing wood use. They are looking at housing. Housing is one of the largest areas of wood use. Any wood reduction in housing would mean large savings.

The two principal researchers in the housing area are Forest Products Laboratory and the National Association of Home Builders. The National Association of Home Builders has a research foundation in Rockville, Maryland.

The National Association of Home Builders has done lumber-saving research. Their findings were presented in the *Manual of Lumber and Plywood Saving Techniques.* This publication lists many techniques for saving lumber.

QUESTIONS FOR REVIEW

1. What is research? Why is research important to woodworking?
2. What is the focus of today's wood research?
3. What are some ways researchers have found to increase our wood supply?
4. What uses have researchers found for small logs?
5. What uses have researchers found for forest residue? Could wood residue be an important energy source?
6. What are the advantages of laser cutting? Is laser cutting widely used in wood industries?
7. What are the advantages of lumber slicing? Where is lumber slicing commonly used?

SUGGESTED ACTIVITIES

1. Look through newspapers and magazines to find articles dealing with wood conservation. Write a summary of the article and report to your class.
2. List some ways in which students might conserve wood while working in the shop.

SECTION 9

Woodworking Projects

54 Building Woodworking Projects

CHAPTER 54

Building Woodworking Projects

Building a project helps you learn about wood. A project allows you to apply what you have read. When you build a project, it is wise to review material in the text that relates to the project. Your book can help you do a better job. It will help you decide the best and safest way to build your project.

The projects in this section require the use of many different tools. When you are working with pieces of stock shorter than 4" (100 mm) long, use hand tools. Hand tools are safer than power tools when working with small pieces.

GENERAL WOODWORKING HINTS

Woodworkers often make the same mistakes when they build their first projects. Some of the following hints will help you avoid the common mistakes.

1. Study the plans before you begin. Make any needed sketches or notes before you begin.
2. Measure and lay out stock carefully. If you are not sure, measure twice.
3. Look over your stock carefully. Keep the best side visible.
4. Cut your stock carefully. If you are not sure of your setup, check it on a scrap piece.
5. Before you glue pieces together, assemble them dry. Make sure the pieces fit well.
6. Sand internal parts before they are glued together. They will be difficult to sand after assembly.
7. Make sure the assembled product is square. Adjust it before the glue dries.
8. Use very little glue. Excess glue can make finishing difficult.
9. Install fasteners and hardware carefully. Make sure they are aligned correctly. Remove hardware before sanding or finishing.
10. Sand your stock carefully before finishing.

PROJECT 1—THE PENCIL BOX

The pencil box is easy to build. You may use either metric or inch dimensions. Decide which dimensions you wish to use.

You can design a method for opening the box (Figure 54-1). You may also want to add an inlay or veneer strip to your pencil box (Figure 54-2). The lid may also be carved (Figure 54-3). These final touches make your pencil box unique.

Figure 54-1. *You may want to design a method for opening your pencil box.*

Figure 54-2. *An inlay will give your pencil box a special look.*

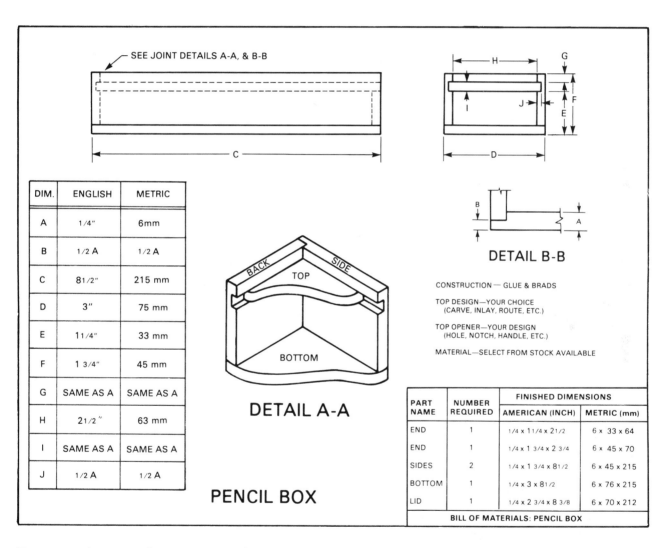

Figure 54-3. *A chip carved lid also makes your pencil box look special.*

DIM.	ENGLISH	METRIC
A	1/4"	6mm
B	1/2 A	1/2 A
C	8 1/2"	215 mm
D	3"	75 mm
E	1 1/4"	33 mm
F	1 3/4"	45 mm
G	SAME AS A	SAME AS A
H	2 1/2"	63 mm
I	SAME AS A	SAME AS A
J	1/2 A	1/2 A

SEE JOINT DETAILS A-A, & B-B

DETAIL A-A

PENCIL BOX

DETAIL B-B

CONSTRUCTION — GLUE & BRADS

TOP DESIGN—YOUR CHOICE
(CARVE, INLAY, ROUTE, ETC.)

TOP OPENER—YOUR DESIGN
(HOLE, NOTCH, HANDLE, ETC.)

MATERIAL—SELECT FROM STOCK AVAILABLE

PART NAME	NUMBER REQUIRED	FINISHED DIMENSIONS	
		AMERICAN (INCH)	METRIC (mm)
END	1	1/4 x 1 1/4 x 2 1/2	6 x 33 x 64
END	1	1/4 x 1 3/4 x 2 3/4	6 x 45 x 70
SIDES	2	1/4 x 1 3/4 x 8 1/2	6 x 45 x 215
BOTTOM	1	1/4 x 3 x 8 1/2	6 x 76 x 215
LID	1	1/4 x 2 3/4 x 8 3/8	6 x 70 x 212
BILL OF MATERIALS: PENCIL BOX			

Figure 54-4. *(Project #1).*

Study the drawing (Figure 54-4) before you begin. Notice how the sides fit the ends. Notice also that there is a right and left side. Lay these out so they fit correctly.

Be sure to read the bill of materials and plan of procedure. The bill of materials will tell you the size of each part. The plan of procedure will outline the building steps.

Plan of Procedure

1. Obtain stock and lay out parts. Use the Bill of Materials to lay out each piece. Cut the lid and bottom slightly oversize. This will allow you to fit them to your box.
2. Cut out all parts. Make sure you allow enough to plane the ends and edges.
3. Cut a groove joint in the end and sides. Make sure the groove is smooth.
4. Cut rabbets in the two ends. Hint: There is a right and left side. If you cut the rabbets incorrectly you will have two left or two right sides.
5. Dry fit the ends and sides. Make sure the grooves line up. Check all corners to be sure they are square and fit well.
6. Sand the inside of the sides and ends. They will be difficult to sand after assembly.
7. Glue the sides and ends together. Use clamps to hold them. You can also use brads to hold the pieces together. Hint: Make sure the parts are square after clamping. Use very little glue. Be sure to clean up excess glue. Always protect your bench with newspaper when gluing.
8. Check the fit between the bottom and the assembled ends and sides. Make sure there is a good fit. Hint: The bottom can be slightly longer and wider than the assembly. You can plane, file or sand it to size after assembly.
9. Sand the inside face of the bottom.
10. Glue and clamp the bottom to the sides and ends. Brads may also be used.
11. Fit the lid to box. It should slide smoothly in the goove. Do any special work on your lid now. Hint: You may want to design a way to

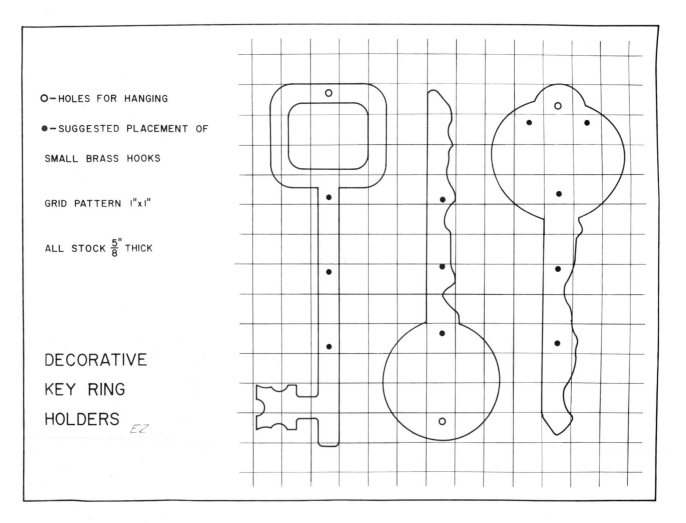

O — HOLES FOR HANGING

● — SUGGESTED PLACEMENT OF

SMALL BRASS HOOKS

GRID PATTERN I"x I"

ALL STOCK $\frac{5}{8}$" THICK

DECORATIVE

KEY RING

HOLDERS *EZ*

Figure 54-5. *(Project #2).*

Figure 54-6. *Attach cup hooks to your work to hold the keys.*

Figure 54-7. *Sand your work well before you apply the finish.*

Figure 54-8. *The sanding block is a two-part project. It is a fine tool. It fits your hand and is easy to use.*

open your box easily. You can also add an inlay or carve the lid.

12. Sand the lid and the outside of the box.
13. Stain and finish the box as you desire. Hint: If you have an inlay in your lid, seal it with shellac before staining. The shellac will protect the inlay from stain.

PROJECT 2—THE KEYHOLDER

The keyholder is easy to build. It makes a nice Christmas or birthday gift. You may want to use the keyholder as a class project, or your class may want to manufacture the keyholder.

Procedure

Study the key shapes in the drawing (Figure 54-5) and select the one you like best. Make a template for the shape you like.

Develop a bill of materials and plan of procedure before you begin working. Use Project 1 as an example.

Obtain some cup hooks (Figure 54-6). These hooks are attached to your work to hold the keys.

Lay out all holes carefully and drill them accurately. Be sure to sand your work well 54-7) before you apply the finish.

PROJECT 3—THE SANDING BLOCK

The sanding block (Figure 54-8) is a fine tool. It fits your hand and is easy to use. There are two parts to this sanding block. Study the drawing

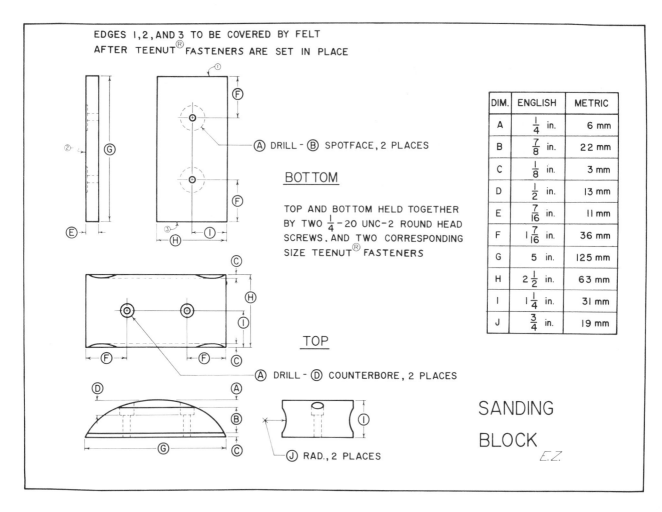

EDGES 1, 2, AND 3 TO BE COVERED BY FELT
AFTER TEENUT® FASTENERS ARE SET IN PLACE

Ⓐ DRILL - Ⓑ SPOTFACE, 2 PLACES

BOTTOM

TOP AND BOTTOM HELD TOGETHER
BY TWO 1/4 - 20 UNC-2 ROUND HEAD
SCREWS, AND TWO CORRESPONDING
SIZE TEENUT® FASTENERS

Ⓐ DRILL - Ⓓ COUNTERBORE, 2 PLACES

TOP

Ⓙ RAD., 2 PLACES

SANDING

BLOCK

E.Z.

DIM.	ENGLISH	METRIC
A	$\frac{1}{4}$ in.	6 mm
B	$\frac{7}{8}$ in.	22 mm
C	$\frac{1}{8}$ in.	3 mm
D	$\frac{1}{2}$ in.	13 mm
E	$\frac{7}{16}$ in.	11 mm
F	$1\frac{7}{16}$ in.	36 mm
G	5 in.	125 mm
H	$2\frac{1}{2}$ in.	63 mm
I	$1\frac{1}{4}$ in.	31 mm
J	$\frac{3}{4}$ in.	19 mm

Figure 54-9. *(Project #3).*

(Figure 54-9) and you will see how the parts fit together.

The sanding block could be manufactured in your shop. Your classmates can develop a flow chart and route sheets. If you build the sanding block, a bill of materials and a plan of procedure will be needed. Study the plans carefully before you begin.

A penetrating oil finish works well on the sanding block.

Procedure

There are two Teenut® fasteners inserted in the bottom half. These provide metal threads to hold the two parts together. Felt is glued over the bottom after the Teenut® fasteners are in place (Figure 54-10). Use masking tape to hold the felt while the glue dries.

Figure 54-10. *Felt is glued to the bottom half after the Teenut® fasteners are inserted. Masking tape holds the felt while the glue dries.*

PROJECT 4—THE MITER BOX

The miter box is used with a back saw (Figure 54-11). It helps you make accurate cuts. It is built using butt joints reinforced with glue and wood screws.

The front of the miter box is wider than the back. This allows the miter box to be clamped or hooked over the edge of a bench.

Procedure

Select a hardwood for your miter box. Hardwoods resist wear. They will remain accurate for a long time.

Study the drawings shown in Figure 54-12 before you develop a bill of materials and a plan of procedure.

A miter box is not usually finished. The wood remains raw. This is so no finish rubs onto the pieces you cut.

Figure 54-11. *The miter box is used with a back saw. It helps you make accurate cuts.*

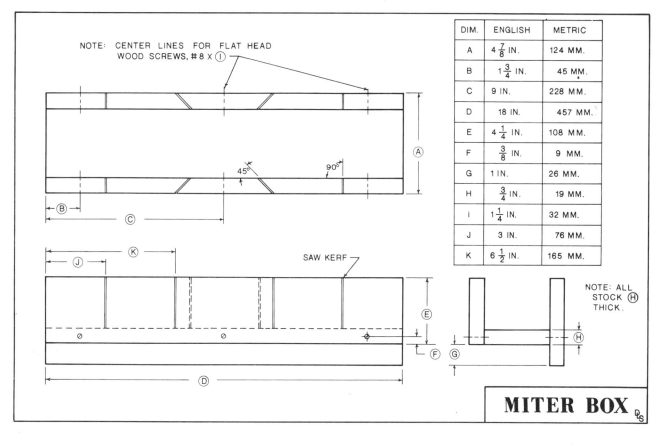

DIM.	ENGLISH	METRIC
A	$4\frac{7}{8}$ IN.	124 MM.
B	$1\frac{3}{4}$ IN.	45 MM.
C	9 IN.	228 MM.
D	18 IN.	457 MM.
E	$4\frac{1}{4}$ IN.	108 MM.
F	$\frac{3}{8}$ IN.	9 MM.
G	1 IN.	26 MM.
H	$\frac{3}{4}$ IN.	19 MM.
I	$1\frac{1}{4}$ IN.	32 MM.
J	3 IN.	76 MM.
K	$6\frac{1}{2}$ IN.	165 MM.

NOTE: CENTER LINES FOR FLAT HEAD WOOD SCREWS, #8 X ①

45° 90°

SAW KERF

NOTE: ALL STOCK Ⓗ THICK.

MITER BOX

Figure 54-12. *Miter box (Project #4).*

Figure 54-13. *This planter can be hung anywhere in your home.*

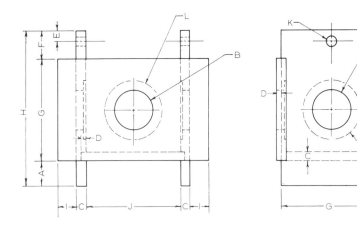

Figure 54-14. *This hanger could be used to hold your planter. The base is 3" (75 mm) wide and 5" (125 mm) long. The arm is 3" (75 mm) wide and 15" (375 mm) long. A ¼" (about 6 mm) dowel holds the pieces together.*

PROJECT 5—HANGING PLANTER

This hanging planter (Figure 54-13) enables you to display plants anywhere in the house. The leather strap can be attached to a metal or wood hanger. You may also want to design a hanger (Figure 54-14).

The holes in the sides have colored plastic in them, but you may choose some other material.

Procedure

Study the drawing (Figure 54-15) and develop a bill of materials and plan of procedure. You will also want to develop a finishing schedule.

Choose a stain that will complement the color of the plant. If the planter is hung outside, you will need a waterproof finish. Drill two small holes in the bottom so it will not hold rain water.

DIM	ENGLISH	METRIC	
A	1½"	38mm	
B	2" dia.	51mm ⌀	FOR PIECE OF PLASTIC
C	½"	12mm	
D	¼"	6mm	
E	1"	25mm	
F	1¼"	32mm	
G	5¼"	133mm	
H	8"	203mm	
I	1"	25mm	
J	7"	129mm	
K	½" ⌀	12mm⌀	
L	3" ⌀	76mm⌀	✳

⌀: MEANS DIAMETER

✳: APPROX. 1/4"(6mm) DEEP FOR PIECE OF METAL TO BACK-UP "B"

PLANTER

Figure 54-15. *Hanging planter (Project #5).*

Figure 54-16. *This picture frame is easy to make. It can be made any size you wish.*

Figure 54-17. *The parts of the picture frame are shaped in the planer using a carrier board. Cut the rabbet before planing.*

PROJECT 6—THE PICTURE FRAME

The picture frame (Figure 54-16) is easy to make. You can make it any size you wish. A carrier board is used with the planer to shape the frame parts (Figure 54-17). The rabbet is cut while the stock is rectangular. Miter corners are used.

Procedure

Determine the size of the object you wish to frame. Use these dimensions to help you develop a bill of materials.

Make sure the finish will match the colors in the room where the frame will hang. You may have to make a finishing sample and a finishing schedule.

Remember to include the carrier board in your plan of procedure. The carrier board must be 2" (50 mm) longer than your longest part or at least 14" (350 mm) long. Study the profile in the drawing (Figure 54-18).

When assembling your frame, measure the length of the rabbet and not the length of the part. The picture fits inside the rabbet.

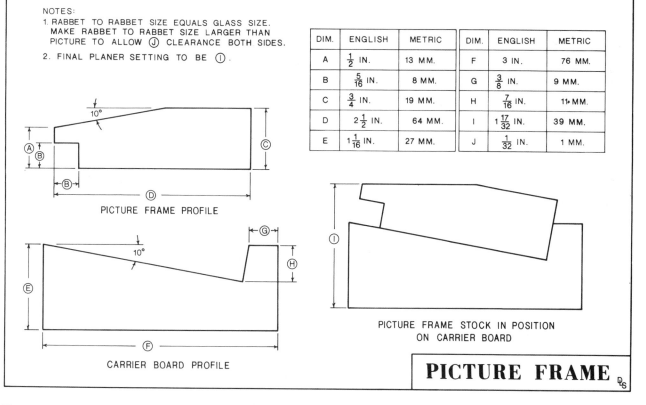

NOTES:
1. RABBET TO RABBET SIZE EQUALS GLASS SIZE. MAKE RABBET TO RABBET SIZE LARGER THAN PICTURE TO ALLOW Ⓙ CLEARANCE BOTH SIDES.
2. FINAL PLANER SETTING TO BE Ⓘ.

DIM.	ENGLISH	METRIC	DIM.	ENGLISH	METRIC
A	$\frac{1}{2}$ IN.	13 MM.	F	3 IN.	76 MM.
B	$\frac{5}{16}$ IN.	8 MM.	G	$\frac{3}{8}$ IN.	9 MM.
C	$\frac{3}{4}$ IN.	19 MM.	H	$\frac{7}{16}$ IN.	11 MM.
D	$2\frac{1}{2}$ IN.	64 MM.	I	$1\frac{17}{32}$ IN.	39 MM.
E	$1\frac{1}{16}$ IN.	27 MM.	J	$\frac{1}{32}$ IN.	1 MM.

PICTURE FRAME PROFILE

CARRIER BOARD PROFILE

PICTURE FRAME STOCK IN POSITION ON CARRIER BOARD

PICTURE FRAME

Figure 54-18. *Picture frame (Project #6).*

PROJECT 7—THE COAT RACK

The coat rack (Figure 54-19) is a challenging project. It includes bending, laminating and turning. There are operations on many power tools such as the band saw, jointer, surfacer, disc sander, drill press, router and lathe.

You may only want to use part of this plan. Any part of the plan may be added to your own design. You may want to add a mirror to the backing board (Figure 54-20).

A shelf (Figure 54-21) or towel bar (Figure 54-22) or a frame (Figure 54-23) may be used with parts of the plan.

Figure 54-21. *This backing board has a shelf. A towel bar is attached to the hooks.*

Figure 54-22. *This backing board was designed to be used as a towel bar.*

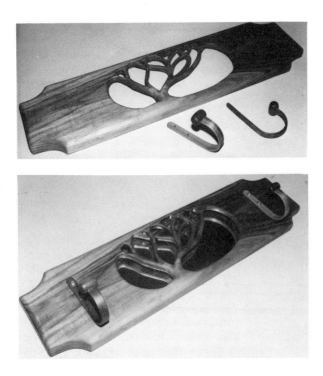

Figure 54-19. *The coat rack is a challenging project. Many operations and tools are needed to build it.*

Figure 54-20. *A mirror could be added to the backing board. Many designs could be developed.*

Figure 54-23. *A framed mirror is used as the backing board for this towel bar.*

Figure 54-24. *These coat racks use pegs instead of hooks. The pegs were turned on the lathe.*

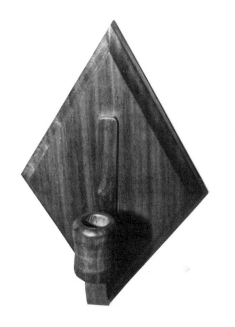

Figure 54-25. *This candle holder uses the hook from this plan. Always use a metal liner between the wood and the candle.*

Figure 54-26. *This form allows two hooks to be clamped at one time.*

The backing board may also be used with pegs (Figure 54-24) instead of hooks. Design a profile for the pegs and turn them on the lathe.

A candle holder (Figure 54-25) may also be designed using the hook from this plan. Always place a metal liner between the wood and the candle to avoid fire.

Manufacturing

If your classmates wish to manufacture coat racks, several hooks will be needed. Design forms that allow two hooks to be clamped at one time (Figure 54-26).

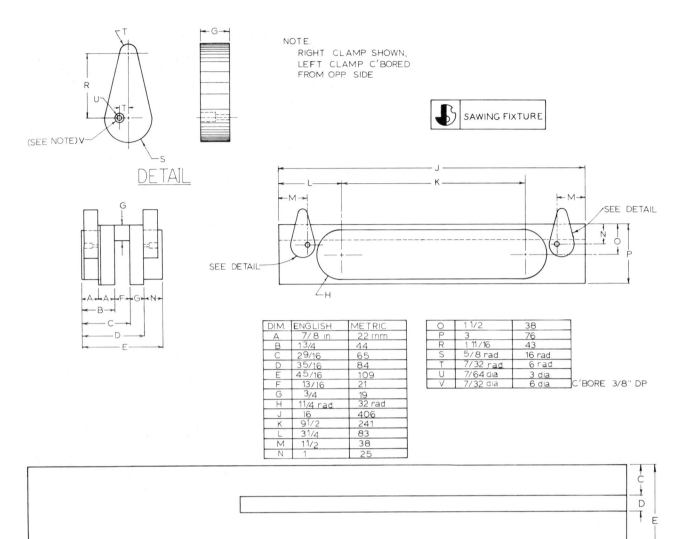

NOTE.
 RIGHT CLAMP SHOWN,
 LEFT CLAMP C'BORED
 FROM OPP SIDE

SAWING FIXTURE

DETAIL

SEE DETAIL

SEE DETAIL

DIM.	ENGLISH	METRIC
A	7/8 in.	22 mm
B	13/4	44
C	29/16	65
D	35/16	84
E	45/16	109
F	13/16	21
G	3/4	19
H	11/4 rad	32 rad
J	16	406
K	91/2	241
L	31/4	83
M	11/2	38
N	1	25

O	1 1/2	38
P	3	76
R	1 11/16	43
S	5/8 rad.	16 rad
T	7/32 rad.	6 rad
U	7/64 dia	3 dia
V	7/32 dia	6 dia

C'BORE 3/8" DP

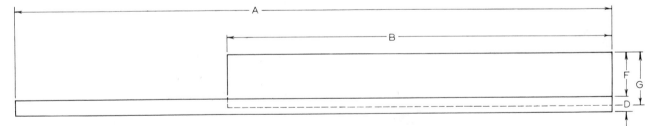

DIM	ENGLISH	METRIC
A	28 in.	711 m m.
B	18	457
C	13/8	35
D	3/4	19
E	6	152
F	2	51
G	23/8	60

SAWING FIXTURE
BASE

Figure 54-27. *Sawing fixture (Project #7).*

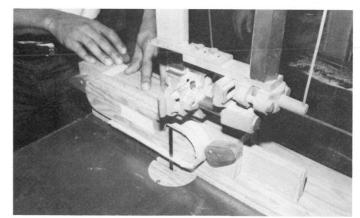

Figure 54-28. *The fixture trims 1/16-1/8" (about 2mm) off the first edge.*

Figure 54-29. *The fixture is reversed to trim the second edge. The first edge is placed against the fixture. The hard board spacer moves the hook 1/8" (about 3 mm) closer to the blade.*

Make these forms using the dimensions on a sawing fixture (Figure 54-27).

The base of the sawing fixture is clamped to the band saw. The sliding part moves the hooks past the blade. Side one trims 1/16" to 1/8" (about 2 mm) off the first edge (Figure 54-28). The fixture is then reversed. Place the first edge against the fixture and trim the other edge (Figure 54-29).

After the hooks are sanded to finished width, the ends are trimmed using cutting jigs (Figure 54-30). One jig trims the hook end (Figure 54-31) and the other jig trims the end that is mounted (Figure 54-32).

Figure 54-30. *A cutting jig is used to trim the ends. There is one cutting jig for each end of the hook.*

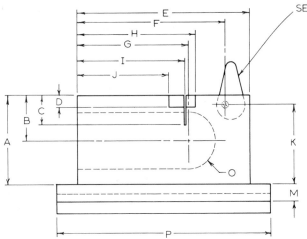

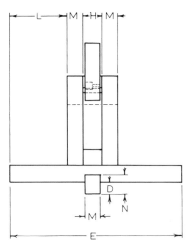

SEE DETAIL ON SAWING FIXTURE

CUTTING JIG

DIM.	ENGLISH	METRIC
A	4 inch	102 mm
B	2	51
C	11/4	32
D	1/2	13
E	8	203
F	6 7/8	175
G	5 5/8	143
H	7 1/8	181

I	7	178
J	6 1/4	159
K	3 5/8	92
L	2 3/4	70
M	3/4	19
N	7/8	22
O	11/4 rad.	32
P	10	254

Figure 54-31. *Cutting jig to trim the hook end. (Project #7).*

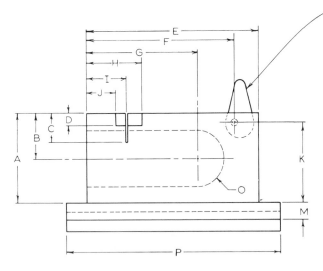

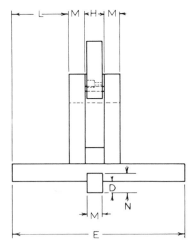

SEE DETAIL ON SAWING FIXTURE

CUTTING JIG

DIM.	ENGLISH	METRIC
A	4 inch	102 mm
B	2	51
C	11/4	32
D	1/2	13
E	8	203
F	6 7/8	175
G	5 5/8	143
H	25/8	67

I	17/8	48
J	13/8	35
K	35/8	92
L	23/4	70
M	3/4	19
N	7/8	22
O	11/4 rad.	32
P	10	254

Figure 54-32. *Cutting jig to trim the mounted end. (Project #7).*

438

The holes in the mounted end are held in a fixture for drilling. The fixture is clamped to the drill press (Figure 54-33). The sliding member (Figures 54-33 and 54-34) is used as a stop for the first hole. When it is moved, the dowel acts as a stop.

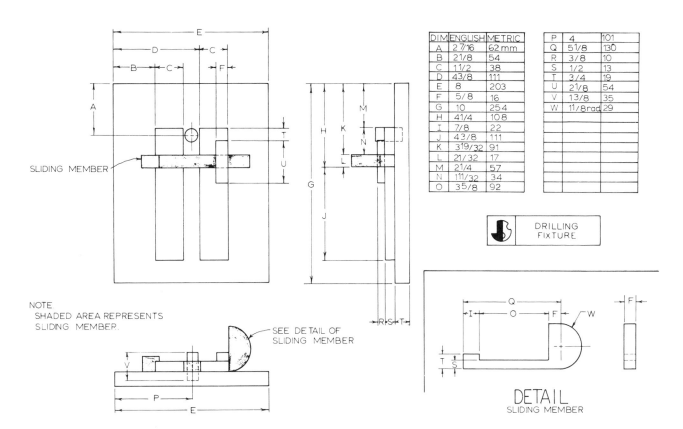

Figure 54-33. *The drilling fixture holds the hooks while they are drilled. When the sliding member is moved to the right, the dowel acts as a stop for the second hole.*

DIM	ENGLISH	METRIC
A	2 7/16	62 mm
B	2 1/8	54
C	1 1/2	38
D	4 3/8	111
E	8	203
F	5/8	16
G	10	254
H	4 1/4	108
I	7/8	22
J	4 3/8	111
K	3 19/32	91
L	21/32	17
M	2 1/4	57
N	1 11/32	34
O	3 5/8	92

DIM	ENGLISH	METRIC
P	4	101
Q	5 1/8	130
R	3/8	10
S	1/2	13
T	3/4	19
U	2 1/8	54
V	1 3/8	35
W	1 1/8 rad	29

SLIDING MEMBER

DRILLING FIXTURE

NOTE
SHADED AREA REPRESENTS
SLIDING MEMBER.

SEE DETAIL OF
SLIDING MEMBER

DETAIL
SLIDING MEMBER

Figure 54-34. *Drilling fixture (Project #7).*

The sanding fixture (Figure 54-35) is used to radius the mounted end of the hook. The hole near the hook's end is used as a pivot point. The

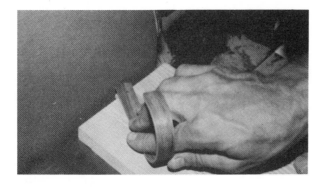

Figure 54-35. *The sanding fixture is used to radius the hook. The hole in the hook is used as a pivot point.*

sliding part of this fixture (*Part B,* Figure 54-36) has a shoulder that stops fixture travel. The base of the sanding fixture (*Part A,* Figure 54-36) is clamped to the disc sander.

When these jigs and fixtures are built accurately and set up carefully, hooks can be manufactured very quickly.

Procedure

Decide upon a design for your coat rack. Develop any needed drawings. Study the drawings (Figure 54-37). Prepare a bill of materials and a plan of procedure from the drawings.

Lay out any needed templates and decide what type of finish you wish to use. Plan the finishing schedule and write it down.

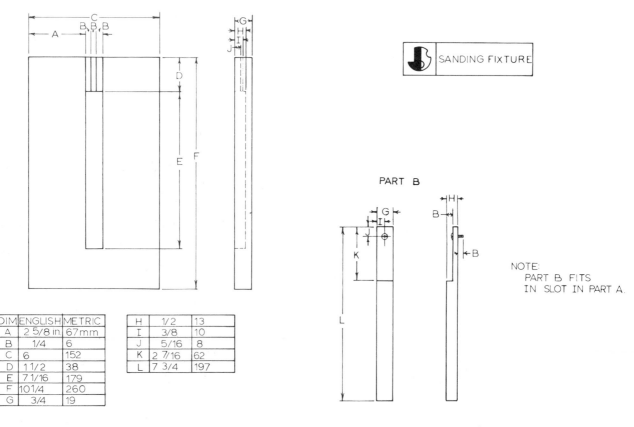

DIM	ENGLISH	METRIC
A	2 5/8 in.	67mm
B	1/4	6
C	6	152
D	1 1/2	38
E	7 1/16	179
F	10 1/4	260
G	3/4	19

H	1/2	13
I	3/8	10
J	5/16	8
K	2 7/16	62
L	7 3/4	197

NOTE:
PART B FITS
IN SLOT IN PART A.

Figure 54-36. *Sanding fixture (Project #7).*

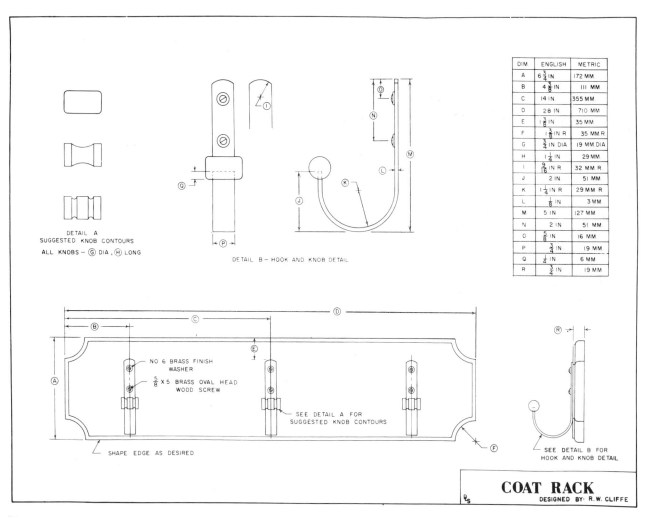

DIM.	ENGLISH	METRIC
A	6¾ IN	172 MM
B	4⅜ IN	111 MM
C	14 IN	355 MM
D	28 IN	710 MM
E	1⅜ IN	35 MM
F	1⅜ IN R	35 MM R
G	¾ IN DIA	19 MM DIA
H	1¼ IN	29 MM
I	9/16 IN R	32 MM R
J	2 IN	51 MM
K	1¼ IN R	29 MM R
L	⅛ IN	3 MM
M	5 IN	127 MM
N	2 IN	51 MM
O	⅝ IN	16 MM
P	¾ IN	19 MM
Q	¼ IN	6 MM
R	¾ IN	19 MM

DETAIL A
SUGGESTED KNOB CONTOURS
ALL KNOBS — Ⓖ DIA , Ⓗ LONG

DETAIL B — HOOK AND KNOB DETAIL

NO 6 BRASS FINISH WASHER

⅝ X 5 BRASS OVAL HEAD WOOD SCREW

SEE DETAIL A FOR SUGGESTED KNOB CONTOURS

SHAPE EDGE AS DESIRED

SEE DETAIL B FOR HOOK AND KNOB DETAIL

COAT RACK
DESIGNED BY: R.W. CLIFFE

Figure 54-37. *Coat rack (Project #7).*

Design and build your hook forms. Make sure they are smooth and accurate. Coat your forms well with penetrating oil. Glue does not adhere well to an oil finish.

If you are manufacturing several hooks, you may want to manufacture the forms. Manufacturing the forms could provide valuable experience. Planning is very important. Develop route sheets and flow charts before you begin.

Backing Board. Edge glue stock for the backing board. Square up your work after the glue dries. Use a template to lay out your cuts (Figure 54-38). Cut stock and smooth the edges. Route the edges if desired. Prepare your work for finishing.

Figure 54-38. *Use a template to lay out your backing board.*

Hooks. Use enough veneer. There should be 5 to 7 layers. The hook should be ⅛″ to ³⁄₁₆″ thick (about 3 to 4 mm). Cut the veneers about ½″ (about 12 mm) wider than finished size will be (Figure 54-39).

Figure 54-39. *Cut your veneers about ½″ (12 mm) wider than finished size.*

Figure 54-40. *Apply glue evenly to each strip. Be sure to wrap the veneers in waxed paper before clamping.*

Figure 54-41. *Use a spring clamp to hold the veneers in place while tightening the band clamp.*

Coat the strips with glue (Figure 54-40) and wrap the group in waxed paper. Tighten the band clamp around the veneers. Use a spring clamp to hold them in place (Figure 54-41).

The band clamp holds the veneers against the curved ends of the form. Use a parallel clamp to hold the veneers against the sides of the form (Figure 54-42). Leave the clamps in position for 16 to 24 hours. The waxed paper makes the glue dry slowly.

If you plan to cut the hooks on the band saw, make a fixture. Do not cut them without one! If no fixture is available, use a dovetail saw or a coping saw.

Figure 54-42. *A parallel clamp holds the veneers against the sides of the form.*

Knobs. The knobs are glued to the hooks (Figure 54-43). A mortise is cut in the knob. This may be cut with a router. A drill may also be used. Use a chisel to clean up the edges.

Kerf square stock for the lathe (Figure 54-44). Cut the mortises in the stock (Figure 54-45) and turn to desired shape (Figure 54-46). Do not separate the knobs on the lathe. Use a back saw.

Figure 54-43. *A mortise is made in each knob. The hook is glued into the mortise.*

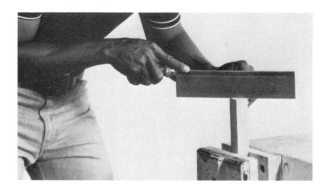

Figure 54-44. *Kerf square stock for turning in the lathe.*

Figure 54-45. *Lay out square stock like this and cut mortises. After the mortises are cut, the stock may be turned.*

Figure 54-46. *Turn stock to desired shape. Do not separate the knobs on the lathe. Use a back saw.*

Figure 54-47. *Install the brass screws carefully because brass is soft. It will damage or break easily. Test your pilot hole first with a steel screw.*

File the ends of each knob and fit them to the hooks. Glue the knobs in place. Use masking tape to hold them in place.

Attaching hooks. Lay out the backing board carefully. Make sure the hooks are spaced correctly.

Brass screws and finishing washers are used to attach the hooks (Figure 54-47). Be careful when installing them because brass is soft. The screws will damage or break easily.

Make sure the pilot hole is large enough. Install a steel screw of the same size first, then install the brass screw.

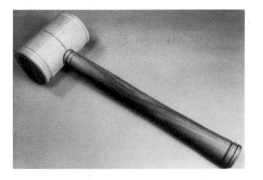

Figure 54-48. *This mallet was turned on the lathe. It is a handy tool for driving chisels.*

PROJECT 8—MALLET

The mallet (Figure 54-48) is turned on the lathe. It is a handy tool for driving chisels. It may also be used to drive stock into position. You can use a large turning square for the head or you can glue several thin pieces together.

There are two head designs and two handle designs for the mallet (Figure 54-49). Study those designs and decide which one you wish to build.

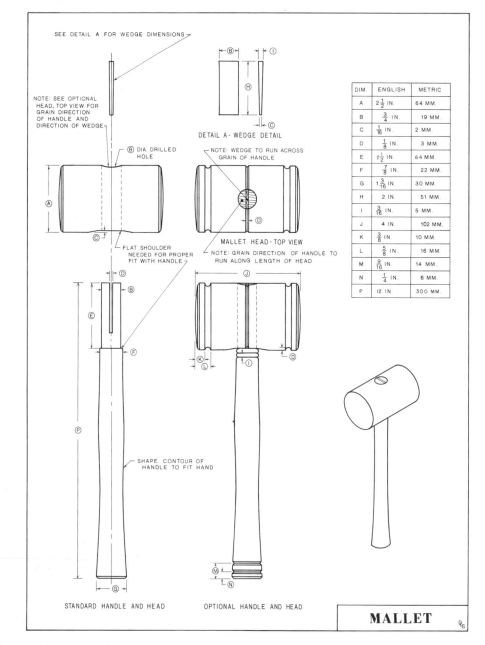

DIM.	ENGLISH	METRIC
A	2½ IN.	64 MM.
B	¾ IN.	19 MM.
C	1/16 IN.	2 MM.
D	⅛ IN.	3 MM.
E	2½ IN.	64 MM.
F	⅞ IN.	22 MM.
G	1 3/16 IN.	30 MM.
H	2 IN.	51 MM.
I	3/16 IN.	5 MM.
J	4 IN.	102 MM.
K	⅜ IN.	10 MM.
L	⅝ IN.	16 MM.
M	9/16 IN.	14 MM.
N	¼ IN.	6 MM.
P	12 IN	300 MM.

Figure 54-49. *Mallet (Project #8).*

Procedure

Study the plans (Figure 54-49). Develop a bill of materials and a plan of procedure. A French polish finish or penetrating oil finish will work well on your mallet.

Select a hard, easy turning wood like maple. The wood must be strong. It must withstand heavy mallet blows. If you glue several pieces together for the head, make sure they are glued securely.

Plane the corners off your stock before turning the head. The stock should be shaped like an octagon (stop sign). This makes it safer and easier to turn. Remember to rough out your stock at low speed.

Notice that the ends of the head are crowned (high in the center). This allows you to drive plugs and wedges without denting the work. Make sure that you turn the head with a crown.

A hole is bored in the head for the handle. This hole should be perpendicular to the annular rings. Check the hole size in scrap stock before boring the head. The handle should fit snugly in the hole. If it is loose, bore a smaller hole.

Make a cut in the handle for the wedge. Make this cut perpendicular to the annular rings. Study the plans to see how the handle fits in the head. Note the direction of the annular rings.

File a flat on the head where it meets the handle. Use glue and a wedge to secure the handle to the head. You may want to use a wedge of a different species for accent.

PROJECT 9—BOWL

This bowl (Figure 54-50) is a faceplate turning. Four thicknesses of cherry were glued face-to-face to make the turning blank. There are more pictures of this project in Chapter 43.

The size of this bowl makes it ideal for salads. If you enlarge the squares in the plan (Figure 54-51), you can make a template for a larger bowl. You may want to turn a serving bowl and a set of salad bowls.

Procedure

Glue up stock for turning blanks. Cut the blanks to a circular shape slightly larger than the bowl. Glue a piece of ¾″ plywood to the bottom of the block. Note: Two layers of brown paper should be glued between the plywood and the turning blank. This makes them easy to separate after turning. This procedure is pictured in Chapter 43.

Screw the faceplate to the plywood block. Make sure the screws are long enough. Mount the faceplate on the lathe and set up the lathe for turning.

Study the drawing and your plan of procedure before you begin. If you are turning several bowls, make hardboard templates of the inside and outside profile. Use a safe finish such as salad bowl finish for your bowl. This finish is described in Chapter 24.

Figure 54-50. *This is a faceplate turning. It is the right size for a salad bowl.*

DIM.	ENGLISH	METRIC
A	$6\frac{5}{8}$ in.	166 mm.
B	$4\frac{1}{8}$ in.	103 mm.
C	$2\frac{7}{8}$ in.	72 mm.
D	$2\frac{1}{2}$ in.	63 mm.
E	$\frac{1}{4}$ in.	6 mm.
F	$5\frac{1}{8}$ in.	128 mm.
G	$5\frac{1}{4}$ in.	131 mm.
H	$\frac{1}{2}$ in.	12 mm.

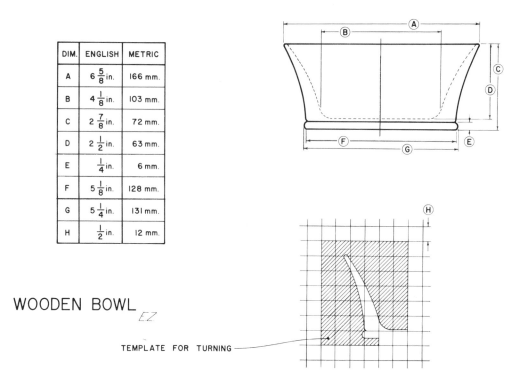

WOODEN BOWL *EZ*

TEMPLATE FOR TURNING

Figure 54-51. *Wooden bowl (Project #9).*

Turn the outside profile first. Then shape the inside of the bowl. Work slowly. Use the scraping method to turn a bowl. Keep your tools sharp. This reduces the amount of sanding needed. Sharp tools require less pressure. This makes them safer. Always wear a face shield when working on the lathe.

PROJECT 10—BOWL WITH COVER
This bowl (Figure 54-52) is about the right size for a desk or bookshelf. It can be used for candy, paper clips, safety pins, or other small objects. If you wish to make the bowl larger, you can enlarge the squares in the plan (Figure 54-53).

This is a faceplate project. After the outer shape is turned, then the cover is cut off the top (Figure 54-54). A parting tool is used to separate the bowl and cover.

The rabbet on the bowl is the same diameter as the inside diameter of the bowl.

Study the drawings before you begin. Work carefully with sharp tools. Rough out stock at low speed. Always wear a face shield when working on the lathe.

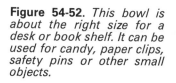

Figure 54-52. *This bowl is about the right size for a desk or book shelf. It can be used for candy, paper clips, safety pins or other small objects.*

Procedure

Study the drawings and develop a plan of procedure. Use a bill of materials to select the correct stock for the job. Glue up turning blanks carefully. Make sure all joints are tight.

Mount the turning blanks on a faceplate. Use the procedure described in project nine for mounting stock to the faceplate.

Turn the outside of the bowl first. Then make the lid. Cut the lid off using the parting tool (Figure 54-54).

Turn the inside of the bowl to match the rabbet on the lid. Sand the bowl and finish. Use a safe finish such as salad bowl finish if food is to be stored in the bowl. Any finish may be used if the bowl will not be used for food.

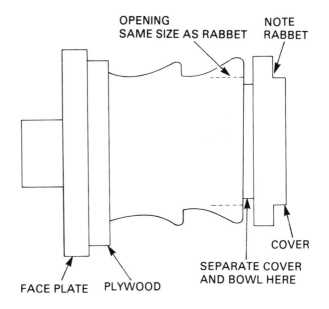

Figure 54-54. *Turning method for bowl with cover.*

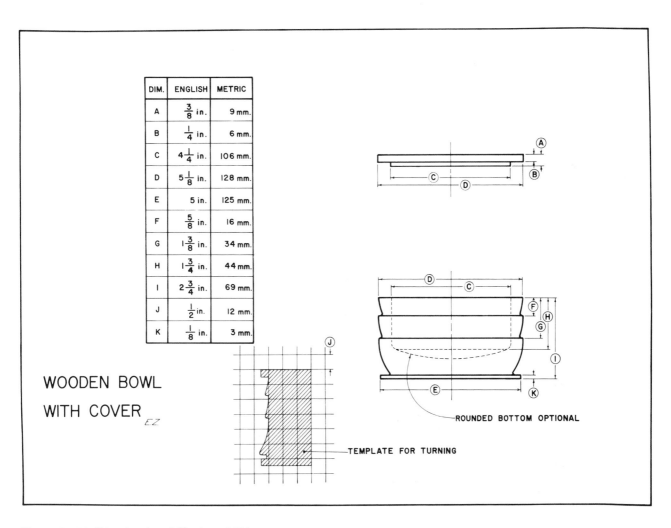

DIM.	ENGLISH	METRIC
A	$\frac{3}{8}$ in.	9 mm.
B	$\frac{1}{4}$ in.	6 mm.
C	$4\frac{1}{4}$ in.	106 mm.
D	$5\frac{1}{8}$ in.	128 mm.
E	5 in.	125 mm.
F	$\frac{5}{8}$ in.	16 mm.
G	$1\frac{3}{8}$ in.	34 mm.
H	$1\frac{3}{4}$ in.	44 mm.
I	$2\frac{3}{4}$ in.	69 mm.
J	$\frac{1}{2}$ in.	12 mm.
K	$\frac{1}{8}$ in.	3 mm.

WOODEN BOWL WITH COVER

ROUNDED BOTTOM OPTIONAL

TEMPLATE FOR TURNING

Figure 54-53. *Wooden bowl (Project #10).*

Figure 54-55. *This trophy makes a nice award for schools, clubs or other organizations.*

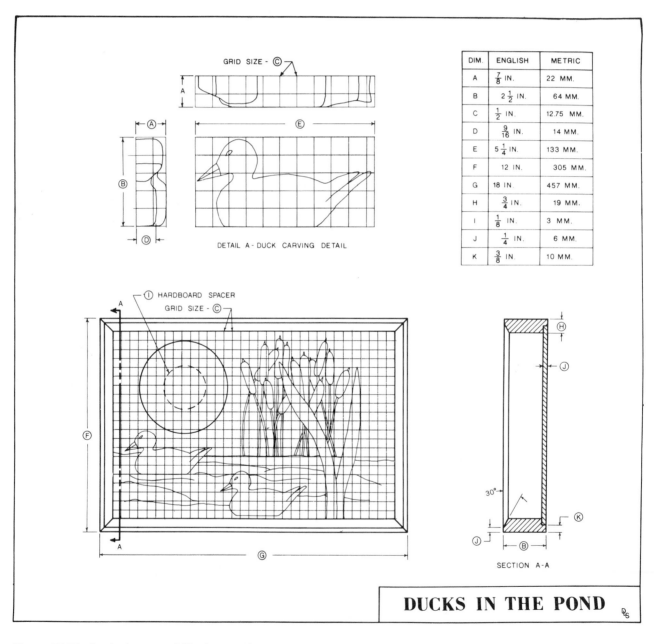

Figure 54-56. *Ducks in a pond (Project #12).*

PROJECT 11—SPLIT TURNED TROPHY

This trophy (Figure 54-55) makes a nice award for schools, clubs, or other organizations. The gavel is turned in two parts: the head and the handle.

Both parts are glued up with brown paper in the center. After the parts are turned, they split through at the brown paper. The flat surface is glued to the backing board.

Procedure

Develop a drawing, bill of materials, plan of procedure and a finishing schedule. The gavel is about 10″ (250 mm) long. The handle is about ⅜″ to ½″ (9-12mm) in diameter. The head is about 2 ⅜″ (60mm) in diameter and about 3 ⅜″ (80mm) long. The backing board is 11″ (275 mm) by 17″ (430 mm).

Prepare stock for split turning. Glue two thicknesses of brown paper between the pieces. See Chapter 43 for a description of this process.

Glue stock edge-to-edge for the backing board. Cut to size, and make decorative cuts. Rout the edge and prepare the board for finishing.

Turn the handle and the head. Split the pieces carefully using a utility knife and a chisel. Glue the handle and head to the backing board. Mark and drill holes for the brass plate. Apply finish and install the brass plate.

PROJECT 12—DUCKS IN A POND

"Ducks in a Pond" (Figure 54-56) is a wall scene. This project will develop many skills. Carving, woodburning, mitering and rabbeting operations are all part of this project.

You may wish to add a clock to the moon in the background, or you may wish to change the scene. Plan any changes carefully. Make drawings of these changes.

Procedure

Study the drawings (Figure 54-56) carefully. Develop any needed grids and templates. Write a plan of procedure and a bill of materials. The project pictured has an oil finish, but most finishing schedules will produce a nice finish.

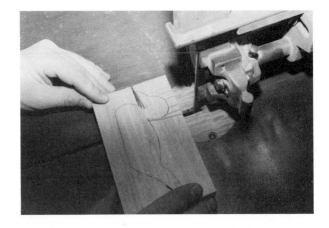

Figure 54-57. *Make relief cuts before cutting along the layout line.*

Figure 54-58. *Relief cuts make it easy to cut along the layout line.*

Figure 54-59. *Shape the ducks with carving tools.*

Cut out the ducks on the band saw. Make plenty of relief cuts (Figure 54-57) and then cut along the layout line (Figure 54-58). Use carving tools (Figure 54-59) to shape the ducks. Smooth the carving with abrasives (Figure 54-60) and then make decorative cuts.

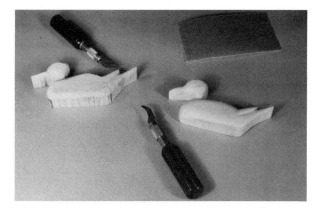

Figure 54-60. *After the ducks are shaped, they may be smoothed with coated abrasives.*

Figure 54-61. *This project will develop many skills. Carving, woodburning, mitering and rabbeting operations are all part of this project.*

Cut frame parts and miter. Glue up the frame and fit the back to it. Lay out the scene lightly in pencil and woodburn it.

Cut out the moon and apply veneer to the edge. Glue the moon and ducks to the backing board. Attach the backing board to the frame. Apply the finish. Make sure all parts are sanded well before finishing. Figure 54-61 shows the completed project.

PROJECT 13—WOODEN JEWELRY

Wooden jewelry (Figure 54-62) is very attractive. It is a nice gift that is easy to make. Wooden jewelry is made from small pieces of stock or veneer. Make the jewelry any shape you wish.

Procedure

Glue several thin pieces of stock together. Use stock of different colors. This will make the jewelry more attractive.

Figure 54-62. *Wood jewelry makes an attractive gift. It is easy to make.*

Cut the stock to desired shape. Sand, file or carve the edges of the piece. Drill a mounting hole. Larger holes or irregular holes can be cut with a fret saw.

Smooth your piece with very fine abrasives and finish. Use a commercial penetrating oil for best results. Buff the piece after the finish dries. Apply more finish or wax if desired.

PROJECT 14—WOODEN SPOON

A wooden spoon (Figure 54-63) is an ideal kitchen tool. The handle does not get hot and it is very strong. The spoon can be made to suit your needs. Any size or shape may be designed. The spoon (Figure 54-64) shown in the drawing is average size. You could enlarge this drawing by enlarging the squares.

Procedure

Use a close-grained hardwood. Lay out the spoon and band saw to rough size. Use carving tools to shape the spoon (Figures 54-65 and 54-66). Smooth the spoon with coated abrasives.

Apply salad bowl finish to the wooden spoon before use. Be sure to follow the manufacturer's directions.

Figure 54-63. *This wooden spoon is an ideal kitchen tool. It is easy to design any size or shape.*

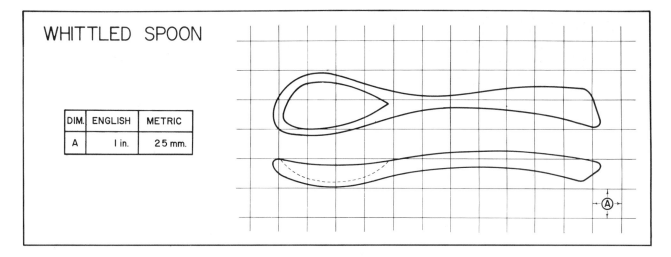

WHITTLED SPOON

DIM.	ENGLISH	METRIC
A	I in.	25 mm.

Ⓐ

Figure 54-64. *Wooden spoon (Project #14).*

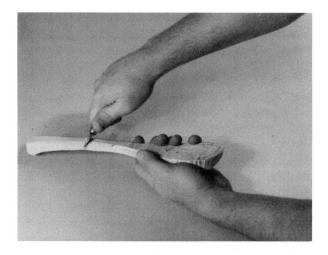

Figure 54-65. *Curved whittling blades work well for shaping the handle.*

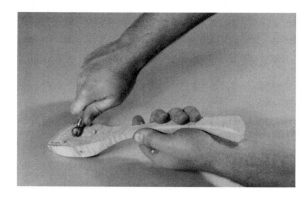

Figure 54-66. *A circular shaped whittling blade or gouge can be used to carve out the bowl of the spoon.*

PROJECT 15—DOLPHIN

The dolphin (Figure 54-67) is a project that is fun to make. It can be displayed on a bookcase, shelf or desk. A nice finish makes this carving look very pleasing.

The dolphin is suspended above its base with a piece of 1/8″ brass rod. The base has a routed edge and a lacquer finish.

Procedure

Study the drawing (Figure 54-68) and develop a bill of materials and a plan of procedure. Select

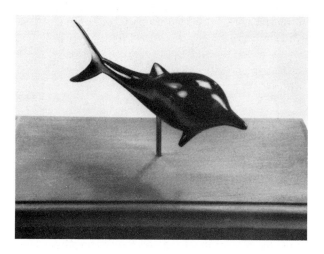

Figure 54-67. *The dolphin is a carving project that is fun to make.*

451

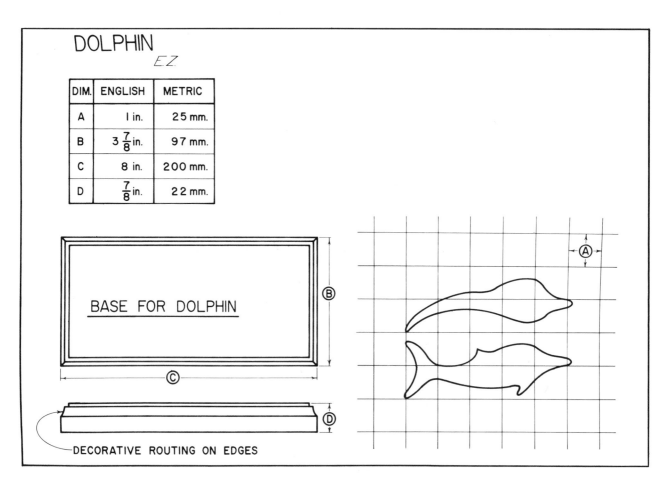

DOLPHIN *E.Z.*

DIM.	ENGLISH	METRIC
A	1 in.	25 mm.
B	$3\frac{7}{8}$ in.	97 mm.
C	8 in.	200 mm.
D	$\frac{7}{8}$ in.	22 mm.

BASE FOR DOLPHIN

DECORATIVE ROUTING ON EDGES

Figure 54-68. *Dolphin (Project #15).*

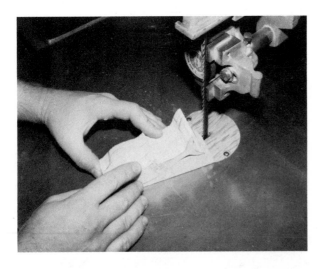

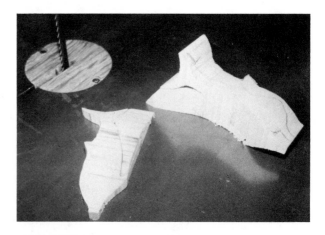

Figure 54-69. *The dolphin is cut to rough shape. Compound sawing on the bandsaw is the best method. Cut away the bottom in one cut. Then tape the waste stock back to the work. The second cut produces a rough shape ready to be carved.*

an easy carving wood such as basswood for the dolphin. Make the base of any hardwood.

Dolphin. Lay the dolphin out on a block. Cut the dolphin to rough shape on the band saw. This is done by compound sawing (Figure 54-69).

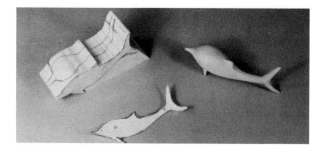

Figure 54-70. *Use carving tools and abrasives to shape the dolphin.*

Carve and smooth the dolphin (Figure 54-70). Drill a hole for the ⅛" rod in the bottom of the dolphin. Raise the grain on the dolphin and sand. Use 220 grit silicon carbide abrasive.
Stain the dolphin with nigrosine stain (alcohol base). Use two coats if necessary. Apply lacquer finish rubbing between coats.

Base. Cut the base to size and rout the edge. Drill a hole in the center for ⅛" rod. Sand and finish. Use a finish (and stain) that makes the base look like an expensive hardwood.

PROJECT 16—CHESSBOARD

The chessboard or checkerboard (Figure 54-71) will develop machine, gluing and layout skills. Your work must be accurate; all pieces should fit snugly with no space between parts.

METRIC CHESSBOARD

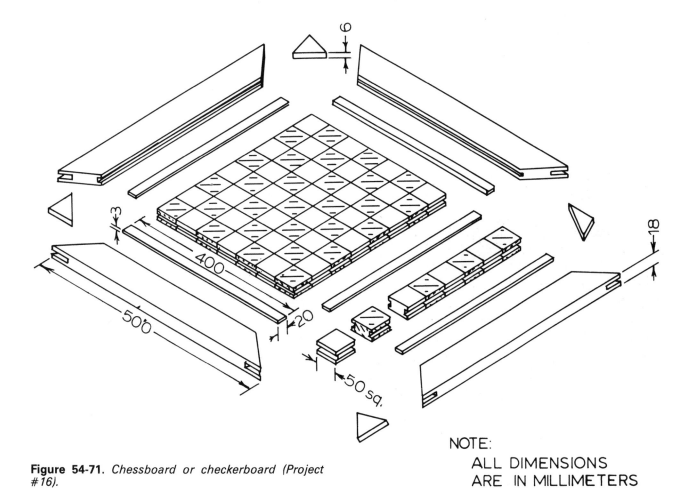

Figure 54-71. *Chessboard or checkerboard (Project #16).*

NOTE:
ALL DIMENSIONS
ARE IN MILLIMETERS

Procedure

Select two different species for the squares in the board. Use a light colored wood such as birch or maple and a dark colored wood such as cherry or walnut.

Develop a bill of materials and plan of procedure. Your finishing schedule should specify a clear finish. Study the drawing before you begin to work.

Square up the stock and glue it together. Cut the stock into strips and join them together. Sand the board and prepare it for finishing.

Attach the frame to the board and install the keys. Sand the frame, prepare for finishing, then apply the finish.

PROJECT 17—THE DART BOARD CASE

This beautiful case contains a dart board (Figure 54-72). The door includes a rack for storing darts (Figure 54-73). Both doors have cork glued to them. They keep stray darts from hitting the wall.

The different door styles are shown (Figures 54-72 and 54-74). Interior details of both cases are the same (Figures 54-73 and 54-75). Other door styles may also be designed. If you wish to turn knobs for the doors, this will reduce the hardware cost.

Figure 54-73. *A rack for darts is located on one door. Cork is glued to both doors. The cork catches most stray darts.*

Figure 54-74. *A curved door has been added to this dart case.*

Figure 54-72. *A dart board is hidden behind this case. The furniture finish makes it suitable for use anywhere.*

Figure 54-75. *Interior details are the same on both dartboard cases.*

Procedure

If some of your classmates like the dart board, you could manufacture them. Or you could manufacture everything but the doors. Each person could then make a pair of doors to fit the case.

Study the drawings (Figure 54-76). Develop a bill of materials and a plan of procedure. Decide what type of finish you wish to apply and make a finishing schedule.

Purchase your dart board before you begin. The cork board must be fitted around the dart board.

Square up stock and make the frame. Glue the back into position. Fit the dart board and cork board in position. First glue the cork in place (Figure 54-77). Then glue the dart board in place (Figure 54-78). Use panel adhesive to hold the dart board in place.

Build the doors to fit the case. Fit and install hinges (Figure 54-79). A screw starter can be used to make the pilot holes. Remove the hardware before finishing.

Prepare the surface and apply the finish. Note: You may want to stain and finish the inside before you install the cork.

Glue the cork to the doors, and attach the hinges.

DIM.	ENGLISH	METRIC
A	$20\frac{1}{4}$ in.	506 mm.
B	$10\frac{1}{8}$ in.	253 mm.
C	$\frac{3}{4}$ in.	19 mm.
D	28 in.	700 mm.
E	$19\frac{1}{4}$ in.	480 mm.
F	$\frac{1}{4}$ in.	6 mm.
G	$2\frac{1}{4}$ in.	56 mm.
H	$\frac{3}{8}$ in.	9 mm.
I	$\frac{7}{8}$ in.	21 mm.
J	$1\frac{3}{8}$ in.	34 mm.
K	$\frac{7}{16}$ in.	11 mm.
L	$6\frac{1}{8}$ in.	153 mm.

INSIDE OF CASE AND DOORS LINED WITH CORK

USE SMALL HINGES TO FASTEN THE DOORS

TO THE CASE, 2 OR 3 PER SIDE

DART BOARD & CASE
EZ

Figure 54-76. *Dart board and case (Project #17). Continued on next page.*

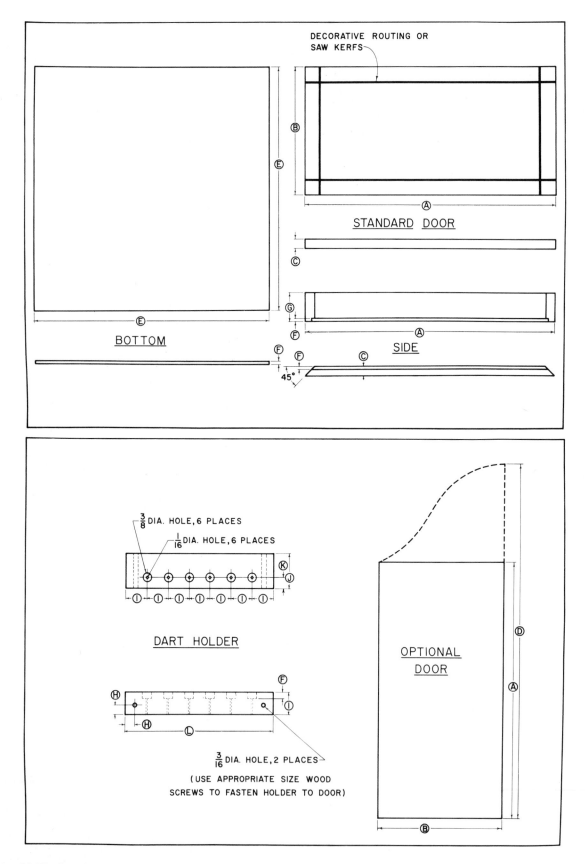

Figure 54-76. *Continued.*

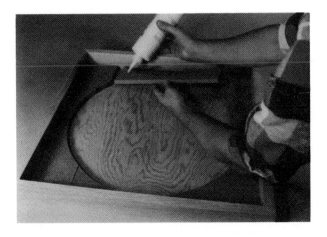

Figure 54-77. *Cork is glued to the back before the dart board is installed. White glue or panel adhesive both work well for this job.*

PROJECT 18—GAME ROOM CLOCK

The game room clock (Figure 54-80) is a nice project for manufacturing. By changing the numerals, the entire look of the clock may be changed (Figure 54-81, 54-82 and 54-83). Many hobby types of symbols such as fishing lures, shotgun shell casings, buttons, coins and stamps may be used instead of dominoes. These make the clock an individual project. There are other clock faces pictured in Chapter 50.

Figure 54-78. *Anchor the dart board in place with panel adhesive.*

Figure 54-80. *This game room clock makes a nice manufacturing project. Chapter 51 pictures many clocks made by modifying these plans.*

Figure 54-79. *Use a screw starter or drill to install hinge screws. Use a screwdriver that fits the screw properly.*

Figure 54-81. *Arabic numerals give this clock a clean appearance.*

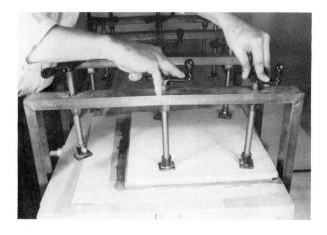

Figure 54-84. *The clock faces and backs may be veneered as part of the project. Hardwood plywood may also be used.*

Figure 54-82. *Upholstery buttons change the clock's appearance.*

Figure 54-83. *The dark Roman numerals are a pleasant contrast with white oak.*

This project also provides an opportunity to use veneer. You can veneer your own clock faces and backs (Figure 54-84). This will reduce the cost of your clock and provide valuable experience.

Procedure

Study the drawings (Figure 54-85) before you begin. Plan your work carefully. If you plan to manufacture the clock, develop your flow charts and route sheet early.

Design jigs and fixtures (Figure 54-86) before you begin. Make sure they are accurate. Select your stock carefully so there is very little waste. Excess waste will raise the unit cost of the clocks.

Use a simple finish on the clock. Penetrating oil works well. It dries fast and does not attract dust. There is little waste with penetrating oil finishes.

Cut frame parts to size first. Chamfer (Figure 54-87), rabbet (Figure 54-88) and miter (Figure 54-89) each frame part. Sand all parts before assembly. Assemble each frame (Figure 54-90) with white or yellow glue.

Cut the back to size, and rout a motor hole in it (Figure 54-91). Then glue the back into the frame (Figure 54-92). Finally glue spacer blocks to the back (Figure 54-93).

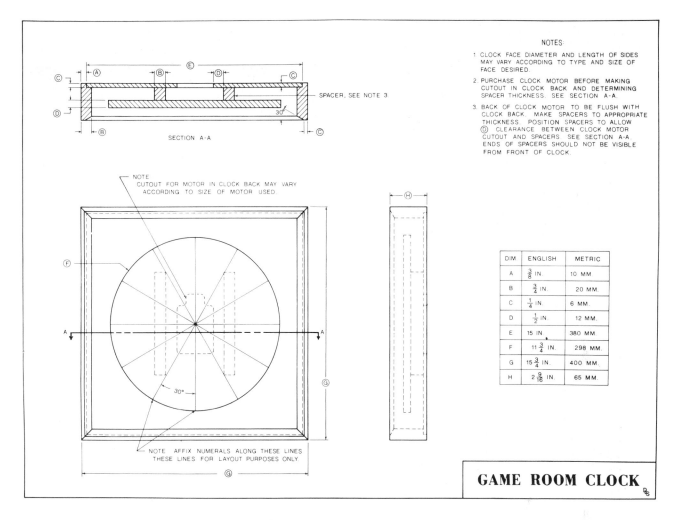

NOTES:

1. CLOCK FACE DIAMETER AND LENGTH OF SIDES MAY VARY ACCORDING TO TYPE AND SIZE OF FACE DESIRED.

2. PURCHASE CLOCK MOTOR BEFORE MAKING CUTOUT IN CLOCK BACK AND DETERMINING SPACER THICKNESS. SEE SECTION A-A.

3. BACK OF CLOCK MOTOR TO BE FLUSH WITH CLOCK BACK. MAKE SPACERS TO APPROPRIATE THICKNESS. POSITION SPACERS TO ALLOW Ⓓ CLEARANCE BETWEEN CLOCK MOTOR CUTOUT AND SPACERS. SEE SECTION A-A. ENDS OF SPACERS SHOULD NOT BE VISIBLE FROM FRONT OF CLOCK.

SECTION A-A

SPACER, SEE NOTE 3

NOTE CUTOUT FOR MOTOR IN CLOCK BACK MAY VARY ACCORDING TO SIZE OF MOTOR USED.

NOTE AFFIX NUMERALS ALONG THESE LINES THESE LINES FOR LAYOUT PURPOSES ONLY.

DIM	ENGLISH	METRIC
A	$\frac{3}{8}$ IN.	10 MM.
B	$\frac{3}{4}$ IN.	20 MM.
C	$\frac{1}{4}$ IN.	6 MM.
D	$\frac{1}{2}$ IN.	12 MM.
E	15 IN.	380 MM.
F	11$\frac{3}{4}$ IN.	298 MM.
G	15$\frac{3}{4}$ IN.	400 MM.
H	2$\frac{9}{16}$ IN.	65 MM.

GAME ROOM CLOCK

Figure 54-85. *Game room clock (Project #18).*

Figure 54-86. *Jigs and fixtures speed the manufacturing process. The gluing jig, left, holds the numerals in the correct place. Hot glue speeds the operation. The routing fixture routs out the clock back for the motor. A panel cutting bit rides on the template below.*

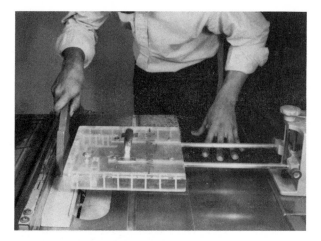

Figure 54-87. *Chamfer the frame parts after they have been cut to size.*

Figure 54-88. *Cut the rabbet on each frame member. This can be done on the table saw or with a router.*

Figure 54-89. *The ends of each frame member are mitered. Make sure the miters are accurate. A stop rod assures uniform length.*

Figure 54-90. *Glue the frame members together. Make sure the frame is square. The frame can be clamped or nailed. Nails reduce assembly time, but they must be hidden.*

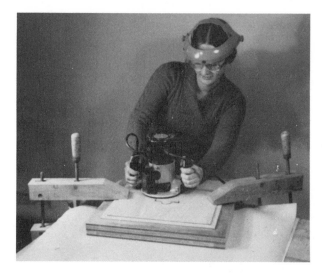

Figure 54-91. *Cut the motor hole in the back before assembly.*

Figure 54-92. *Hot glue acts like a clamp. It holds the back while the stronger glue dries.*

Figure 54-93. *Spacer blocks are glued to the back before the clock face is mounted.*

Figure 54-94. *The clock face can be cut on the bandsaw. A circle cutting fixture could be designed for this purpose. (See Chapter 36.)*

Figure 54-95. *The clock face is veneered or a decorative face is attached.*

Figure 54-96. *The motor and hands are attached last. If you are manufacturing the clock, test the motor.*

Cut the clock face on the band saw (Figure 54-94) and sand the edge. Veneer the face, or attach a clock face (Figure 54-95). Glue the face in position, and apply the finish.

Attach the motor and hands (Figure 54-96). Test the motor to be sure it runs correctly.

PROJECT 19—TOOLBOX

This toolbox (figure 54-97) was designed to hold most common carpentry tools. Edge cutting tools are protected from damage during storage. The framing square is stored on edge. This reduces the chance of it being bent or damaged.

Figure 54-97. *This toolbox was designed to hold common carpentry tools. The holders protect cutting tools from damage during storage.*

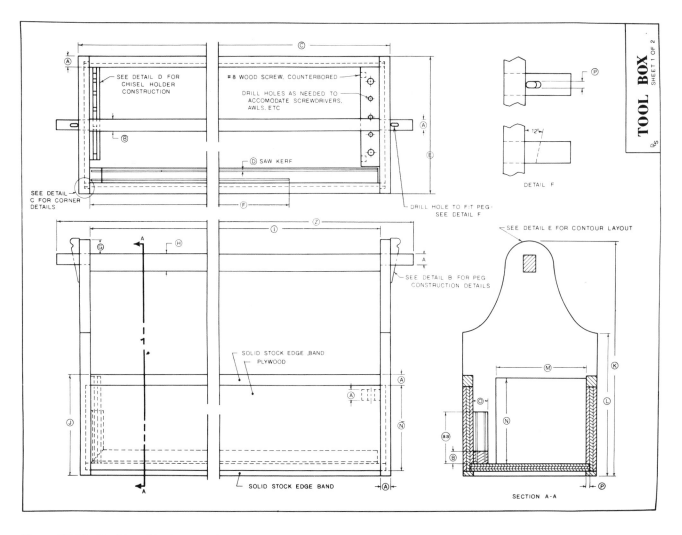

Figure 54-98. *Tool box (Project #19).*

Wooden toolboxes are desirable because they do not bend or rust. They are also very nice looking. A toolbox is an example of your work. People will use it to judge your ability. A nice looking toolbox helps sell your skills.

Procedure
Study the drawings (Figure 54-98) carefully. The parts of this toolbox must be cut accurately. It is easy to rout the wrong side of a part. Plan your work and mark your stock. This will reduce the chance of error.

Develop a bill of material and a plan of procedure. Use an oil finish on your toolbox. It is easy to apply and easy to maintain. Cut stock to size and begin.

You may have to glue several pieces together to make the ends. Cut the handle and radius the corners while the glue dries. Cut the tenon on the end of the plywood sides and glue the solid stock strips in place (Figures 54-99 and 54-100). Note: The two strips are not the same width. The narrower strip goes on the bottom. Mark your pieces and chalk to avoid error.

After the glue dries, rout a groove on the bottom of each side. Make sure the groove is on the inside (Figure 54-101).

Rout the mortise in both ends. A dado connects the mortises (Figure 54-102). The bottom fits in the dado. Locate the handle hole, and bore it (Figure 54-103). Square the hole (Figure 54-104) and cut it out (Figure 54-105).

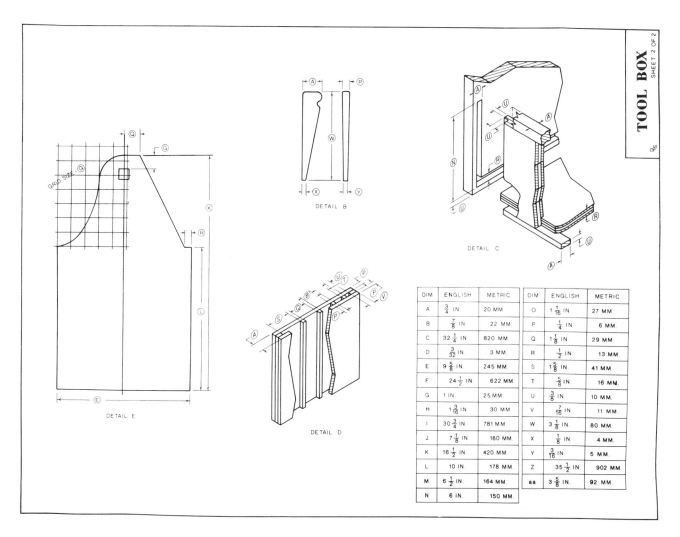

DETAIL B

DETAIL C

DETAIL D

DETAIL E

DIM	ENGLISH	METRIC	DIM	ENGLISH	METRIC
A	$\frac{3}{4}$ IN	20 MM	O	$1\frac{1}{16}$ IN	27 MM
B	$\frac{7}{8}$ IN	22 MM	P	$\frac{1}{4}$ IN	6 MM
C	$32\frac{1}{4}$ IN	820 MM	Q	$1\frac{1}{8}$ IN	29 MM
D	$\frac{3}{32}$ IN	3 MM	R	$\frac{1}{2}$ IN	13 MM
E	$9\frac{5}{8}$ IN	245 MM	S	$1\frac{5}{8}$ IN	41 MM
F	$24\frac{1}{2}$ IN	622 MM	T	$\frac{5}{8}$ IN	16 MM
G	1 IN	25 MM	U	$\frac{3}{8}$ IN	10 MM
H	$1\frac{3}{16}$ IN	30 MM	V	$\frac{7}{16}$ IN	11 MM
I	$30\frac{3}{4}$ IN	781 MM	W	$3\frac{1}{8}$ IN	80 MM
J	$7\frac{1}{8}$ IN	180 MM	X	$\frac{1}{8}$ IN	4 MM
K	$16\frac{1}{2}$ IN	420 MM	Y	$\frac{3}{16}$ IN	5 MM
L	10 IN	178 MM	Z	$35\frac{1}{2}$ IN	902 MM
M	$6\frac{1}{2}$ IN	164 MM	aa	$3\frac{5}{8}$ IN	92 MM
N	6 IN	150 MM			

Figure 54-98. *Continued.*

Figure 54-99. *Solid stock strips are glued to the plywood edges. The wider strip goes on top. Mark your work to avoid error.*

Figure 54-100. *A groove is routed on the inside of each side at the bottom.*

Figure 54-101. *The finished sides should look like this.*

Figure 54-102. *Two mortises are routed in the ends. The sides fit in these mortises. The bottom slips in the dado.*

Figure 54-103. *Locate the center of the handle hole and bore. Bore from both sides to avoid splitting.*

Lay out and cut the ends (Figure 54-106). Sand the edges (Figure 54-107). Dry clamp the box together to check the fit. Lay out the holes for the peg or wedge. Connect the two holes with a coping saw. Fit the pegs to the hole.

Glue up the box and install the pegs. Cut the holders and install them. Apply the finish.

Figure 54-104. *Lay out a square around the hole.*

Figure 54-105. *Cut the hole into a square. A coping saw or jig saw may be used.*

Figure 54-106. *Lay out the ends and cut them. An accurate template speeds layout.*

Figure 54-107. *Sand the edges after cutting. A file may also be used.*

464

Figure 54-108. *A level is a precision tool. It must be built accurately. Purchase the vials before you begin.*

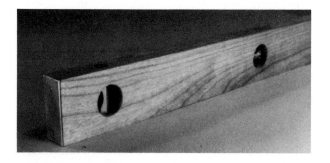

Figure 54-109. *The ends of the level are brass-capped to protect them from damage.*

PROJECT 20—THE LEVEL

If you build the toolbox, you may also want to build this level (Figure 54-108). The level is a precise tool. It must be built accurately. The vials must be plumb and level or the tool will not work.

Notice that the ends are capped with brass (Figure 54-109). This is to protect them from damage. This level will give years of service when built correctly.

Procedure

Purchase the vials before you begin. Many woodworking suppliers have these. All holes must be cut to fit the vials. Study the drawing (Figure 54-110). Develop a bill of materials and a plan of procedure. Choose a wood that does not warp easily. Use a penetrating oil finishing schedule.

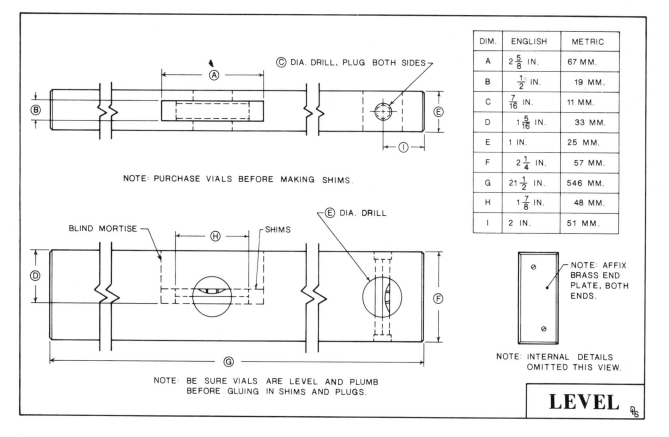

DIM.	ENGLISH	METRIC
A	$2\frac{5}{8}$ IN.	67 MM.
B	$\frac{1}{2}$ IN.	19 MM.
C	$\frac{7}{16}$ IN.	11 MM.
D	$1\frac{5}{16}$ IN.	33 MM.
E	1 IN.	25 MM.
F	$2\frac{1}{4}$ IN.	57 MM.
G	$21\frac{1}{2}$ IN.	546 MM.
H	$1\frac{7}{8}$ IN.	48 MM.
I	2 IN.	51 MM.

© DIA. DRILL, PLUG BOTH SIDES

NOTE: PURCHASE VIALS BEFORE MAKING SHIMS.

BLIND MORTISE

SHIMS

Ⓔ DIA. DRILL

NOTE: AFFIX BRASS END PLATE, BOTH ENDS.

NOTE: INTERNAL DETAILS OMITTED THIS VIEW.

NOTE: BE SURE VIALS ARE LEVEL AND PLUMB BEFORE GLUING IN SHIMS AND PLUGS.

LEVEL

Figure 54-110. *Level (Project #20).*

Square up your stock first. Make sure the edges are straight and true. Sand your stock well. Check it frequently to be sure it remains straight and true.

Drill and mortise your stock. Fit the vials into it. Make sure they are seated correctly. Plug the holes. File the plugs off even with the work.

Install the brass end caps. Make sure they are even with the ends. Apply the oil finish.

PROJECT 21—GUMBALL MACHINE

The gumball machine (Figure 54-111) is fun to build. It makes a nice gift. Your class may wish to manufacture the gumball machine. If so, you may wish to make a prototype so that you may analyze the parts (Figure 54-112).

If you decide to manufacture the gumball machine, develop your flow charts and route sheets early. Build your jigs and fixtures accurately so that all parts fit together.

Procedure

Study the drawing (Figure 54-113). Cut parts to size. Measure the jar before cutting the hole in the top. It should fit snugly. Test the setup in scrap stock if you are not sure.

After routing and cutting each part, begin assembly. Use glue sparingly. The wheel must turn freely inside the assembly.

Excess glue could bind the wheel. Be sure to glue the two veneers to the lower side of the top. They keep the gumballs from falling out.

Figure 54-112. *A prototype will help you analyze the parts. This will make it easier to manufacture.*

Figure 54-111. *The gumball machine is fun to build. It makes a nice gift.*

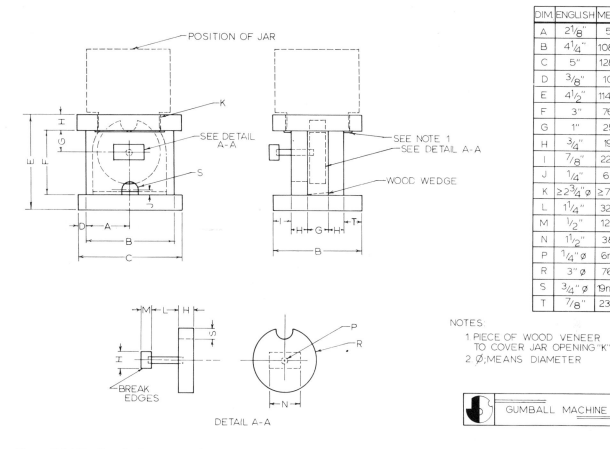

DIM.	ENGLISH	METRIC
A	$2\frac{1}{8}$"	54mm
B	$4\frac{1}{4}$"	108mm
C	5"	128mm
D	$\frac{3}{8}$"	10mm
E	$4\frac{1}{2}$"	114mm
F	3"	76mm
G	1"	25mm
H	$\frac{3}{4}$"	19mm
I	$\frac{7}{8}$"	22mm
J	$\frac{1}{4}$"	6mm
K	$\geq 2\frac{3}{4}$" ∅	≥ 70mm ∅
L	$1\frac{1}{4}$"	32mm
M	$\frac{1}{2}$"	12mm
N	$1\frac{1}{2}$"	38mm
P	$\frac{1}{4}$" ∅	6mm ∅
R	3" ∅	76mm ∅
S	$\frac{3}{4}$" ∅	19mm ∅
T	$\frac{7}{8}$"	23mm

NOTES:
1. PIECE OF WOOD VENEER TO COVER JAR OPENING "K"
2. ∅; MEANS DIAMETER

GUMBALL MACHINE

Figure 54-113. *Gumball machine (Project #21).*

An oil finish works well on the gumball machine. Salad bowl finish is a safe finish to use on items that contact food.

PROJECT 22—THE STEP STOOL

The step stool (Figure 54-114) is a handy item. This one has a colonial style. Many power tools will be used to make this project. All irregular edges must be sanded. Dadoes must be cut. Much gluing and clamping will be done.

This stool has a furniture finish. This requires careful application. The work must be sanded carefully before staining.

Figure 54-114. *This step stool is handy around the house. It has a nice furniture finish.*

467

Procedure

Study the drawings (Figure 54-115) before you begin. Make a bill of materials, plan of procedure, and a finishing schedule. Make templates for all irregular cuts before you begin.

Glue up stock and lay out the parts. Cut dadoes to fit the step. Check the cut in scrap stock first. Be sure you have a tight fit.

STEP STOOL

DIM.	ENGLISH	METRIC
A	$23\frac{1}{4}$ in.	581 mm.
B	6	150
C	$5\frac{1}{4}$	131
D	$6\frac{1}{4}$	156
E	$11\frac{5}{8}$	291
F	$\frac{3}{8}$	9
G	$\frac{3}{4}$	19
H	$\frac{1}{2}$	13
I	$6\frac{3}{8}$	159
J	$5\frac{7}{8}$	147
K	13	325
L	$11\frac{1}{8}$	278
M	1	25
N	$10\frac{5}{8}$	266
O	$6\frac{3}{4}$	169
P	11	275
Q	$5\frac{1}{8}$	128
R	$11\frac{3}{8}$	284
S	$1\frac{1}{8}$	28
T	3	75
U	$\frac{7}{16}$	11
V	$2\frac{1}{2}$	63

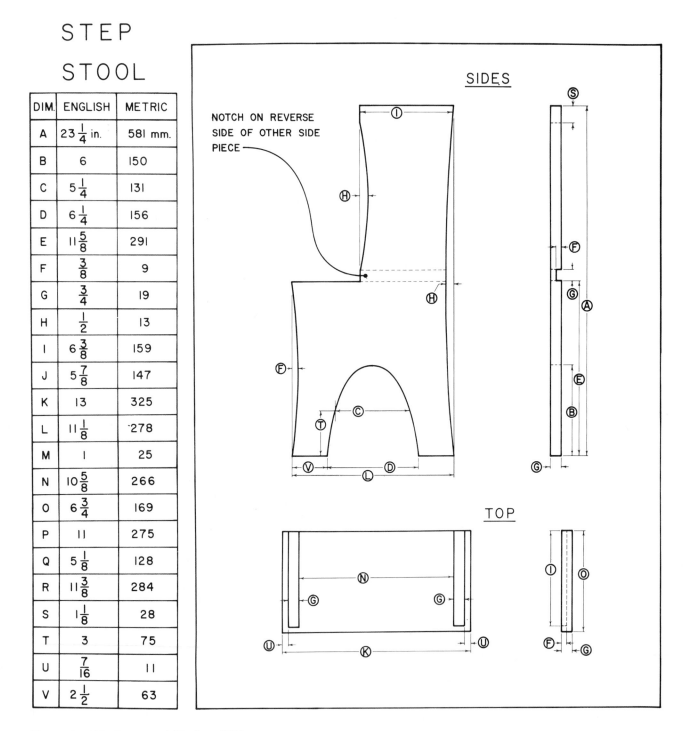

NOTCH ON REVERSE SIDE OF OTHER SIDE PIECE

SIDES

TOP

Figure 54-115. *Step stool (Project #22).*

The two sides are not the same. There is a right side and a left side. Mark each side. Lay them out carefully. Make all irregular cuts and sand.

Sand the insides of the sides and the steps

before you assemble them. You may even want to stain them to avoid glue blemishes.

Apply the finish and rub it out. Be sure to polish it after rubbing. This will protect the finish.

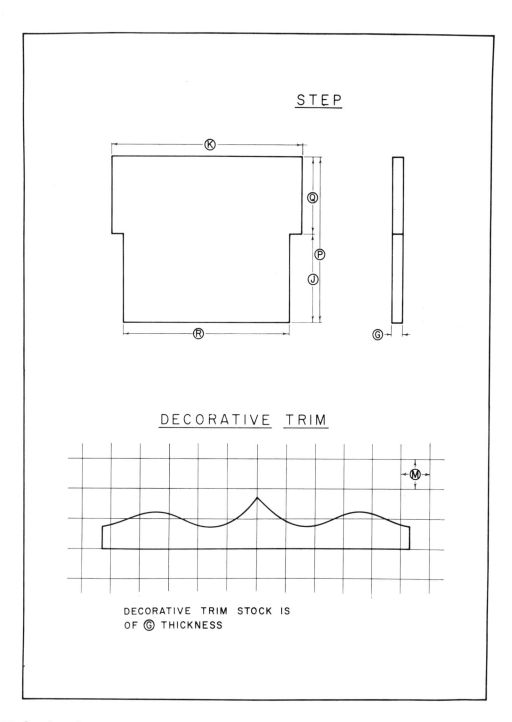

Figure 54-115. *Continued.*

PROJECT 23—THE MIRROR FRAME
(Reprinted from *Man/Society/Technology.*)

The mirror frame (Figure 54-116) is a nice addition to a hallway or bedroom. It has a furniture finish. Some frames have raised corners (Figure 54-117). These add to the decorative look.

The eagle and the corner rosettes are made of plastic. They have been stained and finished to match the wood. The eagle and the rosettes may be purchased.* If you enjoy carving, you can carve your own eagle. The rosettes could be turned on the lathe and then carved.

---

*(Outwater Plastics, 99 President St., Passaic, NJ 07055)

Finish is very important. A nice clear finish makes the frame look much better. Plan a finishing schedule that accents the wood.

Procedure
Study the drawing (Figure 54-118) before you begin. Develop a bill of materials, plan of procedure and a finishing schedule. Cut the frame parts to size. Rout the sides and cut the radius on the top.

Lay out the dowel joints and fit the parts together. Glue up the frame. Use a rabbeting bit to rout the rabbet for the mirror.

Prepare the frame for finishing. Add eagles, rosettes or raised corners if desired. Apply the finish. Rub it out and polish it. Install the mirror.

Figure 54-116. *This mirror frame is a nice addition to a hallway or bedroom.*

Figure 54-117. *The raised corners on this frame add a decorative look.*

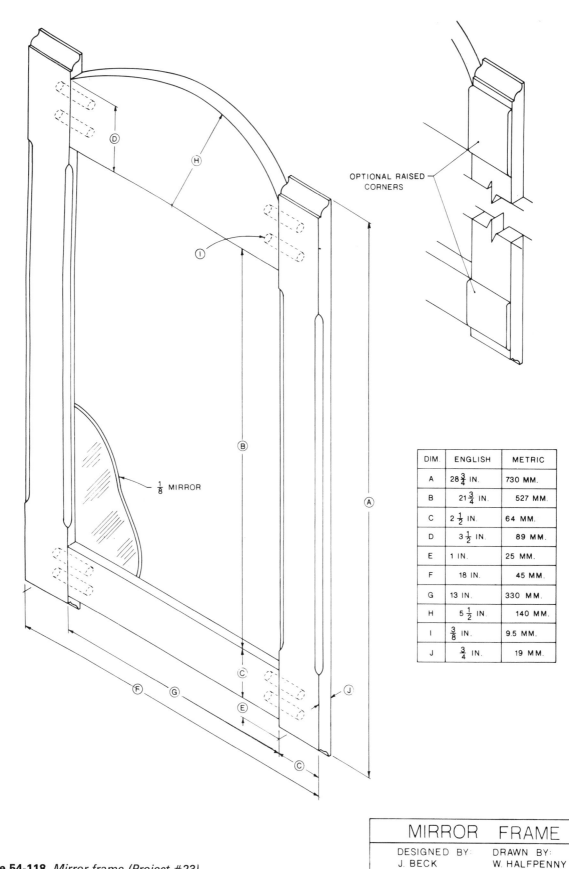

OPTIONAL RAISED CORNERS

$\frac{1}{8}$ MIRROR

DIM.	ENGLISH	METRIC
A	28 $\frac{3}{4}$ IN.	730 MM.
B	21 $\frac{3}{4}$ IN.	527 MM.
C	2 $\frac{1}{2}$ IN.	64 MM.
D	3 $\frac{1}{2}$ IN.	89 MM.
E	1 IN.	25 MM.
F	18 IN.	45 MM.
G	13 IN.	330 MM.
H	5 $\frac{1}{2}$ IN.	140 MM.
I	$\frac{3}{8}$ IN.	9.5 MM.
J	$\frac{3}{4}$ IN.	19 MM.

MIRROR FRAME

DESIGNED BY: DRAWN BY:
J. BECK   W. HALFPENNY

Figure 54-118. *Mirror frame (Project #23).*

PROJECT 24—THE BREAD BOX
(Reprinted from *Man/Society/Technology*)

The bread box (Figure 54-119) has a tambour type rolling door. The tambours pictured on the bread box are made of plastic. They lock together (Figure 54-120) and will turn sharp corners. These tambours are commercially available. (One source is Outwater Plastics, address given earlier.)

If you prefer wood tambours, you can make your own or use screen moulding. The tambours should be glued to canvas or held together with tape.

Procedure
Study the drawing (Figure 54-121) then develop a bill of materials, plan of procedure and finishing schedule. Notice that the right and left side are different. Mark them so that you rout the correct side. (Use a template like the one in Figure 54-124 to rout the sides.) A follower guide attached to the router rides along the template.

Fit the pieces together. Sand the inside well, then glue up the case. Do not install the back. The ¼" (6 mm) back is installed after the tambours are fitted to the case.

Fit the tambours to the case. Sand and finish the tambours, case, and back before assembly. Note: plastic tambours do not need to be sanded or finished.

Wax the grooves in which the tambours slide. Test their operation before assembly. Then attach the back.

Figure 54-119. *This bread box has a tambour-type rolling door.*

Figure 54-120. *The tambours used on the breadbox are plastic. They are designed to lock together. Wood tambours may also be used.*

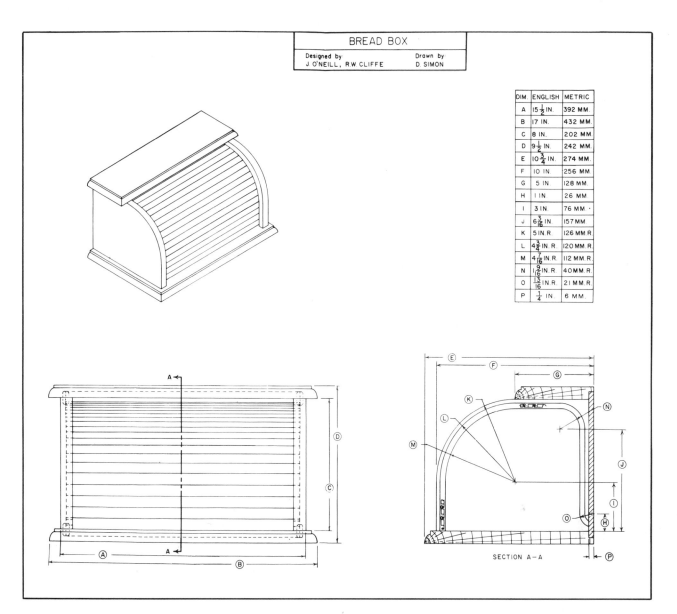

DIM.	ENGLISH	METRIC
A	$15\frac{1}{2}$ IN.	392 MM.
B	17 IN.	432 MM.
C	8 IN.	202 MM.
D	$9\frac{1}{2}$ IN.	242 MM.
E	$10\frac{3}{4}$ IN.	274 MM.
F	10 IN.	256 MM.
G	5 IN.	128 MM.
H	1 IN.	26 MM.
I	3 IN.	76 MM.
J	$6\frac{3}{16}$ IN.	157 MM.
K	5 IN.R.	126 MM.R.
L	$4\frac{3}{4}$ IN.R.	120 MM.R.
M	$4\frac{7}{16}$ IN.R.	112 MM.R.
N	$1\frac{9}{16}$ IN.R.	40 MM.R.
O	$\frac{13}{16}$ IN.R.	21 MM.R.
P	$\frac{1}{4}$ IN.	6 MM.

Figure 54-121. *Bread box (Project #24).*

PROJECT 25—CASSETTE HOLDER
(Reprinted from *Man/Society/Technology*)

The cassette holder (Figure 54-122) protects tapes from dust and dirt when not in use. The cassette holder is designed to work in the upright position or on its back.

This project is a challenge to build. The tambours must fit correctly and travel smoothly. Plastic tambours were used in this one, but you could make your own out of wood. They must be attached to canvas or tape. Tambours are discussed in Project 24.

Figure 54-122. *This cassette holder was designed to protect tapes from dust and dirt. This project is a challenge to build.*

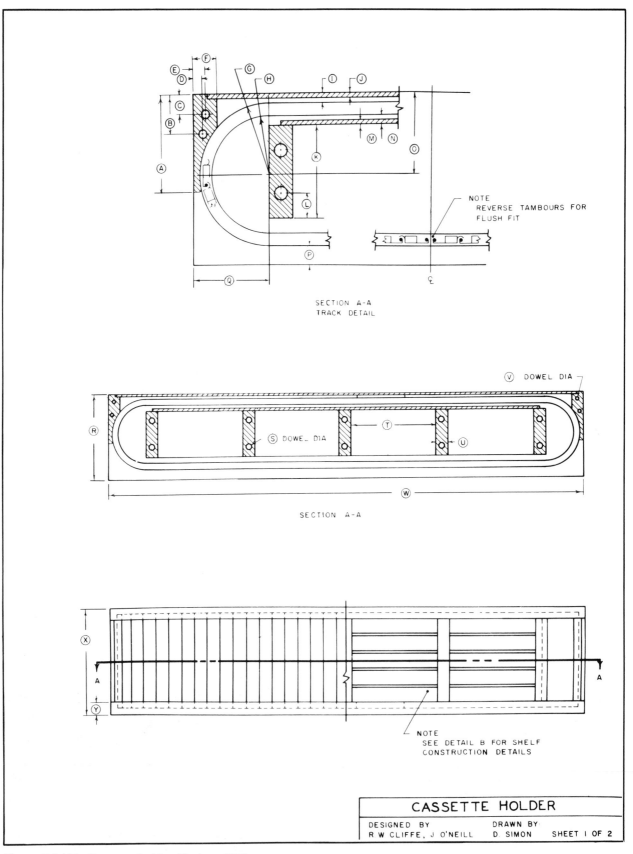

SECTION A-A
TRACK DETAIL

NOTE
REVERSE TAMBOURS FOR
FLUSH FIT

SECTION A-A

NOTE
SEE DETAIL B FOR SHELF
CONSTRUCTION DETAILS

CASSETTE HOLDER

DESIGNED BY
R W CLIFFE, J O'NEILL

DRAWN BY
D SIMON   SHEET I OF 2

Figure 54-123. *Cassette holder (Project #25).*

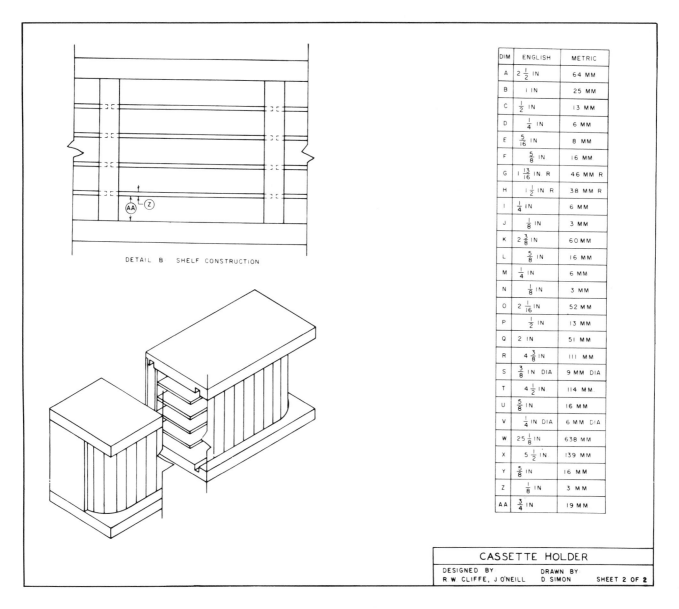

DETAIL B SHELF CONSTRUCTION

DIM	ENGLISH	METRIC
A	2 1/2 IN	64 MM
B	1 IN	25 MM
C	1/2 IN	13 MM
D	1/4 IN	6 MM
E	5/16 IN	8 MM
F	5/8 IN	16 MM
G	1 13/16 IN R	46 MM R
H	1 1/2 IN R	38 MM R
I	1/4 IN	6 MM
J	1/8 IN	3 MM
K	2 3/8 IN	60 MM
L	5/8 IN	16 MM
M	1/4 IN	6 MM
N	1/8 IN	3 MM
O	2 1/16 IN	52 MM
P	1/2 IN	13 MM
Q	2 IN	51 MM
R	4 3/8 IN	111 MM
S	3/8 IN DIA	9 MM DIA
T	4 1/2 IN	114 MM
U	5/8 IN	16 MM
V	1/4 IN DIA	6 MM DIA
W	25 1/8 IN	638 MM
X	5 1/2 IN	139 MM
Y	5/8 IN	16 MM
Z	1/8 IN	3 MM
AA	3/4 IN	19 MM

CASSETTE HOLDER		
DESIGNED BY R W CLIFFE, J O'NEILL	DRAWN BY D SIMON	SHEET 2 OF 2

Figure 54-123. *Continued.*

Procedure

Study the drawings (Figure 54-123) and develop a bill of materials, plan of procedure and finishing schedule.

Make a router template for cutting the tambour groove (Figure 54-124). Square up the top and bottom, then rout the tambour groove.

Square up the ends and back. Fit the case together, then build the tape shelves. Sand all parts carefully.

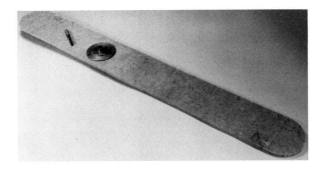

Figure 54-124. *The template guides the router. The follower guide rides against the template while the bit cuts the groove.*

Fit the tambours to the case. They must slide smoothly. Finish all parts before assembly. Install the tambours between the top and bottom when the case is glued together. The back is installed last.

Attach knobs to the tambours. These may be purchased or turned on the lathe.

SUGGESTED ACTIVITIES

1. Develop a bill of materials for one of the projects in this section. Ask your instructor to check your work.

2. Develop a plan of procedure for one of the projects in this section using only hand tools.

3. Develop a plan of procedure for one of the projects in this section using both hand tools and power tools.

Glossary

A

acrylic finish: A clear wood finish that can be thinned with water.

adhesive: Any material that joins two or more substances together. Adhesives are also known as *glues* or *cements*.

air drying: Drying wood in the open air without steam or heat.

assembly time: In gluing, the length of time allowed to position stock after spreading the adhesive.

B

bed: The smooth surface of a machine on which the wood rests when it is processed. Also see *Table*.

bevel: An incline between two faces or edges.

bill of materials: A list of materials (with their dimensions) used to build a project.

bit: A cutting tool (usually cylindrical in shape). Bits are usually driven by rotary motion.

blade: A flat piece of metal used for cutting wood. Saw blades have teeth, but knife blades usually do not.

bleach: Any material used to lighten or remove color from wood.

board foot: The measure of the volume of wood in solid stock: 12″ × 12″ × 1″.

board stock: Any wood (usually softwood) solid in a 1″ (25 mm) thickness and any width of 2″ (50 mm) or more, such as 1 × 2, 1 × 6, 1 × 8.

bristle: The hair-like part of a paint brush that spreads the finish.

burnishing: Glazing of the wood's surface usually caused by heat. Dull abrasives will burnish wood.

C

chamfer: An incline between two right-angled surfaces.

check: A crack that runs perpendicular to the annular rings. Usually found on the ends of a board.

chuck: A device used to hold a bit or blade in place.

clamping time: In gluing, the length of time two pieces must be held together.

coated abrasives: A paper-backed material used to smooth or prepare wood for finishing. See *sanding*.

collet: A chuck-like device used to hold a bit. Usually found on a router.

crosscutting: Sawing wood across the grain. Cutting stock to length.

D

dado: A square channel cut through a piece of stock.

decoupage: A clear finish used to embed pictures, printed pages or small articles.

design: The overall appearance or style of a product.

dimensional stability: A description of the amount of shrinkage and swelling in solid stock or sheet stock.

dimension stock: Any wood (usually softwood) sold in a 2″ (50 mm) thickness and any width of 2″ or more, such as 2 × 4, 2 × 6, 2 × 8.

distressing: Denting, scratching or marking the wood to make it appear older.

dowel: A round piece of stock used to reinforce a wood joint.

driver: The part of a finish that caused it to harden.

F

feather board: A shop-made device used to hold stock against the table or fence.

fence: A smooth, straight surface perpendicular to the table that guides the wood when it is machined.

finishing schedule: A plan of procedure for sanding, staining and finishing wood.

fixture: A device built to hold the work while it is machined.

flexing: Pulling the paper side of an abrasive sheet across a sharp corner. Flexing is done to make the sheet more flexible.

footing: The concrete base on which a house is built.

foundation: The walls of a basement or crawl space.

function: A product's intended job.

G

glaze: A thin paint used for shading (darkening) moldings and carvings.

gluing: The use of an adhesive to hold two or more substances together.

grain: The figure or pattern on a piece of wood caused by growth conditions.

groove: A dado that runs with the grain.

H

hardboard: Sheet stock made up of wood fibers pressed into sheets.

hardwood: The name for any wood that comes from a tree that has broad leaves.

heartwood: The darker colored wood in the inner annular rings.

honeycomb: A group of separations in wood that run perpendicular to the annular rings.

I

isometric drawing: A drawing that has the side and front views turned 30° from the horizontal axis.

J

jig: A device built to guide a tool.

joist: Horizontal framing member in a house.

K

kerf: The cut made by the saw blade.

kiln drying: Drying wood in a sealed chamber (kiln) using steam and heat.

knot: A defect in wood stock caused by branch growth.

L

lacquer: A clear wood finish that dries by solvent evaporation.

laminating: The process of gluing two or more thin pieces together.

M

manufacturing: Building a product in large quantities.

material order sheet: A list of all materials needed to build your project. This list enables you to compare prices.

mechanical drawing: A formal drawing made with drawing tools.

miter: An angular crosscut in wood. A wood joint with no exposed end grain. Commonly used in picture frames.

miter gage: A device used to control stock when it is machined. The miter gage travels in a slot in a table of the machine.

modern furniture: Furniture known for its simplicity. "Scandinavian" and "Danish Modern" are two modern furniture designs.

O

oblique drawing: A drawing that has the side view at a 45° angle to the front view.

P

paint: A colored opaque (not transparent) finish.

paneling: Sheet stock used to decorate the walls of a home.

particleboard: Sheet stock made up of small wood chips and glue pressed together.

penetrating oil: A wood finish that goes into the wood. Also an ingredient in varnish. Common oils are linseed oil and tung oil.

pitch: A sticky resin found in most softwoods.

pitch pockets: Cavities in the wood containing pitch.

pith: The stem or first growing part of the tree. The first annular ring.

planing: Smoothing rough or uneven lumber.

plan of procedure: A written guide to building a project. An outline of construction steps in the correct sequence.

plastic laminate: A thin piece of plastic used for counters and table tops over sheet stock.

plug: A cylindrical piece of wood used to cover a wood screw.

plywood: Sheet stock made up of several layers of veneer or solid stock.

polishing: Protecting a finish after rubbing with wax, lemon oil or other material.

pot life: In gluing, the usable length of time a glue may be used after mixing.

primer: A special paint applied to raw wood. It is used to improve the bond between the wood and additional coats of paint.

problem statement: A description of needs and limitations related to a product that is to be designed.

prototype: A full-size working model of a product designed to be manufactured.

provincial furniture: Furniture of the following styles: Colonial, Duncan Phyfe, Italian Provincial and French Provincial.

push shoe or stick: A shop-made device used to feed stock into the bit or blade.

Q

quarter-sawn lumber: Solid stock with the annular rings running from one face to the other face.

R

rabbet: A right angle notch along the end or edge of a piece of wood.

rafter: The dimensional stock used to support roof sheathing.

resawing: Cutting a thick piece of stock into two or more thinner pieces.

resin: An ingredient in varnish made from tree sap.

ripping: Sawing wood with the grain. Cutting stock to width.

rubbing: Leveling a finish to increase gloss or light-reflecting quality.

run: A long drip in the finish caused by heavy application.

S

sag: A ridge formed in the finish caused by heavy application.

sanding: The use of a coated abrasive to smooth or prepare wood for finishing.

sapwood: The lighter colored wood in the outer annular rings.

set: The bend or offset in a saw tooth.

shake: A separation between the annular rings.

shelf life: The maximum length of time a product such as paint or glue may be stored before use.

shellac: A clear surface finish for wood produced from resin from the lac bug.

sheet stock: All wood materials sold in sheets four feet wide and eight to twelve feet long (1200 × 2400 to 3600 mm).

shoulder: A step cut in a piece of wood.

sketch: An informal drawing usually done free-hand.

softwood: The name for any wood that comes from a tree with needle-like leaves.

solar drying: Drying wood with heat from the sun. Solar drying is faster than air drying and uses less energy than kiln drying.

solid stock: The name for all wood that has been cut into boards.

solvent: The part of a finish that evaporates after application.

springwood: The softer part of an annular ring usually lighter in color than the summer wood.

square: A tool used to mark right angles on stock.

square foot: The measure of area: 12″ × 12″.

stain: Any material used to darken or add color to wood.

stain varnish: A finish that does the job of stain and varnish in one application.

stock cutting sheet: A plan for cutting sheet stock usually made on graph paper.

stud: The dimensional stock used for vertical supports in a wall.

summerwood: The harder part of an annular ring usually darker than the springwood.

T

table: The smooth surface of a machine on which the wood rests when it is processed. See also *bed*.

tang: The pointed end of a file or chisel to which the handle is attached.

taper: An inclined surface that runs from end to end of a piece of stock.

template: A pattern used to draw a curved line or design onto your work.

thin: Reduce the thickness of a finishing material by adding solvent.

traditional furniture: Furniture developed by English designers such as Chippendale, the Adams Brothers, Hepplewhite and Sheraton.

V

varnish: A clear waterproof surface finish for wood. It is made from oil, resin, solvent and drier.

V block: A piece of wood or metal with a V-shaped notch in it. A V block is used to hold irregular shapes during machining.

veneer: Solid stock thinner than ⅛″ (about 3 mm).

W

wane: Bark on the edge of a piece of stock. Often considered a defect.

warp: Any deviation from a true (straight) plane in a piece of stock.

Index